From Tribulation to Triumph

The Revelation of Jesus Christ

by

Norman Mellish

CONTENTS

Preface 3

Chapter 1 The Unveiled Christ 5

Chapter 2 The Seven Churches 23
    Ephesus - A Loveless Church 25
    Smyrna - A Loyal Church 31
    Pergamos – A Liberal Church 34
    Thyatira - A Lawless Church 38

Chapter 3 The Seven Churches continued 43
    Sardis - A Lifeless Church 43
    Philadelphia - A Living Church 47
    Laodicea - A Lukewarm Church 55

Chapter 4 The Throne of Heaven 60

Chapter 5 The Coronation of Christ 70

Chapter 6 The Seal Judgements 80

Chapter 7 Tribulation Saints 89

Chapter 8 The Trumpet Judgements 100

Chapter 9 The Trumpet Judgements continued 108

Chapter 10 The Magnificence of the Angel 119

Chapter 11 The Mourning Prophets and the Majestic Christ 125

Chapter 12 The Woman, her celestial purpose and terrestrial experience 138

Chapter 13 The Two Wild Beasts 150

Chapter 14 The Wrongs Rectified 160

Chapter 15 The Preparation of the Vials 173

Chapter 16 The Pouring of the Bowls of Wrath 178

Chapter 17 Babylon, her flagrant rebellion 186

Chapter 18 Babylon, her fall recorded 203

Chapter 19 The Worship, the Wedding, the War 213

Chapter 20 Future Destiny Settled 223

Chapter 21 The Descent and Description of the City 233

Chapter 22 The Final Call 254

Preface

This book has been written over a number of years and in various parts of the world, as it has been my privilege to serve God both in the gospel and in a teaching ministry in a fairly wide sphere.

The fact that I have not often had the use of my own study and library may account for some of the ways that the book has taken. It will also account for the repetition of truth, which occasionally occurs, as I seldom if ever had the whole manuscript to hand. I trust that the reader will bear this in mind as they peruse its pages.

The main reason for writing this volume is that in my studies of prophecy I found certain things set forth as the teaching of the passage difficult to accept. A further study of these scriptures with the help of expositors who also found the same problems caused me to reach the conclusions set forth here. I have not concentrated my thought too much on Ch 2-3, giving just a brief outline of the contents of these verses.

The problems arose from Ch 4 onwards as, who are the 24 elders? What is the church's destiny according to Ch 5 v 10? Who make up the saved multitude of Ch 7? Is the Lord Jesus ever set forth as an angel in this book? Which beast is the antichrist and from where will he rise? What is Babylon - is it literal or symbolic? The same can be asked regarding the city of Ch 21. If one agreed with the teaching of exclusive brethren of a century ago, then there is no point in adding to the plethora of books written on the subject. One is very thankful for the likes of Kelly and Darby who were instrumental under the hand of God to re-establish prophetic truth, and to unfold the general character that it takes, but one does not have to agree with all that they propound. In fact there are grave problems with many of their interpretations regarding certain events of prophecy. It is understandable that, in the day they lived many of the events recorded in the book of Revelation would have been difficult to envisage happening literally. Hence the constant desire for these writers to spiritualise so much of the book. We of course have no difficulty in being able to see them taking place with the advent of modern technology. If man can do the amazing things that he can then there is no difficulty for God to fulfil His word as he states. This commentary takes where it can a literal view; where it differs from that, the context makes it plain that a figure is being used to explain the truth.

The few Greek words that are quoted will be in the main from the Englishman's Greek concordance, or directly from the Englishman's interlinear Greek text. Again one is thankful for the many Greek aids that are available to the ordinary student, to understand at least something of the language that our bible was written in.

I must add a word of thanks to the many that have encouraged me in my study of prophecy, and to put some of it into writing.

This volume could not have been produced but for the great labours of Lois, who undertook to type my indiscernible handwriting and turn it into the present volume. It was no mean task, and I am very grateful to her. Also to Bruce Rodgers of Canada, who did the same with the latter chapters and e-mailed them to Lois to help bring the work to a conclusion. Also to Mike Baker for his willingness to proof read the work and edit the text. There were also others to whom I am thankful for the time and labour put into the production of the book, like Ruth and Eunice Haugh.

We trust that the writing will be a help to some of God's children.

Norman Mellish
Newcastle under Lyme
Staffs
UK

This work is dedicated to my wife, a true helpmeet, and a constant encouragement in the work of the Lord.

Also to Quartus and his wife who stood by us, and gave great support in a time of grievous trial. The Lord was good to us through them. They like Lois wish to remain unidentified.

Chapter 1
The Unveiled Christ

Introduction

The opening words give to us not only the title of the book "The Revelation of Jesus Christ" but also the character of the book, for the word "Revelation" simply indicates an "Unveiling", an eye opener. The curtain is to be drawn aside to bring before the saints the great purpose of God in his dealings with the earth.

The Revelation is singular, and was to form one book (v. 11), sent to, though not necessarily about the churches, vv. 4, 11. It is comprised of 4 visions given to John whilst on the Isle of Patmos, (v. 9). From the expression: "your companion in tribulation"; he appears to have been there in exile, yet, from the divine standpoint he was there for the express purpose of receiving this revelation. As verse 10 says, "For the word of God, and the testimony of Jesus Christ". The 4 visions are preceded by the expression "I was in the spirit".

These occur in Ch 1:10; 4:2; 17:3; and 21:10.

➢ Vision 1 - Ch 1:10 - Ch 3   Great patience with the saints.
➢ Vision 2 - Ch 4:1 - Ch 16   Grievous peril for sinners.
➢ Vision 3 - Ch 17 - Ch 21:8   General punishment of the Sacrilegious.
➢ Vision 4 - Ch 21:19 - Ch 22   Glorious prospect for the saints.

The Grace - Gloom - Government - Glory, of God's dealings

A friend once told me he doubted the value of prophecy for the believers of this present age, and felt that the truth taught was for those who will believe after the church's rapture, only then would its truth be made plain. He saw no point in studying prophecy, yet, Ch 1:4 and v. 11 make it plain that this book is for the believers of this dispensation. It must also be noted that only 3 short, personal epistles, do not touch prophecy in the New Testament, Philemon and 2 & 3 John. Though there is but a single verse about it in Galatians, (5:5), all other books bring out many aspects of prophetic truth. If I do not study this subject, I am closing my mind to much that God by the Spirit has unfolded. There are various reasons given in scripture to encourage us to study prophecy. It produced Prayer in Abraham (Gen. 18), Preparation and Preaching in Noah (Heb. 11:7; 2 Pet. 2:5), it gives a Prospect and brings Peace (2 Pet. 3:14), and should produce Purity in the saints (2 Pet. 3:11 with v. 14). Thus prophecy will exercise us to do more for God here, for the good of our family, friends, and our personal life. The book opens with a blessing (1:3), and closes with a curse, (22:19). Prophecy will prove to be one or the other to men.

The book makes its own division of the subjects it unfolds. Ch 1:19 states, "Write the things which thou hast seen"; this is the vision of Christ in the midst of seven golden lampstands in Ch 1. Then, "the things which are", which unfolds the condition of Christian testimony in Ch 2-3, "and the things which shall be hereafter". Ch 4:1 interprets this for us, when all Gods dealings with men after this present church age has run its course are revealed to the saints. Ch 1:5 can also be linked with this division. "The faithful witness", indicates the Christ of Ch 1. "The first begotten from the dead", speaks of his relationship to the churches in Ch 2-3, and, "The Prince of the kings of the earth", relates to his authority displayed to the world in Ch 4-22.

Ch1 brings us a prologue vv.1-3, a penman vv. 4-8, and a preparatory vision vv. 9-20.

Prologue (vv. 1-3)

The Revelation of Jesus Christ, which God gave unto him, to shew unto his servants things which must shortly come to pass; and he sent and signified it by his angel unto his servant John: Who bare record of the word of God, and of the testimony of Jesus Christ, and of all things that he saw. Blessed is he that readeth, and they that hear the words of this prophecy, and keep those things which are written therein: for the time is at hand. (Revelation 1:1-3)

The book begins simply, "The Revelation of Jesus Christ". Revelation is the word *Apokalupsis,* it occurs 18 times in the New Testament (Wigram), 7 times with Christ, and 7 with Paul; there are 3 references with the saints, and 1 with God.

In relation to Christ:

1.	Luke 2:32	Purpose of incarnation - to lighten gentiles
2.	1 Cor. 1:7	Passing of gift in the saints.
3.	2 Thess. 1:7	Punishment of the persecutors of the saints
4.	1 Pet. 1:7	Prospect of honour for the saints
5.	1 Pet. 1:13	Purity in the saints
6.	1 Pet. 4:13	Persecution endured by the saints
7.	Rev. 1:1	Prominence of Christ, and purging the world

His revelation is going to have this sevenfold effect.

In relation to Paul:

1.	2 Cor. 12:1; 7	his visions MANIFOLD, he had many revelations
2.	1 Cor. 14:6	his MINISTRY clear, precise, edifying
3.	Gal. 1:12	his MESSAGE, the gospel to sinners
4.	Gal. 2:2	his MOVEMENTS, always led of God, Acts 13:2; 16:6-10; 21:11
5.	Rom. 16:25, Eph. 3:3	the MYSTERY, committed to Paul to fill up the Word of God

In relation to saints:

1. Eph. 1:17   Our appreciation of Deity
2. Rom. 8:19   Our manifestation in Glory
3. 1 Cor. 14:26   Our participation in the Assembly

In relation to God:

1. Rom. 2:5   His judgement upon ungodly men in tribulation days

The prologue of vv. 1-3 unfolds 5 salient facts.

The Subject of the Book - Christ

Luther doubted the authenticity of the book, "for Christ is neither taught nor recognised in it." How strange, to those who have found much of Christ in it. A book has been written solely on "Christ in the Apocalypse" (Page, G.L.P. Glasgow). To say that Christ is,"neither taught nor recognised" indicates that little has been understood of this book that is a Revelation of Himself.

In Ch 1   We have his Authority as Judge.
In Ch 2-3   He is the Author of letters.
In Ch 4-5   He is the Acknowledged King.

It is agreed that little is seen of him in Ch 6-18. Judgement is his strange work, and in this section of the book, the full outpouring of divine fury is seen as God says, "Vengeance is mine I will repay" (Rom. 12:19, Heb. 10:30), yet we find the Lord acting in Ch 6 - In Retribution, Ch 7 - Rescuing, Ch 11 - Returning and Reigning, Ch 14 - Residing and Rejoicing, Ch 14 - Reaping.

In Ch 19-22 he is seen as a husband, a king, a judge, a rewarder, we need not go into details any further, but this is truly the Revelation of Jesus Christ and to say that Christ is not in it manifests a lack of appreciation for the character of the book.

The Source of the Book – God

Elsewhere in the epistles the source is the Holy Spirit in answer to the Lords statement in John 14:26 where he says that the Holy Spirit will be given, "To remind", this the Spirit did bringing to light the four gospels. In John 16:13 the Holy Spirit's work will be, "To reveal", (a) "All truth", giving us the epistles, and (b) "Shew you things to come", in which the book of Revelation is clearly before us. Even though in v. 4 the Spirit is among the senders, God becomes prominent, for all the past promises foretold in the Old Testament are now going to be fulfilled, the ever-existent God of v. 4 is moving, bringing to fruition his eternal purpose.

The Servant of the Book – John

John is chosen to write about every aspect of the Lord Jesus. He records his past movements among men in the gospel, his present ministry for saints in the three epistles, and his future majesty when revealed to the world in Revelation. This is the only book to which he pens his name.

In the Gospels he is unnamed, these are days when he is a relatively young man.
As a young man he will not parade himself, to make much of self. He hides behind his Lord; he simply calls himself the disciple that Jesus loved.

In the Epistles he calls himself the elder. He is now an older man and held in esteem amongst the saints. He did not need to advocate his name to let all know who is the elder, they knew him by his work and care.

The book of Revelation alone declares that it is John that is the writer.
Three times over in Ch 1 he appends his name to the writing. Such a book needs the full weight of such a man as John.

In the gospel he is the beloved in relation to the Son.
In the epistles he is the bishop in relation to the saints.
In Revelation he is the bondman in relation to the sovereign.

The Signs of the Book

Signified in v. 1, indicates "to give sign or signal", it is the root from which the word that John uses in his gospel for "signs" originates. It denotes "optical impressions that convey thought" (Kittel). The Revelation is not merely verbal, but also visual, hence the expressions: "to shew" v. 1, "I saw" v. 12, "write the things thou has seen" v. 19, also Ch 4:1, 17:1, 21:9-10, 22:1-10, "I will shew". The signs are often self-explanatory, 1:20 interprets the sign of the stars, and the lampstands, Ch 12:9 leaves us with no doubt as to who the dragon is, in Ch 17:15 the waters are distinctly said to be "peoples and multitudes and nations and tongues, whilst in Ch 21:2 the city is said to be the bride. Other signs in the book have appeared elsewhere in scripture, which is its own interpreter. Though difficulties will be seen in some of the signs, they should not be impossibilities, nor keep us from the general truth taught in the book.

The Satisfaction of the Book - Blessed

The blessing of v. 3 is said to be threefold. It is for, (a) the public reader, (b) those hearing it read, (c) the obedient hearer, though the last clause could be linked to those who hear and keep, for blessing is only for those who take heed to what they hear, (Matt. 7:24-29), making it two classes of people and not three.

There are seven blessings in the book (and fourteen woes) these are for:

1:3	The Versed
14:13	The Valiant
16:15	The Vigilant
19:6	The Valued
20:6	The Victors
22:7	The Virtuous
22:14	The Vindicated

The term speaks of the joy and happiness to be enjoyed by those who will participate in the divine kingdom.

We notice these things "must shortly come to pass" v. 1, and "the time is at hand" v. 3. The former has to do with the rapidity in which the events of Revelation will come to pass, when it pleases God to begin his dealing with the earth. The present period of silence, and God giving men up, and over, to reprobate minds, and to work uncleanness (Rom. 1:24-28), will soon terminate, then events will happen speedily. The time *(kairos)* infers a set proper time, an occasion (Strong). It is used of the time that saints will be rewarded in Ch11:18, of Satan knowing he has but little of it left Ch 12:12, and of the period that the woman is going to be nourished in the wilderness Ch 12:14. The book ends with the same statement Ch 22:10. The coming is near. In Gods reckoning all will shortly come to pass.

The writing is not only apocalyptic and symbolic it is also prophetic. Unfolding the mind of God to his own. Again like much in the book there are seven references to the word prophecy. The prophecy begins here in v. 3, not in Ch 6:1, leading me to believe that there is a prophetic character to the churches of Ch 2-3. Some would deny that the seven churches in any way display the way church history would unfold. But as Ironside has aptly put it, "if the key fits the door, and the door opens, none can deny it is the right key" and the prophetic key certainly fits in relation to the seven churches.

John was a faithful writer; his record is the word of God, and a testimony of Jesus Christ, which testimony is a prophetic testimony Ch 19:10. The "and" following Jesus Christ should be omitted, it is simply "of all things he saw", making it two statements not three.

Another interesting feature is to see angelic ministry restored in the book. In the epistles the angels seem to be looking, and learning (1 Cor. 11:10, Eph. 3:10, 1 Pet. 1:12), but now they are labouring. It is through an angel John receives the revelation. Note the fivefold way the book comes, from God, to Christ, via an angel, unto John, to show unto us. Old Testament ground is again taken. Moses received the law through the mediation of angels (Acts 7:38, Heb. 2:2). Angels are seen throughout the book, for God is taking up his dealings with the earth again, the time of his longsuffering is over, and angels are linked with God's earthly dealings. "Are they not all ministering spirits SENT FORTH to minister for them who shall be heirs of salvation?" (Heb. 1:14).

Vv. 4-20 bring before us four divisions: vv. 4-8 His Authority, vv. 9-11 His Testimony, vv. 12-18 His Discovery and vv. 19-20 His Ministry.

His Authority - The Trinity (vv. 4-8)

John to the seven churches which are in Asia: Grace be unto you, and peace, from him which is, and which was, and which is to come; and from the seven Spirits which are before his throne; And from Jesus Christ, who is the faithful witness, and the first begotten of the dead, and the prince of the kings of the earth. Unto him that loved us, and washed us from our sins in his own blood, and hath made us kings and priests unto God and his Father; to him be glory and dominion for ever and ever. Amen. Behold, he cometh with clouds; and every eye shall see him, and they also which pierced him: and all kindreds of the earth shall wail because of him. Even so, Amen. I am Alpha and Omega, the beginning and the ending, saith the Lord, which is, and which was, and which is to come, the Almighty. (Revelation 1:4-8)

The Recipients of the letter (v. 4)

These are said to be the seven churches, though we are not told which seven until we come to v. 11. The word church is Ecclesia, which simply means a called out company, indicating their separation. They are said to be in Asia, meaning slime pit or mire, indicating their standing. Verse 11 which names the seven churches indicates they were selected and significant for there were other churches in this western part of Asia i.e. Colosse, (Col. 1:2), Hierapolis, (Col. 4:13), Troas (Acts 20:6). As we look at the seven churches we shall see these were chosen because they give a prophetic outline of this present church age.

The church's blessing is bestowed, which is grace and peace. Grace is that which causes "leaping for joy" and peace is that which brings into unity (Young).

The Revelation of the Lord (vv. 4-6)

We see that all the Godhead is fully involved in the great unveiling. All the expressions in vv. 4-5 show divine dealings with the earth. "He which is and which was and which is to come" is the ever-existent God, the Eternal, and the covenant keeper. He who will do all he has promised. The seven spirits must speak of the Holy Spirit; John would hardly have interjected other forms of spirit in between two obvious members of the Godhead! Why is he seen as the seven spirits? Ottman says, "It is the perfection of his energy as linked with the throne", Scott declares that he is seen in this way as, "Fullness of spiritual activity", Kelly adds to this the expression, "The plenitude of His power". In Isaiah 11:2 the Holy Spirit is brought before us in a sevenfold way, beginning with "The Spirit of the Lord", Isaiah 11 is a chapter bringing in the millennial Kingdom of our Lord Jesus. It is fitting then, that as the millennium is soon to be brought in, the Holy Spirit is seen in this way. Here we have the

Spirit's position, in Ch 3:1 the thought is that of Possession, he is seen in the hand of Christ, whilst in Ch 4:5 Power is the theme, when he is seen as "lamps of fire", Ch 5:6 sets forth his Purpose, when he is "sent forth into all the earth".

The Lord Jesus is manifested in relation to his past, present and future. As the faithful witness he is the Prophet in relation to Israel in the past, as the firstborn from the dead we have his present position as a Priest which ministry is the blessed portion of the saints, and the Prince of Kings of the earth would tell us of his future glories when manifested to the world.

Not only his person, but also his work is brought before us. As to the past, he is the faithful witness, in the present the firstborn from the dead. The word firstborn does not speak of a time born, but that the supreme place has been given to the Lord Jesus. That "time" is not involved in the word is clearly seen from Ex. 4:22, Israel went into Egypt a family, they came out a nation. When they came out, God made it abundantly clear to Pharaoh that God counted them the firstborn, Joseph gets the birthright, the place of the firstborn, it should have belonged to Reuben but he lost it "forasmuch as he defiled his father's bed" (1 Chron. 5:1-2). In Ps. 89:27 David has the honour of the firstborn as the king, though Saul was their first king. The Lord Jesus must have the firstborn place in everything. Col. 1:15 gives him that place in Incarnation, Col. 1:18 links it with the Resurrection, and Rom. 8:29 with his Exaltation, whereas Rev. 1:5 anticipates his future Manifestation, Heb. 1:6 would unveil the Veneration that will be his, "let all the angels of God worship him" and not only they but all who own him. The Prince, (*arkon*), ruler of the Kings of the earth, assures us that the future belongs to him. Note, all is put in the present, what Christ was, is what he will be, "he is", he has carried all to the throne, he changes not. An anthem of praise rises in John as he thinks of the revealer, his rank and his rule. He cannot help remember he is our redeemer. Motivated by love, loosing us from our sins, breaking sin's power, (Rom. 6:18), or removing its defilement and likening us to himself who is a King Priest. He has made us Kings and Priests, Kings to the world, and Priests to God, power before men, and praise to God. The faithful witness, "loved us", the firstborn from the dead "loosed us" and the Prince of the Kings likened us unto himself.

God is not seen as our father in the Revelation, we are seen as servants in v. 1, and Kings and Priests in v. 6. Priesthood is ever God-ward, but the Lord Jesus always abides before him who is his father. Glory, personal (glory is simply a public display of honour, Christ's glory will one day be seen) is ascribed to him, Dominion, universal, is also his by sovereign right; the thought is "might", (*kratos*). This might is not for men, and apart from Heb. 2:14 where Satan has the power of death, the word is only used of God's might in the New Testament. This glory and dominion will last as long as Christ exists unto the ages of the ages, in v. 18 he is alive for evermore (aeons as in v. 6), and John gives his Amen to this blessed truth.

John gives his Amen on three occasions in this chapter. Here it is an Ascription of Praise, in v. 7 it is on the Assumption of Power and in v. 18 Ascension with Permanence.

A Return to the Land (v. 7)

Behold he cometh, blessed prospect, with clouds - clouds ever symbolise the divine presence. It was a pillar cloud that directed Israel (Ex. 13:21-22), it was a cloud that came on Sinai at the giving of the law to discipline Israel (Ex. 19:16), it was a cloud that covered the tent (Ex. 40:34) for God to dwell with Israel. When the Lord ascended it was a cloud that received him out of their sight (Acts 1:9). When the Lord returns it will be with clouds. When he left, God's presence left, now his presence is restored to men. The coming here is not the rapture, taking the saints away from the tribulation period, it is his coming in manifestation, to a world that has rejected him.

Three things will mark the coming; it will be visual, national and universal.

Visual - "Every eye shall see him". Some wonder at the possibility of this, given that the world is a globe. This is no problem to God. In Matt. 4:8 Satan could take the Lord Jesus up an exceeding high mountain and show him all the kingdoms of the world and the glory of them, a miracle indeed; for no one can see all the kingdoms of the world from a mountain, however high. If Satan can show kingdoms to Christ, God can show Christ to the kingdoms.

National - "They also which pierced him". Then shall be fulfilled the prophecy of Zech. 12:10-14 - they shall see the Jesus they rejected is none less than Jehovah, "they shall look on ME whom they have pierced and mourn for Him, as one mourneth for his only son". Also Zech 13:6 when Israel will gaze upon him and one shall say unto him, "What are these wounds in thine hands?" Then he shall answer, "those with which I was wounded in the house of my friends", the wounded one here is evidently our Lord Jesus Christ, and not the wounds of the false prophets of vv. 2-4. Unger has a very clear appreciation of this in his commentary on Zechariah when he says "The word for wounds in Zechariah 13:6 is not the technical word for the self-inflicted "cuttings" connected with idolatrous ritual"

Universal - "All kindreds of the earth". Some make this "the kindreds of the land", Israel, but as Scott justly says, "It is a question of interpretation not translation", for in 5:9, 7:9, 11:9, 13:7 and 14:6 Gentiles are before us. "Their mourning will be a time of great lament, a beating of the breast. Universal mourning combines remorse for the death of Christ, with grief at personal loss in the Judgement" (Kittel) (Matt. 24:30).

A Resplendent Life (v. 8)

How can any deny the deity of the Lord Jesus with such a verse before us? That he is the subject of the passage should be evident to the simplest reader. The opening statement, "I AM", is itself a divine title (*ego eimi*). It is how God revealed himself to Moses at the bush in Ex. 3:14. If Israel were to be delivered by *ego eimi* (LXX.), so this world is to be delivered by the same person. It is a favourite expression with John, occurring some 23 times in his gospel. The first time it is used is to the Samaritan women (John 4:26). It is lost in the translation, it should read, "I AM that speaketh to thee"; she had found the "I AM" that the Jews had rejected. The Lord Jesus became the seventh man in her life, her search ended with the fact that she had found the Christ.

The Lord Jesus is seen as the "Alpha and Omega", which are the first and last letters of the Greek alphabet, all wisdom and intelligence is found in him, Col 2:3 "In whom are hid all the treasures of wisdom and knowledge". The Lord Jesus has the monopoly of wisdom and knowledge, to miss him is to leave man bereft of true enlightenment.

He is also the "Beginning and the Ending", the origin and destiny of all things are found in him. Col. 1:16 teaches that all things found their origin in him, came into being through him, and were for him, note the prepositions, (*en, dia, eis*). It is a divine statement, "saith the Lord" is added, and many reputable manuscripts add "God". It is the Lord God speaking which is and which was, which is to come, the ever existent, eternal God of v. 4 is the Christ of v. 8 telling of his eternal being. To this is added to what is said in v. 4, "the Almighty", as if adding emphasis to the deity of the Lord Jesus. The Almighty occurs nine times in Revelation, bringing before us various aspects of deity.

1:8	Person of Christ
4:8	Pure, powerful, permanent
11:17	Power to reign
15:3	Preserving saints
16:7-14	Pouring judgements
19:6-15	Punishing Babylon, and the world
21:22	His presence in the city

His Testimony (vv. 9-11)

I John, who also am your brother, and companion in tribulation, and in the kingdom and patience of Jesus Christ, was in the isle that is called Patmos, for the word of God, and for the testimony of Jesus Christ. I was in the Spirit on the Lord's day, and heard behind me a great voice, as of a trumpet, Saying I am Alpha and Omega, the first and the last: and, What thou seest, write in a book, and send it unto the seven churches which are in Asia; unto Ephesus, and unto Smyrna, and unto Pergamos, and unto Thyatira, and unto Sardis, and unto Philadelphia, and unto Laodicea. (Revelation 1:9-11)

The Companion in Tribulation (v. 9)

Like another greatly beloved who had future events given to him, "I Daniel" (Dan. 9:2, 10:2), he writes "I John". He introduces himself as a brother, he recognises the relationship that exists in the family of God, he also says he is their companion in tribulation, which indicates the fellowship with them in their suffering. He is both in the family and also in the fight. It is lovely to see the simplicity of "brother". Men love their titles for they love to distinguish as they seek place and honour. It is a sad thing when seen in Christian circles, causing a hierarchal system to be put in place that was unknown and unpracticed in apostolic times. They have not learned what Paul did in Phil. 3:3-8, to count worldly honour as dung.

John was a companion in three things: suffering, sovereignty and steadfastness. Though some would make this but one thing, he was in tribulation on account of the kingdom, and was doing it with endurance. Yet it is true, "all that will live Godly in Christ Jesus shall suffer persecution" (2 Tim. 3:12). All have been "translated into the kingdom of his dear Son", (Col. 1:13) and Paul would exhort us "to endure hardness as a good soldier of Jesus Christ" (2 Tim. 2:3).

God loves to take note of where his people are, we are always in his thoughts, and our circumstances mean much to God. Note the places named in David's flights in 1 Samuel and the prophet's visions (Ezek. 1:1; Dan. 10:4). John is in Patmos, men say in banishment, hence "your companion in tribulation". John says he is there "for the word of God and for the testimony of Jesus Christ". There is advantage in adversity; the prison at Rome yields the rich ministry of Paul's prison epistles. Paul says his experience "had fallen out rather unto the furtherance of the gospel" (Phil. 1:12); to pioneer the way, open up the track. We are indebted to Paul for three things that came out of his imprisonment. If Philippians speaks of his preaching in prison, we then have his prayers from prison as seen in Ephesians, and his pen is the pen of a ready writer as he brings to us the prison epistles. Here, the glorious truths of Revelation are unveiled in exile, and banishment. God uses every circumstance for the blessing of his own.

If John is on the Isle "for the word of God and for the testimony of Jesus Christ", when he is there he must be "in the Spirit", for divine revelation comes through the Holy Spirit (1 Cor. 2:10; 2 Pet. 1:21). He "became in the Spirit", every believer receives the Holy Spirit upon believing (Eph. 1:13 [RV]). This is a special movement by the Spirit to unveil truth. As noted earlier, this marks the first of John's four visions.

"The Lord's Day", has posed problems to a few expositors, some make this expression "The Day of the Lord", a term first found in Isaiah 2:12 and many times after in the Old Testament. It occurs four times in the New Testament:

Acts 2:20	The promise of the Spirit	-	in the millennium
1 Thess. 5:2	Punishment for world	-	its judgement
2 Thess. 2:2	Prospect for saints	-	removed from it
2 Pet. 3:10	The passing of creation	-	all will be destroyed

The Day of the Lord is always associated with God's judgement of living men and of the universe. The book of Zephaniah 1: 14-18 gives a very definite interpretation of the Day of the Lord, "The great day of the Lord is near it is near and hasteth greatly, even the voice of the day of the Lord: the mighty men shall cry there bitterly. That day is a day of wrath, a day of trouble and distress, a day of wasteness and desolation, a day of darkness and gloominess, a day of clouds and thick darkness, a day of the trumpet and alarm against the fenced cities and against the high towers. And I will bring distress upon men, that they shall walk like blind men, because they have sinned against the Lord: and their blood shall be poured out as dust, and their flesh as dung. Neither their silver nor gold shall be able to deliver them in the day of the Lord's wrath; but the whole land shall be devoured by the fire of his jealousy; for he shall make even a speedy riddance of all them that dwell in the land". It takes us into tribulation days, which in the Revelation begins from Ch 6. That the Day of the Lord also takes in the universe is the subject of 2 Peter 3: 10 where the dissolving of all things is brought before us as being another aspect of the Day of the Lord. " But the Day of the Lord will come as a thief in the night; in the which the heavens shall pass away with a great noise, and the elements shall melt with fervent heat, and the earth also and all the works that are therein shall be burned up". Many other verses of scripture could be added to these to show that the Day of the Lord is a time of judgement and destruction. It is said by some, (Bullinger and his followers) that John was projected into the Day of the Lord, and that the scene before us carries us beyond the church age. This first vision is dealing with Christ and his Church, not the future judgement of ungodly men. Ironside says simply "it is an adjective, not a possessive", Grant "an adjective not a noun". It is the same form of expression as that found in 1 Cor.11: 20, where it speaks of "the Lord's supper". The term is descriptive both of the supper and the day, "the first day of the week", which is the day of Christ's resurrection; it is also the day the church was formed, (Lev. 23:15-16, Acts 2:1). It was evidently the day the saints met in the assembly gatherings (Acts 20:7), and the day the collection has to be laid aside by the believers (1 Cor. 16:2). All these are connected with the church of this dispensation in its witness for God. On such a day John has his vision.

The Call as of a Trumpet (vv. 10-11)

"In the spirit", John hears the sound of a trumpet behind him. Trumpets are used with many major dealings of God with men: such as the giving of the Law, (Ex. 19:13-19, Heb. 12:19). The trumpet will sound at the churches rapture, (1 Thess. 4:16). It is said to sound at the change of the living believers (1 Cor. 15:51-52), and though we know that this coincides with the rapture, yet there is no word of the saints leaving the earth in these verses. At the world's judgement in Revelation Ch 8 the sound of the trumpet is also heard, and again when Israel is re-gathered (Matt. 24:31) the trumpet will be blown. John's vision of Christ in the midst of the seven golden lampstands (Rev. 1:13) is preceded by the, "voice as of a trumpet", it is also seen in His vision of the throne room in Rev. 4:1

Men have built their doctrines around the blowing of trumpets, teaching that saints will pass through the tribulation, because trumpets are used with the rapture and the tribulation and the Lord's coming to Israel, but the truth is, all God's major dealings are heralded with a trumpet sound.

The sound is behind him, like Moses in Ex. 3:3, John is going to have to turn. Interest will give him intelligence. Perhaps one reason for the lack of understanding in the truth of God today is because we are not prepared to turn!

The opening words of v.11 are omitted by many scholars, they say they are "an interpolation" from v. 8. Young's literal translation retains them, as does the received text. If they are retained, they show that the Lord Jesus spoke to John, as he did to the churches in Ch 2 and 3. What he is to see, must become a faithful record for the benefit of the seven churches. The Lord is dealing directly with the churches. He desires that we appreciate what the divine intention is.

His Discovery (vv. 12-18)

And I turned to see the voice that spake with me. And being turned, I saw seven golden candlesticks; And in the midst of the seven candlesticks one like unto the Son of man, clothed with a garment down to the foot, and girt about the paps with a golden girdle. His head and his hairs were white like wool, as white as snow; and his eyes were as a flame of fire; And his feet like unto fine brass, as if they burned in a furnace; and his voice as the sound of many waters. And he had in his right hand seven stars: and out of his mouth went a sharp two-edged sword: and his countenance was as the sun shineth in his strength. And when I saw him, I fell at his feet as dead. And he laid his right hand upon me, saying unto me, Fear not; I am the first and the last: I am he that liveth, and was dead; and, behold, I am alive for evermore, Amen; and have the keys of hell and of death. (Revelation 1:12-18)

On turning, John sees seven golden lampstands - (*luknia*) - a standing one, v. 20, states these are seven churches. Seven is the number of completion. Three things can be seen regarding the seven churches:

Autonomy v. 11; Divinity v. 12; Responsibility v. 13

Their Autonomy (v. 11)

Unlike the lampstand in the tabernacle, which had seven branches, speaking of the unified testimony of Israel before God, these are seven individual churches. Each stands alone before God, there is no papal head, no royal head, but all are under the authority of the risen head, Christ Jesus. Each stand accountable to him alone, and not to the other churches, nor can any interfere with another's affairs, or tell another assembly what to do. The word of God knows nothing of a federation of churches. Autonomy never indicates independency, if there is no federation, there is a fellowship. This is based on obedience to the word of God, and a common desire to practice its teachings. Paul left one pattern for all to follow (1 Cor. 7:17). In 1 Cor. 11:16 and in Ch 14:33, the practice of other churches is set before those at Corinth, to follow. The Thessalonians are set forth in Ch 1:7 as an ensample (type) to other believers in their zeal, and they were followers of the churches in their suffering (2:14). It must be noticed that the spirit's voice in Ch 2:3 is not only a voice to the church addressed, but "what he saith to the churches", showing that all truth is for all believers and that the Lord expects us to follow the same pattern.

Divinity (v. 12)

Golden lampstands. Gold is ever a symbol, when used with what is for God, of divine character. Every assembly has the Lord as its gathering centre (Matt. 18:20). Every assembly grows only as the Lord adds to it (Acts 2:47). He determines where they shall be (Acts 16:6-9). They exist as long as it pleases him (Rev. 2:5). It pleases God to exercise and bless the efforts of men, but we must never forget each church is a divine work. They bear divine names, the church of God (1 Cor. 1:2), and also the churches of Christ (Rom. 16:16). They do not belong to men, and it is sad when men link them to systems, nations or to eminent men, rather than give them the titles which scripture gives them.

Responsibility (v. 13)

John sees in the midst of the lampstands "one like unto the Son of Man". Evidently the Lord Jesus Christ is not now in the midst as in Matt. 18:20, where we are said to be gathered to him. Would that saints could value being gathered to the Lord's name, and all it stands for; many displace Christ today, and make anything but him the mode of gathering. Here the Lord is presented as a walking Priest, scrutinising leprous conditions. Whenever a priest is walking, (Lev. 13-14), it is to expose uncleanness. In the sanctuary he stood daily (Heb. 10:11). The leprous conditions of Ch 2 and 3 are about to be exposed. It is a night scene that is before us for lamps are for the night. In this present age, the age when the Lord is not present, the light of the world is no longer here, for the Lord said, "As long as I am in the world, I am the light of the world" (John 9:5). This is the age when prince of darkness rules, we wait for the morning star to appear to remove us from this present evil world (2:28.) The world waits for the Sun of Righteousness (Mal. 4:2) to usher in the millennial day, at that time the light of the world will return in the fullness of glory. Whilst we wait we have a responsibility to shine for God in testimony. The Son of Man, his title of responsibility, is trimming the lamps in Ch 2-3 to see that a true testimony is given to men.

The title Son of Man is fitting, it is an Eternal title (John. 6:62) showing Christ is divine in character, (Matt. 16:13, 16) and authoritative in power (John 5:27). That power is demonstrated in the churches, for judgement must first begin there, (1 Pet. 4:17). Well might Peter say, "If it first begin at us, what shall the end be of them that obey not the gospel of God"? Something of that end is seen in Ch 6-20. May we move carefully under his eyes of fire.

Having caught sight of the Lord Jesus, the vision of him dominates the scene. How different from the one on whom he was happy to lay his head, this will cause him to fall at his feet as dead. In vv. 13-18 He is displayed in:

Majesty (v. 13) - His garment speaks of the honour he holds, the robes of a prince and a priest. Garments display character, he is a glorious Lord.

The Girdle: The priest (Ex. 28:39) wore a linen girdle symbolising that purity must mark him. The prophet, John, (Matt. 3:4) wore a leather girdle, speaking of the inflexibility of his ministry. The pilgrim, (1 Pet. 1:13), wears one of sobriety, he is told to gird up the loins of his mind. The Lord Jesus in John 13 wore a practical girdle, when he draped himself in a towel, the symbol of his humility. He is now seen as a prince and it is a golden girdle in majesty. The paps would speak of the tender affection that marks him. These are controlled by divine righteousness, the golden girdle.

Deity (v. 14) - The head and hair being white, do not speak of senility and decay, but rather holiness and purity. Here is the Ancient of Days of Dan. 7:9, where his garments are white as snow. In Daniel, it is the personal glory that is emphasised; in the book of Revelation, it is his wisdom and knowledge that are before us, that is why his head is the prominent feature.
The eyes as a flame of fire, would portray his omniscience, all knowing, all searching, nothing can escape his fiery glance.

Potency (v. 15) - Here his might is demonstrated, feet to conquer and to crush, fresh from the furnace as brass burning. Brass is ever the symbol of judgement. Those feet which are going to divide the Mount of Olives in twain at his return (Zech. 14:4), and are going to tread the wine press of the fierceness of Almighty God in Ch 19:15, here they are seen in connection with Christian testimony, in Ch 3:1 he is standing to judge the sins of Thyatira. His voice, not as in v. 10, as the sound of a trumpet in revelation, but now as many waters, which, as Ezek. 43:2 and Ps. 93:4 show speaks of his glory and might. John on the Isle of Patmos, hears and sees the relentless power and might of the surging waves, nothing can stay their power, what a glorious picture of the authority displayed by the Lord Jesus.

Superiority (v. 16) - In his right hand, the hand of power and authority are seven stars, which are seen as the Angels of the Churches in v. 20. We shall look at this in v. 20.

From his mouth went a sharp two- edged sword, Heb. 4:12, and Eph. 6:17 interpret this for us. It is the word of God, piercing and dividing. Nothing can stop its penetrating and exposing power. That word which brings salvation to sinners (Rom. 10:8-21; 1 Pet. 1:23-25), brings death to the armies of the beast in Ch 19:21. In Rom. 13:4, the sword speaks of judicial power and authority, when seen in the hands of men in government.

His countenance resplendent as the sun in all its power, in its brilliance, causing all other heavenly bodies to fade into obscurity so the Son of Man stands supreme, alone, all pale before him.

Sympathy (v. 17) - The august presence of the Lord Jesus does for John what such appearances did to Isaiah in Ch 6:5, also to Ezekiel in Ch 1:28, to Daniel in Ch 10:8 and to Saul in Acts 9:3-4. A true realisation of Deity will humble us. If a servant is going to be used of God, it must be against the backcloth of realising the character of him whom we serve, and that it is his hand that sets us up. The hand that holds the stars is the hand that lifts John. If divine revelation is given to a man, it is not to leave him prostrate but to raise him up to use it for God's glory. Let men wait until it pleases the Lord to stand them on their feet.

How sweet it is to hear "Fear not", such was the message of the Angel in Matt. 1:20 to Joseph, to Mary in Luke 1:30, and to the shepherds in Luke 2:10. It is the word of the Lord to Paul in Acts 27:24, even John must know this from the Lord Jesus, for the presence of the Lord in such majesty causes him to recognise his frailty, when in the presence of deity.

If John is going to be raised to serve, he must learn that the Lord must have the first place. Sadly, men who have been raised up of God sometimes overstep the bounds, as Diotrephes in 3 John. It is a blessed honour to be gifted and used of God, but we must ever remember it is a gift of grace, given by the sovereign will of the Spirit (1 Cor. 12:4, 11), or by the risen Head (Eph. 4:11), all we are and have is of God. The word of God in 1 Cor. 1:26-31 teaches us of those whom God uses, and states that he has moved among the foolish, the weak, the base and the things which are not, "that no flesh should glory in his presence", and that we should glory in the Lord. I believe it is to this end that the Lord Jesus is set forth as the First and the Last. If in v. 8 "the beginning and the ending" has to do with time, the "first and last" has to do with place, he takes the supreme place. It is the same in Col. 1:17 where it is recorded "He is before all things". This has nothing to do with time, though that is true, it has to do with place, it is the place God has given him in the creation. As my wife comes before all in the family, so Christ is before all in creation.

Victory (v. 18) - The sight that fills John's eyes is that of a victorious Christ, he is the living one. Seiss, admirably puts it when he writes "this is another title of Deity. It refers not to mere manifested life, but to life inherent and un-derived". Paul pens it well when he says, in 1 Tim. 6:16, "who only hath immortality", or John who says, (John 1:4), "In Him was life", yet though the Lord Jesus has no liability to death, he had the ability to die. The reading is, "and became dead". Let mortal man tread this road with care. Mystery unfathomable, the mind tells us, God cannot die, yet he who is God, became dead! "That through death he might destroy him that had the power of death, that is, the devil, and deliver us who through fear of death were all our lifetime subject to bondage", (Heb. 2:14-15). He who became dead is alive for evermore. "Death could not keep its prey, Jesus my Saviour, he tore the bars away, Jesus my Lord". The great work for our redemption has been finished; he lives in the power of an endless life. In resurrection power, all authority is given unto him. In the temptation the Devil said, "All this will I give thee" it was the easy road to kingdom glory, but the Lord Jesus according to Ps. 2:8 will ask his father, and far more is given to him. Not only the kingdoms and the glory of them, but also, "all power in heaven and earth", (Matt. 28:18). Also here all power in the unseen world. The keys speak of absolute authority, this over the bodies and souls of men. Some texts put death, the body, before hell, the soul. The power over these realms is in the hand of the Lord Jesus. In Ch 3:7 he has the added power of Universal Dominion, the "keys of David". The blessed one who, "became dead", now in the power of his resurrection, has supreme authority invested in himself. Well may we say Amen!

John's Ministry (vv. 19-20)

Write the things which thou hast seen, and the things which are, and the things which shall be hereafter; The mystery of the seven stars which thou sawest in my right hand, and the seven golden candlesticks. The seven stars are the angels of the seven churches: and the seven candlesticks which thou sawest are the seven churches. (Revelation 1:19-20)

Authority (v. 19)

The command of the Lord Jesus to write is fulfilled by John. As we have already seen, the verse has been well spoken of as giving the three main divisions of the book, the three statements also sum up John's three ministries (a) The Gospel, "the things which thou hast seen", (b) His Epistles, "the things which are", and (c) The Revelation "the things which shall be hereafter.

Mystery (v. 20)

The word mystery appears 27 times in the New Testament. Someone has said, a mystery is not something mysterious, but that which was not revealed in the Old Testament, but now revealed in the New. Something that Eph. 3:9 states was hid in God and Col. 1:26 hid from ages, time, and generations, people, but is now made manifest to his saints. Campbell Morgan has said "not only revealed in this present age, but only revealed to faith" which seems to bring out the truth of the word "mystery" with clarity and succinctness, for the world cannot receive the truth of God.

The New Testament mysteries can be summed up by four headings:

(1) Doctrinal, these have to do with the word of God, as in 1 Tim. 3:9, "the mystery of the faith". There are also, (2) Dispensational mysteries, which bring before us God's dealings with the truth of the Church, as seen in Eph. 3:1-10. There are also mysteries, (3) Devotional, mysteries which relate to the person of Christ, which are brought before us in 1 Tim. 3:16. God also unveils others that are, (4) Diabolical in character, to do with evil as in 2 Thess. 2:7, Rev. 17:5. Many other scriptures could be added to these that have been quoted, we are merely giving examples of the truths before us.

The mystery here is seen to be twofold, "the mystery of the seven stars which thou sawest in my right hand, and the seven golden lampstands", thus, something that has not been seen in Old Testament times, is now revealed as the linking of the stars with the lampstands. The second part of the mystery is very simple. The lampstands are the seven churches, which is quite evidently those of v. 11, and who are going to be addressed in Ch 2 and 3. The problem lies with the former part of the mystery, the seven stars, it is here that men differ. Some find no difficulty, for again we are told, the stars are the Angels of the seven churches. They say if a symbol is interpreted, you cannot interpret it to become something else, therefore, these are seven literal angels. To some this presents a problem as angels are never seen to be responsible for a church, and Ch 2 and 3 make it very plain that these Angels are responsible for the character the church displays. Angels are seen in the epistles as looking on the activities of the church, learning from them, but never responsible for them. In 1 Pet. 1:12 they crane their necks to look into the gospel. In 1 Cor. 11:10 they look upon the gatherings of Christians and desire to see the restoration of divine order set in creation, that was ruined by the fall, when a woman stepped out of her place. They delight to see a spiritual woman manifesting the place of subjection, by wearing a veil. It is a sad day when intelligent men look at 1 Cor. 11 as merely local conditions, telling us that the immoral woman of the day went with uncovered head, and this practice of head covering by women is not followed. As one notable man F. F. Bruce says, "the veil has only 'cultural relativity' ". 1 Cor. 11 speaks nothing of the veil being merely a cultural thing to cover local conditions, its whole teaching is based on God's creatorial order as seen in Gen. 1-2. Let men remember, an unveiled woman exposes the male, as her head, to shame, bringing dirty, base, lewd things upon them, which is the strength of the word "shame". Also in Eph. 3:10 angels look upon the church dispensational, seeing the manifold wisdom of God in uniting Jew and Gentile. No, they are not responsible for, but they learn from, the church. As far as the kingdom is concerned, angels have a very definite part to play, but here we are on church ground. I cannot conceive these to be literal angels. Kelly writes, "they are the responsible element in the church", but he does not define who this responsible element is. This is understakable when we know his teaching regarding elders causing the pendulum to swing too far away from the doctrines of the established church with its state appointed bishops. He says, bishops can only be appointed by an apostle, or an apostolic delegate, and as we have no apostles today, they being in the foundation of the church (Eph. 2:20), so we can have no bishops today. However, Acts 20:28 shows that bishops/elders are made by the Holy Spirit, not by men, and the Spirit is still very active. I believe the stars, angels, a word indicating messenger, are certainly not seven carriers of the letters from John to the seven churches as others teach. There was only one book to carry anyway (v. 11). Others put them as the individual pastor, or minister, but the bible knows nothing of individuals ever being in charge of a church, the local assembly is so precious to God, that he always desires a number of men to be responsible for its care and teaching. Acts 13:1-2 declares that at least five ministering men functioned in the assembly at Antioch, 1 Cor. 12 shows the spirit gave nine different gifts to different men to function for God, Phil. 1:1 would teach that the church is composed of saints, plural, bishops, plural, and deacons [ministers], plural, and 1 Tim. 3 would indicate a plurality of bishops and ministers (deacons). These are responsible for the church, which is never placed into the hands of one man who is supposed to have all the gifts that are necessary to build up and protect the flock. These men have to give account to the Lord for their ministry in a coming day at the Judgement seat of Christ, bishops in Heb. 13:17 and teachers (ministers) in 1 Cor. 3:11-15.

Taking the figure of the star we know these are set to guide the traveller, so elders are termed your guides, and the purpose of these that are responsible for the church is to guide them as they testify for God. "Obey them that have the rule over you, and submit yourselves: for they watch over your souls as they that must give account, that they may do it with joy, and not with grief" (Heb. 13:17). The word "rule" is "guide", in the marginal reading. The responsibility of the guides is to see that the church moves in a manner that is consistent with bearing testimony for God. False teachers are also called "Wandering Stars" (Jude v. 13). They give no guidance to their followers. The Priest, in Mal. 2:7, in his teaching ministry is seen as a messenger (LXX Angel). The same is said of the one who was to prepare the way for the Lord Jesus in Mal. 3:1, and also of the Lord Jesus himself in the same verse. Thus scripture would seem to indicate that the stars, messengers, are the elders and teachers of the assembly. These are responsible to the Lord for the character the assembly takes. Identified with it not a representative of the church.

Chapter 2

The Seven churches

Introduction

We now come to "the things which are", the present testimony of God's light bearers in the world. As we scan the messages to the churches, we see all is not well. Things are not as the Lord desires them to be. We hear calls to repent, we hear of threatened judgements, carelessness, high-handedness, indifference, and lukewarmness, are all exposed. Evils, moral and doctrinal are seen. Such has been Christian testimony this past 2000 years.

There are at least three ways to look at the seven churches

(a) Present, (b) Practical, (c) Prophetic

(a) Present - These were actual churches present in John's day. Each church is responsible to the Lord for the character of testimony they give. In Ch 1, they come under his sovereignty, in Ch 2-3 they are subject to his scrutiny.

(b) Practical - The voice of the Spirit to each church, proves that these churches convey more than a local interest. For he speaks to the churches, not just to the church addressed. His voice is for every assembly to take heed to. P.W. Grant writes, "If we were to do what the Lord commends and to judge what he condemns, we would have the perfect church". Let those who shepherd and teach look well to the character of the assembly in which they serve God. Trench admits these chapters are not read in any circumstance whatsoever in the congregation of the Church of England. We need to read them often and be exercised to act by them.

(c) Prophetic - That the seven churches have a prophetic character, giving an outline of the history of the Church on earth from Pentecost until the rapture, presents no difficulty to me. There are many who would object to this form of interpretation but as W. Rodgers has said in connection with another matter "they are welcome to their opinion". H. Ironside gives the illustration of finding a key to a door that has been fastened for years and has written, "If the key fits without forcing, evidently it's the key for the door". I do not suppose John understood the prophetic character seen in the churches but he spake as a prophet, and prophets always spake better than they knew, "Enquiring and searching diligently" (1 Pet. 1:10) - but as we look back over the pages of time, church history has followed the order and pattern that each church displays. As the seven feasts of Jehovah (Lev. 23) teach us Jewish history, and the seven parables of the kingdom (Matt. 13) teach Kingdom history, it would be strange if God did not delineate somewhere church history. I believe this is done in these chapters. The prophecy of the Revelation commences in Ch 1:3, "the words of this prophecy", not in Ch 6:1 which starts the prophecy relative to the tribulation which is to try the earth dwellers.

That these seven churches are chosen is in itself significant, other churches were evidently in the area (Col. 2:1, 4:13). The Lord has chosen these seven because of the message they convey to the churches. Seven, the number of completion, tells the character the churches would bear from losing their first love soon after apostolic departure through the persecution it would bear under Roman Government until Constantine. The linking of church and state by this Emperor seen in Pergamos, and the rise of religious evil dominantly in the 6th century, left but a few who held truth for God. The majority were steeped in idolatry under the guise of Christianity in Thyatira, the deadness of reformation days in Sardis, separating for political expediency rather than to obey the word of God, bringing with it much of the trammels of that idolatry so that some men who speak most against it love its garb, its ecclesiastical system, its distinctions to honour men, using its names and titles that the New Testament knows nothing of. Well might it be said that "thou hast a name that thou livest and art dead". We rejoice before God for the great movement in churches and men, when in the last century many sought again to move in true brotherly love, to honour the name of our Lord Jesus Christ and seek even in much weakness to honour the word. A great fervour was seen to take the gospel to the world. Vast continents were opened to the gospel. Possibly millions have been redeemed as a result of the plain declaration of the word of God. The truth of God has been honoured by many who search the scriptures, and the great hope of the Lord's return has been rekindled. Would that Philadelphia closed these messages to the churches. Sadly, Laodicea has yet to follow, it is the church of the last days. The spirit of democracy and the rights of the people prevail, indifference marks those who profess salvation, they boast much, but it is of materialism not spirituality. The Lord stands outside the church that has organised itself so much it can do without him. Christianity can flourish without Christ. He must spew this out, whilst he still longs for fellowship with his own (3:20). In this manner present testimony ends. The trumpet is soon to sound and the saints to be taken to heaven, as typified in John (Ch 4:1). When a door is opened in heaven and the voice as of a trumpet says, "Come up hither and I will show thee things which must be hereafter".

In the seven churches we see:

1. The Exactness of Ephesus   A Loveless Church
2. The Executions at Smyrna   A Loyal Church
3. The Exposure of Pergamos   A Liberal Church
4. The Excesses of Thyatira   A Lawless Church
5. The Expiry of Sardis   A Lifeless Church
6. The Example of Philadelphia   A Living Church
7. The Exasperations of Laodicea   A Lukewarm Church

In them we see:

1. The Faithlessness of Saints   Personal
2. The Fury of the Devil   Physical
3. The Flattery of Balaam   Moral
4. The Fanaticism of Jezebel   Doctrinal

5. The Fallacy of Testimony   Fatal
6. The Faithful Fellow Labourers Spiritual
7. The Fantasy of Prosperity   Material

Note: The kind of persons within the Church - "Eyes as a flame of fire" (1:14).

Chapter 2:2 Evil - Liars, v. 6 with deeds the Lord hates, v. 14 sacrilegious fornicators, v. 15 holding false doctrine which the Lord hates, v. 20 seducers, v. 22 adulterers (spiritual and doctrinal seduction), v. 24 those which have known the depth of Satan, Ch 3:1 dead, v. 2 decaying, v. 16 lukewarm, v. 17 self-satisfied.

Note the drastic actions of the Lord who has, "Feet as Burning Brass" (1:15).
Ephesus   2:5   Remove the Lampstand
Pergamos   2:16   To make war against them with the sword of his mouth.
Thyatira   2:22   Cast her and her associates into great tribulation.
            2:23   Kill her children with death.
Sardis   3:3   Where he will plunder as a thief.
Laodicea   3:16   Spew them out of his mouth.

These are "the things which are". As we are linked to this present testimony of the Church, what contribution do we make to its well being for the glory of God?

We take a look at the seven churches in a brief way in the following pages. There are similarities found in each of them as:

1. The commission to the angel.
2. The character of Christ displayed to each.
3. The commendation of the saints.
4. Condemnation of failure by the saints.
   Only Smyrna in suffering and Philadelphia in simplicity are not condemned.
5. Correction given.
6. A call to repent.
7. A challenge of blessing to the one who overcomes.

Ephesus - Desirable
A Loveless Church

In the message to Ephesus we see:

Destination of the Letter (v. 1a)

Ephesus means desirable. There was much about it that must have been desirable to the Lord. Note its:

(a) Privilege, There are at least four occasions when scripture is directed to them after the record of the forming of the assembly in Acts 19. They are, the address to the Elders by Paul in Acts Ch 20 at Troas, then there is the epistle that bears the name, Ephesians, another letter that has the Ephesians in view is 1 Timothy, (1:3), and here in Rev. 2.

Paul addresses to the shepherds (Acts 20), the saints in the epistle of Ephesians, and the servant in 1 Timothy.

The final message is by the Lord himself to the stars or angel (Rev. Ch 2).

(b) Progress, This is seen by the high ground they reached as the truth of the "Church which is His Body" is unfolded to them in Ephesians. This truth was given to Paul by revelation (Ch 3:3) and should be understood by the saints (v. 4). This mystery, was hid in God and unknown to Old Testament saints, but revealed to the believers of the present day.

(c) Problems, No work of God is safe either from the flesh or satanic activity. Both evils are seen in the address of Acts Ch 20 and also recorded in I Timothy. In Acts Ch 20 it is men who are the source of the problem (vv. 28-31), in 1 Timothy the attack comes from "seducing spirits and doctrines of devils" (1 Tim. 4:1).

(d) Possibility, There was a danger that for all the privileges that they enjoyed and the blessings bestowed by God, such was the lapse into formalism, that the lampstand would be removed. The gold has become dim in many testimonies, he who causes the lampstand to shine, (Acts 2:47), also has the right to remove a lampstand.

Description of the Lord (v. 1b)

Unto the angel of the church of Ephesus write; These things saith he that holdeth the seven starts in his right hand, who walketh in the midst of the seven golden candlesticks; (Revelation 2:1)

The character the Lord displays is drawn from the features seen in Ch 1, as it is in each of the churches addressed. The promises to the overcomer can all be found at the end of the book of Revelation. The Lord is set forth as the holder of, and the one who walks in the midst of the seven golden lampstands, holding the stars, who are responsible to him for the well being of the testimony and walking in the midst of that testimony. He is a walking priest with the snuffers in his hand. The stars are light for God in the church, and the lampstand is a light for God in the world. The lampstand will only shine as the stars do their work aright.

Definition of their Labours (vv. 2-3)

I know thy works, and thy labour, and thy patience, and how thou canst not bear them which are evil: and thou hast tried them which say they are apostles, and are not, and hast found them liars: And hast borne, and hast patience, and for my name's sake hast laboured, and hast not fainted. (Revelation 2:2-3)

One could not do better than quote what one has said in this regard. "They were sound in Doctrine v. 2, strict in Discipline v. 2, and steadfast in Duty". The Lord says, "I know". Only he knows the true character of the testimony we bear (Heb. 4:13). "Their works" v. 2, would speak of what is done by them, the thought is that of, "labours", with how it's done (*Kopon*). Vine says, it primarily denotes a striking, a beating, then, toil resulting in weariness. Divine service is never easy (2 Cor. 2:23-28). "Patience" is the attitude whilst doing it. The word has the thought of endurance.

We are living in a day of compromise, many no doubt love truth but sadly they do not hate sin. For evil to come in it is enough for good men to say nothing. Those responsible for the Ephesian church looked well to their responsibilities as far as men were concerned.

Three classes are seen:

v. 2, (a) Evil men are exposed, indicating moral failure. (b) Then there were those who sought the highest place in the church, the supreme ruling body among the saints, the Apostles. These were "tried", a concrete discovery was made, for they found them to be liars. How often men seek place above the gift that is given to them, and try to lord it over the assembly. Rom. 12:3 needs to be kept in mind "For I say through the grace given unto me, to every man that is among you, not to think more highly of himself than he ought to think; but to think soberly, according a God has dealt to every man the measure of faith". These exhibited doctrinal failure. (c) The third evil that is seen is that of the Nicolaitanes in v. 6. These demonstrate Ecclesiastical failure. Something of this will be seen when commenting on it.

v. 3 - If they could not bear evil in v. 2, they could bear and endure as seen in the faithful labours when toiling for God to the point of weariness. "Labour" has this thought in view. If in vv. 2-3 we are taught they had a fine head, in v. 4 they had a faulty heart.

Dismissal of Love (v. 4)

Nevertheless I have somewhat against thee, because thou hast left thy first love (Revelation 2:4)

How sad that as the Lord searches he finds heart trouble such as can be the death of the assembly. JND Translation omits "somewhat". This is no small matter. It seems this was a definite act, "didst leave", is better rendered, "to send away". It is used in Matt 4:11 of the devil leaving Christ and Matt. 26:56 of the disciples forsaking and fleeing from Christ.

Their first love has the thought of the foremost love. There are some twenty references to love in the Epistle to the Ephesians, their heart was warm then. By the time Paul addressed the elders in Acts 20 it seems to be on the wane.

Some were drawing away disciples after themselves, like Diotrephes in 3 John. These men sought the pre-eminence.

Disaster for the Lampstand (v. 5)

Remember therefore from whence thou are fallen, and repent, and do the first works; or else I will come unto thee quickly, and will remove thy candlestick out of his place, except thou repent. (Revelation 2:5)

Four things are seen in this verse; as the Lord looks over their testimony he says:

Remember the fall - Does this indicate they knew the time when love was dismissed? One wonders what had influenced the assembly to cause that the love had been lost, but when love has gone it makes for a fallen assembly.

Repent of the failure - We often call sinners to repent, but seldom see a need for it in saints. The Lord calls four of the seven churches to repent, and to Laodicea he also offers counsel.

Recover the fellowship - "Do" = Repeat the first works. That is, to put energy into the love they had in v. 4, their first love.

Remove the Facade - He who forms assemblies has the right to remove them. It is a divine act, both to establish and to remove. "I will", how sad when the risen Christ would rather there was no testimony to his name in a locality, when formal legalism takes over from fervent love, or as in 1 Cor. 11:17 in failing lives. It causes us to wonder how many testimonies have been removed because of failure to move in love and according to the will of God.

Deeds of the Lawless (v. 6)

But this thou hast, that thou hatest the deeds of the Nicolaitanes, which I also hate. (Revelation 2:6)

If there was a need to take sides with God against themselves in v. 5, for repentance means agreeing with God by a change of mind, here they are in full harmony with the Lord. They hate what he hates, Nicolaitaneism, here they loathe their deeds. Deeds if left unchecked soon become doctrines which are acceptable as they do in the letter to Pergamos as seen in v. 15. Little is known about the Nicolaitanes. Some have cast a slur against Nicholas, one of honest report, and full of the Holy Ghost, (Acts 6:3-5) saying he became debauched and decadent, the leader of a licentious sect. To speak against him is both unwarranted and unreasonable, being mere conjecture.

Many have seen here the rise of the clerical system that has prevailed in the church for centuries. "Nicolaitanes" comes from two words, *nikao* to conquer, and *laos* the people, from which we get our laity. Together they have the meaning, "a conquering of the people"; this makes for a hierarchy, and makes a distinction between the ministers and the people, of which the scripture knows nothing. If this is the true interpretation of the word then we must realise that such a system is hated in heaven, and sadly has become a doctrine revered in Christendom.

Desire to Listen (v. 7)

He that hath an ear, let him hear what the Spirit saith unto the churches; To him that overcometh will I give to eat of the tree of life, which is in the midst of the paradise of God. (Revelation 2:7)

A young lady said to me on one occasion regarding preaching she had listened to, but which was not heeded (Matt. 7:26-27), "I'm not saying I did not hear, but I did not listen". How often do we fail to respond to the truth that is ministered to us.

In the first three churches, the Spirit's call "to hear" is placed before the promise to the overcomer. In the last four it is reversed. Here the Spirit is pressing home the message of the risen Christ. Notice it is a personal word, "he", and yet it is to be a word spoken to all, for it is a word to "the churches". This indicates that what is said to one church is for all to take heed too.

The promise to the overcomer is an inducement to faithfulness, not a promise of reward. It is the carrot that is set before the donkey to encourage it to keep moving. These promises are for all believers, for none can be lost, and all who are saved will enjoy the tree of life (Rev. 22:2-14). Just as in the promise to Smyrna, no believer can ever be hurt of the "second death" (20:14) which is the "lake of fire". These promises are not distinguishing marks among believers, as if some will not overcome, and find themselves swallowed up by carelessness, and as a result will not enjoy the promise that is set before the believer. A doctrine has been formulated which in part is founded on these promises to the overcomer; it is called the doctrine of the partial rapture. Those that hold this teaching would tell us that only those who are living the kind of life that merits the salvation of God will be in the rapture. We know that many a child of God has failed miserably as far as his personal testimony is concerned, and others know little of separation from the world like Lot (2 Pet. 2:8). Let us be assured, our salvation does not depend on our standing, but on the finished work of Christ. A brother let me read a letter that he had received from a missionary not long after my conversion. The missionary had penned a footnote to his letter stating, "if we believe 1 Thess 4:14, that is all we need to be in the rapture". We thank God that our salvation did not begin with works, and neither does it depend on works, the work of Calvary is sufficient!

The word "overcomer" is (nikao), to conquer. It occurs ten times in the Gospels and Epistles, and sixteen times in the Revelation. In such a day as the Revelation depicts there is a need for overcomers. It is used of the Lord Jesus, and of his right to take the book out of the hand of the throne sitter, he "hath prevailed" (Ch 5:5). It is used of the "rider on the white horse", the man of sin in Ch 6:2, who, "went forth conquering and to conquer". It is used of saints in Ch 12:11, Ch 15:2 and Ch 21:7, who are said to have, "overcome", or "Have gotten the victory", it is also used in 1 John2:13 of believers overcoming the Devil, and the same epistle in Ch 4:4 writes of overcoming his Deceivers, and also his Domain in Ch 5:4. In these verses we find that the Lord gives the believer power over all the efforts of the adversary to destroy us. This last verse tells me all believers are overcomers for they are born of God. Man in innocence did not eat of the tree of life, man in sin could not (Gen. 3:22-24), man redeemed, will (Rev. 22:2, 14).

Another interesting feature of the Churches is how they span the Old Testament. Ephesus takes us back to the Garden of Eden; Smyrna to the brick kilns of Egypt; Pergamos to the wanderings in the desert. In Thyatira we are brought into the land with Jezebel in the ascendancy; Sardis, the captivity with a few like Daniel which have not defiled their garment; Philadelphia, the return to the land under Ezra, and Laodicea brings before us the sad decline as seen in Malachi.

Smyrna - Sorrow/Suffering/Myrrh
A Loyal Church

Place of Correspondence (v. 8a)

Thayer tells us, that Smyrna was an Ionian city on the Aegean sea, about 40 miles north of Ephesus. It had a harbour and flourished in trade, commerce and the arts. The International Standard Bible Encyclopaedia states, "It was celebrated for its schools of science and medicine and for its handsome buildings. Polycarp was martyred there, the Jews being more antagonistic than the Romans, for even though murdered on the Sabbath, it was the Jews who brought the wood to fuel the fire. The city still exists as IZMIR with a large population. Its present name is a Turkish corruption of the ancient name".

Smyrna simply means myrrh; to which there are three other references in the New Testament.

(a) Matt. 2:11   -   Where it is linked to the birth of Christ,
(b) Mark 15:23 -   Seen with His death,
(c) John 19:39 -   In His burial.

No record is given of how the assembly was formed, but that it was to endure violent persecution is evident from this letter.

The Person of Christ (v. 8b)

And unto the angel of the church in Smyrna write; These things saith the first and the last, which was dead, and is alive; (Revelation 2:8)

1 Thess. 2:13 records the blessed truth of "the word of God which effectually worketh also in you that believe". How blessed for saints who are to know persecution to know the Lord in this capacity. He is over all; he is the first and the last. He has passed through it all, "I am he that became dead" ("became" is better, it speaks of death under his control) "and is alive". With possible death before them through persecution, hope is placed in their heart. The God of the Smyrnians was Dionysus, the dispenser of life and the dispenser of death. Guests were given crowns at his celebrations, what vain hope for the world, but Christ gives a glorious prospect to the saints.

The Poverty of the Christians (v. 9)

I know thy works, and tribulation, and poverty, (but thou art rich) and [I know] the blasphemy of them which say they are Jews, and are not, but [are] the synagogue of Satan. (Revelation 2:9)

The Lord knows all, the energy put into their works Godward, the enmity endured from the world, and the extremity of need selfward. Physical persecutions make for material poverty, (Heb. 10:32-34).

Prosperity in Calamity

Some Christians are very poor, all they have is money, (Ch 3:17). A man once told me he was stopped in his tracks when someone asked him, did he want to be rich or enriched. Many feel money is the answer to all of life's problems, rather than a cause, for the love of money is the root of all evil, (1 Tim. 6:9-10). Look what Naomi found through adversity, (Ruth 4:14-15), Moses also when "Choosing rather to suffer affliction with the people of God, than to enjoy the pleasures of sin for a season; esteeming the reproach of Christ greater riches than the treasures of Egypt" (Heb. 11:26). The Lord Jesus also knew the same experience in Heb. 12:2-3, "who for the joy that was set before him endured the cross, despising the shame, and is set down at the right hand of the throne of God. For consider him that endured such contradiction of sinners against himself, lest ye be wearied and faint in your minds". The Lord says to these believers that they have a wealth far beyond anything this world can give, "thou art rich", and we recall his words in the Gospel of John that he does not give as the world giveth.

The source of the enmity is exposed. Those who once enjoyed nearness to God, Jews, are now seen at a great distance, they are exposed as "the synagogue of Satan". The title given to the devil is that of Slanderer, Adversary. He once stirred up all against the Jews when they stood in the place of privilege, but now like himself having lost such a place (Ezek. 28:13-15), he uses them to oppose what is of God. The blasphemy here is toward man not God, though I suppose ultimately it is against God and Christ - (John 15:18-21; Acts 9:4). The body may suffer on earth but the Head in heaven feels it.

Persecution Coming (v. 10)

Fear none of those things which thou shalt suffer: behold, the devil shall cast [some] of you into prison, that ye may be tried; and ye shall have tribulation ten days: be thou faithful unto death, and I will give thee a crown of life. (Revelation 2:10)

The devil is to stir up trouble; as the roaring lion he will persecute the saints; when this fails to silence the Church's testimony he will seek to nullify its power through patronage in Pergamos, where he becomes the Angel of light.

Period Confined

The persecution is both allowed and allocated by God, as also its duration and intensity, they shall have tribulation, "Ten days", and it should read "even" unto death, their sufferings were to be severe during this period. God always defines, and confines the period of testing, and we can rest assured that "God is faithful, who will not suffer you to be tempted above that ye are able, but will with the temptation also make a way to escape, that ye may be able to bear it" There were thirty-eight years of trial for Israel in the wilderness, Israel was to know seventy years of captivity in Babylon, and there are seven years of tribulation for the world, and ten days for the saints. During the Roman powers from Nero to Diocletion there were 10 distinct edicts to persecute Christians, the last and most ferocious lasted 10 years. The persecutions are set forth in a four-fold way:

(a) National   - Jew,
(b) Diabolical - Devil,
(c) Institutional - Prison,
(d) Fatal   - Death.

Like those of Dan. 3:25, the saints never walk alone in such an hour of trial.

Promised Crown

The Lord selects the Crown of Life as encouragement in such a day, (James 1:12) - given not as some say to the martyr; but it is given, "to those who love him". Every believer will get this crown. In James 2:5 there is a Kingdom in which we will wear the crown, this is also promised to them that love him. There are five crowns set forth as goals for believers (see Ch 3:11).

A Personal Call

As in all the churches, if the angel is responsible for the church and the testimony it gives, so is every believer responsible to respond to the word of the Lord, "he that hath ears to hear let him hear".

A Prospect to Comfort

The Lord Jesus in commissioning the 12 (Matt. 10) - warned of the hostility they would receive as they serve him. The worst man can do is to destroy the body (v. 28), but God can destroy both body and soul in Gehenna, this teaches that Gehenna corresponds to the lake of fire of Rev. 20:14 and that the body is also eternal, not only the soul. I notice there is no mention of the spirit being cast there. Perhaps Ecc. 12:7 would teach that every man's spirit goes back to God that gave it, and this is the reason that the spirit of a man is not seen to join the body and soul in eternal punishment. To the believer is given the assurance that the final, eternal judgement can never be theirs, we have an eternal salvation.

Pergamos – Elevation/Actual Marriage
A Liberal Church

And to the angel of the church in Pergamos write; These things saith he which hath the sharp sword with two edges; (Revelation 2:12)

Sending Address (v. 12a)

As we know, the word church is a word that simply means a called out people. Sadly Pergamos seems to have lost this ground. It had become like its name, elevated in the world and married to it. The period depicted is the days of Constantine, 313 AD and onward, when he adopted Christianity, and made it favourable to the people. The persecutions of Satan in Smyrna change to patronage from the government in Pergamos. A bishop in the church was given a leading role in society, church and state become one. The church's position in the world is relinquished and, to hold its new ground, it has to compromise the truth of God, which it has done ever since.

Saviour's Appearance (v. 12b)

The Lord is seen to have "the sharp sword with two edges" (Heb. 4:12). The word of God, is the sword that goeth out of his mouth Ch 1:16. Here it is used toward the saints. It has two edges, one edge, to lift saints out of the world, and the other, to lift the world out of the saints. In Ch 19:15 the sword is to be used again against sinners.

Settled Abode (v. 13a)

I know thy works, and where thou dwellest, [even] where Satan's seat [is]: and thou holdest fast my name, and hast not denied my faith, even in those days wherein Antipas [was] my faithful martyr, who was slain among you, where Satan dwelleth. (Revelation 2:13)

The Lord knoweth their works; sadly their activity is matched by their abode. He knows where they dwell, this word means to dwell fixedly, and the world had become a settled state for the Christians. They were dwelling where Satan's seat-throne was; this is no place for the saints. They had lost their pilgrim character and with it their ability to discern and judge evil. It is little wonder the Lord takes them back to Israel's wilderness experience. In such a place the church was still faithful to the fundamentals. The Lord says, "Thou holdest fast my name and they have not denied my faith", unlike Jezebel who has done this in Thyatira. They did this in days when Antipas was martyred. (Antipas means everyone against), one man at least was faithful to the Lord in such a day. The world will soon silence his voice and testimony.

Satan's Authority (v. 13b)

Satan's throne was there, that which had formally been at Babylon and from where he indoctrinated the world, and he occupied the throne to influence nations against God. It now seems that the centre of Babylon's teaching has been moved and was established in Pergamos, having moved from Babylon. Was the devil interested in having his power now in the midst of Christianity, as it was moving westward? Thus leaving Babylon for a time, first to corrupt the church in the Grecian provinces, later to move the headquarters of Babylon's cults to just north of Rome, where the Caesars ultimately had them brought into the church at Rome, and through these two areas of Christianity, Eastern and Western to pervade the whole of Christendom with its doctrines, and Christendom adopted its practices. The ISBE states that there was an altar 40 foot high to ZEUS and it was one of the wonders of the world. It had temples to Dionysius, Athene and Aesculopius, to the latter, invalids from all over Asia flocked. The priest and physicians received dreams in the night about remedies to dispense to cure them. An easy way to get rich it would seem! It was the chief religious centre of the province.

Sanctioning Affiliations (vv. 14-15)

But I have a few things against thee, because thou hast there them that hold the doctrine of Balaam, who taught Balak to cast a stumblingblock before the children of Israel, to eat things sacrificed unto idols, and to commit fornication. So hast thou also them that hold the doctrine of the Nicolaitanes, which thing I hate. (Revelation 2:14-15)

Those who are responsible for the church, The Angel, have been failing in their ministry. There had become a false toleration of two evils. The doctrine of Balaam (v. 14), and the doctrine of the Nicolaitanes (v. 15). The Lord makes it known that he is against them for such laxity. It is apparent that the two doctrines were not necessarily being taught. The reason the Lord is against them is that they have there those who "hold" the doctrines. There is no word that they were being taught publicly. It is enough for a man to hold false doctrine for him not to be acceptable in God's assembly. It would also seem that these people were not recognised by the Lord as part of the church. "Thou hast there them", indicating they should not be there, and that these men of responsibility had no right to let them defile God's assembly by their presence in it. The compromise led to corruption. Doctrines held will be taught somewhere; if they cannot teach publicly, they will privately; such men should be shunned.

Balaam means, destroyer of the people. He was hired by Balak, who feared God's people Israel; he sought out Balaam "who loved the wages of unrighteousness" (2 Pet. 2:15), to curse the Children of Israel. How can they whom God has blessed be cursed? God would not curse Ham after his sin with his father, but put the curse on his son Canaan (Gen. 9:25). Neither would David touch God's anointed in Saul, even though he was appointed King in his stead (1 Sam. 24:4-7). David's heart smote him because he had dared to cut off a piece of his garment. What Balaam could not curse (God turned his curse to a blessing Num. 23-24) he could corrupt. This he did in a two-fold way, which affected the associations and affections of the people of God. He set a trap, for such is the word "stumblingblock", to snare the Israelites, linking them with the idolatry and women of Moab. False doctrine in any form is anathema to God. Its source is seducing spirits, and it is a doctrine of demons (1 Tim. 4:1). Its object is to link the saints with what is satanic in origin, and will take away the heart from what is of God. Num. 25 shows that a princely man was prepared to openly flaunt his sin in the presence of the people. The judgement of God was already moving through the camp. The heads of the people were hung up before the Lord, yet Zimri persists in his sin with Cozbi. It took true priestly energy by Phinehas, who used the javelin to good effect, not only to destroy him who sinned, but also the source of the failure, the Midianitish women, to slay the plague.

It cost Israel dearly as the judgement of God fell upon them, 24,000 were slain as a result of this grievous sin, (1 Cor. 10:8), 23,000 of them in one day. It seems there was no Phinehas in the assembly at Pergamos, no one to thrust in the javelin. Not only Balaam, who taught a doctrine of mixture, but also the Nicolaitanes who had a doctrine of mastery were tolerated. The deeds hated in Ephesus were now doctrines held in Pergamos. It will not take long before they will be taught in Thyatira; such is the progression of evil. Corruption and clerisy are combined in these two characters.

Slaughter Assured (v. 16)

Repent; or else I will come unto thee quickly, and will fight against them with the sword of my mouth. (Revelation 2:16)

The Lord calls for repentance from those men who had allowed evil into the assembly. He was looking for a Phinehas to stop the plague. If they will not act and put out those who practice evil the Lord will. These people would be far safer if they returned to their native sphere, (1 Tim. 1:20), Satan's domain. By allowing them a place in God's assembly, they are exposed to divine judgement. As Balaam died by the sword at the Lord's command (Num. 31:8), so these would perish with the sword that goes out of the Lord's mouth, when he makes war against them.

The Spirit's Adjustment (v. 17a)

He that hath an ear, let him hear what the Spirit saith unto the churches; To him that overcometh will I give to eat of the hidden manna, and will give him a white stone, and in the stone a new name written, which no man knoweth saving he that receiveth [it]. (Revelation 2:17)

As to all the churches, there is a personal word to all, not just the angel. A little leaven leaveneth the whole lump. As Israel wept at the failure of Num. 25, so we should be exercised when such evil is present among us.

Satisfaction Assured (v. 17b)

Two things are promised to the overcomer: first my enjoyment of him, "the hidden manna" and second His enjoyment of me, "the white stone".

The food of the wilderness is set before them; they had lost their pilgrim features, they, like Israel had let Balaam take a foothold. To have the Lord before you is the antidote to this. The hidden manna was that which was laid up in the ark in a golden pot (Heb. 9:4; Ex. 16:32-36) speaking of Christ in glory, hidden now from the world, but the source of sustenance to his own (Col. 3:1-3).

God tends to use stones as symbols of his acceptance, approval and appreciation of his people. Onyx stones on the shoulders of the high priest, variegated stones on his breast, representing the saints held in power on the shoulders and in affection on the breast. Here it is a white stone, the symbol of purity and acceptance. Some say that in certain guilds that flourished in Pergamos, acceptance or rejection to the guild depended upon the stone you received. A black stone meant there was no place for you. A white stone on which would be graven your private guild name was handed to one who was accepted. This stone may symbolise the personal approval of our Lord Jesus of those who are not spotted by the world. He himself has a name that no man knows Ch 19:12.

Thyatira - Incense Offering - Continual Sacrifice
A Lawless Church

In Thyatira we have:

The Favoured Tenants (v. 18)

And unto the angel of the church in Thyatira write; These things saith the Son of God, who hath his eyes like unto a flame of fire, and his feet [are] like fine brass; (Revelation 2:18)

Every assembly has a great privilege to serve God. It is in possession of divine truth and knows the presence of divine persons. Many may not hold to the high ground they are brought to, nor appreciate the honour God has put on them to represent him in the world; such was the church in Thyatira. The Lord does not differentiate between churches as to the privileges given to them, and oftentimes it is those in the position of responsibility who fail to grasp the honour God has placed in their hands, and through carelessness allow the glory to be tarnished by allowing error.

The Figure Testing

As in all the churches, the features of the Lord Jesus are suitable for the conditions seen in the church. The Lord is presented in three ways.

His Deity: He speaks as the Son of God. Jezebel has undermined his authority, the Lord of the churches would remind the men of responsibility of his *power*.

His Discernment: "His eyes like unto a flame of fire". There is nothing hid from the eyes of him with whom we have to do. As they pierce and scan this assembly everything is exposed before him. He would remind the men of responsibility of his *perception*.

His Destruction: His feet as fine brass. Not only walking to survey the scene, but treading down in Judgement all that is opposed to his mind and will. He would remind the many who fail in their responsibility of the *punishment* that awaits those who are careless with divine truth.

Jezebel sets the Deity of the Lord Jesus aside (v. 20) as she promotes idolatry. His Destruction of those who are linked to her is seen in vv. 21-23. The Lord never judges in a hurry, it is only after giving, "space to repent" that the Lord act in judgement. His Discernment is seen in v. 23 when all the churches shall know he is the one that, "searcheth the reins and hearts".

Fruitful Testimony (v. 19)

I know thy works, and charity, and service, and faith, and thy patience, and thy works; and the last [to be] more than the first. (Revelation 2:19)

Verse 19 is addressed to the angel, not to Jezebel. Could not these statements be seen in Elijah and Elisha who represented God in Jezebel's day? These works were characterised by a love for God, and service before the King at Carmel, when Elijah withstood the prophets of Baal. We see the faith that looked to the skies both before the drought, and after Carmel, when he looked for the cloud the size of a man's hand that held the promised blessing of rain. Patience, as always, should be translated endurance. This is seen in Elijah at the brook, in the widow's house, under the Juniper tree and in mount Horeb. God never leaves himself without a witness who will be faithful to him in days of adversity. The last works that are more than the first, both in quality and quantity, could be seen in Elisha who received a double portion of Elijah's spirit (2 Kings 2:9-11).

The False Teacher (v. 20)

Notwithstanding I have a few things against thee, because thou sufferest that woman Jezebel, which calleth herself a prophetess, to teach and to seduce my servants to commit fornication, and to eat things sacrificed unto idols. (Revelation 2:20)

There are four women in the Revelation, two good and two bad. They are never individuals though some have tried to make Jezebel the bishop's wife. At this stage in the church's history, the ecclesiastical system of human devising had not yet risen. The seed had been sown in Nicolaitaneism, but as yet the tree had not grown. There was still a plurality of bishops, elders, shepherds, which are differing titles for the same men in one church. The day was yet to dawn when you would have one bishop over many churches, as in many systems forged by man. As the woman "clothed with the sun, and the moon under her feet" of Ch 12, the whore of Babylon of Ch 17-18 and the bride of Ch 19, she is a representative woman, setting forth a system of evil that has dominated the church. This has been allowed by men "thou sufferest", but abhorred by the Lord. Like those in Pergamos, she should not have been there, and was to come under divine judgement. The doctrines held become doctrines taught. Links with idolatry and spiritual fornication are openly taught.

There are three kinds of fornication:

(1) Actual - 1 Cor. 5:1, (2) Mental - Matt. 5:28, (3) Spiritual - James 4:4.

Any association with doctrinal error falls into the latter category. God was ever accusing Israel of playing the harlot as they fell into the sins of the nations around them. As the church progressed in time, battles for supremacy between the Greek church of Constantinople, and the Roman church resulted in a rift that affected both the East and the West. Both practice heathen doctrines, the Babylonish system is fully lodged in both and in all who outwardly may have separated from them for one reason or another. They certainly did not separate from their doctrines. We see today how far reaching has been the effect of "suffering"; here the word means to leave unchecked. The saints and the testimony have suffered as a result, if you suffer false doctrine, you will suffer at its hands.

Jezebel means no habitation, she will not settle, but must be on the move until she has proliferated everything. A glimpse of how she came in should be a lesson to us all for she came by:

(1) **Division**, caused by a hard legal spirit (1 Kings 12), (2) **Destruction**, in 1 Kings 15 Nadab and in 1 King 16 Elah, Zimri, and Tibna were all murdered, (3) **Drunkenness**, when we see Tirzah drinking himself drunk in the house of Arza (1 Kings 16:9), (4) **Disobedience**, when Ahab walked in the sins of Jeroboam, and also took Jezebel to wife and counted it but "a light thing" (1 Kings 16:31). Her history is one of open opposition to all that is of God. She stopped a divine ministry, as she killed the prophets of the Lord (1 Kings 18:4). She promoted false teachers and encouraged them to influence the people (18:19), and she also opposed a ministry of recovery to God (19:2). To add to her sins she would rob Israel of its inheritance (21:1-16), when she had Naboth murdered and stole his vineyard.

Foolish Tempted

Jezebel is still abroad and many saints still suffer these things at her hand. Many true children of God have come under her influence. She still teaches and seduces (Strongs, leads astray), my servants. Much profession is seen in the churches as men make their glib professions, (2:2), "say they are apostles and are not", vv. 9, 39 - "them which say they are Jews and are not", v. 20, "calleth herself a prophetess" and (3:17) "because thou sayest thou art rich". May the Lord enable us to be real in our life and service for him.

Forbearance Terminated (v. 21)

And I gave her space to repent of her fornication; and she repented not. (Revelation 2:21)

I gave her space to repent, God is never in a hurry. Often we look to God to vindicate us immediately when we are opposed, He ever gives space to repent. Even after Carmel, there were many years that passed before God intervened and had Jezebel eaten with dogs (2 Kings 9:30-37). The repentance was out of (ek), to escape her fornication. If her affection could be kindled for God, her idolatry would cease. Love for him will cause us to keep his commandments (John 14:23). Divine mercy only caused her to harden her stance, "she repented not".

Foreseen Terror (vv. 22-23)

Behold, I will cast her into a bed, and them that commit adultery with her into great tribulation, except they repent of their deeds. And I will kill her children with death; and all the churches shall know that I am he which searcheth the reins and hearts: and I will give unto every one of you according to your works. (Revelation 2:22-23)

"Behold!" a word used to arrest the attention. What will her end be? If she has used the bed to seduce his servants, God will cast her into one, the Great Tribulation. In the hour when the wrath of God will be unleashed both she and her associates will suffer the same fate. It is interesting that Elijah was caught up (2 Kings 2), before she is cast down (2 King 9). The coming of the Lord is prominent in these last four churches. The character that marks these four churches will continue to the end of church testimony, Thyatiran conditions remain even to our day, but God will judge it. By this it will cause the churches to know - come to know - to learn by experience, that the affections are tried, "the reins and hearts". Do I keep my heart for him? Profession is not enough; Jezebel professed much but produced nothing. The Lord will give unto every one of according to their works, this seems to refer to those who have cohabited with Jezebel, who are assured that the Lord will one day bring them into judgement.

Faithful Testimony (v. 24)

But unto you I say, and unto the rest in Thyatira, as many as have not this doctrine, and which have not known the depths of Satan, as they speak; I will put upon you none other burden. (Revelation 2:24)

A clear division is seen in Thyatira, "the rest", these could be like Elijah heralding, or Obadiah halting, there were also the 100 prophets hiding, or the 7000 (1 Kings 19:18) that had not bowed or kissed Baal. These had stood firm against the doctrine that is termed "the depth of Satan". The devil's throne is prominent in Pergamos, his teaching in Thyatira, who can plumb the depth of such evil as displayed here? Satan can go no lower in his efforts to corrupt the work of God. Millions have been duped by the established churches of East and West. Whether Greek Orthodox, or Roman Catholic, they have produced many children (v. 23), no hope is seen for them, but in the midst of Satanic delusion there are still "the rest", who have not known this doctrine.

Fidelity Tested (v. 25)

But that which ye have [already] hold fast till I come. (Revelation 2:25)

To the faithful remnant "who have", the desire of the Lord is that "they hold", to keep a grip on, and hope. He is coming; the Lord longs for these to keep faithful till his return. We are living in a day with the rapture imminent when certain teachers seem to be letting go of truth they once held, a spirit of compromise has arisen. I notice even leading expositors who have given much pleasure in their writings have started to adopt the new evangelicalism which makes God a "friendly pal". Using versions and language that descends to the level of the street and are not becoming to divine glory, seeking it seems, to please the masses rather than "hold fast".

Future Triumphs (vv. 26-29)

And he that overcometh, and keepeth my works unto the end, to him will I give power over the nations: and he shall rule them with a rod of iron; as the vessels of a potter shall they be broken to shivers: even as I received of my Father. And I will give him the morning star. He that hath an ear, let him hear what the Spirit saith unto the churches. (Revelation 2:26-29)

What a glorious prospect is set before the overcomer. He that keepeth the Lord's words to the end, that end must be the coming of Christ in v. 25. He is given:

Responsibility - power over the nations is given to him. That is a place of authority in the coming Kingdom of the Lord Jesus. The sphere of authority is over (epi) the nations, those who are saved during the tribulation days, and who are the sheep at the judgement of the living nations in Matt. 25:31-46.

Rule - This rule will be inflexible, "with a rod of iron". It will correspond to that of the Lord Jesus (19:15). The will of man will be kept under, broken in pieces. This is the rule spoken of in 1 Cor. 6:2, when "The saints shall judge the world" and the time of 2 Tim. 2:12, "if we suffer with him, we shall reign with him". Both the Son and the saints receive and do not take authority, and these scriptures would again emphasise the future place that the saints of this dispensation will occupy with Lord Jesus, as they are associated with him in governmental authority.

Rapture - Blessed hope, the Lord is coming as "the morning star", for the church. The morning star shines the brightest just before the dawn. This present night season of Christian testimony will end with the appearance of the Lord Jesus to rapture his own out of the sleeping world. The world sleeps on, to be awakened by the Sun of Righteousness (Mal. 4:2), when in the full blaze of His glory the Lord Jesus returns to restore Israel to its rightful place among the nations in that great millennial day. The morning star is Christ coming for the church, he is our portion, and we are given Christ himself. The object of the coming of our Lord Jesus for the church is never to take us to a place, but to link us to himself (see John 14:3 and 1 Thess. 4:17).

Notice the call of the spirit comes after the promise to the overcomer in the last four churches. It is this that divides this seven into a three and a four. All sevens seem to do this in scripture.

Chapter 3

The Seven churches (continued)
Sardis - Those who escaped - A Remnant
A Lifeless Church

And unto the angel of the church in Sardis write; These things saith he that hath the seven Spirits of God, and the seven stars; I know thy works, that thou hast a name that thou livest, and art dead. (Revelation 3:1)

The Recipients of the letter (v. 1)

There is no commendation from the Lord for the work done in Sardis. A dead church cannot be commended, and such was Sardis. Not just in the opinion of men who are quick to judge, but by the Lord himself, it is a divine record that says "thou hast a name that thou livest, and art dead." There are no assailants, Satan will not bother a dead church, and he might bring it to life if he stirred the church. There is no progress of evil, the depth has been reached in Thyatira, evil may be there but it cannot progress any further.

The Resplendent Lord

The Lord Jesus presents himself as having "the seven spirits of God, and the seven stars". The seven spirits of God, speaking of the Holy Spirit, would remind this assembly of the power and energy that is available to the saints. This power and energy are with our Lord Jesus whom we serve. Does he set before us that there can be life received if we will move in the Spirit's power? He also has "the seven stars", these speak of responsibility and authority. If these knew something of what it meant to move in the Spirit's power things might be different in Sardis, for they are dependent on the Spirit to function aright.

The Renounced Life

Every assembly must begin its service on the grounds of new birth. God can only accept that which is consistent with himself, "in him is life". The flesh cannot produce anything for God (Rom. 8:8). All worship acceptable to him (1 Pet. 2:5) must begin with new birth (1 Pet. 1:23). Here they just bear the name that they live; exercise in the church has gone. They were dead; their works are dying and deficient in v. 2.

Receding Labours (v. 2)

Be watchful, and strengthen the things which remain, that are ready to die: for I have not found thy works perfect before God. (Revelation 3:2)

As they are lifeless, their works also are lingering but ready to die. The Lord would call them to be watchful, as those who know of his return in glory (Matt. 24:42), or as Peter, James and John in the garden of Gethsemane were asked to "watch" (Matt. 26:38).

"Strengthen" - to fix, establish the things about to die (JND), the word is used of the Lord in Luke 9:51 as he "set" his face to go to Jerusalem, also of "a great gulf fixed" (Luke 16:26), so must the saints move with the same resolve to establish things for God. It seems as if hope has gone for the assembly, but evidently recovery is possible if they will rise and do something.

Their works were not complete (JND). The Lord's work was finished, he was not like us, we too often begin and leave things half finished, often promising much and performing little. All work is done before God, "before" means in the presence of, in front of, used in Luke 5:25 of the sick of the palsy who "rose up before them", (Luke 8:47) and of the woman with the issue, "falling down before him". It is also used in Rev. 4:5 of "lamps of fire burning before the throne". Perhaps this had been lost sight of as they failed to see all was done in the sight of God. Had this been recognised perhaps greater energy and care would have been put into their service.

The Last Resort (v. 3)

Remember therefore how thou hast received and heard, and hold fast, and repent. If therefore thou shalt not watch, I will come on thee as a thief, and thou shalt not know what hour I will come upon thee. (Revelation 3:3)

"Remember", the same word as in Ch 2:5 to Ephesus where it is to recover affections lost, here to Sardis it is to recover truth received. The cause of the failure is exposed here, they were not acting on the truth received and heard. The word "received" is in the perfect tense, it is a permanent deposit. If Thyatira sets forth corrupt apostate Christendom, both East and West, Sardis speaks of formal Protestantism, they have a name to live indeed, but they are dead. A few mighty men seeing the truth of regeneration by faith sought to recover things for God, where did it lead? Much of Romish idolatry was brought over, its ecclesiastical order, its vestments, altars, crosses etc. Soon Protestantism is to be simply Rome without its Pope, though a man is still placed as its head, be it a King or Archbishop. The Lord has lost his place; much is done for the eye of man, and not before God. The work of the reformation period was incomplete, it did not go far enough! The Lord calls for repentance, if not the church will be judged like the world though not with the world. The thief in the night is the Lord coming to the world, not for the Church. The coming as a thief is always unexpected, and with judgement in view. They were like the world, dead, they would be judged like it, not knowing what hour he would come upon them. This reminds us of the three hours in Matt. 24:36 and v. 42 - the unknown hour, v. 44 - the unexpected hour, and v. 50 - the unprepared hour. Only repentance and watching, the first God-ward, the second self-ward could offer hope. Twice in its history the Acropolis at Sardis had been scaled by the enemy (around 549 BC by Cyrus and 218 BC by Antiochus though historians differ in their dating), both occasions it fell because it failed to set a watch.

Little Remnant (v. 4)

Thou hast a few names even in Sardis which have not defiled their garments; and they shall walk with me in white: for they are worthy. (Revelation 3:4)

God ever keeps for himself a remnant; there are always the few who will be faithful. If the Assembly had a discredited name in v. 1 it had an honoured name in v. 5, secured and confessed before the Father and angels. Four things mark the few:

Faithfulness - "they had not defiled their garments". Garments always speak of character in the scriptures; they speak of the public testimony of what a man is in himself. Joseph's garments display his morality, Aaron's his ministry, In Ps. 45 it is the King's majesty that is seen in his garments. These had not mingled with the rest in Sardis; one we move for God and need not be swallowed up with the evil that marks the day we live in, may the Lord enable us to be faithful to him in our service here.

Fellowship - "they shall walk with me". How blessed, God and Christ enjoying the company of such. Linked with Enoch (Gen. 5:23), and Noah (Gen. 6:9), who walked with God, these men were prepared to move against the mainstream of the world for the fellowship of God. They walked with him by taking a place outside a world that rejected him; we shall walk with him in the day of his regal glory.

Fitness - "in white". This is always the emblem of purity, and purity will be upon every believer in the day of the Lord's glory when we shall enjoy the fellowship of the presence of divine persons.

Favour - "for they are worthy". Such is the Lord's appraisal of those who delight to serve him faithfully.

Loyalty Rewarded (v. 5)

He that overcometh, the same shall be clothed in white raiment; and I will not blot out his name out of the book of life, but I will confess his name before my Father, and before his angels. (Revelation 3:5)

This verse brings out two customs that would be well known to the saints. When the Romans wished to honour a citizen, they were draped in a Roman Toga, their exploits and names were written in gold in the citizen's roll and they were presented to the sovereign. Also many saints had been humiliated, being stripped and publicly disowned by having their names blotted out. The Lord guarantees the preservation, and presentation of those who overcome. Purity - clothed in white, and Security - not blotted out, will ever mark them, faithful is he who promised.

Lasting Record (v. 6)

He that hath an ear, let him hear what the Spirit saith unto the churches. (Revelation 3:6)

The final word, the word of appeal is again to hear the Spirit's voice, it is to all the saints in all churches, and it is for all saints as we bear testimony for the Lord here.

Philadelphia - Brotherly Love
A Living Church

And to the angel of the church in Philadelphia write; These things saith he that is holy, he that is true, he that hath the key of David, he that openeth, and no man shutteth; and shutteth, and no man openeth; (Revelation 3:7)

Introduction

The name of this church gives us its character. The Lord and his word mean much to them, such desires will lead to a love of the brethren. To Philadelphia there is no condemnation, such a church that rose above the dead formalism of Sardis, and did not sink into the lukewarmness of Laodicea, needs all the encouragement it can get to keep the conditions here stated alive. In its dispensational character, rising from the morass of the reformation, it sets forth the believers who sought to restore Christ to his proper place, and the word to its rightful place of authority. This was a church with a door of opportunity that was open and that it grasped with both hands. Let us look at:

The Church's Unity (v 7)

This unity is borne out of love; love ever unites.

1 Thess. 4:9	Love is common to all - ye are taught of God.
James 2:6-17	Love cares; to love thy neighbour is to care for saints in need
1 John 3:10-12	Love controls, it controls the temper, not as Cain who is of the wicked one.
Rom. 14	Love carries the weak.
1 Pet. 4:8	Loves covers failure.

Well might Paul call love the "bond of perfectness" (Col. 3:4).

Christ's Sovereignty (v. 7)

Three things are said of the Lord Jesus, they are the only references to him that are not directly linked in some way to the revelation of him as seen in Ch 1. Though they would epitomise what is seen there as "The Holy" his head of purity, his eyes piercing, and his feet punishing all would tell us of one who is holy. His "countenance as the sun" would manifest the perfect holiness of "him in whom is no sin". Holiness must mark deity, well might the Lord Jesus speak of his father as Holy Father - John 17:11 and well may the Spirit of God ever be called Holy Spirit. I believe the constant repetition of this name to the Spirit is because he is so directly linked with the believer. Whenever the priest of old was handling the sacrifices, and when these directly affected him, he is reminded they are most holy (Lev. 12:3, 6:25, 6:29). The same is said of other things the priest is directly linked with. The Altar (Ex. 29:37), the

Shewbread (Lev. 24:9), the Anointing Oil (Ex. 30:23-33), the Dwelling Place of God in the tabernacle is called the Most Holy (Ex. 26:34). When speaking of the presence of the Holy Spirit in the life of the believer, (1 Cor. 6:9) we are called to live a life consistent with it. Well might the cry which rises to the throne in Ch 4:8 be Holy, Holy, Holy.

But he is not only "The Holy" he is also "The True". Again though not directly linked to Ch 1, nevertheless how wondrous is the thought summed up in the never failing character of "He who liveth, and was dead", "who is the Amen", "who holds the stars in his hand". He is one who cannot fail, for he is the truth and he cannot deny himself. In his epistle John speaks of the Lord Jesus as "him that is true" (1 John 5:20), he delights to bring this facet of his Lord before his readers. In John 1:9 he is the "True Light", 6:32 the "True Bread", 15:1 the "True Vine", here "Holy and True". In John 1:9, it is to school men in truth, in 6:32 he satisfies saints, in 15:1 he is the source of fruit, here in Rev. 3:7 he is the support of the assembly. Twice over in this book (3:14, 19:11), "he is Faithful and True". To the Church at Laodicea he is all they fail to be and in Rev. 19:11 it is not saints but sinners, who are reminded of this fact. In both passages imminent judgement is due, first to spew out what is nauseous to him, and then to wield the sword of divine judgement against the Godless world. All should remember "He is Faithful and True", he will not fail. God himself is set forth in 6:10 as "Holy and True" in his support of persecuted saints. In 15:3, he is "Just and True", speaking of his ways in his purpose with men. Twice more (16:7 and 19:2) he is "True and Righteous", both verses telling of his punishment of sinners in tribulation days. Is not the Holy Spirit the "Spirit of Truth" (John 14:17, 15:26, 16:13)? The whole of the Godhead is marked by truth; well may it be enjoined upon the believers (Eph. 4:25) "wherefore putting away lying, speak every man truth with his neighbour".

The verse not only sets forth the Holiness of Christ in his character, and the Honesty of Christ in his conduct but also the Honour given to Christ in his commission, he holds "the key of David". In Ch 1 he has "the keys of death and hell", the key is always a symbol of authority and right. The devil in Matt. 4:8-10 offered the Lord Jesus limited authority as he showed him all the kingdoms of the world and the glory of them. It would have been the glory without the sufferings, a short cut to honour, but it would still be a fallen world, dominated by sin, he would have been just the devil's vassal. This is not for Christ, had not God said in Ps. 2:8, "Ask of me, and I will give thee the heathen for thine inheritance"? The Lord takes it from the Father's hand, but in this there is no limitation, (Matt. 28:18) "all power is given unto me in heaven and in earth". See Jacob's ladder established, see a kingdom brought in, remember Eph. 1:10 "that in the dispensation of the fullness of times he might gather together in one all things in Christ both which are in heaven, and which are on earth; even in him". All things gathered up in Christ, both in heaven and in earth. No limitation here, the purpose of God for the world fulfilled, heaven and earth linked in our Lord Jesus; but not only heaven and earth under his dominion, but also the unseen world of death and hell, coming into being as a result of sin, one day to be banished into the lake of fire (Ch 20:14). The authority of the Lord Jesus does not stop here, "the keys of David" - these give him authority over the monarchs of earth. This quotation from Isaiah 22:22 speaks of rights given to Eliakim, whose name means, "whom God will raise up". When linked to the Lord Jesus as here, they show the verses are prophetic of the place the Lord Jesus is to occupy. When clothed in majesty, fulfilling God's mind in service, (the girdle), all government will be put into his hand, and none can resist his power. He opens, he shuts, and everything is in his control.

So here, the Lord Jesus is moving to encourage these who move in brotherly love, who have but little strength, the power is not theirs but his. One considers the evangelical fervour that marked the last century. Vast continents opened to the gospel, men suffering great privations to spread the word. Millions swept into the kingdom, mighty men raised up and used of God. Many great philanthropic works were established, the Lord opened a door, and no man could shut it. If the devil brings out his champions, Darwin's voice is heard, Voltaire pours out his vitriol, higher critics attack the word of God, still he opens and no man shuts. Here is where power lies, all in the hands of him who opens and no man shuts. Let those of our day read and mark the closing phrase, "he shuts and no man opens". The fervour has gone, the door has closed. Lands refuse the missionary entrance, the gospel is despised, and the Christ is ridiculed in a western world. The way of God for such a time, "Preach the word; be instant in season and out of season" (2 Tim. 4:2), has been set aside. Today, to cover seeming weakness, the world and its ways are all brought into evangelism, film stars, pop singers, sports stars, prelates and politicians are all used to prop and bolster special campaigns. A leaflet to hand even as I write invites all to a gospel concert "which has the atmosphere of the last night at the Proms". How sad to bring spiritual things down to a worldly show. No longer do we hear the cry, "come ye out and be ye separate", or "ye are not of the world even as I am not of the world". Today the world and its ways must be allied to spiritual things to give the things of God a veneer of attraction to the unconverted. Church services have lost their dignity, the Lord has been brought down to the level of the man in the street, the congregation has become an audience, entertainment has taken over from worship, dubious translations proliferate, and, sadly, I find writers to whom I am indebted seem to be following the trend. Today the Lord has shut, and every base effort of men will not open. If we could only rekindle Philadelphia conditions, perhaps we would see the door open again!

Conditions of Testimony (v. 8)

I know thy works: behold, I have set before thee an open door, and no man can shut it: for thou hast a little strength, and hast kept my word, and hast not denied my name. (Revelation 3:8)

Four things are set forth in the verse, their witness, weakness, watchfulness and winsomeness.

Witness and Weakness

If the Lord holds the keys and opens a door he draws their attention to it, "Behold". The Lord recognises the weakness that marks them, they have "but little strength", but what is human strength in divine service? (Phil. 3:13), "I can do all things through Christ which strengtheneth me", or as in the epistle to the Hebrews Ch 11:34, "out of weakness were made strong". It is from the prison that Joseph is going to be brought to the throne. It is from the backside of the desert that Moses is to lead Israel from Egypt, in spite of his claims to weakness, (see, Ex. 3 and 4). See Deborah and Barak, as they fight against Jabin king of Canaan, also Gideon by the winepress threshing wheat to hide it from the Midianites, see blind Samson in seeming weakness slay more in his death than in his life. Many more could be referred to but when Christ opens a door, weakness will not hinder the task.

Watchful and Winsome

What a delight to the Lord to see those who manifest adherence to the word and allegiance to himself. The word "keep" occurs 75 times in the New Testament, and is used 35 times by John in his writings, 25 of these having to do with keeping the word. Christ kept the word (John 15:10), those with no love for him fail to do so (John 14:24). It is love for Christ that brings obedience (John 14:23). It is little wonder that these two themes of keeping his word and not denying his name go together, the Lord now appreciates that they have not denied his name. I take it in this, that they have stood for and maintained the character of it. They upheld all that the name would indicate. We are saved in his name (Acts 16:32), baptised in his name (Matt. 28:19), we gather to his name (Matt. 18:20; 1 Cor. 1:2). Many have denied his name in this respect and gather in the name of systems, of doctrines or of men. The name of Christ has been usurped. Some think it of little account to meet under a banner other than Christ, even men who ought to know better, they have read much, but to maintain a position they will not give Christ his glory.

Again, how would I feel if my wife told me one day she was changing her name to that of another man in the street? She may protest her love and fidelity, but my heart would be cut. Paul makes his appeal to those at Corinth in the name (1:10), he teaches that all government in the assembly should be carried out in the name (5:4), and how we are cleansed, claimed and cleared in that name (6:11). Oh! Do not deny that name.

A Chronicle of Humility (v. 9)

Behold, I will make them of the synagogue of Satan, which say they are Jews, and are not, but do lie; behold, I will make them to come and worship before thy feet, and to know that I have loved thee. (Revelation 3:9)

Again we are confronted by the term "synagogue of Satan". Interestingly it occurs in both churches to which the Lord gives no rebuke, Smyrna (2:9), and here in Philadelphia. At Smyrna we see they are the source of opposition. The Jews always set themselves against the gospel, and were at the forefront of the persecution that befell the saints. The book of the Acts reveals it from end to end. In the gospels, it is the Lord Jesus they oppose, the disciples are left fairly much alone, but once they come under the blood, as in Egypt long before (Ex. 12:39) when "they thrust them out", as soon as they were covered by blood Egypt had no place for them. So, once the disciples came under the blood of Christ, the Jews moved in bitter enmity against them. It is the blood that moves the world, the life of Christ holds but a little stigma, but the death of Christ proclaims a world guilty before God, with a need of a Saviour. The flesh rejects the very idea of it, and moves against those who confess it. But now the tide has turned, those who were the source of opposition, become the subjects in veneration. As a synagogue of Jews it would speak of their former nearness, now in degeneration we have their present distance, "the synagogue of Satan". Now they come to worship at the feet of the saints. Obviously they do not worship the saints, they worship God. Of the 60 occurrences of the word, it is of worship either to God, the devil, idols, or the Man of Sin. It was proffered to Peter (Acts 10:25) and refused, the apostle John sought to do the same to an angel in Ch 22:8–9 but was told in definite terms, "Do it not...worship God". In a day to come, God is going to be glorified, and the saints vindicated, as these of the synagogue of Satan take their place in humility to confess they opposed what God loved.

Confidence and Adversity (v. 10)

Because thou hast kept the word of my patience, I also will keep thee from the hour of temptation, which shall come upon all the world, to try them that dwell upon the earth. (Revelation 3:10)

The Lord now brings blessed promises to his own that have "kept the word of my patience". Ch 1:9 speaks of, "the patience of Jesus Christ", this is the present attitude of the Lord whilst waiting to take up his rightful place of public glory, soon to be manifested to wondering worlds. The saints also will be linked with him in this day of his splendour; we wait also, but with great assurances from the Lord of our future role with him. These verses cover three spheres: v. 10 - The Tribulation, v. 11 - The Judgement Seat of Christ, v. 12 - the Coming Millennial Reign, in which we shall have a vital part to play. Here the promise is to be kept from (ek - out of) "the hours of trial which will try the earth dwellers". Could scripture be more explicit? This, along with 1 Thess. 1:10 makes it abundantly clear that believers of this dispensation will not be here during the tribulation period. 1 Thess. 1:10 - "to wait for his Son from heaven our deliverer from - (apo - away from), the wrath to come". Wrath is ever the outpouring of God's anger upon living men; this is not a promise of eternal life as against being in the lake of fire. The lake of fire is never seen as the wrath of God, but is the final outcome of his righteous judgement upon ungodly men. Here it is the wrath to come, which is pointing us to the days of tribulation, when divine wrath will be meted out upon rebellious men. In Rev. 6:16-17 it is the wrath of the Lamb, and in 15:1 it is the wrath of God. Those who are linked to the Lord Jesus cannot share the fate of a world that rejects him. Rom. 8:1 "there is therefore now no condemnation", God would deny himself if he brought us into the same condemnation as the world. It is not enough to preserve us through it, as he did with Noah in the flood, but he must take us "away" from it (1 Thess. 1:10), he must also take us "out" of it (Rev. 3:10) as he did with Enoch before the flood, who was taken to where the judgement was coming from, but far above it, not taking part in it.

Nor are believers "earth dwellers", this is God's term for the ungodly. Are we not citizens of heaven (Phil. 3:20) and strangers and pilgrims (1 Pet. 2:11)? We are God's elect (Rom. 8:33), we have been given to Christ, "out of the world" (John 17:6), it is the Lord who says in John Ch 17 "we are not of the world" (v. 14), "though in it" (v. 11), "and sent to it" (v. 18), "to be a witness to it" (vv. 21-23). No, we are not earth dwellers, the hour of trial does not belong to us.

Crowns for Ministry (v. 11)

Behold, I come quickly: hold that fast which thou hast, that no man take thy crown. (Revelation 3:11)

The Lord now sets before "his own" how they will be kept from the hour of trial. The hope of his coming is set before the eye of the believer. For the child of God it is not retribution but reward, not trial but triumph. For the world there is only wrath, for the believer there are crowns. With this in view the exhortation is "hold that fast which thou hast", keep the end of the race in view, for rewards are only for faithfulness to God here. The Lord gives us a service to render, if we fail to do it, it will still be done, but God will raise up another and the crowns that should be mine another will take.

We have five crowns set before us in the New Testament. They are:

James 1:12 - The Crown of Life: Every believer receives this crown; it is for "salvation". Some call it the martyr's crown granted to those who endure trial, but the text makes it clear, it is for "those who love Him".

1 Cor. 9:25 - The Incorruptible Crown: This is for obedience to the "scriptures". The figure is an athlete in a race, as in 2 Tim. 2:5, to run the race, and keep the rules brings the reward. If I carelessly disregarded the Word of God and its affect on my life, I would lose this crown.

1 Thess. 2:19, Phil. 4:1 - The Crown of Rejoicing: This is for "souls" I have led to Christ. Every sinner I have had the privilege of seeing saved makes up this crown. What a stimulus to service in the gospel, knowing that any influence we have had in the conversion of a sinner, will be rewarded at the judgement seat of Christ.

2 Tim. 4:8 - A Crown of Righteousness: This is for "steadfastness" in the faith. Paul knew at the end of a faithful life when he had fought a good fight, finished his course and kept the faith, that this crown was his, but not only his "but unto all them also that love his appearing". That is, they are longing for the hour when the Son of God will return in glory to the earth. They are looking beyond this world, to the world to come. Not like Demas in v. 10, lived and linked with Paul, served with the mighty apostle, but allowed another to take his crown, for he "loved this present world", not the appearing of Christ.

The failure of Demas may have been the reason that Paul encouraged Timothy not to be ashamed of the testimony of Christ (Ch 1:8).

1 Pet. 5:4 - A Crown of Glory: This is the "shepherds" crown for faithful service. Many godly men have suffered greatly as they have sought to preserve things for God, and to watch over the saints. It will not be forgotten, the Chief Shepherd will reward their loyalty to Him with this lovely crown.

These crowns will be given at the Judgement Seat of Christ, the time when every believer must give account, not for sin, Christ settled that at the cross, but for service, and obedience. These crowns will be displayed in the Millennial Kingdom and our sphere of rule then will depend on our faithfulness now. This brings us to v. 12.

Coming Authority (v. 12)

Him that overcometh will I make a pillar in the temple of my God, and he shall go no more out: and I will write upon him the name of my God, and the name of the city of my God, which is new Jerusalem, which cometh down out of heaven from my God: and I will write upon him my new name. (Revelation 3:12)

There is a threefold promise to the overcomer, regarding his stability, security and the seal of approval that will be enjoyed in the coming kingdom. In their present testimony they have "but little strength" (v. 8), what a contrast when in a future day they will be made a pillar. In Gal. 2:9 James, Cephas and John, to Paul "seemed to be pillars". There will be no possibility of misjudgement here, "I will make a pillar", says the Lord. Stability will mark us then. It is "in the Temple of my God", the word used is that for the holy of holies, (naos). It speaks of the dwelling place of God; it is here where we will be displayed in strength. The promise also settles our security. "He shall go no more out". Heb. 11:33-38 teaches what many have endured as they have stood for God whilst outside. Never again will saints be subjected to the enmity of a hostile world. A threefold seal is then placed upon the saints, "The name of my God", the name of his city, and the Lord's new name. These have not denied his name (v. 8). Now they are brought into close association with God and his purposes for this world, in the city in which his governmental authority is owned in the saints, as we shall see in Ch 21. Notice it cometh down out of (ek) heaven, for it is his rule of earth that is in view, a city being a centre of administration. These purposes are all found in Christ. Thus his new name, whatever that may be, will be put upon us. The 144,000 when seen on Mount Sion, a millennial scene, have the fathers name written on them, and in 22:4, we are seen to bear his name on the forehead. As the beast in 13:16 makes unregenerate men make a public proclamation of allegiance to him, so the Lord Jesus will make a public demonstration of faithfulness shown by the redeemed, in putting his new name upon them.

The Call of Responsibility (v. 13)

He that hath an ear, let him hear what the Spirit saith unto the churches. (Revelation 3:13)

If the Lord himself would encourage us by the precious promises he makes to the overcomer, so the Holy Spirit voices his concern for an attentive ear, that saints might maintain divine honour, and keep our eternal blessings before us. May the ear of the saints be like that of the Lord in Ps. 40:6, "Mine ear hast thou opened" (Margin - digged), which becomes in Heb. 10:5 "A body has thou prepared me". If the ear is opened to his word, a body will soon desire to do his will.

Laodicea - The rights of the people
A Lukewarm Church

And unto the angel of the church of the Laodiceans write; These things saith the Amen, the faithful and true witness, the beginning of the creation of God; (Revelation 3:14)

Introduction

We now come to the church of the last days, conditions are seen which are being demonstrated in our own day. I notice a slight change in the opening format from the other six churches; though slight, it is not without significance as to the character of the Laodicean assembly. Rather than write to the church "in" Laodicea, denoting where they reside, it is to the church "of" the Laodiceans, speaking of the character that marks them. Their rights, rather than their residence are prominent. What they are, rather than where they are. The church was like the city it dwelt in, having neither the healing power of the hot water of its neighbour Hierapolis, nor the refreshing cold water to be found at Colosse, but merely lukewarm water, useful only as an emetic. Barkley adds a few interesting points, of its commercial prosperity, and to it being a financial centre. In AD 61, when devastated by an earthquake, rather than take funds from Rome, it financed its own reconstruction. It was rich and had need of nothing. He also draws attention to it being a medical centre. Amongst its claims for fame were its ointments both for the ears and the eyes, the latter eye salve came from a Phrygian powder which was exported world wide in a solidified tablet form. I merely allude to this as it demonstrates that the assembly was like the city it lived in. There is much interesting reading on the subject in encyclopaedias and bible dictionaries.

In all the other churches a difference is made amongst them:

In **Ephesus,** they tried false apostles, and hate the Nicolaitanes. In **Smyrna,** there is a synagogue of Satan. In **Pergamos,** there is both the doctrine of Balaam and the doctrine of the Nicolaitanes. In **Thyatira,** Jezebel and her followers are distinguished. In **Sardis,** there are a few names that have not defiled their garment, whilst in **Philadelphia,** again the synagogue of Satan is distinguished.

But in **Laodicea,** no such difference is found; all are linked in the same common failure. As in all judgements of God, he does not act until sin has reached its zenith. "The iniquity of the Amorites is not yet full" (Gen. 15:16, see also Jer. 14:10). It is not until the time of harvest that he deals with the Tares (Matt. 13:30), "the mystery of iniquity doth already work", but God withholds the judgement until the consummation of it all is seen in the Man of Sin (2 Thess. 2:7-8). Church witness is about to end, her failure is complete, nauseous conditions can no longer be tolerated; the threatened judgement is that it must be spewed out. We will look at the features that marked it.

Democracy in the Church (v. 14)

And unto the angel of the church of the Laodiceans write; These things saith the Amen, the faithful and true witness, the beginning of the creation of God; (Revelation 3:14)

We have already seen that Laodicea means, "the right of the people". God's governmental order as seen in the elders, and that set before us in 1 Tim. 3, Tit. 1, 1 Pet. 5 and Acts 20, is now set aside. The assembly dictates are taken from the desires of men. The tastes of the pew control the teachings of the pulpit. We are living in a day when democracy is rampant in all walks of society; sadly the same principle is dominating the churches in our own day. The authority of the word of God has been set aside as the spirit of the age has gripped the believer. I recall listening to F.F. Bruce in our home assembly saying "what the world does today the church does tomorrow". It would seem that tomorrow has arrived, and, as far as democracy is concerned, we follow the dictates of the world.

The Description of Christ

The Lord is all that the assembly fails to be. In the three statements regarding him, he is the Embodiment of Truth, the Amen, he who will do all that he says. He is the Expression of Faithfulness, to the assembly "he is faithful and true" even where Laodicea fails, to pilgrims "he is merciful and faithful" (Heb. 2:17), to sons "he is faithful and just" (1 John 1:19). The Lord is always faithful to his own children whatever experience they are in. As he returns to take his rightful place on the earth (Rev. 19:11), "he is faithful and true", what he is to the saints he will also be to the world. He is also the Originator of Creation. Col. 1 and Heb. 1 tell of the omnipotent power displayed as the creation which originated "in Him" (Col. 1:16). He thought it; it became the works of his hands (Heb. 1:10). He is the beginning of the creation of God, not as Jehovah Witnesses claim, the first one created, but if the original creation begins with a heaven and earth, and ends with a man, the new creation, the church, begins with a man, Christ, and ends with a new heaven and earth (see Col. 1:18). Here he is set forth as "the beginning, the firstborn from the dead".

Denunciation of Complacency (vv. 15-16)

I know thy works, that thou art neither cold nor hot: I would thou wert cold or hot. So then because thou art lukewarm, and neither cold nor hot, I will spue thee out of my mouth. (Revelation 3:15-16)

Three times in these two verses the expression "cold nor hot" appears, denoting: (1) Their condition, (2) The Lord's concern, (3) The consequences.

What a sad condition, no fervent zeal, no absolute denial; such is modern evangelicalism, professing faith in Christ yet rejecting every simple teaching of his word. Wanting the security of heaven, but no separation from earth. Democracy demands, Evangelicalism obliges, woman's rights are stressed and divine order is thwarted. A new wave of emotionalism crosses the horizon of Christendom and myriads are swept away with experiential Christianity. A "thus saith the Lord" is ignored and no longer do the "just live by faith", the church must see to believe, and experience takes the place of dependence upon God. Such is insipid, tepid Christianity, bringing no blessing to men and no glory to God. Well might the Saviour's voice be heard "I would ye were cold or hot". The consequences must be borne. The revulsion they cause must end in their rejection. JND translates, "I will spue thee out", as, "I am about to spue thee out", and the judgement is not merely possible but imminent. The sad mixture must bring to an end Christian profession.

Delusion of the Conditions (v. 17)

Because thou sayest, I am rich, and increased with goods, and have need of nothing; and knowest not that thou art wretched, and miserable, and poor, and blind, and naked: (Revelation 3:17)

Sadly the Laodiceans little realise their true state, if vv. 15-16 gives their condition, v. 17 manifests the cause, as v. 18 brings counsel. We notice first of all, their **profession,** "Thou sayest". In Ch 2:2, v. 9, v. 20 and 3:9, others were saying in the church. Now it is the voice of the church that is heard. Secondly, their **prosperity,** "I am rich". Men love wealth, and they think it will give them the "desires of their heart, but it sends leanness to the soul", God is not needed, dependence has gone. Thirdly, their **possessions,** "increased with goods", strictly, "increased with riches". They are like the rich men of 6:15, and also like the whore Babylon in 18:3, who, whilst making others rich, was also facing judgement. Did not our Lord Jesus "though rich become poor" (2 Cor. 8:9)? They have fallen "into temptation and a snare" (1 Tim. 6:10). These should heed the warnings of James 5:1, "go to now ye rich men, weep and howl for your miseries that shall come upon you". Fourthly, their **pretension,** "and knowest not". The proverb well describes them, there's none so blind as those who will not see! Seven times the risen head says to these churches "I know", but this church knew not. Fifthly, their **poverty,** what a sight to the eye of the Lord, who died to redeem such, calls them his elect, makes them sons of God, gives them an inheritance, makes angels to do their bidding in a day to come. Worldly prosperity has marred the work of grace in their soul, and such is the degeneration, these five words, wretched, miserable (pitiable), poor, blind, naked, describe their spiritual condition.

Definite Counsel (v. 18)

I counsel thee to buy of me gold tried in the fire, that thou mayest be rich; and white raiment, that thou mayest be clothed, and [that] the shame of thy nakedness do not appear; and anoint thine eyes with eyesalve, that thou mayest see. (Revelation 3:18)

The Lord counsels them, they are not compelled, or commanded, his desire is that these poor, wretched, miserable creatures should come and buy, like Isaiah 55:11, "without money and without price". Yet a cost is involved. In 1 Cor. 6:20 and 7:32 we are "bought with a price", in Rev. 5:9 "redeemed to

God", this same word is used, as also in 14:3-4 - what a price was paid, it cost our blessed Lord his all, is this the price for recovery to a right place before him? The former character of life will have to be renounced, the voice knocking on the door will need to be heard, and a Saviour shut out will need to be given his rightful place. What has to be bought will make them rich, will robe them and recover their sight. "Gold tried in the fire", such is the trial of the believer in 1 Pet. 1:7, which is, "much more precious than of gold that perisheth though it be tried with fire". The fire only removes the dross, and leaves a pure lump, all placed to our account in a future day. In Matt. 2:11, wise men bring gold, in 1 Cor. 3:12, wise servants build gold, here wise saints will buy gold. Also white raiment, ever a symbol of righteous character of true purity. The elders sit in white raiment in Ch 4:4, the seven angels with the seven last plagues are so arrayed in Ch 15.6. Thus those who are suitable for his presence, and to serve him are dressed in white raiment. There is an eyesalve with which they can anoint their eyes, giving a vision that will reveal the true values to their gaze.

Directions to Consider (v. 19)

As many as I love, I rebuke and chasten: be zealous therefore, and repent. (Revelation 3:19)

In v. 18 recovery is freely offered, in vv. 19-20 it is divinely urged, in v. 21 recovery is greatly rewarded, what is collective in vv. 14-18 now becomes individual. The love displayed here is not the usual word for Divine love - (agapao) - causeless love, but rather that which has a cause, (philio); it has the thought of affection behind it, to love what is our own. Is this the parental love of Heb. 12:6 "For whom the Lord loveth he chasteneth, and scourgeth every son whom he receiveth", for it is linked with discipline? Here, though failure might mark them, love marks the Lord and he will move for their recovery, he is not casting away his own, but working to bring a zeal for repentance in them.

A Closed Door but a Definite Call (v. 20)

Behold, I stand at the door, and knock: if any man hear my voice, and open the door, I will come in to him, and will sup with him, and he with me. (Revelation 3:20)

How sad to find the place occupied by the Lord in relation to this assembly, he who ought to have his rightful place "in the midst" (Matt. 18:20), has been shut out. Church organisation can leave no room for Christ. Laodicea, boasting in all she possesses, much seen that man esteems, in her wealth, her wardrobe and want of nothing, yet no Christ. Truly, how "miserable, poor, blind and naked she is". The Lord longs for fellowship, it seems it cannot be found collectively, so the appeal is to the individual, "if any man". JND in a footnote says the words "stand and knock" have the sense of the Lord placing himself there and "AM STANDING" and "AM KNOCKING", these are continuous actions. Do we not see a heartfelt desire for fellowship, a longing for someone to be taken up with himself, for the Saviour and not service to fill the life, to hear the voice as in the Song of Songs. In 2:10-11 "My beloved spake and said unto me, rise up my love, my fair one, and come away. For lo the winter is past, and the rain is over and gone", or in v. 14 "Let me hear thy voice, for sweet is thy voice, and thy countenance is comely". In Ch 5:2 - "It is the voice of my beloved that knocketh saying open to me, my sister, my love, my dove, my undefiled". Here in Rev. 3:20, it is the Lord knocking with his voice, for saints to open to him, to eat and drink with him, these are symbols of fellowship. In John 6:53 we eat of him for relationship, in 1 Cor. 11:23-26 we take bread and wine for worship, here like 1 Cor. 10:16-21 it is for fellowship. Do we feel a barrenness of fellowship with the Lord? May we open to him to know Christ sitting with us, to find rest, and in eating to find refreshment?

Destiny Confirmed (v. 21)

To him that overcometh will I grant to sit with me in my throne, even as I also overcame, and am set down with my Father in his throne. (Revelation 3:21)

The last of the precious promises to the overcomers brings before us the hope of the redeemed. We have had the Lord's counsel (v. 18), his chastening (v. 19), his call (v. 20), now we have his challenge. There seems to be definite progress in these seven words to the overcomer. In Ephesus, life is imparted, in Smyrna, life is promised after suffering, in Pergamos, private approval before God, in Thyatira, public approval before men, in Sardis, the victor owned before the throne, in Philadelphia the victor is part of that glory, and now finally seated on the throne with his Lord.

It is well to note, this is not the Father's throne. The Lord Jesus alone sits on that with the Father (Heb. 1:13). That throne is the subject of Ch 4. It is the throne of heaven.

No man other than the Lord will ever sit upon that throne. The throne of the Lord Jesus is on earth, (Matt. 19:28) where the disciples are promised a place in his glorious kingdom. Here every believer will be linked with him in the day of his glory. Such verses as Rom. 8:17, Eph. 1:11, 1 Cor. 6:2-3, Rev. 2:26-27 will then come into effect, the saints sharing in the inheritance of our Lord Jesus, judging in a governmental way this world. The Lord says, "to sit with me IN my throne", the preposition (en), denotes not only a place of honour, but also close association with him. He speaks of the throne he occupies now, the Father's Throne, that is developed in Ch 4.

The Desired Consecration (v. 22)

He that hath an ear let him hear what the Spirit saith unto the churches. (Revelation 3:22)

With such blessed promises before us, would we not do well to hear the call of the spirit, and live for the honour of our Lord Jesus until the day of his glory?

Chapter 4
The Throne of heaven

Introduction

The scene now changes from the darkness of earth and the witness of saints, to the glory of heaven and to the worship of the sovereign. It is well known that the book of Revelation alternates between scenes on earth and scenes in heaven; we have at least seven scenes in heaven:

(1) Ch 4-5 are taken up with Christ's Coronation, (2) Ch 8:1-6 the Appreciation of the prayers of the saints, (3) Ch 12:1-2 Israel's Exaltation, (4) vv. 3-5 the Dragon's Anticipation of destroying the Man child, (5) Ch 15 Earth's Condemnation as seven angels hold the seven vials that contain the final judgement, (6) Ch 19 Heaven's Exultation at the destruction of Babylon, (7) Ch 19:11 Christ's Manifestation when he returns in glory. We shall look at them as we come to them.

The time has now come for the coronation of our Lord Jesus. He is finally to take up the reigns of government; all judgement is committed to the Son. In this present church era, it is the Father who judges his sons (1 Pet. 1:17, Heb. 12:5-9). The Lord Jesus is our Great High Priest, and our advocate, now he takes his rightful place as King. The scene before us is comparable with Dan. 7:9-14, "where the Ancient of days did sit", and "one like the Son of Man came to him with the clouds of heaven, and there was given to him, dominion, and glory, and a kingdom, an everlasting kingdom that shall not pass away", nor be destroyed. Dan. 7, like Rev. 4-5, has tribulation days in view, and brings before us the great powers of the last days, with a beast, "dreadful and terrible and strong exceedingly", answering to the coming beast of Ch 13:1-10. Rev. 4-5 is a further commentary on Dan. 7:9-14. From this point on the church is not seen again in the book until Ch 19 when she is linked to Christ as his Bride and Ch 21, when it is seen in its future roles in administration as a city, in affection to Christ as a bride, and as the abiding dwelling place of God, as a tabernacle. Like Enoch in Gen. 5:24, her walk with God in separation from the world is over, she is translated (Heb 11:5), to the place from which the judgements are proceeding - heaven. The world is to experience conditions exceeding those of the flood, (Matt. 24:21). In the days of Noah, one judgement at a stroke dealt with ungodly men. In tribulation days, successive judgements bringing the ferocity of the wrath of God upon the world are poured out, from which some will seek to die, but there is no escape (8:6). But like Noah, who was preserved through it all, as Enoch was saved from it all, so a remnant will be preserved for God, no harm can come to them; these are evidently the sealed 144,000 of Ch 7. During this period of tribulation the church is safely in heaven.

The Sound of the Trumpet (v. 1)

After this I looked, and, behold, a door [was] opened in heaven: and the first voice which I heard [was] as it were of a trumpet talking with me; which said, Come up hither, and I will shew thee things which must be hereafter. (Revelation 4:1)

The chapter begins with an "after this", (*meta tauta*) an expression which occurs 10 times in the book of Revelation. It seems to always denote another event succeeding that which has gone before.

Ch 1:19	it gives the Setting of the book into the 3 parts
Ch 4:1	we have the Separation of the saints from earth
Ch 7:1	the Sealing 144,000 Jews for preservation
Ch 7:9	tells of the Salvation of Gentiles
Ch 9:12	the Severity of the last two trumpet sounds
Ch 15:5	inaugurates the Seven last plagues
Ch 18:1	the Sentence upon Babylon
Ch 19:1	Scene of rejoicing at Babylon's fall
Ch 20:3	tells of Satan's imprisonment.

The "after this" of this verse denotes that the testimony of the church on the earth has finished, the open door and the trumpet call give a beautiful figure of the saints being carried away to the throne room of heaven to witness the coronation of our Lord Jesus Christ. I notice a door is sufficient to take saints in. When the Lord Jesus comes out in 19:11, John sees heaven open. The glorious majesty of that occasion will fill the heavens. John hears, "the first voice". A writer has said, "there is no significance in the expression". For the Spirit to write anything without significance cannot be. This writing of mine may waste many words, the Spirit of God, Never! It is significant to me that this is the first of seven voices John hears in Ch 4-5. This must be the first; it summons him from earth to heaven. The object of John being caught up is to reveal to him, "things which must be". From this point on in the world's history all MUST be; in Ch 2-3 much is allowed, "the things which are", now everything is assured, it must be. From this time on, all is under divine control, nothing happens without a decree from the throne, God again asserts his rights.

In 2 Cor. 12, Paul is also caught up to heaven and sees "things not lawful for a man to utter" (v. 4), he was "a man in Christ" (v. 2), now John is caught up and he reveals what he saw. John is a prophet, he cannot be silent, and he must speak.

The Sight of the Throne (vv. 2-3)

And immediately I was in the spirit: and, behold, a throne was set in heaven, and [one] sat on the throne. And he that sat was to look upon like jasper and a sardine stone: and [there was] a rainbow round about the throne, in sight like unto an emerald. (Revelation 4:2-3)

Here the second vision commences, he was, "in the Spirit". This vision runs right through to the end of Ch 16. The first things that fill John's eyes are the throne set and the throne sitter. The set throne indicates the immovability of divine purpose, the thrones of earth may tumble and fall, but nothing can move this throne. The throne is filled, Israel's throne has been empty for centuries (Hosea 3:4), and when filled again, it will first be by a usurper (2 Thess. 2:4) - God neither vacates, nor is he usurped.

The one that sits can only be described as "like a jasper and a sardine stone". As jewels they would speak of the preciousness of Deity (1 Pet. 2:4, 7). The jasper would tell us of his purity, 21:11, "a jasper stone clear as crystal". The walls of the city are of jasper, divine glory surrounds the saints (21:8) and the first stone in the foundation is jasper, divine glory upholds us. The second stone is sardine, symbolising power. It is rich red in colour, the first man made in the image of God, Adam (red earth) was given power and authority over the creation (Gen. 1:28, Heb. 2:7-8), which is a quotation from Ps. 8. Ps. 8 ends "O Lord our Lord, how excellent is thy name in all the earth!" His majesty is supreme.

Seven things are connected in some way with the throne:

Around it - a rainbow and 24 thrones, Out of it, lightnings and thunderings, Before it, seven lamps of fire and a sea of glass, About it, four living creatures.

Seven is always significant of perfection. The rainbow, God's token of his covenant with earth (Gen. 9:12-17), encircles the throne. If the wrath of God is to be poured out, it will be tempered with mercy. The bow, like the blood (Ex. 12:13), another token, was for God to see and remember the everlasting covenant between God and every living creature of all flesh that is upon the earth. Like the verdant grass of earth, it is emerald. This rainbow is seen before the storm breaks, not when it is over.

The Sitting Elders (v. 4)

And round about the throne were four and twenty seats: and upon the seats I saw four and twenty elders sitting, clothed in white raiment; and they had on their heads crowns of gold. (Revelation 4:4)

Most commentators, following Kelly or Darby who were instrumental under the hand of God in restoring in a positive way the truth of the coming of our Lord Jesus, will teach here that these twenty-four elders are the redeemed of earth in some form or another. When reading Kelly on Revelation as a young man I found this hard to swallow, and as the years passed and I read his pupils, it got no easier. The teaching is summed up by Gaebelein - Annotated Bible, "They cannot be angels, angels are never seated on thrones (not seats, as in the authorised version), nor are they crowned, nor can they sing redemption's song as the elders do. There is only one possible meaning, they represent the redeemed, the saints in glory. They are priests (clothed in white) and they are kings (crowned); they are the royal priesthood in the presence of the throne. Why twenty-four? It points us back to the work David did for the temple. He appointed twenty-four courses of priests (1 Chron. 24). Twice twelve would suggest the saints of the old and new testaments". Many of the statements are unqualified, and seriously flawed.

Firstly, why make these the redeemed at all? Is not this a scene that John views on his entrance to heaven? Surely John must be representative of the church if there needs to be such. John is gazing on the heavenly order of things. That there is a hierarchical system in heaven is clear from many passages. In Col. 1:16, in the creation the Lord Jesus did not only make the heavens and the earth, but also the ordered government in these spheres. Eph. 3:10 speaks of "thrones and dominions, principalities or powers", it sees a heavenly order of these learning the manifold wisdom of God, through the church. Eph. 6:12 puts the satanic host in the same vein, as Satan moves with ordered strategy. He is termed "the anointed cherub that covereth", (Ezek. 28:14). This denotes the honour he had before his fall when God anointed priests and kings; they were given the place of supremacy. Satan had the highest place of authority in the creation of God. He is still the god of this world, whom men unwittingly worship and the prince of this world whom they serve, there are no scriptures that would indicate that he has lost this title "the anointed cherub that covereth" even if he has lost his position.

Michael is known as one of the chief princes (Dan. 10:13), and the great prince (Dan. 12:1). In Jude 9 he is the archangel, denoting an order of authority in the angelic realm. We know from Job 1:6, 1 Kings 22:19-22, Isaiah 6, that a heavenly court sits. Do not these verses give us a further insight into this, heavenly beings associated with God in the government of the universe?

Secondly, as we saw in Ch 2:21, saints are never seen to sit on thrones in .heaven, but rather linked with our Lord Jesus when his throne is established on the earth.

Thirdly, the redeemed of this age are never seen other than as a compound unity: a body, a building, a bride, one new man, in Ch 21: a city, a bride and a tabernacle. Never is it seen in parts, and as a notable teacher at a conference in England scathingly said "one 24th part of the church brethren, come, come, come", quoting Ch 5:5, making that elder distinct in his being, an individual talking to an individual.

Fourthly, it is stated that these are the saints in priestly order, taking their character from the ordering of the priestly courses established by David in 1 Chron. 24. Yet it seems to me that, rather than heaven take its character from earth, the order of heaven gives character to earth, what was already in existence in heaven becomes the pattern of the things of the temple.

Fifthly, it is said these are representatives of Old and New Testament saints, twelve from each dispensation. Again never at any time do we find Old Testament saints linked with the church. The church of this present age is distinct in all its ways. Eph. 3:5, in other ages not made known to the sons of men, Col. 1:26 hid from ages, time, and generations, men. The saints of the

Old Testament do not even seem to be in heaven as the church is during tribulation days. The resurrection of Old Testament saints is seen after the tribulation is over (Dan. 12:2, Rev. 11:18), on the return of the Lord Jesus to earth is the time to reward his servants the prophets. These cannot be representatives of both companies.

Sixthly, some have said these cannot be angels for they wear the victor's crown, the Stephanos. If indeed this is the victor's crown, why cannot God honour angels as he honours men? Is earth the only scene of conflict? Dan. 10, Rev. 12 teaches otherwise, the very fact of Satan's rebellion, and the fallen angels teach there was a time when heaven knew conflict. Could God not reward angels who accomplished something for him in that day? Again is the Stephanos only given to victors? In Heb. 2:7, the head of the creation, Adam, is so crowned and that before any conflict came in. He is head over creation. Perhaps even here it merely speaks of the honour of place given to these twenty-four.

Seventhly, some have said angels are not seen in white robes. John 20:12, Acts 1:10, answer that without any comment, purity, white, must mark them. Rev. 15:6 also speaks of angels "clothed in pure white linen" but the word is different, it signifies radiant, bright. Again, some say angels do not sing as these do in Ch 5:9, they only speak. Yet did not angels sing on creation's day (Job 38:7)? It is to be noted that in Ch 5:9-10 they are not singing for themselves, the song of redemption is for others. "Thou hast redeemed to God by thy blood out of every tribe and tongue, and people and nation, and made them to our God kings and priests" (JND translation).

Dwight Pentecost "Things to come" page 209 adds, "since according to Rev. 5:8, these twenty-four are associated in a priestly act, which is never said of angels, they must be believer-priests associated with the Great High Priest". Again, if these are redeemed men taken up with the prayers of saints, then it immediately opens the door to the Roman Catholic doctrine of the intercessory prayers of saints, for these are taken up with the prayers of saints. Such a thought would be nauseous to any true believer, yet we must seriously consider this if these are indeed redeemed saints. If they belong to the heavenly order of angels, the difficulty disappears; it is very evident from scripture that angels take a great interest in the prayers of saints. Rev. 8:3 plainly states that angels approach the golden altar in heaven, adding incense to the prayers of saints. It was an angel who came to Zacharias in answer to his prayers, also to Cornelius in Acts 10:3-6. In Dan. 9:21 we find an angel appears to Daniel in answer to his prayer; see also 10:12. It is very clear that angels do have a part to play in the prayers of saints as they serve God, acting as couriers of God's answers to the prayers of his own.

Lang, "Revelation of Jesus Christ" page 125, also adds two interesting points saying "a bride cannot be enthroned before her marriage and this does not take place until Ch 19. Also a bride cannot be enthroned before her royal spouse has taken the throne. She may sit down with him, but not before him and these are seated before the Lion of the tribe of Judah comes on the scene".

These conclusions make it apparent that what we have in these seated elders is the heavenly court. There are seven references to them in Ch 4-5; there are twelve references to them in the book of Revelation.

The Symbol of Majesty (v. 5)

And out of the throne proceeded lightnings and thunderings and voices: and [there were] seven lamps of fire burning before the throne, which are the seven Spirits of God. (Revelation 4:5)

Such are the "lightnings, thunder and voices", (Ps. 97:1-5), they give a graphic picture of the majesty of God; clouds and darkness surround him; a fire goeth before him; his lightnings enlightened the world, the hills melted like wax at the presence of the Lord (see also Ps. 77:18, Job 37:2-5), these accompany the presence of God. They are first seen at Sinai, (Ex. 19:16), causing the people to tremble. His majesty is seen when giving the Commandments, here in Rev. 4 at the Crowning of Christ, in 11:19 before the Conflict with Satan, as seen in Ch 12, (verse 19 of Ch 11 really belongs to Ch 12), again in 16:18 with the Collapse of Babylon. They are intimately linked with the throne coming out from it, (preposition *ek*).

The Seven Lamps of Fire (v. 5)

This seems to be a fitting symbol of the Holy Spirit. We have already seen that the sevenfold character is in keeping with his display in relation to the coming glories of our Lord Jesus in millennial days (Isaiah 11:2). He is the seven Spirits in relation to the church 1:4, 3:1. Now as burning lamps, his testimony is to the judgements of God that are to follow. Newberry says, "He is here in all his divine perfection and sovereignty, and in his transcendent holiness and vehement jealousy for truth".

I do wonder why he is introduced as the fifth of the seven things seen in this chapter; meditation has not yet yielded the fruit of the truth that must be in it.

The Sea of Glass (v. 6)

And before the throne [there was] a sea of glass like unto crystal: and in the midst of the throne, and round about the throne, [were] four beasts full of eyes before and behind. (Revelation 4:6)

How beautiful that as the Spirit is before the throne, so a sea of glass is before the throne. It is as if one is jealous for the holiness of God, the sea would speak of the crystal purity that marks the scene. It answers to the laver of the tabernacle. Before a priest could minister in any way, either at the altar, or in the sanctuary, he had to wash thereat (Ex. 30:20). Here all is pure, "nothing that defileth shall ever enter in", as purity must mark those who serve the tabernacle, so must all who approach the throne be pure.

Many years ago, a friend of mine took us through, "The tabernacle in the book of Revelation", in a series of bible readings. Wiersbe gives a table of some of the comparisons with the tabernacle in his commentary on Revelation in Ch 4.

The Seeing Ones (vv. 6-8)

And the first beast [was] like a lion, and the second beast like a calf, and the third beast had a face as a man, and the fourth beast [was] like a flying eagle. And the four beasts had each of them six wings about [him]; and [they were] full of eyes within: and they rest not day and night, saying, Holy, holy, holy, Lord God Almighty, which was, and is, and is to come. (Revelation 4:7-8)

That there is difficulty in interpretation when looking at these Living ones is evident when Strauss says "I have examined 39 different commentaries on this passage, and they leave me convinced that many of the brethren are engaged in mere speculation and fanciful interpretation" (Revelation page 135).

I trust we shall be preserved from this, as we need to look into the subject before us.

Their position is first brought before us

It would seem that these living creatures are cherubim; they are seen in the midst of, and round about the throne. The thought is being central to it, and surrounding it. They are always seen closely linked to the throne (Ex. 25:22) coming out of the mercy seat, and one with it, being the place of divine communication, "there will I meet with thee". See also Num. 7:89. It is little wonder we are told seven times over that God dwelleth between the cherubim (1 Sam. 4:4, 2 Sam. 6:2, 2 Kings 19:15, 1 Chron. 13:6, Ps 80:1, 99:1, Isaiah 37:16). Such seems to be the position here in Rev. 4.

Their perception is noted

They are said to be "Full of eyes before and behind". Ottman links this with omniscience, but such an attribute is linked with deity only and these are not God. Ezek. 28:13, when speaking of the anointed cherub that covereth, Satan, speaks of "the day of his creation", thus they belong to an order of creation, and though the highest form of it, and closest to the throne, they are still created beings. The thought of intelligence rather than omniscience must be seen. As closely linked to the throne, it is essential that they see before, and behind, scrutinising all that approaches.

Their person is presented

The AV speaks of them as beasts; it is well known that this is an unfortunate rendering of *zoon,* which means living ones, they are not the *therion* of Mark 1:13 which the Lord was with in the wilderness, nor as the beast of Ch 13 which are dangerous animals (Strongs venomous wild). Though, to be fair to the translators, the word is used three times outside the Revelation, where it is exclusively used as of these living ones. Elsewhere, the word occurs in Heb. 13:11, where it is speaking of the sacrificial animal, and in 2 Pet. 2:12, Jude 10, where it is used of sinful men who withstand divine truth. On each occasion they are termed beasts.

John sees them as bearing the character of the four representative heads of creation. The fact that they are "like" a lion, or "as" a man, tell me they are not actually this, the statements are symbolic. They have the **MIGHT** of the lion, Judges 14:18 "what is stronger than a lion?", also see Proverbs 30:30, where it says, "a lion which is the strongest among beasts and turneth not away from any". They have the **MINISTRY** of the calf, for these are seen as bringing home the sheaves, treading out the corn and ploughing the field. It became the object of worship to Israel, the molten calf of Ex. 32. Thus it was a venerated animal. In Ezek. 1:10, where each living creature had four faces, one was of the ox in its maturity; here it is that of the young of the herd in its activity. The third displays the **MAJESTY** of man, who is the head of creation (Gen. 1:26 and Heb. 2). It is evident that the highest form of creation, the cherubim has close association with men. Many would say that Satan, before his fall, was responsible for the world. He has certainly usurped authority now in the fall, dictating its present course in opposition to God (Eph. 2:2). The symbols here seen were in the standards of the four tribes who settled the tribes around the tabernacle, and led them on their march.

Reuben held the man, Judah the lion, Ephraim a young ox and Dan the eagle. These would remind Israel that they were under divine care. In their settlement around the tabernacle, as the protectors from attack, (Num. 1 and 2), they are there as God's army, the hand of God preserved both them and the tabernacle. They would also be preserved on their marching. The fourth brings us the **MOVEMENTS** of the eagle. Prov. 30:19 speaks of "the way of the eagle in the air", Isaiah 40:31 gives us the promise that God gives to those who wait upon him, "mounting up with wings as eagles", movements that lift it toward heaven (Prov. 23:5). Such is the character displayed by the *zoon*, "the living ones". They are associated with the throne, yet linked with responsibility regarding the earth. If, as I feel, these are cherubim, first seen when God drove man out of Eden, then God placed them at the east of the garden. (The Companion Bible says "in booths", Ottman says "they tabernacled there - that is the word used", pg. 120 "Unfolding of Ages"). It would seem it became God's first dwelling place, the place to which Cain and Abel came with their offerings, and from which the voice of God spake, when he appealed to, and judged Cain. From here he spoke to Cain and Abel, (Rom. 10:17 and Heb. 11:4), though Abel alone acted in faith and gave God what he asked for "a Lamb" and it would seem that it was to here that they brought their offerings, thus linking the cherubim with God in His governmental and redemptive dealings. They are still seen in the book of Revelation in the same roles. Chapter 5:8-10 shows their interest in Redemption. Ch 6:1, 3, 5, 7, and finally Ch 19:4 tell of their appreciation of God's governmental workings.

Their Protective Covering

We are told they have six wings about them. The Seraphim of Isaiah 6:2 also have six wings, four of their wings are given to cover their face and feet as they fly before the throne crying one to another "Holy, Holy, Holy". These *zoon* seem to be encircled by their wings; such is the word "about them" (*kuklothen*). No wings are seen in Gen. 3:24, two in Ex. 25:22, four in Ezek. 1:6. All must have a covering as they move before God. It is noticeable that their eyes are seen again; now as within, does this tell of the appreciation of inward purity that must be felt in the presence of God?

Their Praise of God

Such is the character of Deity; again, as with the Seraphim, the holiness of God is the subject of their praise. The Seraphim fly, these living creatures "rest not day and night saying, Holy, holy, holy, Lord God Almighty, which was and is and is to come". Their praise is threefold, as they speak of God's Purity, His Power, "the Almighty", and His Permanence, "which was, which is and which is to come".

The Subjection of the Elders (vv. 9-11)

And when those beasts give glory and honour and thanks to him that sat on the throne, who liveth for ever and ever, The four and twenty elders fall down before him that sat on the throne, and worship him that liveth for ever and ever, and cast their crowns before the throne, saying, Thou art worthy, O Lord, to receive glory and honour and power: for thou hast created all things, and for thy pleasure they are and were created. (Revelation 4:9-11)

Verse 9 shows that it is the actions of the living creatures that bring a reaction from the Elders. Worship begets worship. That is seen beautifully in Ch 5:8-14, also in Ch. 19:1-6. Oh that we might rise in worship, for it must produce similar desires in others. There are three things that are done by the four and twenty elders in vv. 10-11.

Firstly - Their Adoration, falling before the throne in worship. This worship is something for God alone. Peter refused it in Acts 10:25, when Cornelius received a man sent from God. God's servants should neither seek it nor be worshipped. An angel refused it in Rev. 19:10 and in 22:9. Both state "Worship God". Even angels bringing divine truth must not be worshipped. This is a sad reflection on Catholicism, that would direct its adherents to look to men and to worship Mary. The devil seeks such worship, even to desiring the Lord Jesus to fall down and worship him (Matt. 4:9). What a fall that would have been, if such a thing could have been possible, far greater than when Satan himself fell, (Luke 10:18). Satan and the Man of Sin will be worshipped in a day to come (13:4), and that by a delusion sent from God himself (2 Thess. 2:11), "because they receive not the love of the truth that they might be saved".

Secondly - Their Abdication, the casting down of their crowns is not veneration, as many make this act. "They see the saints as realising that they owe their victory to him who sits upon the central throne, thus he alone is worthy to receive their crowns" (Lehman Strauss). The saints are never to cast down what is given to them; their crowns are for governmental authority in the millennial Kingdom. The time has now come for this heavenly order to step aside, the Lord Jesus is to take the book of governmental dealings with the world, he, with his own, will rule, and angelic beings are to come under the government of the saints (1 Cor. 6:3). Up to this time, all government is in the hand of the Father and his throne, even that of the believers of this dispensation, (Heb. 12:5-11, 1 Pet. 1:17). Now that the Lord Jesus has all committed to his hand, the heavenly hierarchy must step aside. From this point on, they are not seen with crowns in the other scenes when introduced in the book.

Thirdly - Their Appreciation, with the act of casting their crowns down they praise the throne sitter for his creatorial power. They have been administrators in that creation, they glorify him who is the creator. Some link the Lord Jesus here with the throne, on account of Col. 1:16 and Heb. 1:10-12, but that is not necessary, for as the Spirit had a part in creation (Gen. 1:2), so also our Bible begins, "In the beginning God". Many other scriptures could be added. The Lord Jesus is introduced in Ch 5, not here, where the purpose of creation is brought before us, "for Thy pleasure they are and were created", not for our happiness, but for God's pleasure, strictly "His will" (JND), his desire. Thus, to have a world according to His will and desire, he must pluck out all that offend. The man who is going to act thus for God to bring it about is now introduced in Ch 5, the Lord Jesus.

It is to be noticed the variety of things that draw out worship from these twenty-four elders. Here they worship him as a creator, in Ch 6:9-10 as a redeemer, in Ch 7:12 as a preserver, in Ch 11:16-17 as a ruler, in Ch 19:4 as a judge. God is glorified in all his works.

The Worth of the Lamb (vv. 5-7)

And one of the elders saith unto me, "Weep not: behold, the Lion of the tribe of Juda, the Root of David, hath prevailed to open the book, and to loose the seven seals thereof." And I beheld, and, lo in the midst of the throne and of the four beasts, and in the midst of the elders, stood a Lamb as it had been slain, having seven horns and seven eyes, which are the seven Spirits of God sent forth into all the earth. And He came and took the book out of the right hand of Him that sat upon the throne. (Revelation 5:5-7)

One of the elders consoles and comforts John. The fact that this elder is seen as an individual acting for God, emphasises that they are not the church. I know we are told to comfort one another, (1 Thess. 4:18), but it would be absurd to think that one twenty-fourth part of the church would be brought in here to comfort twenty-three parts of the church.

If none in the creation can take or look upon the book, he who has been exalted far above all (Eph. 1:21), "has prevailed", gotten the victory, overcome, for this is the word. We are told that it is the Lion of the Tribe of Judah. His monarchy is emphasised, the prophecy of Jacob (Gen. 49:9-10) is here fulfilled in Christ, the world has yet to see it, but his regal rights are owned in heaven. If he is Judah's mighty monarch, he must also belong to the house of David to be the rightful heir, for God has decreed that it is David's house that will reign, (2 Sam. 7:12-16, Isaiah 11:1-9). Is it not interesting that it is not his descent that we see as coming from David, but as the root out of which David himself came? Well might David speak of him as "My Lord" (Ps. 110:1). If Monarchy is seen in the lion, his Deity is seen as the root. John ever brings before us the eternal being of the Lord Jesus. If he writes of John the Baptist, the Lord was before him, (John 1:30). If he writes of David, he is his root, not a branch. If he writes of Abraham, he must say that Abraham rejoiced to see his day, for "before Abraham was I Am", ever existent (John 8:53-59). If he writes of creation, he must give the Lord his proper place, "In the beginning was the Word" (John 1:1), but this is not enough to open the book, he must first gaze upon the man of Calvary, the Lamb that was slain.

That which fills his eyes must bring him great pleasure, as the thought that none from creation could take the book gave him pain, once again he is to see him whom he loved, and in the familiar character of how he had known him here, "a lamb". Was John not one of the two who heard John the Baptist cry "behold the Lamb of God", and leaving John, he followed Jesus into the nameless place (John 1:36-39). These brief hours transformed John's life, he had no desire to leave this blessed one afterwards. Israel ever looked for a lamb. In Gen. 4 the lamb is typified, acceptance can only be found in the blood of the Lamb. In Gen. 22, it is prophesied (v. 8) how beautiful! "Himself a lamb", the lamb is God manifest in flesh. In Ex. 12 the lamb is ratified, redemption only through the blood of the lamb, v. 3 "a lamb", v. 4 "the lamb", v. 5 "your lamb". In John 1, the lamb is identified, "behold the Lamb of God". In Isaiah 53 he is crucified, "led as a lamb to the slaughter". Here in Rev. 5 he is glorified. There is need of a lamb for a man, Gen. 4, a lamb for a house, Ex. 12, a lamb for a nation, Lev. 16. Christ met the greatest need when he became a lamb for the world, (John 1:29). Though John sees a little lamb (diminutive) he sees him in the place of supremacy, he must take his rightful place in the midst. He is in the midst of the doctors in life, (Luke 2:46), in the midst of thieves in death, (John 19:18), he is in the midst of the church in resurrection, (Matt. 18:20), now he is in the midst of glory. He is seen as standing, the "until" of prophecy has been completed, the sitting of Acts 1:13, 10:12-13, is over, his enemies are about to become his footstool, he rises to bring a world into subjection to himself. John sees him as the Lamb that was slain; it is as a result of his death that God can deal righteously with the world. If John saw him die in seeming weakness, that is forever done, he sees his power, and perception. The seven horns and seven eyes would demonstrate both in perfection. The Lamb slain is God, Omnipotent, (there are seven horns), Omniscient, (seven eyes), and the fact that they are sent forth into all the earth would demonstrate his Omnipresence. These eyes are seen as the seven spirits of God. We have already seen in Ch 1:4 his position, in Ch 3:1 his possession, now his purpose, "sent forth".

Now the most momentous event in divine purpose takes place. Heaven has waited in anticipation of it; soon it is to break out in rapturous delight. Prophecy has foretold it, this is the fulfilment of Ps. 2:6-12, and of Dan. 7:13-14. Here we find the true understanding of the parable of the Lord Jesus in Luke 19:12. "A certain nobleman went into a far country to receive for himself a kingdom and to return". Here he receives that kingdom, and the wheels are set in motion for his return. Calvary was essential to it, ere he can reign, he must taste death for every man (Heb. 2:9). If he is going to bring many sons into glory, the captain of our salvation must be made perfect through suffering (Heb. 2:10). Not that imperfection could ever mark the Son of God, but until the redemption price had been paid, the world could not be recovered for God, the future reconciliation of the heavens and the earth must be through the blood of his cross (Col. 1:20). The work was done, nothing remains undone, he has been made perfect, his entitlement to dominion is fully paid, the Lamb can with unfaltering steps approach the throne, God's claims to the earth are recovered in him, the book can be taken, the divine program can begin, Christ's rights are now taken hold of, the book is his, the judgement committed to the son, John 5:22 now becomes a reality.

The Worship of the Elders (v. 8)

And when he had taken the book, the four beasts and four and twenty elders fell down before the Lamb, having every one of them harps, and golden vials full of odours, which are the prayers of saints. (Revelation 5:8)

Immediately the Lamb takes the book, the hierarchy of heaven begin their honour to the Lamb. In Ch 4 it is to the throne sitter, now it is directed to the Lord Jesus. They do three things in the verse:

1. Their Prostration - Heb. 1:6 tells of the occasion when angels are going to worship him, Heb. 1:5 speaks of his incarnation as the only begotten then gladly owned by the father, who irrespective of the shame and sorrow he must bear here, will never forsake his son. Filial affection will be known, but in the days of his humiliation the angels worship, not the son but the father. Glory to God in the highest, is their cry, at last a man is found who will bring glory to God. In v. 6 it is the bringing in again of the firstbegotten, his return in glory, then the angels are to worship him, he will sit as God on his throne, then worship will be directed to the Lord Jesus. What is to be seen in the world begins here in heaven, as they fall before him.

2. Their Praise - Every one holds a harp. Harps are always connected with joy and praise for whatever reason. The first reference to the harp is Gen. 4:21. The first reference to the use of the harp is Gen. 31:27, when Laban chides Jacob for stealing away and for not having the joy of a proper departure. The Psalms give the thought of joy and praise linked to the harp (33:2, 43:4, 57:7-8, 71:22, 81:1-2, 98:5, 150:3). Job, when feeling the weight of sorrow on account of his affliction, says my harp is turned to mourning (30:31), his joy had gone. Israel also in the days of captivity must hang their harps upon the willow (Ps. 137:2), how can they sing the Lord's song in a strange land? Isaiah, speaking of God's judgement on the earth says, "The joy of the harp ceaseth" (24:8). Seiss seems to connect it with the prophetic office alone, (page 118). I think he is too restrictive. I can understand the harp introduced into such passages as he quotes, for surely there is joy in divine revelation. Here there is joy in the honour conferred upon the son.

3. Their Prayerful Interest - They are also seen with golden vials or bowls full of incense, which, we are told, "are the prayers of saints". This again should cause us to see that these beings are not in any way the church or we are brought face to face with Catholicism, and its doctrine of the intercessory prayers of saints. That angels have an interest in our prayers is apparent, Dan. 9:21, Luke 1:13 and Acts 10:4 are but a few of many scriptures which teach angelic interest in the prayers of saints, but if these be the saints in glory as some teach, we immediately have a problem which must be dealt with. Do saints in heaven have a ministry of intercession? We refute even the thought of it. The spirit maketh intercession (Rom. 8:26), and the Lord Jesus does the same in v. 34. I do not see this heavenly order in intercession, but in their ministry they hold in those bowls our prayers. I notice that in Ch 8:3 there are seven angels with priestly censers, to whom much incense is given to add to the prayers of saints, here it is the prayers of saints. The incense of Ch 8 rises before God and brings forth ultimate judgement upon a wicked world because of its opposition to the saints. There are seven vials or bowls full of wrath in 15:7. Here the bowls are Godward in praise; there they are manward in punishment. In Ch 17:4 the woman has a cup full of abominations. All are full, be it the weight of prayers borne heavenward or the wrath of God poured earthward, all because of a full cup of wickedness, in the hand of the woman on the scarlet beast.

Their Whoop of Joy (vv. 9-10)

And they sung a new song, saying, Thou art worthy to take the book, and to open the seals thereof: for thou wast slain, and hast redeemed us to God by thy blood out of every kindred, and tongue, and people, and nation; And hast made us unto our God kings and priests: and we shall reign on the earth. (Revelation 5:9-10)

We come to a beautiful but complex section with divergent opinions. As we approach it, all one can say is, let every one be fully persuaded in his own mind. The main problem is that of the true reading. Not being proficient in the Greek text, we are dependent upon scholarship, but then even those well founded in Greek are not textual critics, that is a lifetime's occupation. Some leave the text as it is; it helps their interpretation of who these elders and living creatures are. One writer simply says, "they speak of their own redemption and this settles the matter, they must be glorified saints". Both Darby, and Kelly who first propounded the thought that the elders were the glorified saints, and who have many adherents, are faithful to their appreciation of the text even though it runs against their teaching of the elders. Kelly realises this, and makes these not the redeemed of the present dispensation, but of those who will remain on the earth after the rapture. He writes, "these will still come under God's rich mercy, that, even in the midst of his judgements, he would have a purchased people, who were to share the glory of the kingdom as a royal priesthood, instead of being swallowed up in the delusions of antichrist" (Kelly, Lectures in Revelation, page 120). The teaching of both of these writers omits "us" in v. 9. Kelly says, he is bound to state his firm impression that in the ninth verse the word "us" was put in by the copyist who supposed that the elders were celebrating their own blessing, (page 118). Both change the reading in v. 10 from, "Thou hast redeemed us" to "thou hast redeemed them", also in the verse "they" shall reign, not "we" shall reign. Kelly, of whom the Expositor Magazine wrote, "had the greatest mind in the Western hemisphere", and said his translation of Revelation was the greatest work on that book, has a lengthy textual criticism on page 118-119. It must be said that Seiss will have none of the changes.

Taking these things into account, we can look at the verses. In them we have:

1. The Song of the Heavenly Hierarchy - Some, to strengthen their teaching that these are not a heavenly order, state, angels do not sing. They did in Job 38:7 on creation's morning. If they rejoice in God's handiwork, is it not fitting that they rejoice in the Saviour's work of redemption? Both must cause those nearest the throne to raise an anthem of praise. It is a "new" song, new in character and constitution, (*kainos*). I note it is a word always linked with the whole tenor of this dispensation. Beginning with the new wine of Christ's ministry, formed on the basis of a new covenant, to make us new creatures, putting us into one new man, and part of that new Jerusalem, which is going to rule the new heaven and earth, in a day when God makes all things new. Another new song is seen in Ch 14:3, this is only known by the 144,000 and they will only sing when the hour of adversity is over and they walk with the Lamb on mount Sion. Those who have gotten the victory over the beast also sing (15:3), the song of Moses and the Lamb. Thus a song is raised for those of this present age, and for the elect remnant of Israel, and for those out of the nations saved in tribulation days. Little wonder that where the goodness of God is seen, we must, "sing and make melody in the heart unto the Lord" (Eph. 5:19).

2. The Saviour of Sinners - None can be the object of praise but our Lord Jesus. He alone is worthy. In these verses all heaven, and soon every creature is going to acknowledge his worth to take the supreme place, all on account of his sufferings.

3. His Sufferings - He is worthy for he was slain. The word would express not only all he suffered as rejected of men, but also what he accomplished as a ransom to God. It is used of Cain's slaughter of Abel (1 John 3:12), of the killing fields of men in tribulation days (6:4), and also of those saints whose souls are under the altar (6:9). What a reminder of our Lord's sufferings at the hands of men is in this word, "Slain", as they abused and ill-used the prince of life. Yet not only is it used of murder, but of the ministry of the altar, in sacrificial death. The Lord Jesus has effected this perfectly before God, never more shall God Jehovah smite the shepherd with the sword, the Lamb is slain no more, he is now in exaltation, and "he is worthy".

4. His Salvation - The song is on account of the redemption accomplished and fully seen in the redeemed now in heaven as seen in John. Others in the book wait for their redemption (7:14), they are not in this company.

5. The Subjects of Redemption - Praise God, he shall see of the travail of his soul, the fruit of his labour stands before him. Calvary was worth it all; out of every kindred, and tongue, and people, and nation; the blood has been effectual, the church is complete. They stand before him, to see his glorious coronation, and hear they were objects of his mighty work.

6. Their Sovereignty - Not only redeemed, but also made kings and priests. As the Lord will be a priest on his throne (Zech. 6:13) reigning, as Melchisedec, a king priest (Heb. 7:1) so the saints in close association with him will be kings in governmental authority toward men, and priests toward God.

7. Their Sphere of Rule - The text in the AV is very clear, they shall reign "on" the earth. Darby and Kelly change the preposition to, they shall reign "over" the earth. Both of these taught that the church as a heavenly people would not return to earth. Israel as an earthly people will be on the earth, taking the first place among the nations, but the church will be in the city of Ch 21 which will be over, rather than on the earth. We will deal with the city when we come to Ch 21, sufficient to say here, I believe it is the church, and not the dwelling place of the church. As for the location of the saints, the passage seems to me to be clear. Why change the AV? The preposition (*epi*) is used frequently in Ch 4-5. Its meaning is consistent throughout. Ch 4:2 - one sat "on" the throne, v. 4 - twenty four thrones, and "upon" the seats, they had "on" their heads crowns of gold, v. 9 - gave thanks to him that sat "on" the throne,

v. 10 - him that sat "on" the throne, 5:1 - "in" the right hand of him, v. 3 - "in" the earth, v. 7 - him that sat "upon" the throne, finally v. 13 - "in" the earth, and "in" the sea. Each of these is the same preposition (*epi*). The evidence implies that these be translated "on". The word does translate "over" in many parts of the Revelation, but when doing so, it refers to the authority that is seen in the passages where it occurs. For instance, 2:25, "to him will I give power over the nations", not locality but the extent of their realm, 6:8 "power was given them over the fourth part of the earth", 9:11 "they had a king over them", 13:7 "power was given him over all kindreds, and tongues, and nations".

Seiss feels very strongly saying: "Some people tell us that it is quite too low and coarse a thing to think of the earth in connection with the final bliss of the saints. They preach that we do but degrade and pervert the exalted things of holy scripture, when we hint the declaration of the wise man, that 'the earth endureth forever', and that over it the glorious and everlasting kingdom of Christ and His saints, is to be established in literal reality. But if the ransomed in heaven, with golden crowns upon their brows, kneeling at the feet of the Lamb, before the very throne of God, and with the prayers of all saints, and the predictions of all prophets in their hands, could sing of it as one of the elements of their loftiest hopes and joys, I beg to turn a deaf ear to the surly cry of 'carnal' – 'sensual' – 'unspiritual' – with which some would turn me from 'the blessed hope'. Shall the saints in glory shout: 'We shall reign on the earth', and we be accounted heretics for believing that they knew what they were saying? Is it come to this, that to be orthodox we must believe that these approved and crowned ones kneel before the throne of God with a lie upon their lips? Shall they, from thrones in heaven, point to earth as the future theatre of their administrations, and give adoring thanks and praises to the Lamb for it, and we be stigmatised as fanatics and Judaizers, for undertaking to pronounce the blessed fact in mortal hearing? Oh, I wonder, I wonder, how the dear God above us can endure the unbelief with which some men deal with His holy word. Shall we then keep silence on the subject? – When the Living ones and Elders fail to sing about it in heaven; when inspired apostles no longer admit the subject into their holy writings; then, but not till then, let it be dropped from the discourses of our sanctuaries, and from the inculcations of them that fear God. And woe, woe, to that man who is convinced of its truth, but, for the sake of place or friendship, refrains from confessing it! Well has it been said of him: 'He barters away his kingdom for the applause of men. He eclipseth the glory of Christ to enhance his own'. He stultifieth the adoring songs of celestial kings, that he may win a little empty favour by base pandering to the pleasure of an ignorant, unbelieving, and godless world".

The Witness of the Universe (vv. 11-14)

And I beheld, and I heard the voice of many angels round about the throne and the beasts and the elders: and the number of them was ten thousand times ten thousand, and thousands of thousands; Saying with a loud voice, Worthy is the Lamb that was slain to receive power, and riches, and wisdom, and strength, and honour, and glory, and blessing.

And every creature which is in heaven, and on the earth, and under the earth, and such as are in the sea, and all that are in them, heard I saying, Blessing, and honour, and glory, and power, be unto him that sitteth upon the throne, and unto the Lamb for ever and ever. And the four beasts said, Amen. And the four and twenty elders fell down and worshipped him that liveth for ever and ever. (Revelation 5:11-14)

The Praise is Extensive - from the throne, in ever widening circles, the praise to the Lord Jesus resounds. As in any coronation, choirs follow the initial fanfare that greets the crowning, until all gathered rise to sing the praise of the monarch. As here, what is begun by those who are around the throne extends to angels, and soon all creation must join in the anthem to our Lord Jesus Christ, Perronet's lovely hymn expresses it well:

All hail the power of Jesus name
Let angels prostrate fall
Bring forth the royal diadem
And crown him Lord of all.

Let every kindred, every tribe
On this terrestrial ball,
To him all majesty ascribe
And crown him Lord of all.

All must bow to God's beloved son, he has done all things well, and all answers to Ps. 69:34 "Let the heaven and earth praise him, the seas, and every thing that moveth therein".

The Praise is Earned - like the four living creatures, and four and twenty elders, the cry is, "worthy is the Lamb". Kittel says of the word worthy, "bringing up the other beam of the scale" simply to be of equal weight. Unlike men who long for all that are here received by our Lord Jesus, he did not strive for it, he suffered for it. This was not his goal, it came from his grief. Nimrod longed for power and led people in rebellion against God. Achan and Gehazi wanted riches and, along with Judas, it ends in their own destruction (1 Tim. 6:9), Solomon desired wisdom, and 1 Kings 11 shows how all failed him because of the multitude of his wives, and that they turned his heart to idolatry. Samson had strength, and died a poor blind captive. Saul sought for honour, but when more honour was given to David (1 Sam. 18:7) he was very wroth and the saying displeased him (was evil in the eye, margin), it put a javelin in his hand. Nebuchadnezzar wanted glory and ended up eating grass as oxen; none were of equal weight to it. But the man that went lower than all, has been exalted far above all; the blessing is rightfully his. It is the word to eulogise. Haman thought it was for himself, but he must lead Mordecai the Jew. No one can take the honours here revealed away from our Lord Jesus Christ.

The Praise is Endless - If the whole creation joins in the praise, it is consistent with the number of the world, fourfold. It begins with blessing, and ends with might, (*kratos*), manifest power, it is frequently rendered dominion in doxologies, the Lord will have this supremely in a day to come. This is going to be eternal, forever and ever, "to the ages of ages" (Darby), both his rule and his praise will be exhaustless.

His Praise is Endorsed - again the four living creatures and the four and twenty elders are united in praise, not now for the work of creation, (4:8-11), and his work for redemption (v. 10), but for his exaltation. They not only give their assent to it - Amen, but as one has said, "their hearts are fully in it, they bow the knee".

Chapter 6
The Seal judgements
The Coming Storm - First Seal (v. 1)

And I saw when the Lamb opened one of the seals, and I heard, as it were the noise of thunder, one of the four beasts saying, Come and see. (Revelation 6:1)

From here on to Ch 16:21, we have the great theme of the second vision which John had. In Ch 4-5, which commence the vision, we have the triumphs of Christ, now begins the troubles of the world. This is the period of time spoken of by the Lord Jesus in Matt. 24, Mark 13, Luke 21. The coming tribulation of the world now begins. Paul adds his testimony to it in Rom. 1:18, Ch 2:3-9, 1 Thess. 5:1-3 and 2 Thess. 2. Much could be added from many portions of the word of God, which tell of the day when God will deal in judgement with this world. It will be seen that there are to be three major judgement scenes: (1) The opening of the sealed book in which the judgements of the world are held, as unfolded in this chapter. (2) This is followed by the blowing of the trumpets in Ch 8-9. (3) Finally there is the pouring of bowls in Ch 16. Each tells of conditions that will prevail in the hour of God's wrath. This triad of judgement scenes are interspersed with other events that will take place in those days. It seems that these judgements are for various reasons. The seals seem to be because of the world's rejection of Christ, the trumpets for the reproach of saints and the bowls for rebellion against God. Are the seals in answer to Heb. 10:29-31? God holds a world guilty for rejecting his son; his vengeance will be poured out one day upon it. Are the trumpet judgements in answer to Rom. 12:19? In both of these scriptures the Lord says, "Vengeance is mine; I will repay". God will not allow his son or his saints to suffer the world's enmity and he takes up their cause and deals with the enmity of man in the book of Revelation. I notice that the care he has for his son is the same care he has for the saints. In 1 Thess. 4:6, God makes it clear that he will not have a spouse sinned against in adultery, and not take up their cause. The wrath of God is manifested in the judgement bowls of Ch 16:1; he will vindicate his own claims. These thoughts are in the verse.

There is a fourth scene of judgement in Ch 10, when 7 thunders are heard but John is told to seal it up and write them not. All fours are divided into a three and a one. Ch 10 differs on that, this judgement is not revealed.

1. The Control of Heaven - From this point on, God is directing all the events that take place in the world. The silence of God which has been such a mystery is now broken. The "giving up" of Rom. 1:24 and v. 26 and the giving over of v. 28, is now ended, and heaven is to take up its rightful place again in the affairs of this world. It is the Lamb that directs the events, from this point, nothing happens without heaven's authority behind it, however strange things might seem.

2. The Crack of Thunder - Thunder accompanies a storm, the fury of God is about to be unleashed, and the clouds presently accumulating will pour out their contents upon the earth. Let the world know that with this sound of thunder, the truth expressed in Romans 2:9 will then be brought to pass, "Tribulation and anguish upon every soul of man that doeth evil, of the Jew first, and also of the Gentile".

3. The Call of the Living One - Not only does the Lord Jesus open one of the seals, but also there is no movement on earth without heaven's command, for it is one of the living creatures that are about the throne that ushers in the first event. If we take the living creatures in the order of Ch 4:7, and vv. 3-7 would seem to indicate this, then this is the lion, the king of beasts, that summons the first rider onto the scene to play his part in tribulation days. At his command, another beast is going to rise who claims monarchy. The call is "Come"; most authorities omit, or bracket, the phrase "and see". This does not appear to be a voice to John to gaze on the spectacle before him, though he does that in v. 2. But rather it is a command to the rider on the white horse to come forth. He is hindered (2 Thess. 2:6-7) until it pleases the Lord Jesus to allow his presence here. It is the same in each of these first four seals. The call is to the rider to come, not for John to see.

The Conquering Sovereign (v. 2)

And I saw, and behold a white horse: and he that sat on him had a bow; and a crown was given unto him: and he went forth conquering, and to conquer. (Revelation 6:2)

William R Newell, along with others, makes this the Lord Jesus and his heavenly host. This cannot be so, for the Lord is directing events from heaven. This is in fact a Warrior that is going to have a significant part in the events of the tribulation.

The Warrior

Here I believe, we have the initial rise of the Man of Sin. Like the Lord Jesus in Ch 19:11, he rides a white horse. This is not so much a symbol of purity that white would generally infer, but rather that of imperial power; a monarch is before us. It is his military prowess that is evident in this verse. In Ch 13 it is his governmental rule that is prominent, whilst in Ch 17 his religious pretensions are the focal point of the chapter. In Ch 19 his catastrophic end is recorded for us. Like its counterpart, the book of Daniel, the book of Revelation brings before us much of the momentous history of the "Man of Sin".

His Weapon

He had a bow, Newberry says, "not a sword, the instrument of indiscriminate slaughter, but a bow to single out and destroy individuals who may resist his will". It has been noted that there is no arrow mentioned, does the bow have the show of power? The fact it has no arrow might tell us that he who is to come will depend more on his craft and guile when he first rises. That he is great and terrible Dan. 7:19 makes clear, whilst Dan. 8:23-25 would give his brilliant mind, understanding dark sentences, in v. 25 it is through his policy, i.e. craft and subtlety, that men will be brought under his control. These will cause him to magnify himself, and set himself above all that is called God, (Dan. 11:39; 2 Thess. 2:4).

His Wreath

Here a *stephanos*, the victor's crown is given to him, in Ch 13 they are diadems, the monarch's crown. He first rises as a vile person (Dan. 12:21), to whom they will not give the honour of the kingdom, but he soon establishes authority by military might, and he becomes a king doing according to his will (Dan. 11:36). He is the kind of man that the world looks to solve all its problems, and they are happy to give him a place of honour when he first rises to prominence. It is evident that he wants more than the *stephanos*, and he will not be content until supreme power is given to him.

His Wars

He went forth conquering and that he might conquer. He is unstoppable. As Hitler walked through Europe at will in the Second World War, so this one will march to supremacy, it is obvious that he is able to crush all, whoever it is that he moves against. There will be no Russian might or western alliance to hinder his progress. It will take the Lord out of heaven to deal with him in Ch 19:20.

Ceaseless Strife - Second Seal (vv. 3-4)

And when he had opened the second seal, I heard the second beast say, Come and see. And there went out another horse that was red: and power was given to him that sat thereon to take peace from the earth, and that they should kill one another: and there was given unto him a great sword. (Revelation 6:3-4)

Again it is divine authority that determines events that must be, the future destiny of this world is not only known, but unmistakably written. Now from the control room of heaven the world must reap what it has sown, the awesome bloodshed that has marked man as they rebel against God, and defy his commandment "thou shalt not kill" will return upon them double during these terrible days, (see Is. 40:2). The second living one, the calf, now calls the second rider to make his appearance, and with his coming to bring great bloodshed upon the world.

His Colour

The horse is ever a beast for battle. Men, in their folly, are as "the horse that rusheth into battle", (Jer. 8:32). With the carnage that is to follow, red is a fitting colour for the bloodshed that is to mark the earth.

The Commotion

What a day for humanity when peace is taken from the earth! The gospel is "preaching peace by Jesus Christ" (Acts 10:36). The Lord made peace through the blood of his cross (Col. 1:20). Justification means we have peace with God (Rom. 5:1). The world will not have either him or it; now in the dealings of God peace is removed. This is all antichrist can give, "for there is no peace saith the Lord unto the wicked" (Isaiah 48:22). It will be a day of anarchy, revolution and civil war, and with no prayers of the saints to temper it.

The Carnage

What an awful statement, "that they should kill one another". The killing fields of earth are small now in comparison. Many wonder if the conditions of the present day, when life is held so cheaply can get worse. This age is but the tip of the iceberg compared with what will be known in the tribulation.

The Cutlass

In each of the first three seals, something is held. It is either, a bow, or a sword, or, in verse 5, it is scales. There is nothing held in the hand of the rider when the fourth seal is opened and the rider on the pale horse takes his place on the scene of time. All fours divide into a three and a one, these divide in this way, this will be seen many times as we read through this book. Or again a dictator is in the first and distress marks the last three. The sword here given again speaks of the carnage seen, but not at a distance, as the bow, but in close proximity, "that they should kill one another" is the result of it. What awful days face the unbelievers of this present age of grace who refuse the gospel and are caught out, rather than caught up at the rapture!

Chronic Starvation - Third Seal (vv. 5-6)

And when he had opened the third seal, I heard the third beast say, Come and see. And I beheld, and lo a black horse; and he that sat on him had a pair of balances in his hand. And I heard a voice in the midst of the four beasts say, A measure of wheat for a penny, and three measures of barley for a penny; and see thou hurt not the oil and the wine. (Revelation 6:5-6)

At the opening of this seal, the third living creature, seen as a man, now calls forth his rider. Man is to come under awful circumstances, as famine is to touch the globe. What pitiful sights have been seen from the famine centres of the world. We see what depths people have sunk to in times of famine, such as that recorded in 2 Kings 6:25-29, when women made a pledge to boil their own sons. The world rejected the man who could feed 5000 with five loaves and two small fishes, now it must suffer the consequences of its folly. John's attention is drawn to three things:

A Black Horse

How fitting the colour of this rider! As Job laments his affliction he says, "my skin is black upon me" (Job 30:30). At the affliction the Lord must suffer to recover Israel, he says "I am black, astonishment hath taken hold on me" (Jer. 8:21). As Judah mourneth, and the gates thereof languish because of divine judgement, scripture records "they are black unto the ground" (Jer. 14:2), concerning the death they knew. Lam. 5:10 describes famine conditions, "our skin was black like an oven because of the terrible famine". As men pass through this aspect of divine judgement, black is a fitting symbol.

Balances in His Hand

These would fully illustrate the days before us. Such is the famine, that the scales would speak of limited quantity and a need to ration the provisions. There is no man at this time who is like Joseph, "in whom the spirit of God is" (Gen. 41:38) to help sustain a world in want, and preserve some of the harvest for the days of famine.

Blight Pronounced

The voice in the midst of the four living creatures, announces the extremity of the situation. Is the one who speaks the Lord Jesus? Is it he who says (5:6) "A measure of wheat for a penny and three measure of barley for a penny"? For the one that speaks is "in the midst of the four beasts", and surely this is the place that belongs to the Son of God. We know from Matt. 20 that a penny (denarius) was a labourer's daily pay. A measure was enough to sustain a man for a day. It would seem that a loaf of bread will cost a man his day's wages, and there will not be enough to sustain his family. But as always in times of want, there are those who will find sustenance and plenty. The oil and wine, the food of the rich goes untouched. In conditions like this, some will reserve much for themselves as the poor starve. Remember what Obadiah did in 1 Kings 18:13, when the famine was sore in Israel, when he hid a hundred men of the Lord's prophets in a cave and "fed them with bread and water". These prophets had not black-coated waiters to dine them like Elijah at the brook.

Consuming Slaughter - Fourth Seal (vv. 7-8)

And when he had opened the fourth seal, I heard the voice of the fourth beast say, Come and see. And I looked, and behold a pale horse: and his name that sat on him was Death, and Hell followed with him. And power was given unto them over the fourth part of the earth, to kill with sword, and with hunger, and with death, and with the beasts of the earth. (Revelation 6:7-8)

This is the last seal in which the living ones are involved. As every four divides into a three and a one (I notice that this is the only one of the first four seals in which a rider is named), so every seven divides into a four and three. The fact of living ones associated with the first four, and not with the last three divides them. The call to come issues forth from the fourth beast, the flying eagle, a carnivorous bird, the king in its realm. Man is going to feel the full weight of divine judgement as a quarter of mankind is destroyed in this judgement alone. With the world's population standing at around six billion people as I write, the judgement will have a great effect upon the world.

The Ashen Horse

Scott graphically states the colour of the horse. "The pale horse implying a cadaverous hue is the new harbinger of approaching judgement. It is the colour of men in death".

The Authoritative Rider

His name that sat upon him was Death. In Rom. 5:4, death reigns, there will be no escape from its tendrils in that day, and in death's train, hell follows fast. These two are seen to be in the hand of Christ, (1:18), they are under his POWER, little wonder he can call them forth. Here they are seen as a PUNISHMENT for godlessness. They are together again in Ch 20 where their PROSPECT is stated, where they are to be cast into the lake of fire. They will have done their work by this time, death has claimed the body, and hell the souls of men, there will be no further need of them in a glorious eternal state in which will dwell righteousness (2 Pet. 3:13), for then sin and judgement will no more be seen.

The Anguish of Men

Ezek. 14:21 relates how God is to pour out four sore judgements upon Jerusalem, "the sword, and the famine, and the noisome beast and the pestilence, to cut off from it man and beast". What he says of Jerusalem will in this day affect the whole world. What a day when the slaughter of the sword, the slow lingering death of famine and the savagery of beasts will unite to bring men to death. Some think the term death here means death by pestilence, as Ezek. 14:21. Think of the sores that will be very grievous, probably far worse than those that afflicted Job and caused Job's wife to say, "curse God and die" (Job 2:9). In this judgement, the world is reduced to 75% of its population, in 9:15 a further third of these are slain leaving just 50% of the world's population after two judgements. These verse would demonstrate the intensity of the suffering that will afflict the world after the rapture.

Many have drawn from Matt. 24, where the Lord Jesus speaks of these events, and have shown how they correspond to these seals.

1st Seal	-	"Many shall come in my name saying, I am Christ" (Matt. 24:5);
2nd Seal	-	"Ye shall hear of wars and rumours of wars" (Matt. 24:7);
3rd Seal	-	"There shall be famines" (Matt. 24:7);
4th Seal	-	"and pestilences" (Matt. 24:7);
5th Seal	-	"They shall deliver you up, to be afflicted and kill you" (Matt. 24:9-22);

6th Seal - "The sun shall be darkened, the moon shall not give her light, and the stars shall fall from heaven" (Matt. 24:29).

I do wonder if there is a perfect correspondence between the two, but at least there does seem to be a link.

The Cry of the Saints - Fifth Seal (vv. 9-11)

And when he had opened the fifth seal, I saw under the altar the souls of them that were slain for the word of God, and for the testimony which they held: And they cried with a loud voice, saying, How long, O Lord, holy and true, dost thou not judge and avenge our blood on them that dwell on the earth? And white robes were given unto every one of them; and it was said unto them, that they should rest yet for a little season, until their fellow- servants also and their brethren, that should be killed as they were, should be fulfilled. (Revelation 6:9-11)

The living ones have done their work, it is fitting they are not seen here, for they could not call persecution upon those who are sheltered by the blood which they have witnessed on the mercy seat. In this seal, we see the destruction of the saints by the world; in the sixth seal it is the destruction of the world by God.

The Rejection of the Godly

Many ask who these martyred saints are. It is evident they are not those of this present church age, for they are in heaven at this time, and not under the altar. Neither can they be Old Testament saints for they are not tried for their testimony as these are, but by God for failures. These must be those who are saved during tribulation days. If the world bears with the child of God now, in tribulation days the word of God is rejected, and the testimony of any who bear witness for God will leave them open to persecution. The Man of Sin will allow no voice but his own to be heard, and all who believe in Christ will be put to death (Rev. 13:7). Their death will be seen as an offering by God, their souls are under the altar, the place of sacrifice, but also in the place of the ashes, (Ps. 20:3) "Remember all thy offerings and accept thy burnt sacrifice; Selah". The margin reads, "Turn to ashes". God will be glorified in their death, and accepts it for himself.

The Request of the Godly

This is not the language of the church, in Rom. 12:14, that is rather to, "pray for those who persecute you", rather than pray against them. Bless them is the word, speak well of. Again, v. 19 "dearly beloved avenge not yourselves", the thought is to stand back and allow God to operate, give him room, for "vengeance is mine; I will repay saith the Lord". There is nothing of vengeance in this day, but then, as seen in the many imprecatory Psalms, the persecuted will cry for vengeance and not turn the other cheek. A Holy God will not allow ungodly men to go unpunished, and true to his nature, he will take up the cause of the persecuted; but the time is not yet, the tribulation is not over, if they have been martyred others are yet to be murdered, so they are given a covering.

Raiment and Rest for the Godly

The white robe, the garment of acceptance and of personal purity is draped upon them, and they are called to "rest" yet a little season. It is the call of the Saviour to the heavy laden (Matt. 11:28), it is also the word spoken to the disciples after what should have been a night of watching, but that is past now, and for them they can sleep on and take their rest (Matt. 26:45), for him the work of redemption lies ahead. It is used for the disciples after the beheading of John, in the distress over the shedding of innocent blood; the Lord says, "come ye apart and rest awhile" (Mark 6:31). The Lord ever gives rest to his troubled saints; the word has also the thought of being refreshed after your trouble. Others are to follow their path as fellow servants and brethren, not until all responsibility to God is over (servants), and opportunity for relationship (brethren), has gone, will God act.

Chaos in the Cosmos - Sixth Seal (vv. 12-16)

And I beheld when he had opened the sixth seal, and, lo, there was a great earthquake; and the sun became black as sackcloth of hair, and the moon became as blood; And the stars of heaven fell unto the earth, even as a fig tree casteth her untimely figs, when she is shaken of a mighty wind. And the heaven departed as a scroll when it is rolled together; and every mountain and island were moved out of their places. And the kings of the earth, and the great men, and the rich men, and the chief captains, and the mighty men, and every bondman, and every free man, hid themselves in the dens and in the rocks of the mountains; And said to the mountains and rocks, Fall on us, and hide us from the face of him that sitteth on the throne, and from the wrath of the Lamb: (Revelation 6:12-16)

In these seals we have seen the things that will characterise the tribulation, the victory of the Man of Sin, anarchy amongst men, the quantity of food diminishing, the destiny of the wicked, as they are brought to death and hell and the testimony of martyred saints. Now the calamity that will be seen at the return of the Lord to the earth. Many of the older writers who unlocked the door to understanding the book, not only here, but elsewhere in the book where such events are recorded, could not conceive that such events could be literal and they tend to spiritualise them, making them the systems of men that fall. We have no difficulty in our day to accept a literal interpretation, and as we were taught; if you can take scriptures literally, do so.

Tempest in the Universe

The events before us are set forth in many parts of scripture as they give the events that will bring to an end the tribulation period. For instance, Isaiah 13:10, Joel 2:10, 30-31, Matt. 24:29, Mark 13:24-25. Some would make Luke 21 a prophesy for Jerusalem's destruction in AD 70 but this is too restrictive for me, vv. 24-27 link it with this seal. Heb. 12:26-27 tells us "yet once more I will shake not the earth only, but also heaven". Remember the events of the flood, what a catastrophic outpouring as the firmament of heaven was broken to let in the flood waters it held, (Gen. 1:7). Was the shaking the tilting of the earth to create the poles that did not seem to exist before the flood, for only afterwards do we read of the four seasons (Gen. 8:22)? Perhaps this second shaking may restore the world to something like it was before the flood, enabling the ploughman to overtake the reaper (Amos 9:13) and bring in the glorious conditions of Isaiah 35. That God has used the cosmos before to execute judgement can be seen at Sodom, Jericho and with Korah's sons in Num. 16. Can any forget the earthquake at the time of the Lord's crucifixion, even to open graves that allowed believers to rise after his resurrection? He must be the first to rise, nor is an earthquake needed to open his tomb! Not only do we have a Tempest in the Universe in vv. 12-14, but also in vv. 15-17 we have Terror in the Unconverted.

Terror in the Unconverted

Here seven distinctions amongst men are seen, the coming of the Lord is a great leveller. From the sovereign to the slave, all will seek a hiding place from the wind, and a covert from the tempest. They caused saints to seek refuge in dens (Heb. 11:38), now there is no refuge, all hope has gone. The wrath of the Lamb has come, and "who shall be able to stand?" The answer to this last question is the subject of Ch 7. The parenthesis between the sixth and seventh seal tells of those who will be able to stand when the wrath of the Lamb is unleashed.

The Lamb is ever prominent; he is seen throughout the book.

Ch 5:9	The Worth of the Lamb
Ch 6:16-17	The Wrath of the Lamb
Ch 7:14	The Work of the Lamb
Ch 19	The Wedding of the Lamb
Ch 21:2	The Wife of the Lamb
Ch 21:27	The Writing of the Lamb - the Lamb's Book of Life.

Chapter 7

Tribulation Saints

Introduction

Two great events are brought before us in this parenthetic chapter, vv. 1-8, events seen before the tribulation begins, and vv. 9-17, which is a wondrous scene of the redeemed before the throne when the tribulation has ended. In vv. 1-8 we have the sealing of the Jews before the tribulation begins, and in vv. 9-17 the salvation of Gentiles seen after the tribulation is over. These are they who fulfil the question asked in Ch 6:17 "who shall be able to stand?" The order in which they are seen is divine, "to the Jew first" (Rom. 1:16). That God is going to reserve a people for himself even in the darkest hour of this world's history is evident from this chapter. All hope is not gone. Even in the hour of his wrath he remembers mercy. As in this day of the non-intervention of God in human affairs, it is plainly seen that there are periods when God acts in judgement, also in the day of his wrath, God will still act in grace and save many. Some would teach that there is no salvation after the rapture; they fly in the face of this chapter. Others tell us it is limited to a certain class, misconstruing many verses that have nothing to do with the rapture. John Heading has a timely statement as he opens Ch 7 of his exposition, "This chapter forms what may be termed a parenthesis, in order to show that God has his people on earth at this time. It is necessary to have a right perspective on this point, since it is often claimed that the gospel opportunity ends when the Lord comes for his church. Scripture does not teach this; Christ is presented both before and after his coming - the difference being that those saved during this period do not enter the church". It is evident from this chapter that we are not in this present church age where there is no Jew or Gentile (Gal. 3:28). Here God reverts to his national dealings with men. This we shall look at in more detail as we come to verses 9-17.

The Sealing of the Jews (vv. 1-7)

And after these things I saw four angels standing on the four corners of the earth, holding the four winds of the earth, that the wind should not blow on the earth, nor on the sea, nor on any tree. And I saw another angel ascending from the east, having the seal of the living God: and he cried with a loud voice to the four angels, to whom it was given to hurt the earth and the sea, Saying, Hurt not the earth, neither the sea, nor the trees, till we have sealed the servants of our God in their foreheads. And I heard the number of them which were sealed: and there were sealed an hundred and forty and four thousand of all the tribes of the children of Israel. Of the tribe of Juda were sealed twelve thousand. Of the tribe of Reuben were sealed twelve thousand. Of the tribe of Gad were sealed twelve thousand. Of the tribe of Aser were sealed twelve thousand. Of the tribe of Nepthalim were sealed twelve thousand. Of the tribe of Manasses were sealed twelve thousand. Of the tribe of Simeon were sealed twelve thousand. Of the tribe of Levi were sealed twelve thousand. Of the tribe of Issachar were sealed twelve thousand.

Of the tribe of Zabulon were sealed twelve thousand. Of the tribe of Joseph were sealed twelve thousand. Of the tribe of Benjamin were sealed twelve thousand. (Revelation 7:1-8)

The Distinction of the Judgements

In vv. 1-3 it is evident that it is the world that is before us. The four angels are standing on the four corners of the earth; north, south, east and west. Nowhere will escape the fury of God when he takes up his dealings with the earth again. We see that it is the four winds that are to blow, four, the universal number, is prominent. The time the Lord Jesus said would come in Ch 3:10, "the hour of temptation, which shall come upon all the world, to try them that dwell upon the earth" has arrived. Perhaps these are the same winds that, "strove upon the great sea" in Daniel 7:2, the winds that brought the four great beasts up from the sea that will have such a prominent part to play during tribulation times.

Delay in the Judgement

In this opening verse, the judgements are restrained, until vv. 2-3, where a people are reserved, and in vv. 4-8 their names are recorded. That the tribulation cannot begin immediately the rapture occurs is clearly taught from 2 Thess. 2:6-7 and Daniel 9:27. The Man of Sin cannot rise to dominate the scene whilst the church is presently in this world. Our presence, and that of the Holy Spirit in us, keeps in check the appearance of the Man of Sin. He cannot come whilst we are here. When he does rise, Dan. 9 teaches he makes a covenant with the children of Israel (a peace treaty). It is when he confirms the covenant, not breaks it, as many say, that tribulation days begin. The seven-year period of tribulation begins, neither with his rise, nor the making of the covenant but when he moves into Israel to give them help, and keep the covenant promise that he has made. Perhaps it is to this period of time, that this verse and these events are pointing. For it must be after the rapture, but before the tribulation begins that the elect remnant are sealed.

The Dispersion of Jews (Global)

The fact that all judgements world wide are held in check would indicate that the 144,000 who are sealed are found scattered throughout the world, and do not consist only of those who have returned to their homeland, Israel.

The Declaration of the Angel

There is a strong influence of angelic ministry in the book of Revelation. Those who are seen primarily as observers in this day of Grace (1 Pet. 1:12), stretching forth their necks as the gospel is preached (1 Cor. 11:10), gazing on divine order established at creation, restored in the local church. It is no light thing for women to have a head covering, and to discard it brings out another demonstration of Eve's failure. Again in Eph. 3:10 they see the manifold wisdom of God in the unity of the church which is his body, but the re-emergence of angelic activity is prominent once the church is raptured, and

God takes up His dealings with the earth again. Angels had a prominent sphere of ministry in the Old Testament, and for the last period of this world's history, God will again resort to using them as vessels of service for him.

This angel ascends from the East. The East is the place of idolatry and rejection of the revealed will of God. Nimrod moved eastward, (Gen. 11:2) (margin) to build a city and a tower that was to introduce Babylonish idolatry into the world. In Ezek. 8:16 men have their backs to the temple of the Lord, and their faces toward the east, Ezekiel gives a graphic display of Israel's failure in this chapter. As the nation has been scattered because of its failure, so rising from the east, with the seal of God in his hand is the angel who is going to identify those who are to be preserved during tribulation days as belonging to God. They are sealed in their foreheads; this speaks of public and prominent acceptance by God. There will be no secret disciples during tribulation days.

Defining the Sealed

First, the number of those sealed come before John, 144,000 Jews, whether this number is literal or symbolic is of no importance, God is able to seal such, we shall see that it is 12,000 from each tribe. Twelve is the number of governmental perfection. The sun rules the day and the moon the night and there are 12 signs of the Zodiac to govern the year. The 12 tribes were to maintain divine order in Israel. There were 13 Judges in Israel, but one, Abimelech, was a usurper, leaving 12 recognised by God to judge Israel. The 12 apostles will be linked with Christ in governmental authority in the coming millennial kingdom; the Lord Jesus said unto them that they "shall sit upon twelve thrones, judging the twelve tribes of Israel" (Matt. 19:28). The gospel of Luke takes the position they will have in the coming kingdom a little further, speaking both of the fellowship that they will enjoy, and also the favour that will be bestowed upon them, "that ye may eat and drink at my table in my kingdom, and sit on thrones judging the twelve tribes of Israel" (v. 30). The implications of this have been lost on many brethren who would deny a return to earth with the Lord Jesus, and would raise an eyebrow at the thought suggested that there will be somewhat of a normal life during this period, as eating and drinking. Yet are the words of the Lord Jesus not to be taken literally, and do not these verses give us an insight into the character of the millennial kingdom? The verses are also an encouragement, when we look at the background, and time, in which they were said. The disciples were to face the most awful events that they would know, and in the following hours would find much to discourage them, as they witnessed the crucifixion and death of the Lord Jesus.

The Holy Jerusalem of Ch 21 is the Bride of Christ in governmental authority during the millennium, and on into the eternal state. It is significant that the number 12 marks it. If there are 144,000 Jews sealed in this chapter, in the city we have the wall of the city that is 144 cubits, 12 x 12, there are 12 gates, and 12 angels are standing at those gates, the names of the 12 tribes are seen there, and the city has 12 foundations and 12 pearls for the gates. The number is not without significance; it is the number of governmental authority.

We not only have them NUMBERED, but also NAMED. There can be no mistaking who they are, though some will pervert scripture to make it fit their neat little doctrines, as the Jehovah Witnesses who make these a select number who are saved during this present time, and are the only people who will be in heaven, even though nothing of the place that they will occupy is even hinted at in these verses. Yet no stretching of the imagination can make these other than what they are, 12,000 Jews from each tribe of Israel mentioned. Let God be true, and every Russellite a liar!

They are placed according to their birth. Kelly shows how they are linked together by their mothers. Leah gives us Judah and Reuben, her handmaid Zilpah gives us Gad and Asher. Bilhah yields Naphtali and instead of her other son Dan, Manasseh is substituted (Joseph's firstborn). Then four sons of Leah, Simeon, Levi, Issachar and Zebulon, and finally the sons of Rachel, Joseph and Benjamin make up the twelve. But not only is their BIRTH set before us, but also their BLESSING. Firstly Judah is before Reuben, though Reuben is the firstborn. He taketh away the first that he may establish the second. It is the Royal Line from whence comes the King of Kings that takes first place. Sin cost Reuben much; even we today must beware of failing God, for sin is not without its consequences. It must be noticed that there is no room for Dan, and Ephraim is not in this list. Dan is the first tribe to go a whoring, (Judges 18) as they take Micah's image and his man-made priest. He is ever given to idolatry. Hosea unfolds Ephraim's follies, and declares the treacherous nature that marked this tribe, nature that causes God to state that it would be desolate in the day of rebuke (Hos. 5:9). This is the day of rebuke, and Ephraim will be bereft of 12000 who will know preservation in the midst of the tribulation.

That both these tribes will enter the kingdom, Ezek. 48 makes clear. Dan is actually placed first in the division of the land, (v. 1) "A portion for Dan". Oh the grace of God that will bring him in, and Ephraim who is recorded in v. 5 as having a place in the kingdom. What the sealing unveils is that there are those who will know no harm and cannot enter into death during the tribulation, they seem to me to be the elect of Matt. 24:22, who will be preserved through the tribulation. Are they the woman of Ch 12:13-17? She cannot be harmed either, in spite of all Satan's persecutions. Dan and Ephraim will know no such protection, their sin has left them exposed to the sorrows and tribulation that will come upon the nation, and neither of their tribes will be sealed. Some would find a difficulty of 12,000 from each tribe being sealed, with the Jews presently not knowing fully all their tribes, but God knows, and he will secure these for himself. If they are sealed before the tribulation begins, it is good to see them on Mount Sion in kingdom glory following the Lamb withersoever he goeth in Ch 14. Scott strangely makes those of Ch 14 a different company, stating they are from Judah. When I first read it as a young believer years ago, I searched to see if this could be substantiated, I am still searching! Perhaps he follows a hint from Kelly to the same effect in Ch 7, but there seems neither scripture nor reason to distinguish them, and make them separate companies.

It must be pointed out that nothing is said of these being responsible to carry the gospel to the world after their sealing. Many make these the preachers through whom the Gentile multitude of vv. 9-17 are saved. To make them the preachers is mere presumption; there is nothing in the text to support the theory. I notice that they are sealed of God, and it is the father's name that is written upon their foreheads (14:1). Their links to Christ are not seen until walking with him in Sion in Ch 14. Here it is their preservation that is in view, salvation must be linked with it, though that is not the great thought as it is with the Gentile multitude in vv. 9-17. Israel's salvation appears to be at the end of the tribulation, at the return of the Lord Jesus. Then Isaiah 53 will be fulfilled, as they see the one whom they pierced, and cry, "he was wounded for our transgressions, he was bruised for our iniquities, the chastisement of our peace was upon him, and with his stripes we are healed". This is confirmed in Zech. 12:10, when God, "will pour upon the house of David, and upon the inhabitants of Jerusalem, the spirit of grace and supplication; And they shall look upon Me whom they have pierced, and they shall mourn for Him, as one mourneth for his only son". Then shall Israel understand that the man they slew was none less than Jehovah himself. It is at that time that "the blindness in part which is happened to Israel", will be dealt with, and all Israel shall be saved; as it is written, "there shall come out of Sion the Deliverer, and shall turn away ungodliness from Jacob", (Rom. 11:25-26). It is on the appearance of Christ that salvation will be known by the nation, and it is at that time "he shall send his angels with a great sound of a trumpet, and they shall gather his elect from the four winds, from one end of heaven to the other" (Matt. 24:31). This seems to correspond with the sealed ones out of Israel.

The Salvation of Gentiles (vv. 9-17)

After this I beheld, and, lo, a great multitude, which no man could number, of all nations, and kindreds, and people, and tongues, stood before the throne, and before the Lamb, clothed with white robes, and palms in their hands; And cried with a loud voice, saying, Salvation to our God which sitteth upon the throne, and unto the Lamb. And all the angels stood round about the throne, and about the elders and the four beasts, and fell before the throne on their faces, and worshipped God, Saying, Amen: Blessing, and glory, and wisdom, and thanksgiving, and honour, and power, and might, be unto our God for ever and ever. Amen. And one of the elders answered, saying unto me, What are these which are arrayed in white robes? And whence came they? And I said unto him, Sir, thou knowest. And he said to me, these are they which came out of great tribulation, and have washed their robes, and made them white in the blood of the Lamb. Therefore are they before the throne of God, and serve him day and night in his temple: and he that sitteth on the throne shall dwell among them. They shall hunger no more, neither thirst any more; neither shall the sun light on them, nor any heat. For the Lamb which is in the midst of the throne shall feed them, and shall lead them unto living fountains of waters: and God shall wipe away all tears from their eyes. (Revelation 7:9-17)

Another vision reveals to John another company, not now Jews but Gentiles. Unlike the former company, these are not preserved from harm during the tribulation, v. 15 shows their suffering, but they are saved during the tribulation. A number of things are brought before us.

The People

They are vast and varied; it is "a great multitude that no man could number". They also come out of "all nations, and kindreds, and people and tongues". It is evident that millions are going to be saved during tribulation days. This is not surprising for, "this Gospel of the Kingdom shall be preached in all the world for a witness unto all nations; and then shall the end come" (Matt 24:14). We are not told who will declare the gospel after the Church's rapture, but that it will be preached faithfully there is no doubt. Matthew 24 itself shows that there will be those who will not bow to the Man of Sin during tribulation days. Some are warned of affliction and hatred that will be shown by a hostile world (v. 9). The warnings of vv. 15-26 are to a faithful remnant that will see the abomination of desolation stand in the Holy Place, (v. 15). These must be of the number who are saved after the Church's rapture, though the context of Matthew 24 is Jerusalem, making these Jews, and we know the multitude of this chapter are from every nation. Nevertheless there are those who can be exercised by God to carry the Gospel world wide, whoever they may be. Let me say again that nothing whatsoever is said about the 144,000 sealed Jews being the bearers of this glad news.

The word of God is very plain as to the source from which this multitude come, for they are said to be from "all nations", there is no nation, no tribe and no tongue that will not be reached. Nations that have closed their doors to the gospel in this era will not be able to stop the mighty surge of faith that will sweep over the nations. Also in lands where there is an open door for the word of God, a response will then be made, as many will turn to the Lord for salvation. Perhaps the great gospel activity of the present day will have effect upon the people in tribulation days. We know that millions of Gospel texts such as John 3:16 lie in homes around the world. The same could be said of gospel tracts that have been distributed, though the main source of blessing will be, "the gospel of the Kingdom", which is said to be heralded *(keerusso)* in the entire world. God's method of saving souls is said to be "by the foolishness of preaching" (1 Cor. 1:21), but who knows what God will use in relation to that gospel to stir this vast multitude to faith in our Lord Jesus Christ, but that they will be moved is without question.

There are some who will advocate that there is no salvation after the rapture. Such people use verses that have no bearing upon the coming of the Lord to the air to remove the saints of this present day from the tribulation. They use verses that have to do with his manifestation in glory, and his return to the earth. Some believers would use Luke 13:24-30 to cut off hope for those who will be left behind at the rapture. The context makes it clear that these verses are related to the manifestation and the coming Kingdom, (vv. 28-29). Again Matthew 24 and 25 are taken out of their context in relation to Israel and applied to this present day, giving the impression that, at the rapture, those who are not "taken" (Ch 24:41), will be left for the judgement of the tribulation. Again these verses relate to the manifestation of the Lord in glory on his return to the earth, they refer to those in Israel at his return to earth, for the chapter relates to the people of Israel, and particularly to those in Jerusalem. The events spoken of in these verses do not take place at the rapture and can in no way be linked to it. They speak of those who will be taken to, and along side the Lord, for *(paralambano)* taken, has the thought of, to take near or to oneself. Whilst the thought behind the word *(aphieemi)* left, would indicate that there will be those who will be left in the city for the judgement of God to fall upon them. Perhaps we might find the thought of being taken to Christ for protection in Zech. 14:4-5, when the Lord's feet touch the Mount of Olives and it cleaves towards the east and the west, providing a passage for the remnant to "flee to the valley of the mountains as ye fled from before the earthquake in the days of Uzziah King of Judah: and the Lord God shall come, and all the saints with thee".

The following are a few further thoughts on the continuation of the gospel in the tribulation.

Hurnard says, "Many professing Christians in the federated churches and in every land, suddenly confronted with the choice of open worship of the "The Beast" or loyalty to Christ will take the advice of 3:18, "Buy gold tried in the fire" (These are recent observations).

Again, some would take the parable of the wise and foolish virgins to be the events that take place at the rapture, when the saved are secured and the rest are shut out. The parable of Matthew 25 must refer to the Lord's coming to earth with his Bride to the great marriage feast, to which only the true remnant will come. This is the second of three parables, which mark Israel's failure as they have lost the hope of the Lord's coming to them. In chapter 24:48-51 some are given to sin, whilst in chapter 25:1-30 it is sleep and slothfulness that are emphasised; all would declare that whether corrupt, clean or careless they will have no place in the kingdom.

Another verse that has been used to sad effect saying that there is no salvation after the rapture is 2 Thess. 1:8, drawing from the fact that judgement is going to be meted out to those "that obey not the gospel of our Lord Jesus Christ." By this they assume that there is a difference in the gospel preached, linking this with "the gospel of the grace of God" (Acts 20:24) and declare that it is a different gospel from the gospel of the kingdom of Matt 24:14. The gospel is an everlasting gospel, it was preached before to Abraham (Gal 3:8) and will continue to be preached after we have been removed from the world. Men who have not responded to the call of the gospel, at the return of the Lord Jesus in flaming fire, will be punished with everlasting destruction. The emphasis on the gospel will differ in every age. Presently it is grace that is stressed. In tribulation days the main burden of the message will be the kingdom. (Though I notice the gospel of the kingdom seems to be emphasised by all the apostles). The Lord Jesus is ever the subject of the gospel, and its source will always be God, "the gospel of God" (Rom 1:1).

These multitudes are not saved to be members of his body the Church, but will enter the kingdom as servants.

Some would ask how are men saved if the Holy Spirit is removed from the world at the rapture (2 Thess. 2:7)? It must be remembered that though the Holy Spirit will not be here in the unique way that he is now, in the believer, he will act upon men as he did in the Old Testament economy.

The salvation of this multitude would seem to take place during the first half of the tribulation week, and in the period of time before the week commences after the rapture. For at the entrance of the Man of Sin into the temple to set himself up as God in the middle of the week, then God sends a strong delusion that they should believe "the lie". The lie being the claims propounded by the Man of Sin that he is God, and that he alone must be worshiped. If after all the events that have taken place up to this point have not had the desired effect of turning the wicked from his way, God will himself cause men to accept the deception of the Man of Sin, for their ultimate destruction. It would seem from this verse that there is no salvation after the Man of Sin moves into the temple.

Another point that must be made is that this in no way gives any man a second chance. The call of God is always "today" and no man can leave the salvation of his soul to the chance that there will always be another opportunity for him to get right with God, for God never gives more than the moment that we live in. No man knoweth what a day may bring forth, and we cannot boast of tomorrow. People cannot hope that they will have further time to accept God's salvation if they reject the offer that the Lord graciously gives to them, for who knows the destiny that is before us. Every sinner must take the Saviour as they have the present opportunity to do so.

Their Position

Having dealt at some length with the people saved, we now see their position. It is to stand before the throne, and before the Lamb. Is not this where Elijah the prophet was in 1 Kings 17:1, standing before the Lord? It is where Priests are in their ministry (Heb 10:11), where the King stood in Ch 5:6, it is the place of being "ready to serve", v. 15 tells us "they serve him day and night in his temple". Some expositors assume that this is a heavenly scene because these redeemed ones are before the throne, but as we have seen there is a throne on earth during the millennium where the Lord Jesus sits and reigns.

Their Purity

They are clothed in white robes, such as the young men wore in the sepulchre (Mk 16:5) (angels seen as young men, they do not age!), the same as given to the prodigal on his return (Luke 15:22), these robes speak of purity and acceptance.

Their Pleasures and Prospect

They have "palms in their hands", the conflict of tribulation is over, the palm would speak of their joyous delight, as that of the crowd who took them up to receive Christ as he came into Jerusalem, (John 12:13). The sufferings would then be compared with Paul's in 2 Cor. 4:17, "Our light affliction which is but for a moment worketh for us a far more exceeding and eternal weight of glory". Their joy will be fulfilled in the millennial kingdom, for palms are also linked with that occasion.

Lev 23:40 has that great day in mind, as the children of Israel enjoy the Feast of Tabernacles. The true king will be in their midst, and again they will wave the palm bough before him.

Their Praise

As they rejoice, they cannot be silent, giving praise to those who have made it possible, they may well join with the psalmist (30:1) "I will extol thee, O Lord, for thou hast lifted me up, and hast not made my foes to rejoice over me". The praise is to the source, God, and the supplier of their salvation, the Lamb. As praise begets praise, so the angelic host standing around the throne fall upon their faces to add to the praise. If the multitude of the redeemed value the salvation they have received, the angels recognise the honour that must be given for this salvation. It begins Amen, it ends Amen, the praise is fully endorsed in this way. The praise will never cease, as redemption is eternal, so the praise must also be eternal, the first amen is in agreement with the multitude, the second is their own assessment of it.

And one of the elders answered, saying unto me, What are these which are arrayed in white robes? And whence came they? (Revelation 7:13)

The Problem

At this point it is evident that John is not aware who these are, it is one of the 24 elders, who seem to be used to reveal the truth to John as Ch 5:5, and also here. If this company is the church as some suggest, and the elders are the church glorified as others suggest, we have utter confusion. The church asking about the church! As neither are the church, as we shall see, this creates no problem as to who it is that asks John "who are they, and from whence came they".

And I said unto him, Sir, thou knowest. And he said to me, These are they which came out of great tribulation, and have washed their robes, and made them white in the blood of the Lamb. (Revelation 7:14)

The Probing

John, in his ignorance, desires to be enlightened, saying, "Sir", a respectful address to one superior in age or station (Robertson Nicol). The word is used of all the persons of the Godhead, but also of masters in relation to servants

(Eph 6:5-9, Col 4:1). Sarah used it of Abraham, when she, "obeyed Abraham, calling him Lord" (1 Pet 3:6). Now of an angel who is "greater in power and might" (2 Pet 2:11), the answer lies with him, and he now makes his proclamation.

Therefore are they before the throne of God, and serve him day and night in his temple: and he that sitteth on the throne shall dwell among them. They shall hunger no more, neither thirst any more; neither shall the sun light on them, nor any heat. For the Lamb which is in the midst of the throne shall feed them, and shall lead them unto living fountains of waters: and God shall wipe away all tears from their eyes. (Revelation 7:15-17)

The Proclamation

The mystery is now revealed, as John discovers who they are, where they came from, and where they stand.

Secured – They "came out of great tribulation", Alford "out of the tribulation, the great one". This leaves no doubt as to their origins. Not being saved at the time of the rapture, and knowing nothing of the security of heaven. As in all God's dealings, he always reserves some for himself. The Man of Sin is not going to subjugate all, but from the deep sufferings of those awful days of tribulation, these have been secured for God.

Their Salvation - They "have washed their robes", what an action in such a day! Many, for reasons of little consequence, refuse to bow to Christ now. In that day, with a world in violent opposition, it will be no light thing to believe in the Lord Jesus Christ. The expression would tell of the faith they exercised to salvation, and its blessed effects, "and made them white". Not only saved but left suitable for the presence of God before whom they stand.

The Source - How can any be saved? Salvation is no different in tribulation days than in ours. The only hope for the sinner is still the Lord Jesus and his precious work on Calvary. The same gospel of the kingdom will be preached. Some try to make distinctions in the gospel that is calling out the church, and that which saves in tribulation days. I would remind my brethren that the term "The gospel of the grace of God" (Acts 20:24) occurs but once, the very next verse equates it with the kingdom of God, not the church. May I suggest that the gospel of the grace of God simply tells of the kindness of God to us? The gospel of the kingdom speaks of the destiny we are assured of. Again if there is a difference, why do we take the beautiful verses in the gospels and preach them to sinners today, if we do not preach the gospel of the kingdom? For all the lovely gospel texts and passages are associated with that message proclaimed before the cross. Whereas brethren tell us, the gospel of the grace of God is now proclaimed since Israel has been set aside, and God is calling out the church God is indeed calling out the church, but, as McClain says, "to be the chief rulers of the kingdom" These also avail themselves of John 3:16, these are born again (John 3:3), these find rest for their souls (Matt 11:28), these are they who strive to enter in, and do so before the door is shut

(Luke 13:24-25), they will be the sheep of Matt 25:33-40, who, from the judgement of the living nations at Jerusalem, will go into the kingdom with eternal life (v. 34).

Their Service - This must be a millennial scene, the throne is that of Zech 6:13, Heb 1:8. It is the throne of the Lord Jesus as he takes his place in this world as God. This cannot be heaven, for nowhere in scripture do we find any who come out of great tribulation, in any other place but in the kingdom. These do not reign like the church (5:10), they serve; it is the word for spiritual priestly service, it will be an unbroken service, day and night. As there was the morning and evening sacrifice, the lighting of lamps, evening and morning, so these will be occupied with divine service. I notice Paul's prayers were night and day, his service was undiminished also.

Their Satisfaction - How different from all they have endured through the tribulation, as they dwelt in the midst of the era of the Man of Sin, they would have known great suffering, and often wondered "where will it all end". Here is the end, and as the hymn writer says, "It will be worth it all when we see him". There is a five fold promise made to them concerning, (i) His Dwelling - as he that sitteth upon the throne shall dwell among them, (ii) Their Diet - never to hunger or thirst again, no praying "give us this day our daily bread". They will have needed that when, without the mark of the beast, they could not buy or sell (13:17). (iii) No Danger - every day would have exposed them to danger, now all is over, the heat of persecution is done. (iv) Their Delight - both fed and led by the Lamb. Usually it is the lamb that needs the shepherd care, but he who bought them will protect them. (v) Their Dried Eyes - no more tears. What a glorious day they will enter! Grief will mark them constantly as they suffer in the tribulation, but what a blessed assurance they will have even as they pass through those days, for they will have this blessed book in their hands, and will understand it far better than we do now.

Footnote:

Newell objects to this being a millennial scene, but puts it all in heaven, simply because the 1000 year reign comes to an end, and he wants to know what you will do with them afterwards. I see no problem, Ch 21 brings in the Eternal State, and it is evident that all the redeemed will be in that new state. They will enjoy eternal blessing at the end of their suffering. Here we are told how they will enjoy that blessing at the end of their suffering.

Chapter 8

The Trumpet judgements

Introduction

After the parenthesis of Ch 7, we now come to the opening of the seventh seal. We shall see that from it come the seven trumpet judgements. Again the Lord Jesus is in supreme command, he opens the seal, but once opened it is the ministry of the seven angels that is brought before us. In the seal judgements it was the four living creatures that were prominent, now it is angels. Their ministry as they sound the alarm is the seventh seal. Unlike the seven seals, none of which can take place without the direct hand of Christ, once these angels start their ministry they follow each other directly. There is an interjection after the fourth trumpet sounds; this divides the seven into a four, and a three. Four of the trumpet judgements are on the environment, and three upon the inhabitants of the earth. Again, as with the seals, there is a parenthesis between the sixth and seventh trumpets. This occurs from 10:1 to 11:14, after which the seventh trumpet sounds. If the seals give the general character that the tribulation takes, in the seven trumpets we see the events that will occur in a closer way. The trumpets enable us to understand some of the events depicted under the seals.

Service at the Altar (vv. 1-5)

And when he had opened the seventh seal, there was silence in heaven about the space of half an hour. And I saw the seven angels which stood before God; and to them were given seven trumpets. And another angel came and stood at the altar, having a golden censer; and there was given unto him much incense, that he should offer it with the prayers of all saints upon the golden altar which was before the throne. And the smoke of the incense, which came with the prayers of the saints, ascended up before God out of the angel's hand. And the angel took the censer, and filled it with fire of the altar, and cast it into the earth: and there were voices, and thunderings, and lightnings, and an earthquake. (Revelation 8:1-5)

In the opening verses, we are given an insight to angelic ministry, and also to the fact that any judgement from God is no light thing. It is "his strange work, his strange act" (Isaiah 28:21), for he is a God who is "rich in mercy", (Eph. 2:4). It is from the altar of incense that God is going to act against the world, he is now answering the cries of his people, that of 6:10, "How long O Lord dost thou not avenge our blood on them that dwell on the earth". The God of Rom. 12:19 is going to act for his own, the time for the vengeance of God to be executed against those who have opposed his people, is about to come, in all its fury.

The Pause (v. 1)

Once the Lamb opens the seventh seal, immediately there is silence in heaven. Prior to this, Hab. 2:20 speaks of, "the Lord is in his holy temple; let all the EARTH keep silence before him". Isaiah 41:1 calls for the ISLANDS to keep silence before him, Zech. 2:13, is a call to men, "Be silent O all FLESH before the Lord; for he is raised up out of his holy habitation". Now it is not the earth, islands or flesh, but silence in heaven, solemn indeed. What must be in store for the world when heaven is silent as it was against Christ during the hours of darkness on the cross! Think of the awesomeness of the occasion, what must be the judgement the world will know when heaven is silent for the space of half an hour!

The Preparation (v. 2)

Judgement is never haphazard with God, all is under divine control. Here are seven angels in the place of readiness to serve, "They stood before God", and it is a deliberate act that hands them the trumpets. God spake to Moses regarding the trumpets that were to be used in connection with the children of Israel when they journeyed through the wilderness, (Num. 10:1-10). There had to be two silver trumpets for Israel, two is always the number of testimony, and silver always a symbol of redemption. It was for an ordered camp, before they set forth from Sinai to go to the Promised Land, that God had them made. They were used in a threefold way; they regulated their walk, warfare and worship. Now God is going to use trumpets in relation to the world, the alarm is about to blow, God is going to war. I notice that in all the major dealings of God with men the trumpet is used, such as:

Ex. 19:13, 19; Heb.12:19	Giving of Law
Rev. 1:10	Christ and Assembly Testimony
Rev. 4:1	For Divine Revelation
1 Thess. 4:16	Church's Rapture
1 Cor. 15:52	Saints' Change
Rev. 8-9	World's Judgement
Matt. 24:31	Israel's Regathering
Rev. 11:15	Lord's Return to Earth

Many who teach that the church will go through the tribulation fail to distinguish the various trumpet dealings of God.

J Sidlow Baxter is typical of this school as he tabulates the events of Matt 24 and 1 Thess 4 in his book "Explore the Bible", page 291, in this way:

Matt. 24	1 Thess. 4
"They shall see the Son of Man coming"	"The Lord Himself shall descend from heaven"
"His Angels with a great voice"	"With voice of the Archangel"
"With a great trumpet"	"With the trumpet of God"
"They shall gather together his elect"	"Caught up together with them"
"In the clouds of heaven"	"In the clouds to meet the Lord"

To the casual reader they seem to offer conclusive proof that these statements speak of the same event, until a closer look at the verses manifests that the writer, to fit his own neat formula, and seeking to convince others that he has found the truth, distorts Matt 24.

First the Lord Jesus is seen as "Son of Man" in Matthew, this is his title to earth. Sidlow Baxter does not speak of those who will look upon the Son of Man, which is recorded in the same verse (v. 30) "Then shall all the tribes of the earth mourn and THEY shall see the Son of Man coming". 1Thess 4 knows nothing of the tribes mourning, though it is a source of comfort for troubled saints who have lost loved ones in death to know they are going to meet the Lord in the air, whereas those of Matt 24 are certainly not caught up to blessing, but caught out in their sin.

The comparison between the angels and the Archangel is invalid also; the one gathers an elect remnant on the earth, and the other summons believers to the heavens. In the first it is the angels that sound the trumpet, in the latter it is the Lord Jesus who speaks bearing the character of an Archangel voice, "In (*en*) the voice of the Archangel". There is no record of angels being seen in 1 Thess 4, it is "The Lord Himself", who gathers his own to meet him in the air. Again there is a vast difference between being "gathered together", and being "caught up". The former never leave the earth, but they are linked to Him to go into His Kingdom.

Also the "clouds of heaven" are associated with the Lord Jesus at his return in glory to the earth, he will come in like manner as he went away, when clouds received him out of their sight, (Acts 1:11). The clouds of Thessalonians are linked to the saints as they meet their Lord in the air. The two scenes differ greatly, and some would teach that "in the clouds" should read "in clouds", and refer this to the believers being caught up in the figure of clouds as they leave the earth from various parts of the globe.

The Presence of the Angel (v. 3a)

Another, *(allos)*, he is distinct from those in v. 2, but of the same kind, now came and stood before the altar. We are told it is the golden altar, the altar of incense. Well might Heb. 9:9 speak of the tabernacle in the wilderness as a "figure, a parable for the present time", and 9:23 tells us that it was "a pattern of things in the heavens". Was that tabernacle of old based on the true tabernacle, heaven? And did God actually show Moses the heavenly tabernacle when he showed him the tabernacle visually (Ex. 25:9)?

Whatever, the tabernacle is quite clearly seen in the Revelation. Kelly makes the first altar the brazen altar because it stands unqualified, but, as the subject is prayer not worship, I prefer to see it as the golden altar. Further it is incense he is given, not fire, the latter is from the brazen altar, but incense is for the golden altar. This incense was given to the prayers of saints, again Kelly shows the expression to be the same as in 11:3, when power was given to the two witnesses, and so the angelic ministry is going to empower the prayers of saints.

I had nearly forgotten that some make this angel Christ, as an angel priest. I had so disassociated myself from this strange theory, and wondered at man's thinking, that I had put it from my mind until refreshing my thoughts as I write the chapter. Some find Christ in many strange places in this book. Some men, to cover doctrines they have never understood, make pretentious claims. We have already seen in 5:8, that angels have a prominent ministry in the prayers of saints.

The Prayers of all Saints (v. 3b)

Is it not a blessed thing here to remember that prayers are never forgotten? It would seem that the prayer of Zacharias and Elisabeth had long since ceased, but their prayer was heard and answered (Luke 1:13). Do not give up on prayer; present delay only means God works in his own time to answer the prayers of his saints.

The Presentation of the Incense (v. 4)

The incense yields smoke, this seems to give the thought of power with God. Outside the book of the Revelation it is only used in Acts 2:19 of the future outpouring of the Spirit after tribulation days. Here we have Power in Prayer. In 9:1-3; 9:17-18; 14:11; 18:9, 18; 19:3 - it is Power in Punishment. Ch 15:8 again links it with power, the power of the Presence of God. Here the power of prayer is evident, we may cry to the throne now and wonder if God hears, but the day is coming when the prayers of all saints will bear fruit.

The Pouring of Fire (v. 5)

In Isaiah 6:6 the angel uses tongs when taking live coals from the altar. Let all see in this, that care must be taken when serving God. Some are very slipshod in divine things, as if anything will do for God. God's way of taking coals was by tongs; they were not just for human frailty, unless I would burn my hands. Angels' hands would not burn, but that gives them no licence to approach other than as God states. Here he takes the censer, and fills it with fire off the altar, and casts it into the earth. Fire - the great consumer, tells of the day when men will burn as an oven (Mal. 4:1). The storm is breaking, as here, thunders are sometimes heard before we see lightning. It causes us to realise what is coming, and then we look for the lightning. This storm rolls on, these are given wormwood. The source of the judgement is heaven, it comes from the great star, and because these have refused the light of God's salvation, it burns as a lamp. The star is called Wormwood, some manuscripts put it emphatically "The Wormwood". Wormwood is a bitter, intoxicating and poisonous herb, and when used freely it produces convulsions, paralysis and death (Seiss). When men die after drinking this, it will be an awful death. Jer. 9:13-15 speaks of a judgement of wormwood on those who forsake his laws, and obey not his voice, "but walk after the imagination of their own heart, and after Baalim, which their fathers taught them".

Darkness in the Heavens (v. 12)

If the first trumpet judgement affects the soil, and the second the sea, and the third smites the streams of water, the sounding of the fourth trumpet affects the solar system.

The event before us is the subject of many scriptures that deal with the last days. Its placing in Isaiah 13:10 and the verses being linked with the Day of the Lord (vv. 6-9) first caused me to see that a literal Babylon is going to be judged and not a spiritual Babylon. For Isaiah 13-14 is devoted to its final fall, and is set against the Day of the Lord, and not when it fell when Darius the Median took the kingdom. Its judgement will be as it was in Egypt when the darkness could be felt (Ex. 10:21-23)! Joel 2:1-2 speaks of the same Day of the Lord, and of Jerusalem's plight in that day, and in verse 10 we are told that "the sun and the moon shall be dark, and the stars shall withdraw their shining". This is recorded as being in the Lord's statements regarding conditions that shall prevail in tribulation times just prior to his return (Matt. 24:29, Mark 13:24, Luke 21:25), causing men's hearts to fail them because of fear. It is evident that this state occurs just before the Lord Jesus returns out of heaven. He knew the hours of darkness to provide our salvation; men refuse him, and now have a foretaste of the eternal habitation that awaits them, "the blackness of darkness for ever" (Jude 13).

In God's first dealings with creation, the first act of God was, "let there be light, and there was light" (Gen. 1:3). He removed the darkness, also in a soul's salvation (2 Cor. 4:6), God causes light to shine in the believer. It must be a sad reflection of the human heart, when one of God's last acts before the coming of Christ is to bring darkness upon those who have resisted his claims, and refused his salvation.

The Decree in the Heavens (v. 13)

At this point, John sees a flying eagle in the midst of heaven. Virtually all scholars tell us, though the Textus Teceptus (TR) has angel, that "eagle" is the correct translation. Ch 14:6 certainly has a flying angel, and much scholarship from USA is today casting doubt on the validity of certain texts which a little over a century ago were seen as "the best texts". Not being qualified to give an opinion on the subject, one feels it is better to be safe and at least honour that which has been instrumental in blessing men since it was brought into being in 1611. I suppose that I was reared reading and studying the authorised version of the bible, and I have only found it to be a blessing in all the years of reading it.

The point is not great, one thing is certain, whether it is an eagle, a bird of prey, rapid in its swoop, denoting the rapidity of the judgement, or an angel bringing a message direct from God, the outcome is the same. Heaven's decree gives character to the last three trumpets as woe trumpets. The former trumpets touched places, these last three, people, "the inhabiters of the earth". They are going to bring upon men Distress, Death, and the Descent of Christ. As the sixth seal brings in the Lord Jesus, so the last trumpet tells of the return of Jesus Christ 11:15-18.

Chapter 9

Introduction

This chapter brings before us the first and second "woe" trumpets. We have to wait until Ch 11:15 before the third "woe" is brought before us. As there is an interval between the sixth and seventh seal, so there is an interval between the sixth and seventh trumpet. Scripture always has a beautiful order.

The two judgements before us have marked differences. In both a voice is heard. With the fifth trumpet it is a voice in the "Midst of Heaven", with the sixth trumpet it is "a voice from the four horns of the golden altar which is before God". Then again, in the fifth trumpet "A star fallen from heaven" is the prime mover of events, whereas in the sixth trumpet it is "four angels". If in the fifth trumpet, the star is "fallen from heaven", in the sixth the angels are bound in the "river Euphrates". It is evident in the fifth trumpet that the authority given to these locust demons is only to "hurt" the people, whereas that given to the angels is to "slay the third part of men". The period of time in which they work also differs. In the former trumpet, the time is limited to "five months" whereas in the latter trumpet the time is lengthened to "an hour, and a day, and a month, and a year". Both together cover a period of 18 months of intense suffering for mankind. How comforting to know that in such a period of the world's history, the saints of this present church age will be in the safety of heaven.

Distress for Men (vv. 1- 12)

And the fifth angel sounded, and I saw a star fall from heaven unto the earth: and to him was given the key of the bottomless pit. And he opened the bottomless pit; and there arose a smoke out of the pit, as the smoke of a great furnace; and the sun and the air were darkened by reason of the smoke of the pit. And there came out of the smoke locusts upon the earth: and unto them was given power, as the scorpions of the earth have power. And it was commanded them that they should not hurt the grass of the earth, neither any green thing, neither any tree; but only those men which have not the seal of God in their foreheads. And to them it was given that they should not kill them, but that they should be tormented five months: and their torment was as the torment of a scorpion, when he striketh a man. And in those days shall men seek death, and shall not find it; and shall desire to die, and death shall flee from them. And the shapes of the locusts were like unto horses prepared unto battle; and on their heads were as it were crowns like gold, and their faces were as the faces of men. And they had hair as the hair of women, and their teeth were as the teeth of lions. And they had breastplates, as it were breastplates of iron; and the sound of their wings was as the sound of chariots of many horses running to battle. And they had tails like unto scorpions, and there were stings in their tails: and their power was to hurt men five months. And they had a king over them, which is the angel of the bottomless pit, whose name in the

Hebrew tongue is Abaddon, but in the Greek tongue hath his name Apollyon. One woe is past; and, behold, there come two woes more hereafter. (Revelation 9:1-12)

The Infamous Star (v. 1)

As the fifth angel sounds, John sees "a star fallen from heaven". The angel is acting for God, who is now intensifying his judgements so that they have direct bearing upon men. The fifth angel's origins are divine, and the star that is "fallen" has origins that are evidently demonic. That this "star" is a person is evident from the fact that "to him was given the key of the abyss". Stars as we have seen are set as guides, and false teachers are called "wandering stars" (Jude 13). Here we have a "fallen" creature, for the verb is in the perfect, telling of a completed action. This star is called "a king" in v. 11, and "the angel of the abyss". Some would make this Satan, said by the Lord Jesus to be seen "as lightning fall from heaven" (Luke 10:18), and who is also spoken of as "Beelzebub the prince of devils" (Matt. 12:24). Walvoord justly states that "the book of Revelation unmasks the true nature of Satan and evil", this will be seen as the key given to this star is used to unleash a host of demons upon the world. Notice, his power is a limited power, for the key is "given" to him, unlike the angel of Ch 20:1 who is said to be "having the key of the abyss", an angel who can bind Satan and imprison him in the place that Satan opens to unloose the demons that will afflict society must be one of great power.

Many have been given to speculation as to the origins of Demons. Some like Ottman (The Unfolding Drama of the Ages, pages 216 – 219) go into great detail to teach they belonged to a prior creation that existed between Genesis 1:1 and Genesis 1:2, which coming under the judgement of God then produced these beings. Whilst scripture remains silent about such a world, so should we. To say that God destroyed a creation of Genesis 1:1 because of Satan's fall, and then began to reconstruct it from v. 3 seems to run contrary to the plain teaching of the Word of God. We are not told how they came into being, that they exist is enough, where God is silent so will we be.

Seiss is worse, saying, "They are the souls of dead men, particularly the spirits of those who bore a bad character of life", (pages 212 – 213). There is nothing to justify either of their statements, and both writers are moving with mere speculation, for the word of God makes no reference to such teaching.

Infernal Origins (v. 2)

The abyss, for such is what the bottomless pit is, (there can be no such things as "a bottomless pit"), is quite evidently the abode of imprisoned demons. Demons in the lifetime of the Lord Jesus feared it, "and besought him that he would not command them to go out into the deep" (Luke 8:31), "the deep" is "the abyss". They recognised the Lord's right and power to despatch them there if he so desired. From these verses it is plain that, though imprisoned there, they can be released from it. Ch 20:1-3 teaches that it will be a prison for Satan during the thousand year reign of Christ, and Ch 20:7 shows how he will be let loose from it for a little season. It is one of four places the New Testament that would speak of as holding places God has for the disobedient creatures of the universe. Hades (Hell) is quite clearly a place for the souls of unsaved men only (Luke 16:19-31).

In 2 Pet. 2:4 another place is spoken of for fallen angels where they are said to be in *tartaros*. This is the only reference to it, and nothing more is known of it. Then there is that which the Lord Jesus spoke of in Matt.5:22-30, as Geenna fire. The Lord says of it, that it is not only for souls but also for bodies (Matt. 10:28), this would surely equate with Revelation 20:14-15, the lake of fire where all, Satan, demons, fallen angel, or man, are going to be in eternal torment for their rebellion against God.

As the abyss is opened, smoke is seen to rise like that from a great furnace. The only occurrence of smoke in the New Testament outside the book of Revelation is in Acts 2:19, which is a quotation from Joel 2, where it speaks of an invading army that will afflict Jerusalem in tribulation days, the smoke speaks of the rising judgement of God. Ottman thinks that the judgement recorded in Joel 2:1-11 is a further description of the scene before us here. With the smoke there is darkness as the sun is affected. Is God justly dealing with men because of that which has dominated them in their rejection of truth. Much is said of darkness in the New Testament of which the following verses are but a few, though they do portray the character that marks men:

Matt. 4:16	Sit in Darkness	Position
John 8:12, 1 Jn 2:1	Walk in Darkness	Purpose
Eph. 4:18	Understanding Darkened	Perception
John 3:19	Men Loved Darkness	Passion
Eph. 5:11	Unfruitful Works of Darkness	Production
Luke 22:53	Power of Darkness	Power
Matt. 8:12	Cast into Outer Darkness	Prospect

"Whatsoever a man soweth that shall he also reap" (Gal. 6:7). Is it any wonder that God now brings such judgement upon the godless?

The Innumerable Invaders (v. 3)

From the smoke emerge locusts, their sphere of operation is seen as these demonic creatures are let loose upon the earth. Locusts increase greatly in numbers, and migrate long distances in destructive swarms. Once developed, a locust plague is almost impossible to control. As such these locusts are a true figure of those that will carry the judgement of God against humanity. But more, they are "given power", here they receive delegated authority to fulfil God's will and the power is "as the power of a scorpion". These are venomous arachnids that carry their poison in the tail. When injected into men it is very painful, and can be fatal.

The Instructions Given (vv. 4-6)

Proverbs 30:27 tells us that "The locusts have no king, yet go they forth all of them by bands". These are said to have a king (v. 11), and they are given very definite instructions that they obey. They are evidently intelligent beings, able to distinguish between persons, for they can only afflict "those men who have not the seal of God in their foreheads". Unlike the natural locust, they must not touch the grass, but only the godless. The whole scene is against nature; here we find demonism at work.

Their Injurious Character (v. 5)

Their business is to inflict suffering not death, they are also given a season in which to do their evil, "five months". I take this to be a literal period of time in the midst of tribulation days. Finally, the severity of the suffering is seen, "Their torment was as the torment of a scorpion when he striketh a man". The word torment is the word that is used of the cry of the Legion of demons to the Lord Jesus in Mark 5:7, "that thou torment me not". They inflict what they do not desire. It is used of the sufferings of men in sickness, as the man "sick of the palsy and grievously tormented" (Matt. 8:6).

Babylon is going to know something of this when God judges her in 18:7. It is used of the torment that men will know eternally (14:10). It is also the portion of any who should "worship the beast and his image, and receive his mark in his forehead, or in his hand" (14:9). Also of those destined for the Lake of Fire after the final assize (20:10). Men speak of hell on earth, it would seem that this is a foretaste of what will be endured eternally.

Their Inescapable Fate (v. 6)

Four things are set forth to portray the hopelessness and helplessness of man as he tries to escape this judgement from God. Firstly his Diligent search, for such is the thought behind the phrase "Men shall seek death". Of 119 references in the New Testament, this is the only reference to "seek" in the book of Revelation. It is used of Herod seeking the young child (Matt. 2:13), to destroy him, of Judas seeking opportunity to betray him (Matt. 26:16), of men seeking first the kingdom (Matt. 6:33). Secondly his Discovery, he "shall not find it". The word is that of making a concrete discovery, as when Mary was found with child of the Holy Ghost (Matt. 1:18), and Pilate when he could find no fault in the Lord Jesus (Luke 23:14) and found no cause of death in him (Luke 23:22). Thirdly, their Desire, a word that denotes intense longing, like many who assume that death ends all suffering, they shall long to die, but the verse ends with their Disappointment, as death flees from them. Does this indicate that death is not natural during tribulation days but it comes as a direct judgement from God? Men cannot determine when they die; this is under divine control as are all things in what might seem to be the most chaotic period in human history.

Their Inflexibility (v. 7)

A description of these demon locusts is brought before us in these verses. They are inflexible "like unto horses prepared unto battle" (armoured and clad in mail). Job 39:19-25 gives graphic details of the horse with the battle before it. So also does Jer. 8:6, speaking of the obdurate heart of Israel that would not hearken to the voice of God and likening them to the horse as it rusheth into battle. They are not turned aside by anything; they have only one thing before them and do it. So these locust demons set themselves to do what is committed to them.

Their Influence

They wear crowns like gold upon their heads. There are three who have these in the book of Revelation, These Locusts, The Elders of 4:4, and one like the Son of Man (14:4), though the latter two have crowns of gold, not one "like gold". Nevertheless surely this would depict the authority given to them.

Their Intelligence

With faces as the faces of men, this would denote the ability to discern, they can receive instructions and carry them out. They have the ability to distinguish between those who have the seal of God in their foreheads and those without it, for it is only these that they can harm. They can also recognise time, for the judgement is for a specified time of five months. They also appreciate how far their responsibility goes as even these infernal beings fulfil God's will, for neither were they allowed to kill men. It might seem as if this was their desire if God did not preclude them from doing so.

Their Insidiousness (v. 8)

After telling us they have the face of a man, the hair is immediately seen, but it is that of a woman. For a man to have long hair is a sign that he is in rebellion against God, for God has put into the very nature of man that he should have short hair (1 Cor. 11:14). For man to move against the natural instinct given at birth by God speaks of casting off all restraint, so these are displayed as moving against their original purpose in creation. Their teeth, "as the teeth of lions" speak of the ferocious savagery that will mark them as they go about their satanic business.

They are Indestructible (v. 9)

Such is the thought behind the breastplate of iron. Breastplates are for defence, the believer is told to put on the breastplate of righteousness (Eph. 6:14), and of faith (1 Thess. 5:8). These are "iron" speaking of strength and power, for both Christ and his own are going to rule with a "rod of iron" (2:27, 19:15). The horsemen of v. 17 have breastplates of fire.

They are Incessant

The incessant movement of their wings causes them to sound like "chariots of many horses running to battle". The sound of their approach will bring terror to the hearts of men, and as the horse turneth not from the battle these will not fail to fulfil the mind of God as they torment those who have not the seal of God in their foreheads. Hurnard has a novel explanation as he says they are "demon possessed men flying aeroplanes and chasing the terrified people about". How fanciful can the minds of men get?

They are Irritating

If there is no respite under the symbol of the wings, here there is no escape. For five months, the natural lifespan of a locust, they sting with their scorpion-like tails, this is their power "to hurt men". The word used is that which means, "to do wrong", as in 1 Cor. 6:7-8, 2 Cor. 7:2-12, Col. 3:25, Phil. 18. Men have done wrong against God; they now reap what they have sown.

Their Inspirer (v. 11)

"The locusts have no king" (Prov. 30:27), such is the plain fact of scripture, but these are satanically inspired and moving under his direct command. As "the angel of the bottomless pit" he is the fallen star of v. 1. Though these demons have been imprisoned, upon their release they immediately come under his authority, they are aligned to him. There is nothing haphazard with Satan, Eph. 6:12 teaches how Satan always moved with ordered strategy; he is never careless and pointless. His name, given in the Hebrew and Greek, indicating "Destroyer" pinpoints this as Satan himself. Is he the same one as in Ex. 12? By linking Jew and Gentile names together, it would express that there is no escape from the terrors of this judgement whoever men are.

One woe is past; and, behold, there come two woes more hereafter. (Revelation 9:12)

This is but the first woe, they will increase in intensity as the tribulation proceeds.

Death for Men (vv. 13-21)

And the sixth angel sounded, and I heard a voice from the four horns of the golden altar which is before God, Saying to the sixth angel which had the trumpet, Loose the four angels which are bound in the great river Euphrates. And the four angels were loosed, which were prepared for an hour, and a day, and a month, and a year, for to slay the third part of men. And the number of the army of the horsemen were two hundred thousand thousand: and I heard the number of them. And thus I saw the horses in the vision, and them that sat on them, having breastplates of fire, and of jacinth, and brimstone: and the heads of the horses were as the heads of lions; and out of their mouths issued fire and smoke and brimstone. By these three was the third part of men killed, by the fire,

Their Appearance (v. 17)

Some would again seek to bring this down to depict modern warfare with its machines of mass extermination. Let it be understood, this is not a scene of warfare before us, there is no battle, we do not read of this army facing opposition, however weak. A commission is given, and they carry this out.

Both the horses and they that sit on them have "breastplates of fire, and of jacinth, and brimstone". It again seems to be the horses that inflict death not their riders. How different these are to the High Priest whose breastplate bears precious stones, speaking of saints held in affection. Instead of affection, in its place are the instruments of destruction. Their bearing is that of a lion's head, terrifying to men and powerful to destroy. Their breath is as fire, smoke and brimstone, the last a gas with a sulphurous smell; these are the instruments of death.

The Adversity (vv. 18-20)

An awesome picture of that which awaits a third of the world's population is drawn in vv. 18-19, and yet judgement is tempered with mercy, for limitations are imposed upon these destroyers, it is but one third that they can harm. The form death will take is positively expressed, it is a visible demonstration of the destiny of the wicked, that which awaits the ungodly. "The lake that burneth with fire and brimstone" (21:8) is the means of death here. The scorching heat of the fire, and the suffocation of the smoke and brimstone will again smite men. We cannot help but ponder the terrors of Hiroshima and Nagasaki that felt the blast of atomic bombs in 1945; destruction of this magnitude had never been seen before. Larkin suggests, "This army of infernal beings will be invisible to the naked eye" (Revelation page 79). They cannot be resisted or warred against; neither will men know the source from which their torment comes. Destruction comes from a double source, for not only does the head kill, but there is power in their tails, "which were like unto serpents and had heads". I notice these are only said "to hurt". Is it that after passing by those who are killed, others than the third of the mass of mankind will suffer, but not suffer death?

The Licentious Allies (vv. 20-21)

The Apathy (v. 20a)

It is evident that neither miracle nor judgement will move the hardness of man's heart, nor cause him to open his blinded eye. The mighty miracles of the Son of God only moved men to envy, and ultimately to cry "away with him". It is also worthwhile to look at the response to the miracles done by the apostles in the Book of Acts; far from bringing the world into submission to Christ, they only provoked men to opposition and bitter persecution. The tongues of Ch 2 brought doubt and mockery (vv. 12-13), the healing of the lame man in Ch 3 brought grief and imprisonment (4:2-3) and finally threatening (4:21). After the healing of many sick folks and the liberating of the demon possessed (5:16), healing "everyone", this again produced indignation and imprisonment (vv. 17-18).

Stephen's miracles recorded in 6:8 only produced disputing, lies and eventually his murder. Some modern charlatans who profess much in the way of healing, and their gullible followers who are taken in by spurious claims, would do well to see the effect of true miracles on the populace. But here the most serious judgements to befall mankind leave a godless world unmoved, they "repented not". Obviously these "plagues", like those on Egypt long ago should have produced repentance, but the heart of man is as obdurate as that of Pharaoh.

Their Activity (v. 20b)

The cause of God's wrath is revealed as the true character of man's life is exposed. Their worship is seen in v. 20, which is base idolatry, and manifests the folly of men when such idols, "neither can see, nor hear, nor walk". Such worship will only produce the wickedness of verse 21. Idolatry is always linked with immorality; they are the handmaids of unclean spirits. There are five traits seen in the sin of men brought forth in these two verses:

Demon Worship

Such is the idolatry of men as they worship inanimate objects, for behind the idol is a demon. 1 Cor. 12:2 emphasises that men are "carried" and "led" to such worship, the demon behind the idol will have worshippers, and exerts his power over the minds of men. August Van Ryan seems to limit this to Catholicism with its many icons, but this is not limited to the practices of Rome. The millions of the east with their many cultures and many temples fall into the same mould, as do the religions of the many Indian groups of North and South America. We often limit the activities of men to what we see around us, and too many writers look no farther than Europe to fulfil all prophesy. God here brings all men into the condemnation of idol worshippers.

Destruction of life

If demonology is first mentioned manifesting that God's rights are violated, he now brings before us the unrepentant nature of man in his evil against mankind. The two tablets of the Law are broken, the first Godward, the second manward. Life has become cheap and murder becomes an every day occurrence. If God is despised, man made in his image is destroyed.

Drugs

Sorceries is the word *pharmakia* translated "witchcraft" in Gal. 5:20. The rise of the occult is startling in our day, even monarchs and political leaders openly confess to consulting spiritists. Devil worship has a respected place in society, and the pop culture promotes tampering with the unseen. It has also become the tool for the promotion of the drug culture that is devastating many lives around the world. The word is our word for pharmacy, as applied to drugs and medicine, but distorted to the illicit use of narcotics to enhance sensual pleasure. Such is the trend among us today that certain politicians and even police officers are seeking to legislate for all laws relating to the use of drugs to be removed, making them legal. It would seem as if they are preparing the way for the scene before us.

Defilement

It is not surprising after exposure of the drug culture that fornication follows, for men throw off all restraint in their desire to gratify the flesh, and often the two go together as men seek to satiate carnal desire to the full.

Dishonesty

If there is a disregard of persons, and a delight in pleasure, there is also dishonesty with property. The greed of mankind is seen. Who amongst us is not appalled at the events recorded in news bulletins of major fraud and consortiums strategically sifting millions from society, or who amongst us has not been the victim of robbery? Bars, bolts and burglar alarms are common features of many homes.

It is because of these features that the sixth trumpet is blown, but in spite of a third of the world's population being slain because of it, man remains unrepentant.

Perhaps it is worth quoting Seiss here when he wrote over 100 years ago "murder will be amongst the commonest of crimes. Sensual and selfish passion will make sad havoc of human life, with no serious thought about it on the part of leaders of public sentiment. Foeticide, infanticide, homicide, and all forms of sin against human life will characterise society, and be tolerated and passed as if no great harm were done" (Revelation, page 215).

His insight was remarkable in light of present events!

Chapter 10
The Magnificence of the Angel
Introduction

Chapter 10 seems to begin the interlude between the sixth and seventh trumpet, which does not sound until Ch 11:15-18. This would correspond with the interval between the sixth and seventh seal recorded in Ch 7, yet Ch 11:14 definitely states that it is then that "the second woe is past". Therefore it appears that the events before us are in some way linked to the sounding of the sixth trumpet, the second woe. This judgement must also be in the last half of the week for that is the period of the ministry of the two witnesses in Ch 11. The magnificence of an angel as he reveals prophetic truth is the subject of Ch 10, whilst we have the mourning of the prophets as they testify for God in Ch 11. We will turn our thoughts to the things revealed in Ch 10.

The Strong Angel Commanding (vv. 1-3)

And I saw another mighty angel come down from heaven, clothed with a cloud: and a rainbow was upon his head, and his face was as it were the sun, and his feet as pillars of fire: And he had in his hand a little book open: and he set his right foot upon the sea, and his left foot on the earth, And cried with a loud voice, as when a lion roareth: and when he had cried, seven thunders uttered their voices. (Revelation 10:1-3)

We are immediately confronted with a remarkable figure that is implicitly stated to be "another angel". Such are the features displayed by the angel that many writers link it with another manifestation of the Lord Jesus himself. Kelly, whom many follow, says "we have Christ taking the form of an angel" (Kelly, Lectures on the Book of Revelation). Why he who has been exalted "far above all principality, and power and might and dominion", (Eph. 1:21), should now lower himself again to be equal to them remains a mystery not revealed, for this one is "Another" (*allos*), another of the same kind of angels who have gone before in the book - he is not unique. As far as I can see, the Lord Jesus is never seen as an angel in the New Testament, even though, as Kelly states in the passage quoted, "In the Old Testament Jehovah had occasionally assumed an angelic form".

That the features seen in the angel by John are linked with Deity is evident. As the divine representative, he must bear the character of him who sends him. That angels have been arrayed in great splendour is plainly seen from Ezek. 1, and Dan. 10. The angel of Dan. 10 has also been mistaken for the Lord Jesus. This one is seen to be a mighty angel, an expression also used of an angel in Ch 5:2 and 18:21. **His capability** is stamped upon him from the outset. **His clothing** is said to be a cloud. Each of the features seen in some way displays the glory of him whom he represents. John the Baptist was so like Christ that Herod thought the Lord was John raised from the dead (Matt. 14:2). Moses could not be in the presence of Deity without his face shining (Ex. 34:29). The cloud always speaks of the presence of the Lord, and this angel carries it as he ministers for God. **His crown** is said to be a rainbow, its colour is not specified as in Ch 4:3, but as there, whenever God is going to sit in judgement it is always tempered with mercy. The book he holds, and the thunders he utters proclaim further outpourings of God's wrath upon the earth. The rainbow again reminds us of God's covenant not to destroy the earth (Gen. 9:12-16). **His countenance** is said to be as the sun, the woman of Ch 12:1 is clothed with the sun. The righteous are said to "shine forth as the sun" (Matt. 13:43). The angel bears righteous character and displays the righteousness of God to deal with a rebellious world. His legs are like "pillars of fire", fire purges, and the judgements of God will purge the earth in preparation for the reign of Christ.

His carrying

He has in his hand a book, some have confused this book with that of Ch 5:1. That they cannot be the same is fairly evident. This is in the diminutive, it is a little book, and whereas that of Ch 5 is a sealed book until put into the hand of Christ, this is open. Also John is going to eat this book in v. 10. It speaks of further prophecies relating to the earth, not the right to dispense this world for God, which Christ alone can do, as seen in Ch 5.

His carriage

The angel has feet that are "as pillars of fire" and the pillars of fire are placed upon the sea and the land. Many speak of this as "claiming the world for God". This is too early for the Lord to come down and claim the earth; he will do that with majestic splendour in Ch 19, not as an angel, but as "King of Kings, and Lord of Lords" (19:16). There is no point in the Lord Jesus demonstrating his rights at this time in the tribulation period, they are fully known to faith and God in his own time will shew "who is the blessed and only Potentate, the King of Kings and Lord of Lords" (1Tim. 6:15), the time to make a public display of Christ has not yet arrived. What is seen here is that scenes of divine judgement are before us, God is going to deal further with the sea and the land and those therein. There is no need to spiritualise these as Kelly does, making the sea "the unformed masses of the outside world", and the earth "that part of the world which is favoured with divine testimony and government". The whole world will be the subject of this further prophecy and the angel demonstrates it with the placing of his feet upon the sea and the earth.

His cry

The principle of Gal. 6:7 is seen here, "whatsoever a man soweth that shall he also reap", Ps. 22:13 speaks of a people who set themselves against Christ in his deep sufferings at Calvary, "as a ravening and a roaring lion" seeking to instil dread and fear into the Son of God. Well might the book of Proverbs (Ch 19:12 and 20:2) states "the King's wrath is as a roaring lion" and "the face of the King is as the roaring of the lion". The question is asked by Amos Ch 3:4, "will a lion roar in the forest, when he hath no prey?" and v.8 of the same chapter adds, "the lion hath roared, who will not fear?" "Vengeance belongeth unto me, I will recompense saith the Lord" (Heb. 10:30). Another series of judgements is to follow as God vindicates his Son, those judgements are heard as, "seven thunders uttered their voice".

The Seven Thunders Concealed (v. 4)

And when the seven thunders had uttered their voices, I was about to write: and I heard a voice from heaven saying unto me, Seal up those things which the seven thunders uttered, and write them not. (Revelation 10:4)

We are now introduced to the third series of judgements that God will bring upon the earth in tribulation days. Alarm will strike at the hearts of men as these thunders roll. John is about to write what he heard, they were obviously intelligible to him, but as far as this series of seven is concerned, like Daniel (Ch 12:4) he is told, "seal up those things which the seven thunders uttered, and write them not". Paul could not unveil the wonders of heaven, (2 Cor. 12:4), nor on this occasion can John unfold wrath poured out from heaven. God does not reveal all he is going to do in tribulation days, but that this is going to be a bitter experience for the world is clear from v. 9.

That one series of judgements should not be revealed is in keeping with the fact that all fours in scripture divide into a three and a one, and whereas we know the content and character of the seal, trumpet and vial judgements, these are not to be written.

The Solemn Oath Completing (vv. 5-7)

And the angel which I saw stand upon the sea and upon the earth lifted up his hand to heaven, And sware by him that liveth for ever and ever, who created heaven, and the things that therein are, and the earth, and the things that therein are, and the sea, and the things which are therein, that there should be time no longer: But in the days of the voice of the seventh angel, when he shall begin to sound, the mystery of God should be finished, as he hath declared to his servants the prophets. (Revelation 10:5-7)

Acknowledged Authority (v. 5)

The identity of the angel is maintained; it is the same angel throughout, v. 2 makes this clear. Now, like the one clothed in linen of Dan. 12:7, who speaks of the duration of the tribulation period "that it shall be for a time, times and an half", this one is to tell of the imminent culmination of that period, both raise the hand to heaven. In this there is an acknowledgement that the history of this world is not dependent upon men, but on the living God. Abraham does a similar act in Gen. 14:22-24, testifying to the fact that this world's temporary treasures offered by the King of Sodom could add nothing to the foretaste of that coming kingdom which he had received from Melchisedec, when taking of the bread and wine, God's guarantee that he could enjoy all that God had promised him in the fulfilment of the promises, when the land would eventually be his.

Acclamation of Supremacy (v. 6)

When the angel sware, (take, or declare an oath, Strongs), he did it "by him that liveth for ever and ever". This in itself should be enough for any to see that this angel is not Christ as many hold. It is plainly stated in Heb. 6:13 "because he could sware by no greater, he sware by himself", thus when God swears he swears by himself. This angel swears by God both in his eternal existence, "Him that liveth for ever and ever", and also by his creatorial power, "who created all things". There is no room for evolution in these statements, it is a living creator God who determines the course the world takes which he has brought into being, and that is the purpose behind the last statement "That there should be time no longer".

The TR puts it as "delay shall be no longer", followed by JND "there shall be no longer delay". The tribulation period is fast climaxing, God is bringing all things to their final goal as v. 7 graphically states. Soon the glorious kingdom of the Lord Jesus will be introduced. There is no thought in the statement that the final dealings of God with man are now complete, and that there will be at this point the establishment of the Great White Throne judgement and then the bringing in of the New Heaven and Earth. The context forbids such an interpretation. It is, that the tribulation period is fast climaxing and there will be no delay in bringing in the Kingdom of our Lord Jesus Christ, which is the great hope of scripture.

The word *chronos* - time, occurs four times in the book of Revelation. In Ch 2:21 "space" is given to Jezebel to **repent**, again in Ch 6:11 a little "season" is given to tribulation saints to **rest,** in this present verse it is to bring in Christ's **rule**, and in Ch 20:3 a little "season" and Satan will be **released** from the abyss. One writer has said that "the only meaning for *chronos* that makes any sense in this context is the sense of 'delay' " (Thomas).

A further note on the hand raised may be of interest - most scholars add that it was "the right hand" that was raised according to some manuscripts, and then presume the book was in his left hand. There is nothing to indicate this in the verses, and as it is but a little book, and this is a strong angel, there is no reason why he could not have raised the hand with the book in it, though this is not stated either.

Accomplished Mystery (v. 7)

The **PERIOD** is defined for us when the history of the world as we know it is to be terminated, it is "in the days of the voice of the seventh angel when he shall begin to sound". This is recorded in Ch 11:15-18, at which time "the kingdoms of this world are become the kingdoms of our Lord and of his Christ". This trumpet is soon to blow. The word used for to "sound" is *mello* and of the 13 times it is used in the Revelation, it always has the idea of that which is about to happen, it is imminent. That there is a close time link between the blowing of the sixth and seventh trumpet is evident from these statements.

The **PERPLEXITY** that has troubled many will be revealed that, "The mystery of God should be finished". A New Testament mystery is not something mysterious, but rather something that in other ages has not been made known, either to time or to men (Col. 1:26, Eph. 3:5) but was "hid in God" (Eph. 3:9). But though hidden from those of former dispensations it is now revealed, not to men in general, "the natural man receiveth not the things of the Spirit of God" (1 Cor. 2:14), but revealed to faith. The world still asks the question "if there is a God - why?" They know not the divine principle that God does not judge unripe evil. Man, "treasurest up unto thyself wrath against the day of wrath" (Rom. 2:5) and "the iniquity of the Amorites is not yet full" (Gen. 15:16). The mystery of God is simply his tolerance of the evil of humanity as motivated by Satanic power. We must admit that for those who delight in God's honour it is difficult to conceive why God does not intervene in human affairs, and allows degenerate humanity its will as it violates every aspect of the revealed will of God. One day it will be "completed", "accomplished, made an end, expire, finish" (Strong).

The **PROMISE**, as the world declares its opposition of Deity, God has proclaimed to his servants, the prophets, the ultimate subjugation of all evil and a glorious kingdom for himself. The word "declared" is that to bring glad tidings to men, used 55 times in the New Testament for the preaching of the gospel. Whether these prophets are Old Testament or New Testament prophets is of no consequence. Down the ages, in every dispensation, God has encouraged his own, through the prophets, that he will bring in a kingdom in which the will of God is done on earth.

The Small Book Consumed (vv. 8-11)

And the voice which I heard from heaven spake unto me again, and said, Go and take the little book which is open in the hand of the angel which standeth upon the sea and upon the earth. And I went unto the angel, and said unto him, Give me the little book. And he said unto me, Take it, and eat it up; and it shall make thy belly bitter, but it shall be in thy mouth sweet as honey. And I took the little book out of the angel's hand, and ate it up; and it was in my mouth sweet as honey: and as soon as I had eaten it, my belly was bitter. And he said unto me, Thou must prophesy again before many peoples, and nations, and tongues, and kings. (Revelation 10:8-11)

The Command to Take (v. 8)

John again in this section defines those who instruct him, the voice of v. 4 again speaks telling him to take the book from "the hand of the angel that standeth upon the sea and upon the earth". This action again emphasises that this is not the book of Ch 5:1, for John would have no right to that book. Christ alone can open that book. That this angel cannot be Christ is also evident, for John would not take what naturally belongs to Christ, and we must remember that when a search was made in the universe for someone who was worthy to open the seven sealed book, John was among those who were, "not found worthy to open the book neither to look thereon" nor would he approach the Lord Jesus without due reverence.

The Call to Give the Book (v. 9)

Here we have John's request and the response of the angel. The response is not only for John to handle the book but also to "eat it up". The book evidently contains divine truth; Scroggie says that its contents are the prophecies of Ch 11:1 to 19:10. This can hardly be true for the seventh trumpet is part of a series that has gone before, and the second vision relates to everything from Ch 6:1 - 16:21.

Any man who ministers for God must imbibe divine truth, he has to know the ministry, and make it his own. This action of John's is not uncommon in scripture. The words of Jeremiah have been a delight to many a believer, "Thy words were found, and I did eat them; and thy word was unto me the joy and rejoicing of my heart". (Ch 15:16), and Ezekiel had a similar experience to John when he is called to eat the roll and then go and speak to the house of Israel. To Ezekiel it is only, "in my mouth as honey for sweetness" (Ezek. 3:1-3). John is told of the bitterness that will be felt internally, though naturally sweet to the taste.

Consuming the Book (v. 10)

John's readiness to take the book is now recorded and its effect on him. What is like honey to the mouth immediately becomes bitter to the belly. Honey, like milk, is that which is digested in the life of another, no man can make truth, though he can make truth his own. Truth when first received is very sweet, but the implications of that truth when known cause us to recognise the seriousness of God's dealings with men. One has said prophecy gladdens, saddens and maddens. The truth of God can both thrill and chill.

Commission to Prophecy

Having tasted and felt the truth, John is now told he must prophecy again. The expression "before" has the sense of "concerning". Prophecy at this stage of the world's history embraces all mankind, and it is noticeable that "Kings" are added to the list of those whom John is to address. The sovereigns of earth are going to feel the weight of God's word, and will ignore it to their peril.

Chapter 11
The Mourning Prophets and the Majestic Christ
Introduction

This chapter begins a section in the book of Revelation that introduces the main actors in the second half of the tribulation "the tribulation the great". Here during the time of "Jacob's trouble" (Jer. 30:7), we see those who will have the chief roles during that period. In Ch 11 we have the Two Witnesses prophesying, Ch 12 brings before us Two Wonders with the Woman protected, whilst in Ch 13 we have Two Wild beasts in all their power, Ch 14 speaks of Two Walking together according to the promise of God. This is another millennial scene when Christ and the 144,000 walk in fellowship together on mount Sion, the city of the great king.

The chapter also brings before us the seventh trumpet in fulfilment of Ch 10:6-7, indicating that the tribulation period is now fast drawing to a close for the time has now arrived for, "the kingdoms of this world are become the kingdoms of our Lord and of his Christ; and he shall reign for ever and ever" (v. 15).

The chapter has four major themes throughout it, (1) **TEMPLE WORSHIP** is seen in v. 1, with (2) a **TRODDEN CITY** in v. 2, whilst during this period in Israel's history there will be (3) the **TESTIMONY BEARERS** (vv. 3-14), and it ends with (4) a **TRIUMPHANT CHRIST** (vv. 15-18). The chapter break here is unfortunate for the last verse strictly belongs to Ch 12, and sets the scene for the two wonders of Ch 12.

An interesting section is written by Ottman regarding this portion of the book in relation to the various interpretations that men make of this section, "Interpreters of the Revelation exhibit more confusion in the exposition of this chapter than elsewhere". He then expounds many of the varied interpretations that abound regarding these verses. It is evident that much confusion is seen here; Alford himself says this chapter is "undoubtedly one of the most difficult in the whole Apocalypse". Yet if we take the scripture as it stands all seems very clear and simple. A footnote by Newell in Ch 14 is weighty in this connection when he says "it is well, when people claim that the scripture does not mean what it says, to ask who then can say what it means?"

The Temple Measured (vv. 1-2)

And there was given me a reed like unto a rod: and the angel stood, saying, Rise, and measure the temple of God, and the altar, and them that worship therein. But the court which is without the temple leave out, and measure it not; for it is given unto the Gentiles: and the holy city shall they tread under foot forty and two months. (Revelation 11:1-2)

As the second half of Daniel's 70th week (Dan. 9:27) is about to commence, at a time when Satan and his Antichrist seem to be in ascendancy, when Israel is now subject to the Man of Sin, and the nation is under Gentile dominion, God sees that a reed is given to John to measure the temple. By this act God is reserving for himself what is still the true worship that is his alone. This is not the same measuring of the temple by Ezekiel (Ch 40-42) for that is the millennial temple, and Ezekiel records the day when "the glory of the God of Israel came from the east" (43:2) and "the glory of the Lord filled the house" (43:5). That will be a day of splendour and honour for God, when all is measured and all is his. The same period is in view when Zechariah is told to measure the city of Jerusalem (Ch 2). Again the Lord will reserve for himself a city full of those who stand redeemed in the coming kingdom, a city without walls, (Zech. 2:4), with no fear of assault from without, for "the Lord will be unto her a wall of fire roundabout, and will be the glory in the midst of her" (v. 5). When John is bidden to measure he has limitations imposed on him, only two things are measured, the temple (the *naos*, the Holy of Holies) and the altar. This altar must be the golden altar of the sanctuary, for the court, the place of the brazen altar, he is told to "leave out". In the midst of satanic evil, when God seems to have been removed from all that is rightfully his, he still retains his rights for praise, the temple, and prayer, the altar. John is not only to measure the place, but also the people "that worship therein". It is evident from this that a remnant are still faithful to him, and though they may not at this time be able to worship in the place God truly desires, for the Man of Sin enters this temple (2 Thess. 2:4) yet God accepts it as his in reality.

It is a definite act that gives John the reed to measure the temple with. The conjunction "and" *(kai)* would seem to link the giver with the angel who told him to swallow the book in Ch 10. This reed is like a staff, *(rabdos, rod)*. It is the word used for governmental authority in the coming kingdom, where it is said both of the saints (2:27) and of Christ (19:15) they shall rule with a "rod of iron", speaking of the inflexible government of that coming day. The fact that the same word is used here bespeaks that God will not yield his rights to the Man of Sin. When John measures the Holy Jerusalem in Ch 21:15, he is given a "golden reed", this would remind us of the divine character that will mark the saints both in the kingdom and in the eternal state.

The court of the temple must not be measured, rather a stronger word is used it is to, "cast out" *(ekbale)*. It must not be measured; God is not reserving this for himself, for it is given unto the Gentiles. It would seem that this is a divine act. Seiss expresses the thought well when he says, "what is measured is from that moment his, and what is outside of these lines, and not measured, is not acknowledged by him, but is rejected and held and treated as defiled". The time of Jacob's trouble begins at this point of time, and Jerusalem is going to feel the full weight of Gentile oppression. It is noticeable that Jerusalem is called "the holy city". It is still "the city of the great king" (Ps. 48:2) and if for a short period of forty-two months it is trodden under foot, God will hold Gentiles responsible for their treatment of what belongs to him.

If the city is trodden under foot during this period, the Lord Jesus will himself tread these Gentiles under foot without its gates at the end of the forty-two months (Ch 14:20). Then during his reign he will suppress all who oppose him (19:15).

What is recorded here has very close links with Daniel's great prophecy of Ch 9, in which, in v. 26, we are told "and the people of the prince that shall come shall destroy the city and the sanctuary; and the end thereof shall be with a flood, and unto the end of the war desolations are determined". Virtually all expositors link this statement with the coming of Titus in AD 70, when the city was ransacked and the people were driven into exile (an exile which lasted until May of 1948, when the UN gave the Jews the right to a homeland). Some like Sir Robert Anderson tell us of this passage "this is conclusive proof that the coming prince must be a Roman". Such an interpretation takes the statement outside Daniel's revealed period of seventy weeks. The first 69 weeks encompass vv. 24-26a, which begin with the edict to rebuild the walls given to Nehemiah in Neh. 2 and end with the presentation of the Lord Jesus to the nation recorded in Matt. 21:1-16, Mark 11:1-14, Luke 19:28-40. To fulfil this prophecy to the letter the events recorded from vv. 26b-27 must be kept within the confines of the last week to make the prophecy complete. To take the statement of v. 26 and use it to relate to AD 70 moves it outside the 70-week prophecy.

There is no difficulty in linking Daniel's prophecy with other scriptures that clearly state what Jerusalem will pass through at the time of the end, where Daniel himself places the fulfilment of this prophecy. Perhaps Dan. 11:16, "But he that cometh against him shall do according to his own will, and none shall stand before him: and he shall stand in glorious land, which by his hand shall be consumed" is speaking of this event, for the prophecies recorded from v. 6 of Dan. 11 seem to be prophetic and not historic, leading up to, and bringing in the Man of Sin who appears from v. 21 of that chapter. The prophecy of Joel 2:3 relates to this same treading under foot by the people of the prince that shall come, which again as in Dan. 11:16 is seen to be a northern army, not Roman. A graphic portrayal of the trouble for Jerusalem is recorded in Zech. 12-14, placing the destruction in the midst of tribulation days, not AD 70. To add to these clear prophecies we have the words of the Lord Jesus telling of the same havoc Jerusalem will know, recorded in Matt. 24, Mark 13 and Luke 21. Each of these relate to what we have here in Rev. 11:2 and all are the fulfilment of Dan. 9:26. We are told in Hab. 1:6 that "the Chaldean" is that bitter and hasty nation. We shall see as we come to look at the coming world ruler in Ch 13, that his origins are Babylon rather than Rome.

The Witnesses' Ministry (vv. 3-6)

And I will give power unto my two witnesses, and they shall prophesy a thousand two hundred and threescore days, clothed in sackcloth. These are the two olive trees, and the two candlesticks standing before the God of the earth. And if any man will hurt them, fire proceedeth out of their mouth, and devoureth their enemies: and if any man will hurt them, he must in this manner be killed. These have power to shut heaven, that it rain not in the days of their prophecy: and have power they should believe the lie", but he raises a witness against it in these sackcloth garbed servants.

The Type (v. 4)

Three things are said of the two witnesses in this verse, as they are seen as "two olive trees", **Receiving a Blessing.** For the olive always speaks of blessing, the fig is Israel's national emblem, the vine is what they are fruitfully, today they bring forth "wild grapes" (Isaiah 5:2), whilst the olive speaks of blessing (Ps. 52:8), and the blessing of children as "like olive plants round thy table" (Ps. 128:3). The present position of Israel is that they are now cut off from blessing, and the Gentiles brought into it as seen in the illustration of the olive tree in Rom. 11:11-24. That Israel is going to be brought into the place of blessing again at the coming of the deliver out of Sion v. 26 (Christ) is the burden of many scriptures. Perhaps these two witnesses are precursors of that blessing.

They are also stated to be the "two candlesticks", **Raising a Testimony**. It is here that the likeness to Zech. 4 stops. In Zechariah, God's "two anointed ones" are seen feeding the Lampstand but are not said to be the Lampstand, whereas these two witnesses also bear testimony for God in Jerusalem's darkest hour.

They are also said to be "standing before the God of the earth", in **Readiness to Serve**, for when any stand before God, it is for this purpose (1 Kings 17:1; 2 Kings 3:14). They serve God when others must needs flee Jerusalem. It is interesting to notice those whom God has raised up in pairs to serve him, Moses and Aaron, Joshua and Caleb, Haggai and Zechariah, Joshua the son of Josedech and Zerrubabel the son of Shealtiel. Also when the Lord Jesus sent the disciples forth it was in twos. Sadly when men go astray and move against God and his truth, it is also in twos (see Lev. 10:1, Num. 12:1). In 2 Timothy we have two men in every chapter who acted against God. We do well to watch our company, we can be a blessing for God or become antagonistic to him, and our friends do help to mould our destiny. Chapter 13 will bring before us the two worst men who ever opposed God.

These are days when men will claim despotic rights to the earth, but we are reminded that it still belongs to God who is "the God of the earth".

Their Torments (vv. 5-6)

It is small wonder, when we look at the activities of the witnesses, that they have been taken for Moses and Elijah, for the miracles that come from their hand correspond with those accomplished by these servants as they stood against Pharaoh and Ahab. The first feats recall those of Elijah in 2 Kings Ch 1, when he called down fire upon two companies of fifty who came to take him captive, and his first act for God, when he prayed that there should be neither dew nor rain but according to his word (1 Kings 17:1); whilst the last two miracles recall those of Moses in Egypt ere Pharaoh let Israel go. Even in these days of the reign of the Man of Sin, the God of the earth will manifest his rights to do with it what he will at the hands of his servants, and men will be reminded what little power is theirs in reality. God again introduces the element of the miraculous after centuries when faith has been the principle of walking with God. But as in other ages, when God has been dealing with Israel to bring them to himself, he used miracles, so again, when he is about to bring them from this dreadful apostasy, he stakes his claim by his demonstration of power. Though it must be remembered that, as Pharaoh's magicians sought to bring the miracles of Moses to disrepute by imitation, so will the false prophet in Ch 13:13-15 do wonders to deceive them that dwell on the earth.

The Beast's Mastery (vv. 7-8)

And when they shall have finished their testimony, the beast that ascendeth out of the bottomless pit shall make war against them, and shall overcome them, and kill them. And their dead bodies shall lie in the street of the great city, which spiritually is called Sodom and Egypt, where also our Lord was crucified. (Revelation 11:7-8)

Four simple statements relate how these two witnesses finally meet their end. We are told firstly, when they die, it will not be until the ministry that God has put into their hands is completed. Only when the thousand two hundred and threescore days have run their course will the beast be able to overcome them. It is a blessed thing when any finish the work that the Father gives them to do.

Then we are told, who causes their death. This is the first time that the Man of Sin is introduced as a beast in the book. There will be thirty-five further references to him as such; it is the dominant title that he carries in the Revelation. The thought is that of a wild beast such as would seek the destruction of a lamb, the Lord Jesus, and those who testify to him. His origin is stressed; he is "the beast that ascendeth out of the bottomless pit". It may have been this statement that causes Walvoord to think this is "Satan himself" (page 181) where he links the trinity of evil together by this word, one out of the sea (13:1) as the great world dictator, and he who rises from the land (13:11) as the religious leader. The latter verse is the only time that the false prophet is called a beast in Revelation. This could hardly be the devil here, for though he is released from the Abyss and raises an army to assail "the camp of the saints about, and the beloved city" (20:9), at the end of the millennium, he is always portrayed as the Dragon, not a beast. It would seem that the reason the beast is seen to be from the pit, is to reveal his satanic and spirit origin. The Lord Jesus, whom he imitates, is "the Lord from heaven" (1 Cor. 15:47).

Further we are instructed as to how they die. If during their ministry it is others who are killed who seek to harm them, it is now going to require a battle to overcome them and kill them. They cannot be taken as others will and be executed by the sword (20:4). The word for war here is that which is used of the beast in Ch 19:19, when he goes to make war against Christ when he returns in glory. On that occasion there is no success, only his inglorious end. It is evident that the beast desires, like many before him, to silence the ministry of God, but the word of God will not cease to be operative just because men cut down those who bear his testimony.

Finally in v. 8 we are told, where they die. Some expositors have tried to deny that this is the literal Jerusalem that is in view, yet the section from v. 1 is dealing with that city. What it is spiritually, Sodom and Egypt, this is not what it is literally. Seiss has well written in this connection, "Men mistake God's mind, and pervert God's word, when they refuse to accept and interpret the bible as it reads". (The Apocalypse page 264). The fact that it is the place "where also our Lord was crucified" settles any argument, and silences the protestors. Jerusalem though called "the holy city" (v. 2) had degenerated morally into bearing the features of Sodom, when it manifests the character of that which is worldly it is likened to Egypt, and spiritually the place of a rejected Lord.

The People's Mockery (vv. 9-10)

And they of the people and kindreds and tongues and nations shall see their dead bodies three days and an half, and shall not suffer their dead bodies to be put in graves. And they that dwell upon the earth shall rejoice over them, and make merry, and shall send gifts one to another; because these two prophets tormented them that dwelt on the earth. (Revelation 11:9-10)

The belligerence of the world's population is seen in their death. It must be remembered that at this time the world is dominated by the beast (13:8), and they move under the strong delusion of 2 Thess. 2:11. As the two witnesses had ministered for three and a half years, so now for three and a half days they refuse them the honour of a burial. This was surely long enough to prove "the reality of their death, of which the representative of the nations were so anxious to be perfectly assured" (Seiss). It is to be noticed that whereas carnivorous birds eat the bodies of those who are slain at the return of the Lord, these two witnesses are not allowed to be so used, for God is going to raise them from the dead.

The bliss of the world at the demise of these two prophets whose ministry tormented them is now recorded. Men who refuse the voice of God cannot help but feel the weight of it as they reject it. They knew the severity of what they will know in eternity, for the torment inflicted by those prophets was as that spoken of in Ch 20:10. It is little wonder that such was the relief known by their death, that the world makes it a time of great rejoicing and festivity by these earth dwellers. Twice they are called such in the verse, speaking not merely of their habitat, but of that which characterises them, as they live for this world, with no thought of the world to come.

Raised Miraculously (vv. 11-12)

And after three days and an half the Spirit of life from God entered into them, and they stood upon their feet; and great fear fell upon them which saw them. And they heard a great voice from heaven saying unto them, Come up hither. And they ascended up to heaven in a cloud; and their enemies beheld them. (Revelation 11:11-12)

These two verses speak of the resurrection the two prophets will know, and the rapture they will experience.

These two, like their Lord, have served God faithfully in the midst of a world that rejects him; they are now going to experience the same things that the Lord Jesus knew. There is a difference, in that none saw the Lord raised and only his disciples saw him in resurrection, and they alone witnessed his glorification as he ascended heavenward. With the two witnesses, the very men who slew them, and gloated over them are going to be witnesses of God's vindication of his servants, not only in "the spirit of life from God entering into them", but also of the positive display of it "when they stood upon their feet". Did these watchers expect a return of the ministry that they had previously been engaged in, would fire proceed out of their mouth and devour these enemies? Little wonder, "great fear fell upon them which saw them". But these "have finished their testimony", the world is not worthy of them (Heb. 11:38), like their Lord they are to ascend up to heaven in a cloud, and the world gazes upon this amazing sight. Shortly they will gaze again, for it is evident that these two witnesses are raptured not long before the Lord himself appears, "in flaming fire taking vengeance on them that know not God, and that obey not the gospel of our Lord Jesus Christ" (2 Thess. 1:8).

It is a great voice that calls these servants to "come up hither". It was a voice like a trumpet that called John to heaven in Ch 4:1. For John it was "in the spirit", for these it is a physical experience. As Enoch and Elijah in a former day, but linked to the same dispensational dealings of God, so these will be raptured toward the end of the tribulation. Those of the Church will have been raptured some years before this, but this does prove that not only the saints of this dispensation are caught up. These witnesses will not form part of the Church, they are distinct from it, but they will share our experience. Their experience is somewhat unique, for most of those redeemed not forming part of the Church will not experience heaven at all, being raised when the Lord appears in glory to enter into the Kingdom (Dan. 12:2-3).

The City's Misery (vv. 13-14)

And the same hour was there a great earthquake, and the tenth part of the city fell, and in the earthquake were slain of men seven thousand: and the remnant were affrighted, and gave glory to the God of heaven. The second woe is past; and, behold, the third woe cometh quickly. (Revelation 11:13-14)

This is the third of five earthquakes mentioned in the Revelation, in each of them God is displaying his power at significant times. The vengeance of God is swift upon those who reject his testimony. Ottman is fairly acute when he remarks, "the truth is a suggestion of the tithe, whose enforced payment is exacted by heavy judgement". A far greater earthquake is to divide the great city into three parts and cause every island to flee away (16:19-20). This judgement is but a foretaste of what the whole world will feel when "yet once more I shake not the earth only, but also the heaven" (Heb. 12:26). This will be accomplished as the Lord returns in great glory, and would seem to be that spoken of in Ch 6:12-14.

The number of men who are slain is also noted, as seven thousand of "Names of Men" (see margin) are slain. Whether the expressions Names of Men refers to men of power and dignity is debatable, certainly God is going to deal with persons who mocked his claims and the witnesses' death.

These events do leave their mark as men are compelled to acknowledge that all these events have the finger of God upon them, and though there can be no thought of salvation, or a desire for it, yet men must give "glory to the God of Heaven".

We are reminded again that all these events are within the orbit of the second woe. Though these events are said to be in the interval between the sounding of the sixth and seventh trumpets, yet we are told that this concludes the second woe, which is the sixth trumpet. That everything is rapidly drawing to a close is evident from the fact that the third woe follows quickly, which is the return of Christ to establish his Kingdom as seen in the remaining verses of the chapter.

Christ's Majesty (vv. 15-18)

And the seventh angel sounded; and there were great voices in heaven, saying, The kingdoms of this world are become the kingdoms of our Lord, and of his Christ; and he shall reign for ever and ever. And the four and twenty elders, which sat before God on their seats, fell upon their faces, and worshipped God, Saying, We give thee thanks, O Lord God Almighty, which art, and wast, and art to come; because thou hast taken to thee thy great power, and hast reigned. And the nations were angry, and thy wrath is come, and the time of the dead, that they should be judged, and that thou shouldest give reward unto thy servants the prophets, and to the saints, and them that fear thy name, small and great; and shouldest destroy them which destroy the earth. (Revelation 11:15-18)

It has been noticed that there was "silence in heaven" with the opening of the seventh seal (8:1) in the anticipation of the coming terrors that await men. Now at the blowing of the seventh trumpet "there were great voices in heaven" at the prospect of the triumph of Christ in taking his rightful place to hold all things for God.

This is the fulfilment of the third woe, though Larkin places all up to (20:3) under this woe finding a place for the vial judgements within its scope (Revelation page 88). Walvoord expresses a similar thought because the reign of the Lord is brought in here "when as a matter of fact the seven vials seemingly are still to be poured out. The answer as indicated previously seems to be that just as the seven trumpets are comprehended in the seventh seal so the seven vials are comprehended in the seventh trumpet. The process of destruction of earthly power is therefore already under way" (The Revelation of Jesus Christ page 184). There does not need to be an incorporation of the future visions brought into the third woe, for the book is constantly bringing us to the point of the reign of Christ, as 6:12-17, or again the reign of the eternal state that is brought before us in 20:1-8, and then from v. 9 relating back to events that are still to be accomplished in the millennial kingdom. As far as the seal judgements are concerned they culminate in the return of Christ. As far as the trumpet judgements go, they also culminate with the reign of Christ. This does not preclude God through his servant from unfolding other events that take place even though he has established that Christ must reign. Tatford puts it well when he says "On more than one occasion, the Apocalyptic seer is carried in thought and vision to the closing scenes, only to revert soon afterwards to events which must necessarily precede them. So here, the judgement upon Jerusalem is followed immediately by the glad picture of the Millennium and even the eternal state, although the book later goes back once more to the events which will occur prior to the millennium" (Tatford, Prophecy's Last Word page 132).

Rule of Christ (v. 15)

With the sounding of the seventh angel, the stage is now set to bring in the glorious kingdom of our Lord Jesus Christ. This has been long awaited in heaven. God's rights have been overthrown under the hand of human governments and now great voices in heaven proclaim three glorious facts. First **the displacing of human government**, the Lord is not going to share his glory with another, as earthly kingdoms do. The stone cut out without hands (Dan. 2:45) will bring all other governments down, and remove them until it itself fills the earth. The hour that Psalm 2 foretold has finally arrived. God's king is to be set "upon my holy hill of Zion" (v. 6). This brings us to the second point of the verse, **the destiny of human government**. What man has wrested for his own glory now become "the kingdoms of our Lord, and of his Christ". Divine purpose is now fulfilled, government that was built into the creatorial order (Col. 1:16) and established on earth with Adam's creation (Gen. 1:26) now finds its true goal as it comes into the hand of God and is administered by his Christ, our Lord Jesus. Finally we have **the duration of Christ's government**. It is "for ever and ever". It is literally "to the ages of the ages". The Lord will neither die or be deposed for his kingdom to pass into the hands of another.

Rejoicing of the Elders (vv. 16-17)

As on other occasions when Christ is honoured in the book the heavenly beings must acknowledge it with delight and devotion. It is another occasion for worship; heaven begins what will be accomplished on earth as they fall on their faces before him, soon to be followed by every creature (Phil. 2:9-11). It is at this point that Heb. 1:6 is fulfilled, when "all the angels of God worship him". It is a time for thanksgiving when a corrupt world is going to be subjugated by almighty power, for it will take this to deal with the whole course of a satanic system, and to remove everything that has opposed God since the fall. The Eternal God finally brings all within his authority.

Retribution and Reward (v.18)

As in v. 15, three thoughts are expressed in this verse:

(a) The distress of nations - Well might Psalm 2:1 ask the question "why do the heathen rage and the people imagine a vain thing?" JND translates the verse before us as "the nations have been full of wrath, and thy wrath is come". A full reward is going to be given when, "then shall he speak unto them in his wrath, and vex them in his sore displeasure" (Ps. 2:5). Man will find "it is a fearful thing to fall into the hands of the living God" (Heb. 10:31). These are they who will be alive at Christ's return.

(b) The distribution of reward - Further, on his return the Lord Jesus will raise the faithful of the Old Testament, and those who have suffered martyrdom during tribulation days. I believe we have here the fulfilment of Daniel 12:2 "and many of them that sleep in the dust of the earth shall awake". The scripture makes it clear that there are various stages to the resurrection of the Just, (1 Cor. 15:23) "but every man in his own order". The first resurrection is not one of time, but of type, it is a resurrection to life and blessing. The Lord Jesus as the firstfruits was the first of that order, the saints of this dispensation, the church, will have their place at the rapture. The two witnesses of this chapter have enjoyed their resurrection at this time, now all the faithful who like the patriarchs "died in faith not having received the promises" (Heb. 11:13) will be raised to enter into the kingdom (Luke 13:28). Along with their resurrection will be their reward for faithfulness during their period of testimony. It is comforting to know that all who serve regardless of office or status will enjoy a reward from the master they served.

There is no need to make this a general resurrection of all men, nor to make the judgement here that of the great white throne of Ch 20:11-15 as some do. The fact that this resurrection is linked with reward links this with the "first resurrection" which is to blessing and not the "last resurrection" which is to damnation.

(c) The destruction of the ungodly - In this church era, men are warned in 1 Cor. 3:17 that "if any man defile (corrupt) the temple of God, him will God destroy" (corrupt). The same word is used here with the preposition *dia* added, which Vine tells us intensifies the word to make it an "utter or thorough corruption". "Whatsoever a man soweth, that shall he also reap" (Gal. 6:7). Men little realise the results of their wickedness, with its final outcome of having to meet God and his Christ. At this time, the judgement of living nations will take place, and the goats, the unredeemed, will be cast into the lake of fire (Matt. 25:31-46). Living men will quickly share the fate of the beast and the false prophet who are cast there at the return of the Lord Jesus to earth, this latter pair without a judgement, such is their wickedness as they have corrupted the earth (see Ch 19:20).

And the temple of God was opened in heaven, and there was seen in his temple the ark of his testament: and there were lightnings, and voices, and thunderings, and an earthquake, and great hail. (Revelation 11:19)

The last verse of the chapter would seem to belong to chapter 12, and begins a new section. Here we are introduced to God's faithful dealings with his people Israel, for the ark of his testament is always linked with the nation, and it embodies the covenants made with Israel alone, the Roman epistle Ch 9:4-5 stresses this fact. In chapter 12 we shall see God's interests in Israel manifested as he preserves them from the devil's assaults. The fact that "lightnings and voices, and thunderings, and an earthquake, and great hail" are seen is consistent with what has gone before, when God unveils his majesty, and faithfulness to deal with the earth in judgement because of the violation of all that is his by wicked men. See Ch 4:5 in connection with the throne, and Ch 8:5 when the scene is from the altar, now it is from the "ark of his Testament".

Chapter 12
The Woman, her celestial purpose and terrestrial experience

Introduction

If Alford finds Ch 11 "undoubtedly one of the more difficult in the whole Apocalypse" then I must reiterate the statement in relation to this chapter, for it is full of difficulties. This is evident from the abundance of interpretations that have been written regarding it, and many faithful and able men differ in their understanding of it. The problem lies in the identities of both the woman and the man child, for the rest all seems fairly discernible. I cannot say that I am fully convinced of that which I set forth, but it has been done with much prayer, and searching, as we seek to understand the mind of the Lord. I put forward the following interpretation by no means with dogmatism, but as a suggestion that spiritual minds will ponder, and one that to me at least seems to answer in some measure the problems. I still wait upon God and look for further light upon the subject, though I have pondered these verses for many years.

The Wonders in Heaven (vv. 1-6)

And there appeared a great wonder in heaven; a woman clothed with the sun, and the moon under her feet, and upon her head a crown of twelve stars: And she being with child cried, travailing in birth, and pained to be delivered. And there appeared another wonder in heaven; and behold a great red dragon, having seven heads and ten horns, and seven crowns upon his heads. And his tail drew the third part of the stars of heaven, and did cast them to the earth: and the dragon stood before the woman which was ready to be delivered, for to devour her child as soon as it was born. And she brought forth a man child, who was to rule all nations with a rod of iron: and her child was caught up unto God, and to his throne. And the woman fled into the wilderness, where she hath a place prepared of God, that they should feed her there a thousand two hundred and threescore days. (Revelation 12:1-6)

The Woman, her Privilege (v. 1)

The chapter begins with two wonders in heaven, the first is said to be "a great wonder", the epithet great is not linked to the second wonder of v. 3. This word *(megas)* is linked to five things in the chapter

In v. 1 we have a **great wonder** connected to the woman; vv. 3-9 **great wickedness** in the dragon; v. 10 **a great word** spoken from heaven; v. 12 there is **great wrath** displayed by the devil and v. 14 **great wings** are given to the woman for flight.

Chapter 12 - The Woman, her celestial purpose and terrestrial experience   139

The reason this is a "great wonder" is that after thousands of years of being under the Gentile yoke, conditions are now being produced that will see Israel once again manifesting governmental authority, for this is evidently the figure that is set before us.

The woman cannot here be the church for though the sign is in heaven, and relates to the woman's position in divine purpose, yet we are going to see the woman's terrestrial experience from v. 6 when she flees into the wilderness. The time of the sojourn there is specified as "a thousand two hundred and threescore days", and in v. 14 as "a time, and times, and half a time" linking her with the last half of the tribulation period of which the church has no part, for it is in the safety of heaven during this period. Yet the woman cannot be all Israel, nor yet the true remnant in Israel, for when she flees and is helped of God to escape the violent attack of the dragon (vv. 13-16), the dragon turns his attention to "the remnant of her seed" (v. 17). These are also part of Israel, and will come into blessing when the kingdom is brought in, so she must be a part of, and some aspect of, Israel. Her governmental role is plain for all to see, she is "clothed with the sun". That which was given "to rule the day" (Gen. 1:16) will once again shine in resplendent glory as the Day of Christ comes in. The moon, "the lesser light to rule the night" (Gen. 1:16), would this symbolise Gentile powers which have dominated world government in this "time of the Gentiles"? The time of the Gentiles is a night season, when God no longer takes responsibility for the government of the nation of Israel but leaves it in the hand of Gentile powers. It is also the period of an absent Lord, who no longer shines as the light of the world (Jn. 8:5). In the vision before us, Gentile powers are seen as being subservient again, "under her feet". The twelve stars must represent the twelve tribes adorning her head; it is with *stephanos* crowns that she is arrayed, crowns of honour, with each tribe sharing in this future glory. That this has nothing to do with Joseph's dream of Gen. 37 is evident, for that speaks of the family bowing to Joseph. But if this woman does not speak of all Israel but of a particular part of that nation, which aspect could she be? I make the suggestions that vv. 13-17 may hold something of a key to unlock this problem. In these verses it is evident that in spite of all the dragon's efforts, no harm comes in any way to the woman, the attacks are all repelled and she is preserved in such a way for the dragon to cede defeat. The only other company of whom we are told that nothing can hurt them during tribulation days are the 144,000 of Ch 7. Again Matt. 24:22 speaks of the tribulation days being shortened for the elect's sake, and the verse seems to indicate that if God allowed this period to be prolonged beyond the time decreed there would be no living man left in the earth. I suggest the 144,000 are that elect, they cannot be harmed; God must act on their behalf. Also when "he shall send his angels with the great sound of a trumpet, and they shall gather together his elect from the four winds" (Matt. 24:31) this would also seem to be the sphere to which she has fled, for "the earth helped her". Surely the nations of men among whom she has fled are those who have helped, and will be rewarded at the judgement of the living nations as those who "have done it unto the least of these my brethren" (Matt. 25:40). So the experience of the woman certainly corresponds to that of the 144,000. Is it that they are sealed before the tribulation begins Ch 7, preserved during the tribulation Ch 12, and seen walking with Christ on mount

Sion when the tribulation ends Ch 14? I leave you to judge. I was somewhat thankful to read Ottman's thoughts as I was preparing to write this chapter. He says, "The sealed company of the seventh chapter preserves Israel nationally during the great tribulation which begins with the violation of the covenant in the middle of the week. This sealed company, constituting the nation, may flee to, and be nourished in, the wilderness during the twelve hundred and sixty days; whilst the rest of the Israelites remaining in Jerusalem would constitute 'the remnant of her seed' that becomes the object of Satan's persecution. This interpretation is in the judgement of the writer, equal to a certainty. It is, at any rate, clear and constant" (Unfolding of the Ages page 293). Evidently Ottman saw the same difficulties. John Heading (From Now To Eternity, page 137) also states "the woman here would denote what is commonly known as the 'Jewish remnant' - not the whole nation which will be sunk in apostasy, but the faithful ones defined elsewhere as the 144,000".

The Woman - Her Pains (v. 2)

The woman is said to be "with child" literally "having in the womb". It is to be observed that this is an internal working not external persecution. Rather it is what is developing within the woman to produce governmental authority, after long years of barrenness in fulfilment of Hosea 3:4 when God said, "the children of Israel shall abide many days without a king, and without a prince". Those days are coming to a close, God's purpose for the nation is now coming to fruition, and the necessary workings to produce conditions for her place of rule are now being manifested. This is not the persecutions from without that she is about to endure from vv. 13-16, but rather God's dealings with her, the sign is in heaven, where she is seen in the glory of governmental power, and she is now in travail to bring this to fruition.

The Woman - Her Predator (vv. 3-4)

Another wonder in heaven is now seen; the word wonder should be translated sign (*semeion*) as also should the word in v. 1. A wonder is rather the effect produced by a sign, which in itself is a direct manifestation of divine movements. The word occurs seven times in the Apocalypse, the first in v. 1. Like all sevens, they divide into a three and a four, three are said to be "in heaven" (v. 1, v. 2; 15:1). The other four are those wrought by the false prophet (13:13-14, 19:20) and by spirits of devils (16:14).

The Dragon - His Character (v. 3a)

This sign is that of "a great red dragon". It is significant that there are thirteen references to the dragon in the book, which is the number of rebellion, defection, and apostasy. All are seen with the devil's movements. There are eight references to the dragon in this chapter in which he is displayed in his:

v. 1	-	Authority
v. 4	-	Malignity
v. 7	-	Ferocity
v. 9	-	Destiny (two references)

v. 13 -   Enmity
v. 16 -   Inability
v. 17 -   Irritability.

It is to be seen that this is a chapter of conflict and a defeated foe. The devil fails in all he proposes to do; this is seen in vv. 5-8, and also in vv. 15-16, when he seeks to **devour the child**, to **defeat Michael** and to **destroy the woman**. This is not surprising, as the Lord annulled his power at Calvary, (see Heb. 2:14; Col. 2:15), the devil is seen very much as a defeated foe. His path is always downward from the heavens to the earth (v. 9), from earth into the abyss (20:3), and ultimately into the lake of fire (20:10). It must be remembered that in his initial fall there was also a downward movement when he fell from heaven to the heavenlies, this is the sphere of his present movements (Eph. 6:12). That this is the devil is beyond argument - v. 9 settles it for us.

The Dragon - His Colour (v. 3b)

The dragon is said to be "red", some, like Larkin, speak of it as "the colour of blood, for he is a murderer from the beginning" (John 8:44) (Revelation, page 90). But the word is derived from that which means fire, and would rather speak of the heated enmity against all that is of God, and the fiery trial he would expose the woman to.

The Dragon - His Crowns (v. 3c)

Another feature that marks him is that which sees him as "the prince of this world" (John 12:31, 14:30, 16:11), the one who is in control of Gentile dominion, for this is evidently what is meant by his "having seven heads, and ten horns, and seven crowns upon his heads". The woman is displayed with heavenly authority in v. 1, whilst the dragon manifests earthly authority. This authority will be put into the hands of the first beast in Ch 13, if in a somewhat altered form, for here the heads are crowned, that is, the seven kingdoms who have held sway during the period of time that is known as "the times of the Gentiles" (Luke 21:24). They are the vassals that hold authority under the devil's control. These began in Dan. 2, when God put into the hands of gentile monarchs the government of the earth because of Israel's failure to act aright for God. The book of Daniel makes it plain who these seven heads are, and we do not have to move outside that book to find them. Some do, by linking all the nations who have oppressed Israel with this seven namely, 1. Egypt, 2. Assyria, 3. Babylon, 4. Media and Persia, 5. Greece, 6. Rome, 7, stating that this is the final power, under the "Man of Sin". Yet Daniel explains the seven whom God has decreed will form this rule, they begin with Nebuchadnezzar, "the head of gold" in the image of Daniel 2. It is from this point in history that the seven must be found, Egypt and Assyria had nothing to do with the image, and can have no part in the seven. Daniel prophesises not only in Ch 2, but also in Ch 8 of those who are going to rise after the Babylonish power has been supplanted, and declares that it is Media and Persia, followed by Alexander and his Grecian power, which power when lost by him then "four stood up for it" (v. 22), making seven distinct powers that will take control of the governmental dealings with the earth as God himself has directed.

Historians tell us of the empire of Alexander, which was divided unto his four generals, Lysimachus who took Thrace and Bithynia, Cassander who ruled Macedonia and Greece, with Seleucus taking Syria and Babylon, and Ptolemy taking Egypt, Palestine, Arabia and Petrea. Further, when Daniel speaks of where the beast is to originate in Ch 11, he again delineates these same powers in vv. 1-4. He then prophesies that the future world ruler will rise from the Selucian dynasty, which is Babylon. All these powers at some time were linked with Babylon, the sphere from which Satan works, it being his centre of operations as Jerusalem is the scene of God's dealings with the earth. It is a fact of history that the Roman power did not encompass Babylon in its territory, and is not mentioned in Daniel's prophecy (in spite of the fact that many expositors seek to place it there), though these seven are, and they are also the great movers in the purpose of God in relation to the times of the Gentiles. In the interpretation of the vision of Daniel Ch 2, the legs are passed over, and the prophecy jumps from the Grecian rule immediately to the fourth and final government which is that seen in Revelation 13, the ten-toed empire of the beast, or the ten horned world empire. In its final phase in Ch 13 it is the horns that wear the crown for it is not now powers that have ruled during the whole period of the time of the Gentiles, but its last phase seen in the Ten Kingdom confederacy. It is interesting that the legs of Daniel's image come out of the thighs which are said to be the Grecian power, and could refer to the two powers which will vie for world supremacy in the end time as set forth in Daniel 11, the Babylonish and Egyptian power, Seleucus and Ptolemy with Seleucus (Babylon) proving supreme. All this is under Satanic control as the "Dragon having seven heads and ten horns".

The Dragon, His Confrontation (vv. 4-5)

And his tail drew the third part of the stars of heaven, and did cast them to the earth: and the dragon stood before the woman which was ready to be delivered, for to devour her child as soon as it was born. And she brought forth a man child, who was to rule all nations with a rod of iron: and her child was caught up unto God, and to his throne. (Revelation 12:4-5)

The dragon is now going to seek the destruction of the man child as soon as he is born. Whether the use of the tail here is linked with the control of nations as seen in v. 3, or used to mass an attack against the man child is difficult to discern. The tail is also linked with the scorpion judgements of Ch 9, and here we have the only other reference to it, in both cases they are destructive. In this verse it is the dragon that draws (drags) the stars. This word is used of the persecuted saints in the Acts when men seek to hinder the progress of the gospel as they hale them to prison or draw them to the authorities for judgement (Acts 8:3, 14:19, 17:6). It is also used of the dragging in of the nets in John 21:8. The casting down to the earth is also the work of the dragon, whereas in v. 9 it is a victorious Michael and his angels that cast the devil and his angels to the earth. Stars are seen as angels in the scriptures, as in Job 38:7, and some have linked this with Satan's fall from his place in heaven, though it does appear to be at the time of his attack on the man child as he purposes to devour the child at the moment of birth.

Many make the man child Christ, and make this historical as to his birth. Ironside who seems to quote Alford verbatim says, "This clearly enough is the Lord Jesus Christ, who is soon to reign over all the earth, and undoubtedly He is the Man child who is to rule the nations with a rod of iron" (Lectures on Revelation page 208). Yet why should history be brought into prophecy? We are told that all from 4:1 has to do with "the things which must be hereafter" but when a difficulty appears some men depart from their normal mode of teaching. Again v. 6 places these events very firmly at the beginning of the last half of the tribulation period when the child is snatched to the throne, then the woman flees into the wilderness to be preserved and fed for "a thousand two hundred and threescore days". Larkin, with others, links this attack by the dragon to Herod's attempt to destroy Christ in Matthew 2, and with Joseph being warned in a dream to flee into Egypt (Book of Revelation page 92-93). There are also various attempts to try to explain why the life and death of Christ are not introduced into the scene, but all this is glossed over. Heading has a unique explanation when he writes, "there is no reference to the death of the Lord Jesus. This is a political section, and his death at the hands of men was really a religious event" (From Now to Eternity page 133). Many other views could be expressed as men clutch at straws to seek to explain a difficulty.

It is apparent that this child is snatched away as soon as it is born, and not many years later. The word rendered "caught up" is the Greek word *harpazo*, it occurs thirteen times in the New Testament and is used of taking by force (Matt. 11:12), of the catching away of seed in the heart (Matt. 13:19), of the wolf catching the sheep (John 10:12) and of no man plucking the saints out of the Lord's or the Father's hand (John 10:28-29). It is used of the Apostle Paul when caught up to the third heaven (2 Cor. 12:2-4), also of the saints "caught up" when the Lord comes (1 Thess. 4:17). It carries the idea, "to seize" or "take by force". Of the Lord Jesus it is said that he is, "received up into heaven" (Mark 16:10), on the ground of his finished work. Again in Luke 24:51 he is "carried up into heaven", in Luke's gospel the Lord Jesus is a dependent man, and it is fitting that he is carried. The book of the Acts Ch 1:9 declares that the Lord Jesus was "taken up", which has the thought of being raised, exalted, or hoisted. This would link well with 1 Tim. 3:16 where he is "received up in glory". The idea of force or violence is absent.

Again this child is taken from a scene of conflict, and preserved from the Dragon's assault. The Lord Jesus never fled from the devil or from the conflict, but rather met him in conflict both in the wilderness and at the cross. In the wilderness, he entered the strong man's house and spoiled his goods (Mark 3:27), at the cross the Lord again vanquished him and also his hosts (Heb. 2:14, Col. 2:15) making a shew of them openly, and in his ascension, rather than fleeing, "he led captivity captive" (Eph, 4:8). The Lord triumphed gloriously, and in no way was he preserved from the conflict as this man-child is, but ascended a mighty victor.

Again, because this man child is "to rule all nations with a rod of iron", it is said to be conclusive that this is Christ. That he will certainly do this is clear from Ch, 19:15, but it is also said of the believers of this present dispensation as they are "joint heirs with Christ" (Rom, 8:17), we are also to govern the world with Christ, "Do ye not know that the saints shall judge the world?" (1 Cor. 6:2), and Ch 2:27 assures the overcomer of Thyatira that "he shall rule them with a rod of iron". It is statements like this that cause Seiss to make this the rapture of the true believer mid way through the tribulation, he calls the woman the "visible church" of all who profess, and the man child "the invisible church" of true believers within her (Seiss Lecture 28). His arguments are seriously flawed and cannot be the correct interpretation. He gives the impression of being a partial rapturist, for which there is no foundation in the word of God. Our salvation depends on the work of Christ and not on any effort of the believer. The professing church is never displayed in regal glory as the woman is, nor are the saints of this dispensation raptured in the midst of the tribulation, but they are removed from the scene of conflict altogether (3:10).

Intelligent minds like Hoste and Newbury also find difficulties in making this Christ. Hoste says this man child is "a select company from Israel, who will have been associated, say, with the testimony of the two witnesses, and will, like them, be caught away from the evil to come" (The Visions of John the Divine page 88). But does this man child have to be a person at all? Could it not be rather God's divine purpose for governmental rule of the nation, for they will also have part in the future government of the world? Is this the internal workings within the nation to produce governmental authority, which when the dragon perceives, he will not allow it to come to fruition, his man is to be set forth in government in Ch 13, the beast out of the sea. There is no way he would allow Israel, in any form, to take dominion. This must be destroyed, for it is the child at this point, not the woman who is to be attacked. If the time is not yet for this rule to be displayed, the purpose of God regarding the nation cannot be destroyed, if there is no place on earth to display it, the purpose of God for them will be in a future day fulfilled by the man who is on the throne, the Lord Jesus. Here that purpose is fully linked to Christ for it cannot come into fulfilment by the woman herself, it is only as the Lord takes his rightful place that the true destiny of the woman can be fully manifested. What she is in celestial purpose as seen in heaven, a woman in governmental authority clothed with the sun, will be fully displayed on earth when the purpose of God is seen in resplendent glory in the millennial reign of Christ.

The War in Heaven (vv. 7-9)

And there was war in heaven: Michael and his angels fought against the dragon; and the dragon fought and his angels, And prevailed not; neither was their place found any more in heaven. And the great dragon was cast out, that old serpent, called the Devil, and Satan, which deceiveth the whole world: he was cast out into the earth, and his angels were cast out with him. (Revelation 12:7-9)

As there were two wonders in the former part of the chapter, so there are two wars in this latter part. We are now confronted with a war in heaven (v. 7). Later in v. 17 we shall see a war on earth.

Again, in vv. 1-6 we have a woman crowned with glory, and a child caught up to the throne. Now we see Satan cast out of heaven, before John introduces the woman cared for in the wilderness.

In these two verses we have a further insight into realms that are beyond the natural knowledge of men. God is again unveiling events that take place in the heavens, as he does in the book of Daniel Ch 10. We could never know, apart from divine revelation, events that take place between angelic beings as they have a part to play in the affairs of men. Chapters like 1 Kings 22, where the heavenly court meets to determine Ahab's death, and the manner of it (vv. 19-22), or Daniel Ch 10, which relates the conflicts between angelic guardians of nations, not all of which are good, that will take place in the middle of Daniel's 70th week. That this takes place then is evident from the fact that the woman is persecuted for the whole of that period, and the devil empowers the first beast of Ch 13 from earth, for the same period of time.

The Commanders and the Conflict (v. 7)

We are now told who are the chief agents in this heavenly conflict. As in other battles, the commanders do not stand alone, they have their angels with them.

Michael means, "who is like God". Whether this is a question or a comparison is difficult to ascertain. That angels bear divine features is apparent from the angel in Ch 10. Perhaps it is that as the believers through gazing on the glory of Christ are changed into the same image, (2 Cor 3:18), so the angels who are ever in the divine presence also bear features of his majesty. There are five references to Michael in the scriptures, each time he appears it is in a scene of conflict.

In Daniel 10:13, he is seen as one of the "chief princes", along with Jude 9, where he is "the Archangel", this tells us of his **supremacy** among the angels. Daniel 10:21 and 12:1 relate to his **responsibility** as having a particular work in regards to the Jewish nation. There he is "your prince" i.e. Daniel's, and one "which standeth for the children of thy people". The book of Jude v. 9 speaks of his **dignity**, when he durst not bring a railing accusation against the devil. We now see his **mastery**, as he overwhelms the dragon's host and casts him to the earth.

The Conquest and Casting (v. 8)

And prevailed not; neither was their place found any more in heaven. (Revelation 12:8)

The defeated foe cannot prevail even against an angel, little wonder all his evil workings against Christ were of no avail. From this point onwards the Devil ceases to be "the prince of the power of the air" (Eph. 2:2) and he who has ever opposed the saints of this church era who are seated in heavenly places (Eph. 2:6) from this realm (Eph. 6:12). He is now "cast out into the earth, and his angels were cast out with him". This is an utter rout, he who was seen "as lightning fall from heaven" (Luke 10:18) by the Lord Jesus, now loses his place in the heavens. His path is ever downward. At the return of the Lord in glory, he is bound and cast into the Abyss (20:2-3). Soon he will have his end in "the lake of fire and brimstone" (20:10). From this point, he turns his enmity against "the inhabitants of the earth and of the sea" (v. 12).

The Character of the Dragon (v. 9)

And the great dragon was cast out, that old serpent, called the Devil, and Satan, which deceiveth the whole world: he was cast out into the earth, and his angels were cast out with him. (Revelation 12:9)

Who the dragon is, is left in no doubt, as four names are given here which portray his full character. As a dragon we have his **savagery** in the "old serpent", his **subtlety** is foremost. Who can forget the display of this in Eden? No doubt the word old (ancient) carries us back to the garden. Then, as "the Devil and Satan", he is known as the **slanderer** and the great adversary of God and man.

The Word in Heaven (vv. 10-12)

And I heard a loud voice saying in heaven, Now is come salvation, and strength, and the kingdom of our God, and the power of his Christ: for the accuser of our brethren is cast down, which accused them before our God day and night. And they overcame him by the blood of the Lamb, and by the word of their testimony; and they loved not their lives unto the death. Therefore rejoice, ye heavens, and ye that dwell in them. Woe to the inhabiters of the earth and of the sea! for the devil is come down unto you, having great wrath, because he knoweth that he hath but a short time. (Revelation 12:10-12)

The Tormentor of the Brethren

As the Devil is cast out of the heavens, it causes one to say with a loud voice the time is now ripe for the coming Kingdom of our God, and the power of his Christ to be displayed. Though the kingdom of the beast must be seen from Ch 13, nevertheless all that God has promised regarding salvation and strength will soon be manifested, for the kingdom of the beast is very short lived. With the heavens being cleared of God's implacable foe, all is in readiness for the Lord's return. The fact of the reign of the Man of Sin being allowed, is only to demonstrate that the best the Devil can produce on earth, is only evil continually. Walvoord draws attention to the various interpretations of who the speaker is, saying, "some have ascribed this voice to God himself, some to angels, some to the twenty four elders, some to the martyred saints in heaven mentioned in 6:10, because they also cry with a loud voice. Support for the latter view is given in that, in the same verse, the loud voice mentions "the accuser of our brethren". This would seem to eliminate angels and indicate saints in heaven. The "loud voice" may very well be the shout of triumph of the tribulation saints longing for and anticipating their ultimate victory and triumph". (Walvoord, The Revelation of Jesus Christ page 193). Over against this, we do have an angel speaking to John in Ch 22:8-9 who says I am, "of thy brethren the prophets" so though Walvoord's suggestion is helpful it is not conclusive.

The accusations of the devil were as a charge in a courtroom, "a complainant at law" (Strong), and constant in character "day and night". That this is of those other than believers of this church age is clear from Romans Ch 8. For God has cleared us of condemnation (v. 1), and will allow none to lay a charge against his elect v. 33, and none can condemn v. 34. That he sought to bring accusation before this church age is seen in Job 1:6-12, and Luke 22:31-32, where Satan desired to sift all the disciples, "you" is plural, but Peter was especially vulnerable, "I have prayed for thee" singular. In these verses we see the value of the AV that is lost in modern translations. His accusations here seem to be against tribulation saints, the devil could bring accusations against those in Old Testament times, and in the tribulation we are taken back to God's dealings with the earth and acting as he did in the Old Testament.

Triumph for the Overcomer (v. 11)

And they overcame him by the blood of the Lamb, and by the word of their testimony; and they loved not their lives unto the death. (Revelation 12:11)

This verse again links the accusations with the faithful martyrs of this period in the world's history. These are seen as overcomers in a threefold way. First through the **value of the blood**, how precious is that blood, ever effectual, bringing to salvation and new life? Second by the **virtue of their testimony**, others will sing in another day "I'm not ashamed to own my Lord, nor to defend his cause", but in defending that cause it brings us to the third point, **valiant in death**, "they loved not their lives unto death". Such are the believers in tribulation days.

Trouble for the Earth Dwellers (v. 12)

Therefore rejoice, ye heavens, and ye that dwell in them. Woe to the inhabiters of the earth and of the sea! for the devil is come down unto you, having great wrath, because he knoweth that he hath but a short time. (Revelation 12:12)

The call is for heaven to rejoice at Satan's defeat, as again they will rejoice over Babylon's destruction in Ch 18:20. They rejoice in the same way as the world rejoices over the death of the two witnesses in Ch 11:10. These are the only three occurrences of this word rejoice in the Revelation. The worlds joy will turn to fear at the resurrection of the witnesses, but there is no recovery for Satan or Babylon.

If these are "woes" for the inhabiters of the earth at the sounding of the last three trumpets, so this is added to at the fall of Satan to the earth. His fury will be poured out as he recognises that time is short, all his efforts to retain a place are futile, and the lake of fire looms large before him. It matters not that "the inhabiters of the earth and the sea" have yielded to his overtures, such is the character he bears that he will pour out his fierce indignation against his own followers, but what is of God on the earth will receive special attention as verses 13-17 prove.

The Wilderness - A Haven (vv. 13-17)

And when the dragon saw that he was cast unto the earth, he persecuted the woman which brought forth the man child. And to the woman were given two wings of a great eagle, that she might fly into the wilderness, into her place, where she is nourished for a time, and times, and half a time, from the face of the serpent. And the serpent cast out of his mouth water as a flood after the woman, that he might cause her to be carried away of the flood. And the earth helped the woman, and the earth opened her mouth, and swallowed up the flood which the dragon cast out of his mouth. And the dragon was wroth with the woman, and went to make war with the remnant of her seed, which keep the commandments of God, and have the testimony of Jesus Christ. (Revelation 12:13-17)

The Devil's Ferocity (v. 13)

The "great wrath" of the devil is directed toward the woman who brought forth the man-child. If the purpose of God for Israel is unassailable, and will be fulfilled at the coming of Christ, the woman is seemingly vulnerable. The devil knows little of God, for He who preserved Israel in a former day is able to deliver from any satanic attack.

The Woman's Flight and Feeding (v. 14)

When Israel came out of Egypt it pleased God to take up their cause and he said "ye have seen what I did unto the Egyptians, and how I bare you on eagles wings and brought you unto myself" (Ex. 19:4). At this period eagle wings are given to the woman for self-preservation. Her escape will be rapid, and as an eagle rides on the storm to assist its flight, so this remnant of Israel will find divine help during the fury of the Dragon's attack. Verse 6 says, "she hath a place prepared"; it is evident that her preservation is not in the land, the wilderness seems to be a barren world with nothing for God. Some would make this literal Petra, in the wilderness of Edom, and speak of it as the place of refuge that God has prepared for those escaping from the attack of the Dragon; I feel that this is too much to accept. Both Larkin and Lockyer, among others, promote the thought that this is the place where God will preserve the woman. Lockyer writes, quoting Sale Harrison's book, The Great Unfolding that says, "Petra, the rock city and one of the wonders of the world (located southwest of the Dead Sea), is a possible hiding place. With its accommodation for a quarter of a million people, such a marvellous cavern would afford an excellent protection". Larkin is quite dogmatic regarding it, "When the time comes for the 'Man-slayer' (Israel), to escape from the hands of the 'Avenger of Blood' (Antichrist), the rocky fastness of the ancient city of Petra will be her 'City of Refuge' ", (page 102). What might have been a place of refuge centuries ago would be no shelter for any in this day of modern warfare, and if we are supposed to know where it is, Satan certainly will, and there would be no difficulty in destroying her there. The place in the wilderness would simply seem to be her protection among the people of the world where she is helped. The woman has not only a place but also a provision, for she is "nourished". As Israel were fed with Manna during their journeying so the Lord will feed the woman. It will not be on a meagre ration program for to nourish is to fatten, to cherish with food, to pamper, rear (Strong). The time of her sojourn is for the whole period of the second half of the tribulation "time and times, and half a time". Again her complete preservation corresponds to that of the 144,000 in Ch 7.

The Flood and the Failure (vv. 15-16)

The Devil will make every attempt to destroy the woman, and here under the symbol of a flood he seeks to drown her. God who opened the Red Sea to deliver from Egypt now sees that "the earth opened her mouth, and swallowed up the flood". As much here is in symbolic language we cannot be sure what this flood represents, sufficient to know "the earth" helped her, is this those who offer protection, and will find a reward at the Judgement of Living Nations (Matt. 25:31-40)?

The Flight (v. 17)

Having been frustrated in his attempts to destroy the woman, the dragon now goes to "make war with the remnant of her seed". These are evidently those in Israel who are not destined for preservation during tribulation days, making a difference between the woman and the rest of Israel. These are the faithful, for they "keep the commandments of God", and to them is given the responsibility "of the testimony of Jesus Christ". His name will be owned and held by some during this time. God does not leave himself without a witness.

Chapter 13
The Two Wild Beasts

Introduction

We now have our attention turned to the two major vessels in the hand of Satan during the last period of the tribulation days. These are the men who will dominate the earth and subject humanity to the most dreadful apostasy that it has ever known. They will lead men in this final phase of Satanic workings to overthrow all that is of God, and bring men to worship the Devil, the first beast, and also the image raised to him (v. 15). At the same time openly opposing all that is of God, and persecuting a faithful remnant that will be overcome during this period. The two beasts rise from different places, which might indicate they are not of the same nationality, though they unite together in one devilish purpose. The first comes from the sea (v. 1), the second from the earth (v. 11).

The Coming Prince (vv. 1-10)

And I stood upon the sand of the sea, and saw a beast rise up out of the sea, having seven heads and ten horns, and upon his horns ten crowns, and upon his heads the name of blasphemy. And the beast which I saw was like unto a leopard, and his feet were as the feet of a bear, and his mouth as the mouth of a lion: and the dragon gave him his power, and his seat, and great authority. And I saw one of his heads as it were wounded to death; and his deadly wound was healed: and all the world wondered after the beast. And they worshipped the dragon which gave power unto the beast: and they worshipped the beast, saying, Who is like unto the beast? who is able to make war with him? And there was given unto him a mouth speaking great things and blasphemies; and power was given unto him to continue forty and two months. And he opened his mouth in blasphemy against God, to blaspheme his name, and his tabernacle, and them that dwell in heaven. And it was given unto him to make war with the saints, and to overcome them: and power was given him over all kindreds, and tongues, and nations. And all that dwell upon the earth shall worship him, whose names are not written in the book of life of the Lamb slain from the foundation of the world. If any man have an ear, let him hear. He that leadeth into captivity shall go into captivity: he that killeth with the sword must be killed with the sword. Here is the patience and the faith of the saints. (Revelation 13:1-10)

We are now introduced to "the prince that shall come" (Dan. 9:26). His people have trodden underfoot Jerusalem in Ch 11:1-2, now the prince of that people is set before the eyes of the saints, as John unveils to us the rise of the antichrist, the Man of Sin.

His Rise (v.1)

The text speaks of John standing upon the sand of the sea to witness the rise from the sea of the beast. Some manuscripts change the "I" to "he" and link this statement with 12:17, making it Satan who stands on the sand of the sea, but as no activity is involved by the one standing he is simply observing the events that are taking place, it matters not who is actually there. It is in keeping with John observing the events which take place from the various stand points of divine revelation, see Ch 1:9-20, Ch 4:1, Ch 17:1-3, Ch 21:9-10. Cohen says "Here as in almost all cases where there is a question about the exact text of a word or verse, the doctrinal difference is NIL (Revelation Visualised).

The beast is seen to, "rise up out of the sea". Here we have the fulfilment of Daniel Ch 7 where "the four winds of the heaven strove upon the great sea and four great beasts came up from the sea, diverse one from another".

(Vv. 2-3) Many expositors have missed the truth of this chapter, and these events, by referring this vision to that of Ch 2 of Daniel where we have Nebuchadnezzar's great image, saying that they are the same thing seen from different stand-points. In Ch 2 it is the time of the Gentiles seen from the human side, where the glory and splendour of humanity is seen, whereas Ch 7 is from God's point of view, the same period, but now seen as rapacious beasts, indicating the moral failure of humanity. This cannot be, for whereas in Ch 2 the kingdoms that are represented by the image are successive, in the vision of Ch 7 all the beasts are contemporaries, and when the last beast is "destroyed and given to the burning flame" (v. 11) the other three "had their dominion taken away: yet their lives were prolonged for a season and time" (v. 12). Also v. 17 emphasises the fact that these beasts "are four kings, which shall rise out of the earth", at this point in Daniel's life the Babylonish empire was all but finished. The vision is for the end time, to be fulfilled in tribulation days.

Now the vision of Daniel is coming to pass with the last beast of that chapter now rising to become the last ruler of "the times of the Gentiles". We have already seen the significance of the "seven heads and ten horns" in Ch 12 when linked with the Dragon, now they are displayed in this beast as he becomes the final head of Gentile dominion. Whereas in Ch 12 it is the heads that are crowned speaking of the seven great powers that rule the world in the purposes of God, here it is the horns that are crowned, for in its final form the ten kings associated with the beast will hold dominion under him. Many writers always turn to a federal Europe to find these horns as 10 kings, who are linked to a revived Roman Empire. But I can look no further than nations from the Middle East, who will come under the control of the Man of Sin.

His Rule (v. 2)

The beast is seen to be a mixture of those beasts that come up out of the sea in Daniel 7. Rising from the lawless heaving masses of humanity as Ch 17:15 shows the sea to be, rising from the Mediterranean region for that is what the

"Great Sea" speaks of. His dominant form is that of the leopard, the third beast in the vision of Daniel 7. The third kingdom in the image is Grecia, it would seem in the last days all the world powers that form the image of Daniel Ch 2 will be revived, so that all will fall together when the stone cut out without hands falls on the feet of the image. The leopard, swift in its movements, symbolising Greece, whose first king Alexander, rose from obscurity with great rapidity, so will the last, the beast of this chapter. Daniel 8 speaks of the last king to rule the earth rising from some aspect of Alexander's divided empire (Dan. 8:8-12). Thus it is not surprising to find the leopard as the dominant aspect of this beast. Yet encompassed within her rule will be the Medo-Persian, the bear treading all beneath its feet, and the Babylonish lion, where the voice of authority is paramount.

His rule is also seen to be empowered and inspired by Satan, as three things are given to him, "His power, and his seat (throne) and great authority". That which the Lord Jesus would not take when on the mount of temptation, there were no short cuts to kingdom glory for Christ. The Lord is prepared to wait his father's time who said "Ask of me and I shall give thee the heathen for thine inheritance" (Ps. 2:8). Nor could true kingdom glory be seen without the cross first taking place, making a righteous ground to remove the curse. This offer is taken from Satan, and we now see a man with all of Satan's power invested in him.

His Resurrection (vv. 3-4)

Here John sees "One of its heads as it were wounded to death". Some like Epp (page 205) tell us that this is only an imitation by the Devil of Christ's death and resurrection using the expression "as it were" as the basis for the argument, it not being so in reality. Others like Scott say of this, "here we have the political death and resurrection of the beast" (Page 273). They make this the demise of the Roman Empire, which ceased to exist around the year AD 476, but will be revived again under this beast. The language used in the verse is too strong to make it other than a literal act that takes places, and which is constantly referred to by John as he writes. The word wounded is (sphatto) meaning to butcher, of an animal for food or sacrifice. To slaughter, to maim violently (Strong). It is used of the Lord as "Lamb as it had been slain" (5:6-9, 12). Also of those that should "kill" one another (6:4), and of Cain when he "slew his brother" (1 John 3:12). The martyred saints are said to be "slain" also (6:9, 18:24). It seems to have the idea of a violent death; verse 14 would substantiate this where we are told his slaying was by a sword. The great point of the verse is that he becomes a resurrected man that causes the world to wonder, and exclaim in verse 4 "who is like unto the beast? Who is able to make war with him?" Men are powerless to destroy him. Later in verse 15 the false prophet is able to give life to an image. It is from this point he is known as the one who ascends out of the Abyss, causing some like Larkin and Strauss to link him with Judas raised from the dead, simply because Judas is said to be "The son of perdition (Jn. 17:12), others say he is a resurrected Nero. There is nothing in scripture to incline us to think that this is anything other than a man raised up for his own time. The wound takes place in the sight of men living at that time, as does the healing, this is not a resurrection of some past being, but of one who will be known at that time.

His resurrection produces what the Devil has always sought; worship, both for himself and the beast. The word used *(proskuneo)* occurs sixty times and is always used of worship, of God, idols, the Devil and the Man of Sin. It was refused by Peter in Acts 10:25, and by an angel from John in Ch 22:8-9, where John is told it should be for God alone.

The Devil's goal is now reached in the resurrection of this man causing the world to wonder and to worship.

His Rebellion (vv. 5-6)

The language of the beast is here pronounced. If blasphemy is linked with the heads of the beast, showing how the very governments that God allowed to hold responsibility for him rejected his authority and blasphemed his name, so now it is continued in an intensified form in this final head of Gentile dominion. The direction of his blasphemy is seen to be God, and his name, that is all that his name would stand for. Nothing of God will be tolerated. The blasphemy reaches even to those who in this present day form his dwelling place, the church, which is now in heaven. The tabernacle and those that dwell in heaven seem to be just one company, the conjunction "and" is by some authorities omitted, making this just one thing, and could be translated the "tabernacle even them which dwell in heaven". The reason for this enmity is because this is the time when he now, "shall cause the sacrifice and oblation to cease" (Dan. 9:27) and when, according to 2 Thess. 2:4, he "sitteth in the temple of God, showing himself that he is God". The Man of Sin will seek to remove all that is against his claim that he is God.

If his language is that of blasphemy, it is encouraging to know that there are limits to his blasphemy. He may be empowered by Satan, but he will only be allowed to continue for forty and two months by God, the time given to the last half of Daniel's seventieth week.

His Rampage and Reign (v.7)

His whole career is marked by woe. It is war that brings him to the fore, when "it devoured and brake in pieces, and stamped the residue with its feet" (Dan. 7:7). This refers to the other three beasts of the chapter and this shows how they come to be, in a subservient way, part of the beast now before us. He is also said to deal with three of the kings that will form this confederacy, for they are "plucked up by the roots" (Dan. 8:8), and "he shall subdue three kings" (v. 24). During his reign he will make a battle plan to destroy those who have been saved before his rise, the tribulation saints. These will seal their faith in blood for he will overcome them. He maintains his war-like character to the end, destroying Babylon also, as God puts it in their hearts to fulfil his will. This is done by his confederate kings, but no doubt at the instigation of the beast. Finally he raises himself "to make war against him that sat on the horse, and against his army" (19:19). This is his last act, for both he and his false prophet are at this point "cast alive into a lake of fire burning with brimstone".

His power seems to have international effect, reaching to be "over all kindred, and tongues and nations".

His Religious Pretensions (v. 8)

Again the scope of his operations is seen to be extensive when, "all that dwell upon the earth shall worship him". As many religions today have adherent's world wide, in the tribulation days no other religion will be tolerated. This will also be strengthened by God himself, who at this time sends the strong delusion upon the minds of men everywhere "that they should believe a lie: that they all might be damned" (2 Thess. 2:11-12). They would not receive the truth, the gospel of the kingdom, as God's efforts to bring men to repentance and salvation are rejected, and now in the midst of the tribulation human destiny is sealed. Those "whose names are not written in the book of life" will receive this delusion to damnation. This delusion will take place mid way through the tribulation at the entrance into the temple by the Man of Sin to proclaim himself God.

That there are differences over the translation of the words "whose names are not written in the book of the Lamb slain from the foundation of the world" is evident from the mass of material written upon it, and, having no ability in textual criticism, it hardly behoves me to pontificate in textual matters. That this statement divides the world is clear, appearance in the Lamb's book of life determines the destiny of humanity; by it men are saved or lost, see also Ch 20:15. Whether it is the names that are written from the foundation of the world (Darby) or it is Christ who is slain from the foundation (AV) matters little. What is important is that their names are written, and that is in virtue of having received Christ's death on their behalf. Certainly all God's dealings with men other than the saints of the church age, who are chosen in him "before the foundation of the world" (Eph. 1:4), all others are blessed "from" or "since the foundation of the world". The Lamb fore-ordained before the foundation of the world (1 Pet. 1:20) is the only one who can redeem, and his work at Calvary is certainly retrospective for it is "for the remission of sins that are past, through the forbearance of God" (Rom. 3:25). The preposition "from" is (*apo*), away from, since. The death of Christ was certainly in view then, even though it occurred some four thousand years later.

A few thoughts on the book of Daniel may help to give us something of the history of this coming prince. His geographical rise is taught in Ch 7, he is to rise from the area of the great sea, the Mediterranean. The following prophecy of Ch 8 brings before us his national rise. He is to come from some aspect of the Grecian empire, when it was divided unto his four generals, though the prophecy does not define which one. Then Daniel is told of his religious rise in connection with his, Daniel's people in Ch 9. The final great prophecy of Daniel covers Ch 10 - 12 and these speak of his actual rise from the Northern Kingdom of Seleucus, the Babylonish Kingdom. He is seen first of all as "a vile person" in verse 21. (Any who want to make this Antiochus

Epiphanes must look again at the history shown, and see how it relates to the Man of Sin). Then he is "the king" in verse 36; by this time a crown has been given him. Finally he is termed "The King of the North" in verse 40. This great chapter unfolds that the rise of the Man of Sin must be from Babylon.

Again a table will compare Christ and Antichrist.

The Lord Jesus Christ		**The Antichrist**	
1.	The Son of God	1.	The Son of Perdition
2.	Anointed of God	2.	Empowered by Satan
3.	Three and a half years ministry	3.	Three and a half years ministry
4.	Signs and wonders	4.	Signs and wonders
5.	Came from obscurity	5.	Came from obscurity
6.	Had a prophet	6.	Had a false prophet
7.	Died	7.	Died
8.	Rose	8.	Rose
9.	Many diadems	9.	10 diadems
10.	Has a bride	10.	Linked to Mother of Harlots
11.	Glory	11.	Lake of Fire

Responsibility to Hear (vv. 9-10)

When reading these verses, we must remember that this is a book to the seven churches (1:11) and, as there are calls in the messages to those churches to give heed to the voice of God, so here, even events that are future still have a bearing upon present day saints. We must remember that prophecy has a practical bearing upon His own, though this will have a very definite message for those who will be alive in the times before us, tribulation days.

Tatford seems to sum up the truth of verse 10 well, "At the same time, God announced the immutable law of retribution. The one who gathered others into captivity should himself become a captive, and the one who slew others with the sword should himself perish by the sword. For forty-two months evil might ride victoriously, and good might be enslaved. But God is not deaf to the cries of his people, and the oppressor must inevitably suffer in the end. In this assurance were the saints to possess themselves in patience, their faith rising undoubting to the faithful God (Prophecy's Last Word page 151).

There may be a warning to the believers of that day also not to resist as Peter sought to do in the garden, showing it will be pointless for them to take up the sword, for he who wields it will only end up slain by it.

The Coming Prophet (vv. 11-18)

And I beheld another beast coming up out of the earth; and he had two horns like a lamb, and he spake as a dragon. And he exerciseth all the power of the first beast before him, and causeth the earth and them which dwell therein to worship the first beast, whose deadly wound was healed. And he doeth great wonders, so that he maketh fire come down from heaven on the earth in the sight of men, And deceiveth them that dwell on the earth by the means of those miracles which he had power to do in the sight of the beast; saying to them that dwell on the earth, that they should make an image to the beast, which had the wound by a sword, and did live. And he had power to give life unto the image of the beast, that the image of the beast should both speak, and cause that as many as would not worship the image of the beast should be killed. And he causeth all, both small and great, rich and poor, free and bond, to receive a mark in their right hand, or in their foreheads: And that no man might buy or sell, save he that had the mark, or the name of the beast, or the number of his name. Here is wisdom. Let him that hath understanding count the number of the beast: for it is the number of a man; and his number is Six hundred threescore and six. (Revelation 13:11-18)

His Description (v. 11)

We are now brought to the second beast, later termed the false prophet (16:3, 19:20, 20:10). We shall see he is also rapacious like the first beast, and is equally evil, and will share the same fate. His origins are different; he is seen as "coming up out of the earth". If the sea would speak of tumultuous nations, the earth tells us he comes from what should have been the land rightly ordered by God, Israel. That his sphere of operation is in Israel and is directly linked with the image, being "the abomination that maketh desolate" (Dan. 9:27, 11:31, Matt. 24:15) seems fairly clear. That he is the one with whom the coming prince "confirms the covenant" (Dan. 9:27) and he with whom he makes a league (11:23), again points to the one in Israel who will promote the coming prince.

Unlike the first beast, he will be a Jew, he is called "the prince of the covenant" (Dan. 11:22), that is, he is responsible to hold for God and his people the covenant relationships. Many assume the first beast must also be a Jew for Israel to accept him, though it is evident at the Lord's crucifixion Israel will accept whoever suits them when they say "we have no king but Caesar" (John 19:15). This second beast is not acting as Messiah, he is not the Antichrist, but he is acting for the Messiah. He is responsible to prepare the nation for him. Sadly he will promote a false Christ when, "he causes the earth and them that dwell therein to worship the first beast, whose deadly wound was healed" (v. 12). He also feigns to bear the character of the lamb, when "he had two horns like a lamb", but there the similarity ends! There is nothing "lamb-like" about him, other than the horns, the symbol of power. That power, which ought to be held for God, is misused as he uses his mouth to manifest that he is of the dragon and his voice is satanic in character.

His Directives (v. 12)

There are great distinctions between the first and second beasts. The first beast is always getting, for everything is given to him. He is given "power and his seat and great authority" (v. 6), "a mouth speaking great swelling words", and "power to continue forty and two months" (v. 5), whilst in v. 7, "it was given to him to make war with the saints". It is as if he has no inherent powers or rights of his own. Whereas, in contrast to this, the second beast is always doing. Eight times over in this section the Greek word *(poiei)*, to do, is used in one of its forms. He comes out of the same mould as the first beast, he is "another" of the same kind *(allo),* but rather than receive honour, he is full of activity.

The first action he "does" is to show his **might** "exerciseth all the power of the first beast before him". Here we see two men who will demonstrate great power, this is delegated power, and it is derived from the dragon. If God gives power to his two witnesses (11:3), the dragon will give power to his servants. The second beast comes behind the first beast in nothing but authority.

His second action relates to his **ministry**, when he "causeth the earth and them that dwell therein to worship the first beast, whose deadly wound was healed". As the false prophet, he has a responsibility to promote his master, as John the Baptist pointed out Christ, so this one exalts the first beast. It is to be noticed that it is as a resurrected man that the first beast is worshipped, and here is where the trinity of evil is displayed, for on resurrection ground it is the Holy Spirit who makes much of the Lord Jesus. This beast is not called a prophet in this section, and it may be so that he could correspond to him of whom the Lord said "he shall not speak of himself; but whatsoever he shall hear that shall he speak" (John 16:13), and in verse 14 "he shall glorify me: for he shall receive of mine, and shall shew it unto you". Similarly, the ministry of the second beast is to make much of the first beast.

His Deception (vv. 13-15)

His third action is that "he doeth great wonders", he makes his impression by the **marvels** he does. The world will be filled with astonishment at his ability to bring down fire from heaven. It is a ministry of imitation like Jannes and Jambres who withstood Moses (2 Tim. 3:8), they also copying the miracles of Moses, so this man follows the workings of the two witnesses, who in Ch 11:5 bring out fire, but only in a protective way, "if any man hurt them". This creature will also imitate the actions of Elijah in 2 Kings 1:9-14 when he called down fire on the captains of fifty and their men. It is little wonder that, "such as do wickedly against the covenant shall He corrupt by flatteries" (Dan. 11:32). Though this relates to the first beast, nevertheless it can apply to the second with such displays of power being manifested.

His fourth action is that he "deceiveth them that dwell on the earth by means of those miracles which he had power to do in the sight of the beast". Thus his **miracles** will enhance his reputation, they are done in the presence of the first beast, as they are carried out to cause men to bow to Him. They are so effective that the Lord Jesus said regarding them that they "shall shew great signs and wonders; inasmuch that, if it were possible, they shall deceive the very elect" (Matt. 24:24). It must be pointed out that the word "wonder" in verse 13 is that for "sign". The Jews require a sign (1 Cor. 1:22), and the Lord said, "except ye see signs and wonders, ye will not believe" (John 4:48). They would not receive the Lord Jesus, but these lying wonders will turn the hearts of men to believe the lie.

The fifth thing he will do is to cause men to make an image to the beast. Here we have his **model**, that which is a pattern of the original (*ikon*), the word that is used of the Lord Jesus as "the image of God" (2 Cor. 4:4) or "who is the image of the invisible God" (Col. 1:15). Again it is the image of a resurrected man "which had the wound by a sword, and did live", much prominence is given to this fact in these verses. What is now rejected and mocked in relation to the Son of God will be extolled and venerated in this Son of Perdition.

In verse 15, we have the sixth thing he will do when he **motivates** this image, and brings it to life. Here is the amazing feature of the image. It is surprising that even modern expositors look at this image as, "that it may be no more than a robot" (Walvoord, The Revelation of Jesus Christ page 208), "or an electronic robot which is equipped with some type of speaking apparatus" (Cohen, Revelation Visualised). These things would not move men in this technological age. The amazing ability of man today to produce what they do at this time, means that what happens here is far beyond what is now considered normal. What man would love to do is to produce life, not merely to clone, which they have done, but to produce life in an inanimate object is beyond them. In spite of all attempts by scholars to get around the clear statements here, many insisting that this is only the appearance of life, the scriptures state, "He had power to give life". The word is *pneuma*, the word that is constantly used of the Spirit. If God allowed life to return to a dead man in the first beast, he now allows power (satanic) to be given to the second beast to animate an inanimate object. As God did this in the creation of Adam, so now spirit is imparted to this image causing it to speak. Men make this image and the false prophet animates it.

The seventh thing that is done, though this seems to originate from the image itself, is to inflict **murder** on those who will not bow in worship before it. The image in the plain of Dura required another to act to bring men into the fire (Dan. Ch 3); this image will act for itself! The conjunction "and" could refer this to the first clause of the sentence, giving not only power to the beast to give life to the image, but also to insist on the worship of it.

The Distinguishing Mark (vv. 16-18)

We now come to the eighth and last of the things that were done in this section, (seven, if not all eight, are the activities of the second beast), when men are compelled to receive a **mark**. It matters not what status they hold, or what substance they have, all, "small and great, rich and poor, free and bond", all will be required to receive the mark, either in their right hand or in their foreheads. This is a mark of subjection; the Lord puts the seal of ownership on his followers. The seal brings men to blessing; the mark brings men to death (14:9-11).

When the mark is in the hand or on the head, this gives ability to buy and sell. However one may interpret the place of the mark is of little consequence. Secret allegiance, the hand, or open allegiance, the head, the fact is that men have submitted to the beast for temporary needs. World markets will be controlled and shopping malls guarded. This day of electronic scanning will make it easy to control sales. The computerised technology, which is now so common, is pointing the way, and leading up to the events here prophesied.

Whether there are three things involved in the subjugation of the masses, or two, is a point for scholars to debate over. The received text as in our beloved authorised version makes it three things that men will have the option to take: (a) the mark, (b) the name of the beast, (c) the number of his name. Many textual critics leave out the first "or" making it to read, "he that had the mark, the name of the beast", in this way stamping upon humanity that which will always remind them of their god, for this is what he insists on being to them. Chapter 14:11 would seem to make the latter preferable when it says "and whosoever receiveth the mark of his name".

The number of his name has caused many to move in speculative folly, as they have sought to prove who this Man of Sin is. Knowing him to be a resurrected man, they assume he is a figure from past history that will rise again. The evil that marked him in his former life will again be set forth. Such are the diversities of names given, all it proves is that evil in the heart of man never changes, and at any time in human history these monsters of evil are continually being seen. By taking the letters of the Greek language and using them in their numerical form, many have pontificated who the Man of Sin is. We do well to leave these things alone.

Perhaps those who will pass through this period of tribulation, when wisdom from God will be given to the people that know their God, will be able to know the truth of verse 18. It is common knowledge that six is the number of man. He was created on the sixth day; he had six days in which to labour when he was set over the works of God. Man can never reach perfection or the divine number seven. Three is associated with what is of God. Perhaps the best we can do with this number is to see that all of man's efforts to rise to deity must always fall short of it. This final world emperor will prove, "that every imagination of the thoughts of his heart was only evil continually" (Gen. 6:5).

Chapter 14
The Wrongs rectified

Introduction

If Ch 11-13 bring before us events that will take place during the final 3½ years of the tribulation, this chapter brings before us the culminating events of that period. Seven scenes are brought before us, each relating to the bringing in of the kingdom, and the final judgements preceding that kingdom. The chapter is a chapter of voices, two voices from heaven (vv. 2-13), and five voices of angels (v. 7, v. 8, v. 9, v. 15 and v. 18). Though six angels are seen in these verses, making it the chapter of heaven's dealings with the earth after we have had three chapters of the events that relate to men. It has to do with the vindication of those who will have suffered during the period of Antichrist's reign, and the subjugation and destruction of those who oppressed them. It also brings before us the "firstfruits unto God" (vv. 1-5), the harvest (vv. 14-16) and the vintage (vv. 17-20).

The Vindication and Glorification (vv. 1-5)

And I looked, and, lo, a Lamb stood on the mount Sion, and with him an hundred forty and four thousand, having his Father's name written in their foreheads. And I heard a voice from heaven, as the voice of many waters, and as the voice of a great thunder: and I heard the voice of harpers harping with their harps: And they sung as it were a new song before the throne, and before the four beasts, and the elders: and no man could learn that song but the hundred and forty and four thousand, which were redeemed from the earth. These are they which were not defiled with women; for they are virgins. These are they which follow the Lamb whithersoever he goeth. These were redeemed from among men, being the firstfruits unto God and to the Lamb. And in their mouth was found no guile: for they are without fault before the throne of God. (Revelation 14:1-5)

Sion, a Scene on Earth (v. 1)

As John takes in the scene before him, all is different from what has gone before, the tribulation is over and a glorious kingdom is now the sight that fills his gaze. The Lord is seen on Mount Sion accompanied by the 144,000. How Scott can make these 144,000 from Judah, whilst those of Ch 7 are from Israel (Scott on Revelation page 291) is beyond our comprehension, and is without substantiation and must be rejected. Also beyond our comprehension is how others like Larkin can introduce heaven here and say "Mount Zion is not Mount Zion of the earthly Jerusalem but of the heavenly of which Paul speaks in Heb 12:22-23". Those of Heb 12 are believers of this present day, and it is the present experience of saints. This is the future glory and kingdom blessing for those who have passed through the tribulation. Those who were preserved during the tribulation, and sealed from Israel so that nothing could hurt them, they were the object of Satan's attack in Ch 12, but now God is vindicated as those who received his name on their foreheads (this unfolds what the seal was in Ch 7) are now seen with the Lamb in the place of his glory, Sion.

Sion is seen to be the capital city from which our Lord reigns. In Psalm 48:2, it is "the city of the great King". From here nations will be controlled as, "The Lord shall send the rod of thy strength out of Zion: rule thou in the midst of thine enemies", (Psalm 110:2). The king priest will reign with a rod of iron, as righteousness is seen in the earth. It is the place **chosen** by the Lord, "the Lord hath chosen Zion, he hath desired it for his habitation" (Psalm 132:13), his King will be **crowned** there (Psalm 2:6). Zion became the "city of David" after it was won from the Jebusites by **conquest**. It is interesting to see how David's claims were mocked and ridiculed, as they implied that David could not even deal with "the blind and the lame" (2 Sam 5:6), just as they mocked our Lord's claims, "He saved others; himself he cannot save. If he be the King of Israel, let him now come down from the cross, and we will believe him" (Matt 27:42). He will come down in majestic splendour, and take his rightful place on the "holy hill of Zion" (Psalm 2:6). He will not be alone, for in close association and in intimate fellowship will stand the 144,000.

The Singers, A Song from Heaven (vv. 2-3)

As in Ch 5 when the Lord Jesus takes the book a song is raised, so now on his glorification on Mount Sion heaven cannot be silent. The song is said to be "from" (*ek*) heaven, coming with vigour, "as the sound of many waters", and volume "as the voice of great thunder". This song could be that of the victors of Ch 15:2. It is evidently not sung by the heavenly host as it is in Ch 5, for here it is sung "before the four beasts and elders" not by them. The song is of value only to the 144,000, for they alone can learn it. This is the second of three songs in the book, the first is raised as a testimony to the redemption accomplished by the Lamb (5:9-10). Now it is on account of the preservation of the 144,000. Further we have the song of Moses the servant of God, and the song of the Lamb (15:3). This is sung by tribulation saints and is a song that testifies of their deliverance. The song of Moses was raised when the Children of Israel had crossed the Red Sea, and saw their enemies dead on the seashore.

The Subjects of the Song (vv. 4-5)

There are a number of things said about the 144,000 in vv. 1-5. The **place** they occupy is seen in v. 1, as they stand with the Lamb on Mount Sion. Their **purchase** is emphasised both in v. 3, where they are seen "redeemed from the earth" and in v. 4 where "these were redeemed from among men", they cannot be linked to Christ other than on redemption ground with the purchase price paid in blood. Further their **purity** is described; one would believe that it is doctrinal purity that marks them. The whore of Ch 17:2 has affected both kings and the inhabitants of the earth and, along with her children, has lead many to defile themselves doctrinally. Then we are introduced to their **pursuit**, nothing can turn them aside, they have undivided love and affection for the Lamb as they "follow the Lamb whithersoever he goeth". Christ is all to them, nothing can turn them from him. Their **privilege** is underlined when they are described as "the firstfruits unto God and to the Lamb". Firstfruits are ever a guarantee that a harvest is to follow; they are invariably given to God as an appreciation of his blessing, such was the feast of firstfruits (Lev. 23:10-12). These are a guarantee that all the redeemed of Israel will stand in the Kingdom with our Lord Jesus Christ. The word firstfruits is used of the Lord Jesus in resurrection (1 Cor. 15:20-23), and in itself stands for the fact that all who are Christ's will rise with him. They will not all rise at the same time, but "every man in his own order", that is, they will rise at the time appointed by God, when they shall come into their particular sphere of blessing. The saints of this dispensation, the Church, are said to be those "which have the firstfruits of the Spirit" (Rom. 8:23), telling us that others will receive the Holy Spirit in a future day at the fulfilment of the prophecy of Joel 2:28-29, when all will receive the Spirit of God at the outset of millennial days.

Finally in v. 5 their **perfection** is stated, there is no deceit in their tongue, and no defect in their person. They are made like their Lord of whom it is written, "neither was guile found in his mouth" (1 Pet. 2:22), and again "as of a lamb without blemish (fault)" (1 Pet. 1:19). This is the prospect of all the redeemed, the work of Calvary puts us "faultless before the presence of his glory with exceeding joy" (Jude 24).

The Proclamation of the Angel (vv. 6-7)

And I saw another angel fly in the midst of heaven, having the everlasting gospel to preach unto them that dwell on the earth, and to every nation, and kindred, and tongue, and people, Saying with a loud voice, Fear God, and give glory to him; for the hour of his judgment is come: and worship him that made heaven, and earth, and the sea, and the fountains of waters. (Revelation 14:6-7)

The Movement of the Angel (v. 6)

The former verses, like others in the book, allow us to see the end before it is reached; God's purpose is sure and will be fulfilled. Once again we are now introduced to events that precede the kingdom, as we are told of the things that will occur at the close of the tribulation, the end of the last 3½ years of that period.

This is the first of five angel voices, and his movements like those of the angel of Ch 9:13, are "in the midst of heaven". The other angels follow but we are not told if they also fly in this realm. His flight would indicate the sphere of the angel's work, for his ministry follows his movement.

The Ministry of the Angel (v. 6)

This is to bring the "everlasting gospel" to "them that dwell on the earth, and to every nation, and kindred, and tongue and people". This gospel is for the world, like that of Matt. 28:19-20. Some have sought to limit this gospel, and even though the term gospel has the idea of good news, they propound that there is no good news here; it is a message of judgement. But does the gospel differ? Flanigan states, "we must not fall into the snare of seeing different gospels. There is ever but one gospel in God's dealing with men; but the emphasis differs from one age to another" (Notes on Revelation page 85). This seems to be a true appraisal of what is here. Ottman links this gospel with the Old Testament message and seeks to make it a message of judgement and repentance, and states that the gospel of "salvation by faith through Christ, with a corresponding heavenly inheritance, is not found in this proclamation of the angel, nor is it, except in veiled speech, found anywhere in the Old Testament." (Unfolding of the Ages page 143). Yet this is a contradiction of 1 Pet. 1:10-12, and in opposition to the fact that, "the scripture, foreseeing that God would justify the heathen through faith, preached before the gospel unto Abraham, saying, In thee shall all nations be blessed" (Gal. 3:8). That Abraham was justified by faith is the whole subject of Romans 4. Abraham also looked for "heavenly things" (Heb. 11:16) though he was not looking for heaven but that which was characterised by it. Does not the gospel of the grace of God carry a message of judgement? Rom. 1:17; 2:16; Acts 10:42; 17:31 are but samples of numerous verses that could be brought to prove the case. It is also a message that calls for repentance, for without that there is no salvation (Acts 17:30, 20:21, 26:21). Again much emphasis is placed on the fact that it is an angel who carries this gospel, and we are told by wise men that no angel can preach the gospel of the grace of God for that is given to men alone. They quote Acts 10 to substantiate their claims, when the angel appeared to Cornelius and said "call for one Simon whose surname is Peter" (v. 5), "he shall tell thee what thou oughtest to do" (v. 6). This was not because the angel could not preach the gospel, but because to Peter had been given the "keys of the kingdom", and it was his responsibility to open the door to the Gentiles here, as to the Jews in Ch 2.

Seiss says the reason angels do not preach today but will in this future dispensation is because "it is no longer the meek and entreating voice, beseeching men to be reconciled to God, but a great thunder from the sky, demanding of the nations to fear God" (Lecture 34 page 355). We do not see how this can be reconciled with Acts 17:30, which Paul proclaimed, saying of God's requirements "but now commandeth all men everywhere to repent" or again the truth expressed in Rom. 1:18, "for the wrath of God is revealed from heaven against all ungodliness and unrighteous of men, who hold the truth in unrighteousness". These are terms linked to the "meek and entreating gospel". We in our day must proclaim that which the angel in a former day cried when he said, "escape thou for thy life" (Gen. 19:17), or the words of John the Baptist who said "O generation of vipers, who hath warned thee to flee from the wrath to come?" The message of John 3:36 carries the same weight, when a warning is raised to the unbeliever that, "he that believeth not the Son shall not see life; but the wrath of God abideth on Him." In every age and dispensation the gospel carries a warning note, whoever proclaims it. Ottman links the everlasting gospel with the gospel of the kingdom, which is "once more taken up and proclaimed as John the Baptist proclaimed it" (page 346), yet tries to make a difference with that of the angels to the shepherds which was "fear not" rather than "fear God". The message of the angels belonged to the same gospel that John preached. Again what a beautiful gospel they did preach! I would that every preacher would proclaim as clearly and plainly the lovely message of Luke 2:10. Angels can preach the gospel, it is just not given to them in this day, rather they are said to "desire to look into" the gospel now preached (1 Pet. 1:12), and they rejoice over sinners repenting (Luke 15:7, 10). Their business in this age is not proclamation, but observation. In Tribulation Days angelic ministry to the earth will be restored.

The everlasting gospel simply tells of God's desire to bring before men the need to "prepare to meet thy God". The gospel of the kingdom speaks of the destiny the gospel brings us to, and was the message of every preacher in the book of the Acts and Paul's final word in Ch 28:23-31. The gospel of the grace of God, to which there is just one reference (Acts 20:24), tells of what brings us to blessing, grace. The gospel of God (Rom. 1:1) speaks of its source, the gospel of Christ, (1 Cor. 9:12) and the gospel of His Son (Rom. 1:9), relate to the theme and originator of the gospel. The gospel of peace (Eph. 6:15) tells of the precious results of the gospel. There is only one gospel, though described in different ways.

The Message of the Angel (v. 7)

The message is clear and plain. With the hour of his judgement before them, men must "fear God", for this is the beginning of wisdom. "The hour of his judgement" would seem to point to the outpouring of the wrath of God in the vial judgements of Ch 16. His creatorial rights have been set aside, men are not only responsible to receive the gospel, but, as we were created for his pleasure (4:11), men have no right to set aside God's creation rights as they do in Romans 1:19-32. This last verse declares how the judgement of God will fall on those who "commit such things". It is the same message that this angel proclaims. The spheres of creation mentioned are those that, along with men, experience the wrath of God (16:1-6).

The Declaration of Another Angel (v. 8)

And there followed another angel, saying, Babylon is fallen, is fallen, that great city, because she made all nations drink of the wine of the wrath of her fornication. (Revelation 14:8)

Another angel is seen, though his position is not stated, but his message is clear, it is obviously in anticipation of the events that take place in Ch 17-18, where a vivid description of Babylon's fall is penned. The identical expression is used in 18:2; the double use of "fallen" would speak of the utter ruin it has known. This is the first mention of Babylon in the Revelation and linked with it the phrase "that great city". We shall see it is a literal city, and a literal Babylon that is meant. If her ruin is described, the reason is also told, as all nations did drink the wine of her fornication. The sin here is not physical but doctrinal, and the wine would relate to the pleasure men had in receiving the false doctrines she propounded.

Chapter 14 - The Wrongs rectified

The Denunciation by a Third Angel (vv. 9-13)

And the third angel followed them, saying with a loud voice, If any man worship the beast and his image, and receive his mark in his forehead, or in his hand, The same shall drink of the wine of the wrath of God, which is poured out without mixture into the cup of his indignation; and he shall be tormented with fire and brimstone in the presence of the holy angels, and in the presence of the Lamb: And the smoke of their torment ascendeth up for ever and ever: and they have no rest day nor night, who worship the beast and his image, and whosoever receiveth the mark of his name. Here is the patience of the saints: here are they that keep the commandments of God, and the faith of Jesus. And I heard a voice from heaven saying unto me, Write, Blessed are the dead which die in the Lord from henceforth: Yea, saith the Spirit, that they may rest from their labours; and their works do follow them. (Revelation 14:9-13)

The Doomed (v. 9)

In this cry of the third angel, the Lord makes clear what lies before those who have worshipped the beast and his image, and receive his mark in their forehead or in their hand.

The tense used for worship here is that which means it has been over a period of time, and is presently continuing. These are doomed to the judgement of God, which is twofold:

(a) Their Drink (v. 10) - this seems to speak of what they shall have to endure in life, "the wine of the wrath of God". This is the outpouring of the vial judgements in Ch 16, where the fifth angel specifically pours out his vial upon the seat of the beast. The wrath of God will not be tempered with mercy; it is undiluted in its mixture.

(b) Their Destiny (v. 10) - the word declares not only judgement in life, but also in death. The end of those who worship the beast is seen to be that of torment, the place of their pains makes it quite clear that it is not on the earth, and as "fire and brimstone" are part of the "second death" (21:8) and are linked with the lake of fire, this must relate to their final end, and must be in their bodies also, for the eternal end of the lost is for "soul and body" (Matt. 10:28). It is evident that this judgement will be appreciated both by holy angels, and by the Lamb, for it is in their presence. As the 144,000 enjoy the bliss of being "before the throne of God" (v. 5), so these will know with grief all they have missed, as the Lord said of the lost in Luke 13:28, "There shall be weeping and gnashing of teeth, when ye shall see Abraham, and Isaac and Jacob, and all the prophets, in the Kingdom of God and you yourselves thrust out". How any can refuse to believe in eternal conscious punishment for the lost, as some leading evangelical teachers of our day do, is beyond me.

The Duration (v. 11)

This verse lays further stress on the extent of their punishment when it says "And the smoke of their torment ascendeth up for ever and ever, and they have no rest day nor night". The words are plain, easy to be understood, and unmistakable. Yet Farrar in a former day wrote a treatise called "Eternal Hope", which sought to deny it on the grounds of God's love, and all intelligent reason. Human reasoning must bow to the divine record, and that God should love us is a mystery, that he does love us should be a magnet drawing us to himself. These have rejected his love, and leave God with no other course but to judge them. God cannot be charged with being unjust, he has written all in very clear tones, and his appeal in the gospel is for all to repent and believe in his Son for salvation, the blessing of eternal life is provided for all who believe. Some would seek to teach annihilation as a hope for the lost. Would men not be better believing God's word and teaching others the plain statements of scripture that souls might avail themselves of God's salvation? Jukes also wrote a book "The Restoration of all Things" (Farrar admits to being influenced by it), wherein he proclaims that all, Devil, fallen angel, evil spirit, and man will one day be restored as a result of Calvary. He uses as his premise Acts 3:21, "the restoration of all things", which speaks of the recovery to be enjoyed in a millennial scene, and does not deal with wicked unbelieving men. There are so many who teach the scriptures who will not believe God and plunge on in their folly, teaching doctrines of devils (1 Tim. 4:1) and damning souls they instruct. Some notable evangelical teachers of our day proclaim the same sad theories.

The Devotees

The section begins and ends the same, making it very clear who are the people who are going to endure the judgement of God. The verses are of course only dealing with those who will, during the tribulation, refuse the message of God's salvation, which leads the multitudes of Ch 7 to faith, and as a result leave themselves no option but to receive the alternative, which is the worship the beast and his image, and receive the mark of his name.

The Delivered (vv. 12-13)

What a contrast now with that which has gone before, when the wicked burn as an oven (Mal. 4:1)! There is a blessedness pronounced upon the faithful, who endured persecution during the days of the beast. The fruit of their patience is now seen. The word patience has the thought of endurance, and during the last half of the tribulation these have been called upon to endure much persecution, but now the prospect of blessing is to be enjoyed. It would seem to be the Holy Spirit himself who speaks from heaven and calls John to write. The enmity of the Man of Sin simply causes them to enjoy the blessedness of rest, rest from their trouble, lament, or beating their breasts in sorrow, for such is the meaning of "their labours". The anguish of bitter persecution is over, and this will not be without its reward for "their works do follow them". This can only be in the sense of receiving praise as the Lord values their steadfastness in the midst of bitter enmity. These would seem to be the saints spoken of in Matt. 24:13, "but he that shall endure unto the end, the same shall be saved".

The Harvest and The Vintage (vv. 14-20)

And I looked, and behold a white cloud, and upon the cloud one sat like unto the Son of man, having on his head a golden crown, and in his hand a sharp sickle. And another angel came out of the temple, crying with a loud voice to him that sat on the cloud, Thrust in thy sickle, and reap: for the time is come for thee to reap; for the harvest of the earth is ripe. And he that sat on the cloud thrust in his sickle on the earth; and the earth was reaped. And another angel came out of the temple which is in heaven, he also having a sharp sickle. And another angel came out from the altar, which had power over fire; and cried with a loud cry to him that had the sharp sickle, saying, Thrust in thy sharp sickle, and gather the clusters of the vine of the earth; for her grapes are fully ripe. And the angel thrust in his sickle into the earth, and gathered the vine of the earth, and cast it into the great winepress of the wrath of God. And the winepress was trodden without the city, and blood came out of the winepress, even unto the horse bridles, by the space of a thousand and six hundred furlongs. (Revelation 14:14-20)

There is a great similarity between the two scenes that are now brought before us. The chapter begins with companions for Christ in the vision of the firstfruits (vv. 1-5). We are now confronted with a crisis for sinners in these visions of the Harvest (vv. 14-16), and the Vintage (vv. 17-20).

We now have the last three of seven proclamations from heaven recorded from v. 6. As in all sevens in scripture, they divide into a four and a three. Four are calls to the world (vv. 6-13), the last three speak of the calamities which befall men because there is little or no response from the world. The first four voices again follow a scriptural pattern, in which every four divides, into a three and a one. The first three messages (v. 6, v. 8, v. 9) are messages of warning; the last is a message of encouragement to the blessed dead. Again the first three are specifically said to be angels, whereas the last voice of v. 13, is simply said to be "a voice from heaven".

That there are differences of opinion regarding the interpretation of these scenes is apparent as one reads various expositions, so we cannot approach these verses with dogmatism, but I trust as with all scripture, with carefulness, and setting forth what one sees as the Spirit's teaching.

Ottman after a lengthy debate (Unfolding of the Ages pages 351-353) begins by saying "A clear distinction between these must be maintained if we are to understand what is before us", and ends stating "it is therefore a judgement of the Gentiles. Such is certainly the harvest of the earth, and may be the harvest referred to in our passage in Revelation. In the vision of the vintage, we have before us what is characteristic of Israel, rather than the Gentiles". On the other hand, John Phillips (Exploring Revelation page 195) says "The

Its Final Brevity (v. 16)

The judgement in the end times will come with great rapidity. This is the thought behind the expression "as it was in the days of Noah" (Luke 17:26), where it is not so much the character that will mark those days, but the rapidity with which the flood came. "They knew not until the flood came, and took them all away; so shall also the coming of the Son of Man be" (Matt. 24:39). The judgement is again linked with the Son of Man. Here the thrusting in of the sickle carries the same idea.

Retribution (vv. 17 - 20)

Seiss draws attention to the fact that, "evil has its harvest as well as good" (The Apocalypse page 359). In neither of these scenes does there seem to be any thought of the preservation of the just, both seem to deal with the destruction of the wicked. These present verses leave no doubt that it is the treading down of those who have opposed God and all his claims upon them, this may be the reason why we have:

The Source of Visitation (v. 17)

This is said to be by another angel who "came out of the temple which is in heaven", not the earthly temple at Jerusalem, for the Man of Sin has not yet been deposed, and he sits as God there. Both the temple and the altar must be those in heaven. From the temple the Lord directs the angel to fulfil his will, and with the angel that comes from the altar, we remember from Ch 8:3 that it is here where the prayers of saints are presented before the throne. God is about to vindicate his own name, and that of those who love him, who have been trodden underfoot by a merciless world, who must now reap what they have sown.

The Stripping of the Vine (v. 18)

Three figures are used in the word of God to describe those with whom God has dealings.

Israel are always seen as "His Vineyard" (Isaiah 5:1), in which was planted "the choicest vine". The vineyard would speak of Israel separated from the world. God hedged Israel in to himself, through divine revelation. The law and its ordinances separated Israel from the nations, and made them unique among the nations. Rom. 9:4-5 tells of the privilege that Israel knew as God hedged them about, a privilege that Gentiles were devoid of (Eph. 2:11-12).

Yet, for every privilege that God gave to them, the sad history of this vine is seen in many scriptures where they are seen to be wanting. I place a table that chronicles the failure that marked them as a fruitless nation:

Deut 32:32	They are wicked
Psalm 80:8-19	They are wretched
Isaiah 5:4	They became wild (see also Jer. 2:21)

Hosea 10:1	They are wanting
Matt 21:33-46	They are wilful

It is because of their wilfulness that Israel are set aside, and another figure is introduced, that of the vine and the branches (John 15). During this present age, this is how believers are seen as they are linked to Christ. There is no vineyard during the present church age; we are not controlled by the law and its ordinances (Israel was a sheepfold, we are a flock, the same principle of liberty is linked with the present dispensation). Nor does the Lord "let it out to husbandmen", (Matt. 21:33) these, the religious leaders who were responsible to God for the nation's spiritual well being failed in the ministry given to them. The father is now the husbandman; he will not let it out again to those who could fail to produce fruit for God.

This leads us to the third figure, "The vine of the earth". Here we have the nations of men who are taken up with the earth and have no regard for God. They are fully ripe; wickedness marks them to the full. God can do no more with them but bring them to the winepress for judgement.

The Subjects of Vengeance (v. 19)

As we have seen, these are again termed "the vine of the earth". The angel gathers them into the winepress. The fury of God is going to be unleashed and men are to feel the full weight of it, as he is to tread them beneath his feet. Men have despised God's claims and those of his Son; having trodden him under their feet (Heb. 10:29) they must now reap what they have sown (Gal. 6:7).

The Scene of the Violence (v. 20)

We are told the winepress is "without the city". It is evident that this is the same scene as that recorded in Isaiah 63:1-6, where the Lord is seen as coming from Edom "with dyed garments from Bozrah". Verse 3 gives a graphic description of how the garments are dyed. "I have trodden the winepress alone, and of the people there was none with me; for I will tread them in mine anger, and trample them in my fury; and their blood shall be sprinkled on my garments, and I will stain all my raiment". Bozrah was the capital city of Edom, a city of great antiquity, mentioned as early as Gen. 36:33, when it produced Jobab who took up the monarchy of Edom. It was another Edomite who was on the throne - Herod - when the Lord Jesus was born, and the final rejection of the Lord took place "without the city". Thus linking Isaiah with Revelation we see that the future judgement of this world is because of the rejection of the Son of God from his birth to his death.

It is fitting that the treading takes place outside the city where they crucified Christ.

The Slaughter is Vast

By depicting the height and length to which the blood flows, "unto the horses bridles, by the space of a thousand and six hundred furlongs", we see the immense slaughter envisaged at this time. It is said the distance covers from Dan in the north to Beersheba in the south. Thus the length of the land will see the evidence of the wrath of God as he summons men to feel it. There is no escape for any; it is an angel does the reaping. In Ezekiel 38, when Gog and Magog are brought to the slaughter, it is said in verse 4 that, God will "put hooks into thy jaws, and I will bring thee forth, and all thine army, horses and horsemen". The flesh hooks could speak of the fact that Gog and Magog have no desire to come, but God controls the events, and they will be there for the slaughter. The whole scene reflects Armageddon (The Hill of Slaughter) of Ch 16:16. This is the last great judgement of God. Such a scene should exercise our hearts to reach out to the lost, as we realise the awesome fate awaiting them.

Note: Some believe that Ezekiel Ch 38-39 takes place in the middle of the tribulation, causing the Man of Sin to be content that he has not got them to deal with. I find this interpretation difficult, as many things stated in Ch 39 could hardly take place in the last three and a half years, as the burning of the weapons of war lasts for 7 years. The sacrifice for the feathered fowl (vv. 17-20) is plainly that of Revelation Ch 19 vv. 17-18, which occurs at the return of the Lord to the earth. Also it is a time when God "will set your glory among the heathen" (v. 21). The fact that "the house of Israel shall know that I am the Lord their God from that day and forward" (v. 22) can only put Ezekiel Ch 38-39 at the end of tribulation days.

Chapter 15
The Preparation of the vials

Introduction

This chapter introduces the final judgement of God in tribulation days. It is the conclusion of the second vision, which began in Ch 4 and ends in Ch 16. The tribulation period began with the "wrath of the Lamb" (6:16), it ends with "the wrath of God" (15:1; 16:1). This wrath is seen as seven plagues, which seem to be the contents of the seven vials or bowls, though this is assumed but not stated, for the angels are said to have the plagues (v. 1), but they are given the bowls (v. 7). The setting for the final outpouring of God's wrath is the subject of Ch 15, with the stream of vengeance poured out being that of Ch 16. In Ch 15 we have the preparation for the punishment of Ch 16.

This chapter is divided into two sections. In vv. 1-4 we have a **triumphant song** and from vv. 5-8 there is a **temple scene**. In the former we have the **joy of the saints,** in the latter the **judgement of sinners.**

The Triumphant Song (vv. 1-4)

And I saw another sign in heaven, great and marvellous, seven angels having the seven last plagues; for in them is filled up the wrath of God. And I saw as it were a sea of glass mingled with fire: and them that had gotten the victory over the beast, and over his image, and over his mark, and over the number of his name, stand on the sea of glass, having the harps of God. And they sing the song of Moses the servant of God, and the song of the Lamb, saying, Great and marvellous are thy works, Lord God Almighty; just and true are thy ways, thou King of saints. Who shall not fear thee, O Lord, and glorify thy name? For thou only art holy: for all nations shall come and worship before thee; for thy judgments are made manifest. (Revelation 15:1-4)

The Sign in Heaven (v. 1)

Again John has a sight of the activity that takes place in heaven as preparation is made for the outpouring of the bowl (vial) judgements. He saw "another sign in heaven, great and marvellous". Of the seven signs in the book of Revelation, only three are seen to be "in heaven". They are **The Woman's Majesty** (Ch 12:1), **Satan's Malignity** (Ch 12:3) and here, where we have **the Angel's Ministry**. The four remaining signs are linked with the false prophet, (13:13, 13:14, 19:20) and with "the spirits of devils" (16:14). The divine principle of dividing sevens into a four and a three is again seen. Three signs with heaven, and four signs demonstrated by satanic power.

This great and marvellous sign reveals seven angels having the seven last plagues. These are the final judgements that God is going to bring upon the earth and particularly upon the seat of the beast, Babylon.

The thought of "in them is filled the wrath of God" is that of bringing them to the finish. The word used, *teleo,* (Wigrams) is linked with the cry of the Lord Jesus in John 19:30 when he said, "it is finished", where we have a finished work of redemption. Now it is a finished work of judgement that is before us.

The Sea of Glass and the Standing Multitude (v. 2)

We were introduced to the sea of glass in Ch 4, where it was seen in relation to Christ's coronation, now is added to it "mingled with fire", for here we have the saints who conquered. In Ch 4, the purity of heaven is predominant, whilst here, the fire would seem to allude to God's vindication of his suffering saints. Heaven is prepared to judge the world for its maltreatment of these who have "gotten the victory".

They have gotten the victory because they have endured to the end (Matt. 24:13). The oppression of the Man of Sin has not caused them to yield to his image, his mark, or the number of his name. These are evidently of the vast multitude of Ch 7:9-17, and those of Ch 14:13 who suffered at his hand.

As they stand upon the sea, they have the harps of God in their hand. In Ch 5:8, it is the four beasts and four and twenty elders who have the harps. Though their song is to the Lamb, it is on account of the redemption of the saints of this present dispensation, the Church. In Ch 14:2 we are not told who the singers are, it is not those of Ch 5:8, for the song is "before the four beasts and the elders", and it is a song only the 144,000 can learn. The present song seems to be sung simply for the Lord's pleasure, but it is by the tribulation martyrs. They are rejoicing after their trial is over. I suppose they must have endured much sorrow during their stand against the Antichrist, often wondering where it would all lead to. Now their sorrows are over, and their sufferings have led them into heaven's courts. Now they can see the hand of God in every circumstance, and their lips and harps cannot be silent.

The Song of the Saints (vv. 3-4)

It is evident that joy fills the heart of these victors, their troubles are over, they stand because of the goodness of God to them through all their adversity, therefore they must raise their voice in praise unto Him. Their song is that of "Moses the servant of God and the song of the Lamb". Many suppose that the song of Moses is either that of Exodus 15 or Deuteronomy 32. The song is quite clearly neither, for we are given its theme here in these two verses. Their praise follows that of Moses, who sang when the power of God had been demonstrated in the deliverance of the prisoners (Ex. 15), and the preservation of the pilgrims (Deut. 32). These triumphant sufferers are also seen as "servants" (Ch 7:15), they also must sing as they recall God's goodness. Their song also follows that of the Lamb. His song is spoken of in Heb. 2:12, this is sung when the Lord comes into his possessions in that great millennial day, which will be the fruit of his sufferings at Calvary (Heb. 2:9). There again, as in the songs of Moses, it will be praise to God for "in the midst of the Church will I sing praise unto thee". Every song is unto God, and is sung when victory from adversity is secured.

The song is fourfold in character when it glorifies God for:

1. His Works - "Great and marvellous are thy works, Lord God almighty";
2. His Ways - "Just and true are thy ways thou King of Saints" (nations or ages, King James margin);
3. His Worth - "who shall not fear thee O Lord and glorify thy name? For thou only art holy";
4. His Worship - "for all nations shall come and worship before thee; for thy judgements are manifest".

Much could be said of the song as it relates the goodness of God, who brought them through their great tribulation under the Man of Sin. It is enough for the purpose of this writing to see how the song emphasises the glories and virtues of God.

1st - His deity is expressed — He is the "Lord God Almighty".
2nd - His monarchy is noted — He is the "King of Nations".
3rd - His purity is seen, for it is said — "Thou only art holy".
4th - His authority is marked — "Thy judgements are manifest".

How precious these victors find the Lord as they stand in his presence! In their sufferings here, the Man of Sin had sought all these for himself, whilst now they are full of praise, and desire to see the God who delivered them glorified in all his creation.

The Temple Scene (vv. 5-7)

And after that I looked, and, behold, the temple of the tabernacle of the testimony in heaven was opened: And the seven angels came out of the temple, having the seven plagues, clothed in pure and white linen, and having their breasts girded with golden girdles. And one of the four beasts gave unto the seven angels seven golden vials full of the wrath of God, who liveth for ever and ever. (Revelation 15:5-7)

The Sanctuary Opened (v. 5)

As we have seen earlier in the book, there are definite overtones of the tabernacle in the Book of Revelation. This is not surprising, when we are given such an insight of the glories of heaven throughout the book. The tabernacle was but a type of what is in heaven, and Moses was given a glimpse of this in Exodus 25:9. The seven Churches are set against the background of the lampstand. The trumpet judgements are set against the altar of incense. Now we are to see the vials poured out against the background of the holy of holies. The temple is the *naos*, the inner sanctuary, and God's dwelling place.

The expression "after that" (*meta tauta*) sets before us another vision, though it is very closely linked with what has gone before. Here we see the inner sanctuary opened and it allows us to see angels who are linked with the final judgement of God coming forth. Are these associated with the presence of God at all times, or were they in the sanctuary only to receive the authority to fulfil God's will? The High Priest was only able to enter the most holy on the day of atonement, and only then to do the work for atonement. When he came out it was not to bring judgement upon the people, but these angels are coming forth with plagues in their hands.

The Seven Angels (v. 6)

The angels are evidently those of v. 1, they are said to have in their possession "the seven plagues". These are not specified, but in some way they seem to become the contents later of the bowls given to them. John is drawn to the attire of the angels, and is struck by their garments and their girdles.

The garments would emphasise the purity that is ever linked with angels, the thought behind the word pure is that of cleanness, it is the word used of the linen that Joseph of Arimathea wrapped the Lord's body in: "clean linen". The whiteness struck John and must have appealed to him again as he remembers the garment they arrayed the Lord in at his trial, the "gorgeous robe" of Luke 23:11. Again it is evidently linked with angelic dress, for the angel of Acts 10:30, who appeared to Cornelius, was also in "bright clothing", the same word as here.

The girdle would tell of the power invested in them. Like the Lord Jesus as he stands to judge the seven churches (1:13), they also have a golden girdle, as they prepare to pour out God's judgement on the earth.

The Seven Vials (v. 7)

One of the four living ones who was instrumental in inaugurating the judgements at the commencement of the tribulation, the seven seals, is now associated with the closing judgements, when he gives the seven golden vials to the seven angels. The word "vial" is properly "bowl", this is to indicate the rapid, local and condensed form the judgements will take, as the final fury of God is unleashed. That these judgements all associated with one who is "just and true" (v. 3), and that they come from the inner temple prove that God is not acting in malice but it is the "judgement of God according to truth" (Rom. 2:2). Men reap what they sow, and having refused every overture of God to lead them to repentance it is said of them, "after thy hardness and impenitent heart treasurest up unto thyself wrath against the day of wrath and revelation of the righteous judgement of God" (Rom. 2:5). That day has now arrived, and the activity of heaven is seen to bring it to pass.

God's enduring character is seen unto the ages of ages. His glory and dominion (1:6), his worship (4:10), his honour (7:12), his rule (11:15), these are all unto the ages of the ages.

It should be seen that the bowls of Ch 5:8 are full of odours, these are full of wrath. The former are for the pleasure of God, these are for the punishment of sinners.

Smoke in the Sanctuary (v. 8)

It is the glory and power of God that produces this smoke that fills the temple; the smoke is evidently produced by both of these. Such smoke, like the Shekinah, speaks of his presence and glory. Sinai saw this smoke (Ex. 19:8), causing men to stand back before it. Isaiah saw it also (6:4) and it caused him to cry, "woe is me". The smoke would indicate that God is acting in judgement and such is his indignation that no one is able to enter the sanctuary until the angels have finished their work. This work will be completed in the following chapter, when the bowls are poured out. The ministry of the angels in Ch 8, when they bring the trumpet judgements upon the world, begins with "the smoke of the incense" (v. 4), but here there is no thought of incense being linked with this smoke. Perhaps it is because the wrath of God is now being poured out in all its fury.

Chapter 16
The Pouring of the Bowls of wrath

Introduction

As we have seen, Ch 15 is the preparation for the scene set before us. The preparation of Heaven gives way to the pouring of the bowls of wrath upon the earth. This is the filling up of the judgement of God in relation to this world. We are now to see the results of the fourth great judgement in John's second vision. The seal judgements, the trumpet judgements and the unrevealed judgements of the seven thunders of Ch 10 have gone before. We now have recorded the final acts of God, which bring to a close tribulation days, and, with this series of seven, the closing of John's second vision that began in Ch 4. From Ch 17, we are introduced to John's third vision, which gives more detail of what is revealed here in relation to the beast and his kingdom. It also unveils the future glories of our Lord Jesus Christ that can be displayed when sin has been dealt with.

The Decree Sounded (v. 1) – The first bowl

And I heard a great voice out of the temple saying to the seven angels, Go your ways, and pour out the vials of the wrath of God upon the earth. (Revelation 16:1)

John hears "a great voice out of the temple". The voice is directed to the seven angels that they will go their way and fulfil the ministry given to them. Their mission is to pour out their bowls of wrath. The fury of God will be swift and concentrated during this period. It is evident from verses 2, 10, and 19 that these judgements will have a particular effect upon all that was associated with the beast and his kingdom. The voice that John heard would seem to be God's voice for 15:8 states that none can enter into the temple whilst it is filled with the smoke of his glory, and until the seven angels had done their work. The voice speaks again in v. 17, to say that all was done, the consummation of the judgements of God is reached, and all that remains is for the Lord Jesus to come forth in great power and glory.

The word great (*megales*) occurs eighty two times in the Revelation, and eleven times in this chapter. I notice it is frequently used of an angel's voice (loud), here of God's voice. Oftentimes one hears criticism of preachers who raise their voice to declare the gospel. A pity such critics do not read this book, and see how heaven makes known its message in no uncertain tones. Attention is drawn by Bullinger to the occurrences of the word in Ch 16-18 and he says, "We are justified therefore in entitling the judgements and subject of these chapters as 'great' " (The Apocalypse page 477).

The Distressing Sore

And the first went, and poured out his vial upon the earth; and there fell a noisome and grievous sore upon the men which had the mark of the beast, and upon them which worshipped his image. (Revelation 16:2)

Like the trumpet judgements of Ch 8, the first four bowls affect the environment, and follow the same order as Ch 8. The earth, the sea, the rivers and finally the sun. To me they differ from Ch 8 in that the trumpet judgements cover the tribulation period generally, whereas these bowls of wrath are a definite series of judgements poured out at the end of tribulation days, and have particular relationships to the kingdom of the beast. The following two chapters, 17-18, see the destruction of his city and centre of working, Babylon. The beast and the false prophet meet their doom in Ch 19, with the Devil himself being incarcerated and finally cast into the lake of fire in Ch 20. This leaves the way open for God to bring in the Eternal State and the final blessedness of the saints from Ch 21.

The contents of this bowl are poured out upon the earth and with it there fell a noisome and grievous sore. The word "noisome" indicates what is evil, wicked. It was the ailment of Lazarus (Luke 16:20) and the cry by Paul to the Philippian jailer when he was warned to do himself "no harm" (Acts 16:28). "Grievous" would relate to its bad and harmful effects. Those who have followed the beast will feel the physical effect of this. It is very much akin to the sixth plague in Egypt (Ex. 9:8-12), when God sent "a boil breaking forth with blains upon them" (v. 9).

Disaster in the Seas (v. 3) – The second bowl

And the second angel poured out his vial upon the sea; and it became as the blood of a dead man: and every living soul died in the sea. (Revelation 16:3)

It will be no problem to God to effect this judgement literally. The seas are still a major source of food, and a major means of the transportation of goods. For the seas to become as blood of a dead one, and to cause the death of all in the seas will prove a great disaster.

Drinking Supply Corrupted (vv. 4-7) – The third bowl.

And the third angel poured out his vial upon the rivers and fountains of waters; and they became blood. And I heard the angel of the waters say, Thou art righteous, O Lord, which art, and wast, and shalt be, because thou hast judged thus. For they have shed the blood of saints and prophets, and thou hast given them blood to drink; for they are worthy. And I heard another out of the altar say, Even so, Lord God Almighty, true and righteous are thy judgments. (Revelation 16:4-7)

(a) The Pouring (v. 4) - As Moses in the first plague upon Egypt turned the waters of the Nile into blood (Ex. 7:19-21), "so that they could not drink of the waters of the river", once again God, through the pouring of this third bowl, is going to give men "blood to drink; for they are worthy" (v. 6). All sources of the water supply in that day will be affected, not only the rivers but also the fountains of waters. This would indicate that not only rivers but also all subterranean waters would be polluted.

(b) The Praise (vv. 5-7) - We notice again the various ministries of angels when v. 5 speaks of "the angel of the waters". Plainly angels are given responsibility over various parts of God's creation. This angel is quick to vindicate the actions of God, when he speaks of His righteousness "who is, who was, the Holy one". The words "shalt be" translate the word for holy (*hosios*), which is applied to human acts, (see 1 Tim. 2:8; Tit. 1:8). The Lord Jesus is referred to in this form, (Acts 2:27; 13:35; Heb. 7:26). Thus God is acting in holiness to cause men to reap what they have sown. "They are worthy". They slaughtered God's saints and prophets as they rejected both the lives and testimony of his own. Man in his folly cannot conceive that there will be a just retribution, but in tribulation days they will drink what they have shed.

The praise is added to by another out of the altar, we take this altar to be that of Ch 8:3, where the prayers of suffering saints are heard. It is in keeping with what he has heard, that this angel should also vindicate the Lord God Almighty for "true and righteous are thy judgements".

Demoralised by Scorching (vv. 8-9) – The fourth bowl

And the fourth angel poured out his vial upon the sun; and power was given unto him to scorch men with fire. And men were scorched with great heat, and blasphemed the name of God, which hath power over these plagues: and they repented not to give him glory. (Revelation 16:8-9)

Their Burning (v. 8)

The pouring of the fourth bowl is upon the sun. The effects are plain and simple to understand. The fires of persecution have been raised against the saints, now God will cause men to suffer for their atrocities. I never forget treating an airman in Egypt who had recently arrived from England and spent a whole day swimming and sun bathing in the Bitter Lakes, little realising that the exposure to the sun could have such awesome results. His back was in an awful state. The loss of body fluids became critical and he was surrounded in ice packs to keep his body temperature down. Such will be the lot of men under this bowl judgement.

Their Blasphemy (v. 9)

The demoralising effect of this plague only confirms the utter intransigence of those who have received the mark of the beast, who now, being past redemption (2 Thess. 2:11), refuse to honour God and instead blaspheme his name.

Distress for the Subjects of the Beast (vv. 10-11) – The fifth bowl

And the fifth angel poured out his vial upon the seat of the beast; and his kingdom was full of darkness; and they gnawed their tongues for pain, And blasphemed the God of heaven because of their pains and their sores, and repented not of their deeds. (Revelation 16:10-11)

The four former plagues were upon the environment; in these three latter plagues they seem to be more political, each in some way affecting the Empire of the Beast. The first affects his kingdom, the second is in connection with the river on which Babylon stands, the Euphrates, and finally the city of Babylon itself comes under the judgement of God in the seventh bowl.

With the pouring of this bowl, God moves directly against the beast, for it is against his throne (seat AV). That which was originally Satan's and was given to the beast (13:2) now becomes the centre of God's judgement and it extends to the whole of his kingdom. As with the ninth plague in Egypt (Ex. 10:21), his kingdom is full of darkness. This is not the darkness that precedes the Lord's manifestation (Matt. 24:29; Mark 13:24); this takes place prior to the Lord's return and is a direct judgement on the beast's kingdom. What is associated with this darkness is not known, but it brings great pain, causing men to gnaw their tongues (the only occurrence of the expression in scripture). They still use their tongues to blaspheme the God of heaven yet again. It is possible that such is the rapidity of these bowl judgements that, with the former pains from the grievous sore, and the scorching with great heat, and because of the darkness when all means of light has gone, men can do nothing or very little to tend their ailments. All they can do is seek relief by biting the tongue. In their misery they refuse to repent or give God glory. Do they recognise the source of their distress, as coming from God?

The New Testament has much to say about darkness in its various forms as:

Matt. 4:16	-	Spiritual Darkness,
Matt. 6:23	-	Intellectual Darkness,
Matt. 8:12	-	Eternal Darkness,
Rom. 13:12	-	Moral Darkness,
Eph. 6:12	-	Infernal Darkness,
Col. 1:13	-	Satan being the power behind it,
Matt. 27:45	-	Providential Darkness.

Here in Revelation we have what is judicial and physical darkness. Walter Scott looks on this as a moral darkness. When comparing it with that in Egypt, he says, "There, however, the darkness was physical, here it is moral" (Exposition of Revelation page 330). Why this should be different from that of Egypt is difficult to see.

Drying of the Euphrates (v. 12) – The sixth bowl.

And the sixth angel poured out his vial upon the great river Euphrates; and the water thereof was dried up, that the way of the kings of the east might be prepared. (Revelation 16:12)

Once again we see God acting to dry up a river. As he dried the Red Sea to deliver Israel from Egypt, and the Jordan to settle the destiny of the nation in Canaan, so he dries up the Euphrates for the destruction of the world's armies. The object of the river being dried is to make an unimpeded access for the kings east of the river, to come to the place called Armageddon. Many and varied are the interpretations regarding the river. One writer infers it is simply the removal of the army then in command of the Euphrates. That it is a literal drying of the river should not be difficult to accept. The other plagues in the chapter are literal, as was the drying of the Red Sea and Jordan. Seiss draws attention to its formidable size when he says, "from time immemorial, the Euphrates, with its tributaries, has been a great and formidable boundary between the peoples east of it and those west of it. It runs a distance of 1,800 miles and is scarcely fordable anywhere or at any time. It is from three to twelve hundred yards wide, and from ten to thirty feet in depth; and most of the time it is still deeper and wider" (Seiss, The Apocalypse, page 377). Many have said that it is not necessary to dry the river to enable a modern force to cross. Though this is no doubt true, it will facilitate and simplify things for the vast hordes that will be drawn from the eastern side of the river to Armageddon.

The Dispatching of Demons (vv. 13-16)

And I saw three unclean spirits like frogs come out of the mouth of the dragon, and out of the mouth of the beast, and out of the mouth of the false prophet. For they are the spirits of devils, working miracles, which go forth unto the kings of the earth and of the whole world, to gather them to the battle of that great day of God Almighty. Behold, I come as a thief. Blessed is he that watcheth, and keepeth his garments, lest he walk naked, and they see his shame. And he gathered them together into a place called in the Hebrew tongue Armageddon. (Revelation 16:13-16)

As we have seen, both with the opening of the seals, and the blowing of the trumpets, there is a parenthesis between the sixth and seventh judgement. Some like Larkin (The Book of Revelation page 144) have seen v. 15 as the parenthesis in this section. It would seem to me, that, as John uses the expression "And I saw", which he uses to give a fresh vision throughout this prophecy, so here we could have something that is entirely unconnected with the sixth bowl, yet having the same end, to bring other kings than those of the east to the battle.

It should also be noted that it is the trinity of evil that produces these frog-like demons, it is not an angel, nor is their origin heaven, they are the direct result of issuing from the mouths of the dragon, the beast and the false prophet.

When we see the judgements in the chapter, everything is associated with heaven, but these would appear to be in opposition to the purpose of God.

Many and varied interpretations have been given regarding these evil spirits or demons and the reason why they come out of the mouths of Satan and his puppets. Lockyer says, "The unclean spirit out of the dragon's mouth symbolises the proud infidelity opposing the Lord and His Anointed (Christ). The unclean spirit out of the beast's mouth represents the spirit of the world in the politics of men, whether lawless democracy or despotism, in which man is set above God. The unclean spirit out of the false prophet's mouth pictures lying spiritualism and religious delusion rampant in the days of satanic deception" (Drama of the Ages page 241).

But we are only told of where they arise and what they do. Coming from the mouth would indicate they act in word and because they are working miracles we see what they do. Thus coming from the wicked trinity and acting on their behalf by word and deed they cast their delusive powers over "the kings of the earth and of the whole world", to gather together all for the battle of that great day of God Almighty. God opens the way for the kings of the east; these evil spirits draw the rest preparing all for Armageddon. The name of the last great conflict is very apt; it means The Hill of Slaughter. Zechariah 14 might give the reason for v. 15 being brought in. Zechariah 14:2 states, "For I will gather all nations against Jerusalem to battle; and the city shall be taken, and the houses rifled, and the women ravished", v. 3 then brings before us the divine intervention that will deliver the remnant. "Then shall the Lord go forth and fight against those nations, as when he fought in the day of battle". We are now told how the Lord will come "as a thief in the night", a dreadful event for a Godless world, but a blessing to a watching and faithful remnant. The three parables of Matthew 24:48 to 25:30 relate how the unjust servant, the foolish virgin and the careless steward were not watching. The garment, ever a symbol of character, speaks of the separation of the remnant who, in spite of fierce opposition, keep themselves pure and endure to the end.

The Dividing of the City (vv. 17-21) – The seventh bowl

And the seventh angel poured out his vial into the air; and there came a great voice out of the temple of heaven, from the throne, saying, it is done. And there were voices, and thunders, and lightnings; and there was a great earthquake, such as was not since men were upon the earth, so mighty an earthquake, and so great. And the great city was divided into three parts, and the cities of the nations fell: and great Babylon came in remembrance before God, to give unto her the cup of the wine of the fierceness of his wrath. And every island fled away, and the mountains were not found. And there fell upon men a great hail out of heaven, every stone about the weight of a talent: and men blasphemed God because of the plague of the hail; for the plague thereof was exceeding great. (Revelation 16:17-21)

Seven great things are associated with the pouring of the bowl by the seventh angel. The judgements of God are brought to their climax in this plague;

Chapter 17

Babylon, her flagrant rebellion

Introduction

We now come to the third vision of the book of Revelation. As we have seen in Ch 1, the expression "I was in the Spirit" (v. 3) opens a new series of revelations given to John. This vision concludes in Ch 21:8, and gives a panoramic view of events that take place from the destruction of Babylon until the bringing in of the eternal state. In this section we see all that has been contrary to the mind of God finally dealt with. Babylon, the Man of Sin, the false prophet, and the devil all meet their end, and, with death and hell cast into the Lake of Fire after the millennial reign of Christ recorded in Ch 20:1-10, the way is clear for God to bring in the new heaven and earth.

The chapters before us (17:1 - 19:4) have been the subject of both sad and poor handling by many expositors. The word of God has been distorted, as men, following exclusive writers of a hundred years ago, have failed to see beyond Rome to interpret these verses, though there is no mention of Rome in any of its forms, pagan or ecclesiastical, political or military. The western world that sees Babylonish evil in Rome, cannot seem to see beyond it to the true sources of opposition to God "BABYLON THE GREAT THE MOTHER OF HARLOTS AND ABOMINATIONS OF THE EARTH". It is Babylon that is plainly spoken of on six occasions as deserving the judgement of God, (14:8; 16:19; 17:5; 18:2, 10 and 21). Rome is nowhere seen in the writings of this book. In fact at the point of writing, Rome had not risen ecclesiastically and could in no way be guilty of the sins enumerated in these chapters. The seven churches to which this book first came could not equate the things said to a papal Rome, it did not exist!

It will be necessary to give an outline of Babylon's history to establish that in these two chapters nothing less than what the Bible states is the true subject of their theme - Babylon.

Babylon is portrayed in a fourfold way in the scriptures: historically, with the captivity, prophetically and in its final apostasy here in Revelation.

Babylon Historically

The city of Babylon is brought before us in Genesis Ch 10-11 where it is known as Babel. It is the capital city of the world's first empire established by Nimrod the "mighty hunter before the Lord" (Gen 10:9). "Before the Lord" means in defiance of him. Nimrod was a hunter of the souls of men rather than animals. His name means "Rebel". He is a grandson of Ham, it seems he is the youngest son of Cush. Ham's name means swarthy, darkened, sun burnt, such was his soul as he sinned against the light God had given him. Ham was the man guilty of perpetuating the sins that were the cause of God's judgement at the flood, practising them after the flood. When he saw his father's nakedness (10:22), far more is involved than that of seeing a naked man, gross immorality was involved. When Noah awoke (v. 24) "he knew what his younger son had done unto him", it was an action not merely a look. This brought a curse on the family of Ham. Noah could not curse what God had blessed (9:1) so the curse moves on to the family. It is from here that Nimrod, a chip off the old block, rises. The history of this family makes sad reading from Ch 10:6 onwards, not only Babylon but from Mizraim came Philistim (v. 14). These were to be inveterate enemies of Israel and oppose all that is of God. From Canaan, the subject of the curse, came all that would speak of Phoenician idolatry. Prized by man for its culture, hated by God for its sin, who told Israel to put them to the sword when they came into the promised land (see Ch 18:16-17). They are also linked with Sodom and Gomorrah (v. 19). Such is the family history that produces Nimrod. His desires for complete dominion over men is seen in Ch 11, where moving eastward toward the rising of the sun, he seeks to establish a kingdom with a religious system that is satanic in the extreme. In the first Babylon, built by artificial means (such is man) with burnt brick and slime for mortar, both a city for commercialism and a tower for worship were established. The tower "whose top may reach unto heaven" (v. 4) seems to have been an observatory to read the message of God recorded in the stars. Psalm 19:1-6 indicates that there was a message for man in them. Rom. 1:19-25 also refers to these days when the known truth of God is refuted and replaced by idolatry. Hyslop's "Two Babylon's" gives the history of Babylon that produced the worship of mother and child in Semiramus and Tammuz. The purpose of this exposition forbids going into all the attendant evils which come from this system, but it had far reaching effect even upon Israel and the temple ministry (see Ezekiel Ch 8). The will of God was overthrown, in its place were put doctrines of demons (1 Tim 4:1) even as they were actively led by evil spirits to worship dumb idols (1 Cor. 12:2). God must act against it, confusing their tongues and scattering them over the face of the globe. In the scattering they took their Babylonish doctrines with them with the result that "the inhabitants of the earth have been made drunk with the wine of her fornication" (Rev. 17:2). Every religious system of earth can trace its origin and doctrines back to the mother of harlots, Babylon. She has given birth to a multitude of children, who all oppose the truth of God. What God scattered in Genesis 11, he is going to shatter in Revelation 17-18.

Babylon and the Captivity

Such is Babylon; it will ever seek to bring under its sway that which ought to be for God's pleasure. If Israel is going to indulge in the idolatrous practices of Babylon there is nothing for it but to be made captive by it. Daniel will tell of the results of this captivity, with its despotic king, type of the Man of Sin, with its image to worship and its fiery furnace, all of this typical of tribulation days. As in the book of Daniel hope is set before the nation, with the promise of the stone cut out without hands bringing to naught all human government and filling the whole earth (Dan. 2:31-45), even so shall the stone whom the builders rejected fill the earth, one day he shall reign in glory in the world.

Babylon in Prophecy

Three great prophecies bring before us what is in store for Babylon. Two portions of Old Testament prophecy, Isaiah 13-14 and Jeremiah 50-51 relate to her future judgement in the time of divine visitation against her. That judgement is fulfilled in these two chapters of Revelation. There is one prophecy that speaks of her restoration and reconstruction in preparation for this judgement (Zech. 5:5-11).

The first of these prophecies, Isaiah chapters 13-14, gives the setting of her judgement as tribulation days. There is nothing in the prophecy that could be linked to the fall of Babylon at the hands of the Medes and Persians as recorded in Daniel Ch 5, yet many expositors use these to teach that its past fall was the fulfilment of this scripture, and state that it will never be rebuilt (13:20). A few simple observations should be enough to establish that the tribulation days are the subject of this prophecy.

1. The period of the judgement is defined as "the day of the Lord" (v. 6, v. 9). The Day of the Lord is tribulation days.

2. There will be disturbances in the heavens (v. 1) when, "the stars of heaven and the constellations thereof shall not give their light: the sun shall be darkened in his going forth, and the moon shall not cause her light to shine". This is a graphic foreshadowing of Matt. 24:29, Mark 13:24, Luke 21:25, Rev. 6:12-14.

3. Pangs and sorrows as a woman in travail (v. 8). The tribulation period is spoken of in these terms in 1 Thess. 5:3, and the word tribulation has the thought of a woman in child labour in it.

4. Fear will grip the hearts of men (v. 7) corresponding to Luke 21:26.

5. The judgement is carried out at the time when God "will punish the world for their evil, and the wicked for their iniquity" (v. 11), showing that the judgement of God is far wider than just on Babylon. This could not refer to its fall in the days of Daniel.

6. It would seem from verse 12, that there would also be international slaughter of humanity, when a man will be more precious that fine gold. Such is the effect of the seal, trumpet, and vial judgements so that Matthew must write "and except those days be shortened, there shall no flesh be saved" (Matt. 24:22).

7. Its final utter destruction (vv. 19-22). At no time in the past did Babylon ever fall as it is described here, when it will be "as when God overthrew Sodom and Gomorrah, it shall never be inhabited" (vv. 19-20). It took centuries for it to fall into gradual decay and Ottman, quoting Stanley's History of the Jewish Church Vol III, page 59 states "It is true that even Babylon has never ceased to be inhabited. Hillah, a town with a

population of five thousand souls is within its walls". This was in the 1800's.

This prophecy can in no way be equated with what happened in the days of Darius the Mede; it must have a future fulfilment.

The prophecy of Jeremiah 50-51 is set, not against the background of the tribulation, but of the Regathering of Israel and Judah back to the land at the outset of the millennium. It will be noticed that it will affect both aspects of the nation, whereas after the victory of Darius in Dan. 5 there was only a remnant from Judah that returned (see Ezra Ch 2).

I merely quote the scripture references for the perusal of any. Jer. 50:4-5 relates how as a nation they shall come "together, going and weeping: they shall seek the Lord their God. They shall ask the way to Zion with their faces thitherward, saying, Come, and let us join ourselves together in a perpetual covenant that shall not be forgotten". Again in verse 20 the prophet is clear as to the time of the prophecy, "In those days and in that time, saith the Lord, the iniquity of Israel shall be sought for and there shall be none; and the sins of Judah, and they shall not be found; for I will pardon them whom I reserve". Verses 33-34 are very specific when they speak of an oppressed people finding deliverance through their redeemer who is strong, "The Lord of hosts is his name: he shall throughly plead their cause, that he may give rest to the land, and disquiet the inhabitants of Babylon". Ch 51:5 also confirms the fact of the restoration of the nation when Babylon is overthrown, "for Israel hath not been forsaken, nor Judah of his God". These verses point to a future recovery of Israel and Judah together in the coming kingdom, not of an event that took place in the past.

Again these two chapters speak of the utter destruction and complete overthrow of Babylon never to recover from the judgement of God. The call to "flee out of the midst of Babylon" (51:6) corresponds to Revelation 18:4. She has a golden cup which made all the earth drunken (51:7). She "dwellest upon many waters" (51:13). Her final destruction is by fire (51:25, 58), and "none shall remain in it, neither man nor beast, but that it shall be desolate for ever" (v. 62). Finally to "bind a stone to it, and cast it into the midst of the Euphrates: And thou shalt say, thus shall Babylon sink and shall not rise from the evil that I will bring upon her" (vv. 63-64). It is quite evident that these scriptures are what John was led to when he wrote of Babylon's destruction in Rev. 18:18-24.

We now touch the third prophecy, which enlightens us as to Babylon's full restoration in preparation for the judgement of God. This prophecy is the subject of Zechariah 5:5-11.

The former part of Zechariah has revealed the blessing that Israel will know when restored to the Lord. The **punishment** of the nations who overstepped their responsibilities when Israel was made subject to them is the theme of Ch 1. The **populating** of Jerusalem in peace and harmony Ch 2, the **priesthood** restored Ch 3, and the **power** of God in the nation Ch 4. We are then told of

purging of evil from the nation, that will precede the blessing, in the flying roll of Ch 5:1-5, and the source of where that evil rose, Babylon, in vv. 5-11.

The vision of the Ephah (the largest commercial measure) would indicate that the commercial centre of the world would be established in Babylon. We are told that a woman, which is wickedness (v. 8) is sitting in the midst of the Ephah. Is she the woman of Rev. 17-18? A lead weight is cast upon the mouth thereof (v. 8), which would seem to indicate a restraining influence imposed upon the woman until the time of the end. The rebirth of Babylon is foretold in verses 9-11, when the Ephah is brought to "the land of Shinar", where the first Babylon stood (Gen. 11:2). At the time of Zechariah's prophecy, historic Babylon had fallen into the hands of Darius the Mede (Ch 1:1). We are now informed of its future restoration. This is in preparation for its final destruction, to fulfil in detail the prophecy concerning its end in Isaiah 13-14, Jeremiah 50-51 and Revelation 17-18. We can now turn our attention to Revelation Ch 17-18.

Many expositors make a distinction between Ch 17 and 18, seeing in Ch 17 Babylon religiously, symbolised by the tower of Gen 11, and in Ch 18 Babylon commercially, representing the city of Gen. 11. They would see two separate judgements each distinct from the other. Ottman goes so far as to make them two distinct things, saying of Ch 17 "that great city of Rome, not merely Rome Pagan, but Rome papal which shall yet from the literal site of Rome exercise the supremacy here spoken of over the kings of the earth". Then he speaks of Ch 18 in this manner "the passing of mystery Babylon is followed by the appearance of Babylon palpable and literal. Literal Babylon on the Euphrates comes into remembrance before God after Mystery Babylon on the Tiber has been overthrown. The passing away of one, and the reappearing of the other, would seem to be indicated in the following prophecy" (Ottman - The Unfolding of the Ages pages 384 and 385).

However it would appear to the author that there would be sufficient internal evidence in these two chapters to make them one thing, and that one judgement is spoken of. I am aware of the expression of Ch 18:1, "After these things" (*meta tauta*) which has caused some to see two distinct things before us, rather than Ch 18 being a description of the effects that the judgement of Ch 17 had. That both refer to one and the same thing seems apparent for the following reasons:

1. Both speak of a single judgement by God (17:1; 18:8). Chapter 18 speaks of the effect of that judgement whilst in Ch 19:1-4 Heaven is rejoicing over the judgement of the whore.

2. In both chapters Babylon is referred to as a woman (17:1; 18:6-9).

3. Both are called "that great city" (17:18; 18:16).

4. Both have the same attire, (17:4; 18:16).

5. The kings of the earth are seen in the same relationship (17:2; 18:3, 9). These are a different company of kings from those linked to the beast.

6. Both hold a golden cup (17:4; 18:6).

7. Both are burned with fire (17:16; 18:8-9).

8. Both are given the same name (17:5; 18:10).

9. Both hold the blood of the saints (17:6; 18:24).

Without developing the theme, it is apparent that the two chapters speak of the judgement that will befall Babylon as it comes into remembrance before God. The great theme of Ch 17 is "Her Flagrant Rebellion" and that of Ch 18 is "Her Fall Recorded". Chapter 17 will be divided into three parts: vv. 1-6 Her Abominations, vv. 7-14 Her Associations and vv. 15-18 Her Annihilation.

Her Abominations (vv. 1-6)

And there came one of the seven angels which had the seven vials, and talked with me, saying unto me, Come hither; I will shew unto thee the judgment of the great whore that sitteth upon many waters: With whom the kings of the earth have committed fornication, and the inhabitants of the earth have been made drunk with the wine of her fornication. So he carried me away in the spirit into the wilderness: and I saw a woman sit upon a scarlet coloured beast, full of names of blasphemy, having seven heads and ten horns. And the woman was arrayed in purple and scarlet colour, and decked with gold and precious stones and pearls, having a golden cup in her hand full of abominations and filthiness of her fornication: And upon her forehead was a name written, MYSTERY, BABYLON THE GREAT, THE MOTHER OF HARLOTS AND ABOMINATIONS OF THE EARTH. And I saw the woman drunken with the blood of the saints, and with the blood of the martyrs of Jesus: and when I saw her, I wondered with great admiration. (Revelation 17:1-6)

As with the vision of the Bride (21:9), it is "one of the seven angels which had the seven vials" that spoke to John. Which of the seven it is, is not specified in either case, enough to know that one of the executors of God's judgement upon the world is now used to reveal the judgement of Babylon, and the glory of the Bride.

John is carried by this angel "in the spirit" into the wilderness. An apt sphere to reveal the judgement of that which would have robbed God of the fruitfulness and fragrance of worship that should have been his, and produced nothing but barrenness.

Being "in the spirit" introduces the third vision of the Revelation, which vision continues to Ch 21:8.

As the judgement of the whore is introduced, John is told of her character that deserves and brings forth her destruction.

Her Sphere of Operation (v. 1)

Babylon is introduced as a whore, an unmarried mother who draws aside all men. Whoredoms are constantly linked to all forms of religious evil, when the affections of men are drawn away from obedience to God, and he is supplanted by idolatrous worship (see Ex. 34:15, 16; Lev. 17:7; 20:5-6; Deut. 31:16; Ezek. 6:9). The extent of these whoredoms is graphically portrayed by where the whore sitteth, "upon many waters". These are interpreted for us in v. 15 as "peoples and multitudes and nations and tongues". The nations of men have all come under her influence and control. Babylon has affected all nations with her evil doctrines and dominates them.

She is seen here sitting **ecclesiastically,** whilst in v. 3 she sits **politically** where she is seen sitting on the beast. In v. 9 she sits **positionally,** not now merely on the beast, but the place where she sits is specified, upon the heads of the beast, and in Ch 18:7 she sits **defiantly,** "I sit a queen and am no widow".

Her Moral Degradation (v. 2)

Though the angel is to reveal to John her judgement, these verses give the reason for that judgement, for God does not punish without cause. If the sphere of her working influenced people globally, we see how their political leaders submitted to her. Kings have a responsibility to act for God, as the powers that be are ordained of God. Here we see how kings and people alike have entered into spiritual fornication with her. Fornication is commonly put for association with idolatry, when men's affections are drawn by evil to refute and reject God's love.

It is a well known fact that the basest of sins are performed in connection with heathen idolatry and lewdness revelled in by so called priestesses, with a view to lifting the spirit of man by sexual ecstasy into union with the gods. Such teaching derived from Semiramus, who alleged that a spiritual union with her dead husband Nimrod produced Tammuz. From this came the worship of mother and child, and opened the floodgates to immorality in heathen worship. It made idolatry acceptable to the masses, "idolatry was no mere sin into which people gradually sank; but it was the creation, by satanic wisdom, of a mighty system, which he intended to use, and to lead up to his own worship" (Bullinger, The Apocalypse page 505). This has caused men to be drunk with the wine of her fornication, to be heady, uncontrolled and besotted by Babylon's teaching.

This idolatry was not something that was yet to rise under a papal Rome centuries later, but that which already dominated the minds of men from the days of Genesis 11 onward. John is reminded of the condition of the world in his day, which is no less evil in ours, and pursues the same doctrines.

The Seat of Occupation (v. 3)

Not only have kings and nations imbibed her doctrines, but she holds a place of prominence, not only ecclesiastically as in v. 2, but also politically as in this verse. The interpretation of what we have here is the subject of vv. 7-14. The spirit of God is his own interpreter. Sufficient to see now, that she produced nothing for God or in men, only barrenness, such is the statement "carried me away into the wilderness". A howling waste is the product of apostate religion.

If she is going to ride the beast, is she controlling it or is it merely upholding her? From the place of prominence upon the heads of this last final conglomerate of Gentile power, as Babylon controlled at the beginning, she seems to want control at the end.

Her Glorious Ornamentation (v. 4)

The woman has much that appeals to the eye of man, with great outward splendour, yet God sees only that which brings her to shame.

Her garment is prominent, arrayed in purple and scarlet colour, both regal and splendid. The gospels portray the Lord Jesus as being thus arrayed as men mocked his claims.

Matthew says a scarlet robe (Matt. 27:28), his kingly glory is spurned, scarlet being the colour that represents suffering and death. Both Mark and John speak of a purple robe in which men arrayed him. The lowly humility of Christ is despised and mocked, as they reject the honour of the true manhood that was his. Purple represents regal glory, Christ is seen in service, and manhood in Mark and Luke. This woman arrays herself with glorious apparel to attract her adherents.

Her girding is apparent, "decked" actually means girded with gold. In the sanctuary of God in the tabernacle both its boards and furniture were covered with gold. It is little wonder that she who would usurp the place of Deity is so arrayed.

Her Golden Cup - The Lord has golden vials in this book, in 5:8 full of odours, the prayers of saints, in 15:7 full of wrath to be poured upon sinners. Now her cup is full of abominations and uncleanness. Her idolatry and immorality fill her cup from which the nations of the earth freely drink (v. 2). Many looking upon these features cannot help but see in them that which is displayed in Rome, but they are equally seen in the Eastern and Russian Orthodox churches, as in heathen temple worship. They all bear the attire of their mother.

Her Personal Revelation (v. 5)

Emblazoned for all to see, her name is written, prominent and unmistakable, such is the fact that it is in her forehead, "Mystery, Babylon The Great, The Mother of Harlots and Abominations of the Earth". No doubt is left as to whom he speaks of; Babylon is Babylon in any language and cannot be spelt R.O.M.E. We are not now faced with one of her children, but with the MOTHER of every harlot and abomination that has polluted the earth ever since Genesis 11. What began in Babylon has spawned many children, of whom Rome is one, but here, it is that which gave them being that is to suffer the judgement of God.

"MYSTERY" is associated with her. Ottman, who as we have seen links her with Rome in this chapter, takes the word to indicate that all the vagaries of Romish mysticism are behind the word. Transubstantiation, the bread and wine becoming the literal body and blood of the Lord. The signs of the cross, turning to the east to worship, candles and incense and holy waters. Though these may be indeed mysteries to the uninitiated, this is not the thought behind the word "Mystery".

A mystery in the New Testament is that which has not been revealed in the Old Testament, but which now, in this present dispensation is revealed. Campbell Morgan has well said "not something merely that has been revealed, but revealed to faith". Only believers can understand God's mysteries. Please note the comma, it is not Mystery Babylon, but Mystery, Babylon the great. Some would omit the latter part of the verse as not being part of the Mystery, but in its simplicity it reveals what was not known in other ages, that the source of all abominations is the same Mother. Rome is not the mother, but one of the children she gave birth to. We are now face to face with that which has corrupted kings and made ALL inhabitants of the earth drunk with the wine of her fornication. The earth, not localised spheres, has been corrupted by doctrines that came from this mother. God unveils this iniquitous mystery to us. We have come across the term Mystery before (1:20 - 10:7), where we saw that the fifteen or so mysteries of the New Testament can be headed under, Mysteries Dispensational, Doctrinal, Devotional or Diabolical.

Of the mysteries diabolical, that of 2 Thess. 2:7 would be linked to the rise of the Man of Sin, the beast of this chapter, "The Mystery or Iniquity". This is when all iniquity finds its culmination in the worship of the beast, when he moves into the temple. The mystery here is linked with the exposure of the source of all spiritual evil, Babylon, and is called "Great". There are but three great mysteries:

Eph. 5:32 - The Union of Christ and His Church, 1 Tim. 3:16 - The Union of God with man "God manifest in flesh" and Rev. 17:5 - The Union of Religious evil with Babylon.

Iniquitous Persecution (v. 6)

(a) The Murders of the Woman - This verse covers far more than the persecution poured out upon the saints of this dispensation. They cannot be linked alone to the blood baths that marked the events that brought in the reformation. That is, to the burning, beheading and battering of believers who were not prepared to bow to the authority of the Pope nor to that of Protestant monarchs in England who sought to eradicate catholic opponents, and who also brought great persecution and bloodshed upon Scottish covenanters because they would not receive the King as head of the church. "The blood of saints, and with the blood of martyrs of Jesus" covers every age from Babylon to now. The opposition through the vagaries of Heathendom as well as Christendom have made her drunk with the blood of saints. Even in recent times we have the chronicle of the murders of missionaries by the Auca Indians of Ecuador, and by the Papuans of Papua New Guinea. The slaughter has never stopped; religious evil emerging from Babylon brooks no rivals, and destroys all who oppose her.

(b) The Marvels of John - This vision had a great effect upon John. The sight of the woman caused him to wonder with great wonder. The two words are akin, and come from the root of the word to see, and speaks of the effects of that sight. It is translated, "marvelled" on thirty of the forty-six occurrences in the New Testament. It is said of the Lord that he marvelled both at faith (Matt. 8:10) and unbelief (Mark 6:6). It is used of the populace who marvelled at his miracles, of a Pharisee when he saw the Lord eat with unwashed hands (Luke 11:38). Pilate marvelled at the silence of the Lord at his trial (Mark 15:3) and at the fact that he was dead already (Mark 15:44). And the disciples marvelled at his resurrection (Luke 24:12, 41). It is evidently the effect of the unexpected. John says it was with great wonder. Such was the unveiling of this mystery to John.

Her Associations (vv. 7-14)

And the angel said unto me, Wherefore didst thou marvel? I will tell thee the mystery of the woman, and of the beast that carrieth her, which hath the seven heads and ten horns. The beast that thou sawest was, and is not; and shall ascend out of the bottomless pit, and go into perdition: and they that dwell on the earth shall wonder, whose names were not written in the book of life from the foundation of the world, when they behold the beast that was, and is not, and yet is. And here is the mind which hath wisdom. The seven heads are seven mountains, on which the woman sitteth. And there are seven kings: five are fallen, and one is, and the other is not yet come; and when he cometh, he must continue a short space. And the beast that was, and is not, even he is the eighth, and is of the seven, and goeth into perdition. And the ten horns which thou sawest are ten kings, which have received no kingdom as yet; but receive power as kings one hour with the beast. These have one mind, and shall give their power and strength unto the beast. These shall make war with the Lamb, and the Lamb shall overcome them: for he is Lord of lords, and King of kings: and they that are with him are called, and chosen, and faithful. (Revelation 17:7-14)

We are now introduced to the second mystery of the chapter. We have the Mystery of Babylon in v. 5, now it is "the mystery of the woman and of the beast that carrieth her, which hath seven heads and ten horns". In the first we see her religious corruptions, we are now introduced to her political affiliations. As we have seen, both are from Babylon, but the beast is to remove his centre to Jerusalem, and sit as God there (2 Thess. 2:4). Babylon must be destroyed; these chapters speak of that destruction.

Confirming the Kingdom (vv. 7-8)

(a) The Ride of the Woman - John is asked why he marvelled at the revelation he had just received. The purpose of God will be fulfilled, and what God had foretold in the prophecies of Daniel must be accomplished. The book of Daniel unveils the political powers that will hold sway during the time of the Gentiles but speaks nothing of the ecclesiastical union that will be apparent in its final form. Hence the word "Mystery", which now reveals the full blown exposure of the source of all demonic doctrines that have corrupted the earth. The mother of all evil begins her final days triumphantly, riding in power. She ends them tragically, ruined and broken (vv. 16-17).

(b) The Rise of the Beast (v. 8) - The prophecy of Dan. 2:40-45 is now to be fulfilled. The fourth kingdom of the time of the Gentiles is to begin its course. It is apparent that the aspect of this kingdom is that under the eighth head as verse 11 states. It cannot be a revived power, but a person, for a power and a kingdom cannot come from the abyss as this person does. As Nebuchadnezzar stood for the Kingdom of Babylon as the head of gold (Dan. 2:37-38), so the eighth head of Gentile dominion will be that Kingdom (v. 11).

Many expositors see here a revived Roman empire, and take great pains to explain the statements of this verse as the three stages in Rome's history. The beast "that was", representing Rome's existence until its destruction in 476 AD, "and is not", its present plight when it holds no power, though the nations it ruled are still in existence, "and shall ascend out of the bottomless pit", as a revived Roman empire empowered by Satan. As has been stated, no empire actually rises from the abyss, and no power collectively will find its end in perdition. This is the course of an individual, verse 11 states that "the beast that was, and is not, even "HE" is the eighth". As we saw in Ch 13, the Man of Sin suffers a deadly wound, a wound unto death, and rises again by Satanic power. This verse confirms all that has been said concerning him. It is only as a resurrected man that he is spoken of as ascending out of the abyss, the prison house of evil spirits. It is only a person that can go into perdition. The Man of Sin is spoken of as "The Son of Perdition" (2 Thess. 2:3). Some have actually thought because Judas is spoken of in the same way (John 17:12), that the Man of Sin is Judas in resurrection, but Ch 13 makes the death and resurrection of the Man of Sin things that the world at that time see and know, causing them to wonder and worship (13:3-4).

(c) The Response of the People - As John wondered at the revelation of the woman, so the world will stand and marvel at the rise of the beast. God himself is to send a strong delusion that they should believe the lie. The man "whose coming is after the working of Satan with all power and signs and lying wonders", will sway the minds of unbelieving men. That it is only such is evident from the fact that it is those, "whose names were not written in the book of life from the foundation of the world", that wonder.

The "book of life" is evidently the record in heaven of those redeemed, the expression occurs six times in the book of Revelation:

Ch 3:5 - Reveals the **security** of the redeemed, "I will not blot out his name out of the book of life".

Ch 20:12, 15 - Unveil the **sentence** on sinners, "whosoever was not found written in the book of life was cast into the lake of fire".

Ch 22:19 - Foretells of those **separated** from blessing when a threefold warning is given to those who tamper with God's word (the TR has book of life, the margin says, tree of life).

Ch 13:8 and 17:8 - Speak of those who are the **subjects** of the beast. These cannot have a place in salvation, having rejected every offer of God's salvation; God sends a strong delusion (2 Thess. 2:11).

The Confederacy of the Seven Heads (vv. 9-10)

As the rise of the beast is the fulfilment of the prophecy of Dan. 2, so in these verses we would seem to have the fulfilment of Dan. Ch 8:8-12 and vv. 20-27. In this prophecy, it delineates where the beast is to rise from. He is to rise out of (*ek*) the seven heads, and to bring their rule to its conclusion.

(d) **The Rule of Gentile Powers** (vv. 9-10) - As wisdom is required to discern the number of the beast (13:18), so wisdom is to be applied to discern what is before us here. That this portion is difficult to understand is evident on account of the divergent thoughts expressed on it. Wisdom is needed for the two interpretations in relation to the Man of Sin that are most difficult (perhaps that is why it is introduced). Wisdom (*sophia*) only occurs four times in the book, twice in relation to the Lamb and to God (5:12; 7:12) and twice in relation to the coming world power (13:18, 17:9).

Many, following a line of teaching laid down by exclusive brethren writers from the close of the last century, see here definite proof that the final kingdom of this world is to be a Roman power revived. The seven heads are seen as either (i) Seven Kings of Rome as "Augustus, Tiberias, Caligula, Claudius and Nero, then Vespasian and finally Titus. The reign of the last is held to be a short one, thus fulfilling the text" (Charles L Feinberg - Liberty Bible Commentary, quoting R H Charles, followed by Barclay, page 836). (ii) The succession of the forms of administration as, Kings, Consuls, Dictators, Decemvirs, Military Tribunes, Emperors (Walter Scott, Book of Revelation, page 352).

Much has been made of the fact that these heads are said to be "seven mountains on which the woman sitteth". Ottman states, "It is generally agreed that the seven heads represent the seven hills of Rome" (page 382). Let Seiss speak on this matter "These are the words which are supposed to fix the application of the picture to the city of Rome, as Rome is called a city of seven hills. But a flimsy basis for such a controlling and all-conditioning conclusion is perhaps nowhere to be found. The seven hills of the city of Rome, to begin with, are not mountains, as every one who has seen them can testify; but the taking them as literal hills or mountains at all is founded upon a total misreading of the angel's words" (The Apocalypse, page 391).

In these seven heads we have the successive governments to whom God has committed the times of Gentile power. These heads are said to be mountains (*eisen*), which is interpreted for us in verse 10 as a symbol. What is written here is the same as continually occurs in this book, which has not caused expositors to read other than is written, except here. The word "*eisen*" occurs in the following places, and is self-explanatory:

1:20	-	The seven stars are the angels of the seven churches,
1:20	-	The seven candlesticks are the seven churches,
4:5	-	The seven lamps of fire are the seven Spirits of God,
5:6	-	The seven horns and seven eyes are the seven Spirits of God,
5:8	-	Golden vials full of odours are the prayers of saints,
11:3, 4	-	The two witnesses are the two olive trees and the two golden candlesticks standing before God in heaven,
16:13, 14	-	Unclean spirits like frogs, they are the spirits of devils,
17:9	-	The seven heads are seven mountains and
17:10	-	and are seven kings, *lit* "and kings seven are" (TR).

Prominent powers are called mountains, the subsequent kings of v. 12 are said to be "Horns". Babylon itself is specifically so called (Jer. 51:25), "O destroying mountain", and after the judgement of God visited on her "a burnt mountain". Such she will become in Ch 18. These heads are those linked to Babylon or the times of the Gentiles, and are prominent features of that rule. When all crumbles as the stone cut out without hands smites it (Dan. 2:33-34), this stone becomes "a great mountain and filled the whole earth". Such will be the greatness of the kingdom of Christ. So we find that the mountains are not the hills of Rome, but those great powers linked with Gentile dominion.

Who are these great powers? Better than the various powers or administrations of Rome is the interpretation that they represent the great powers that have had authority over Israel, namely Egypt, Assyria, Babylon, Medo Persia and Greece, these representing the five that are fallen, Rome, being the one that is, and the future Babylon rising in its first head from out of whom the eighth cometh, being the seventh.

But perhaps another interpretation can be suggested which is not without a little difficulty yet might hold the key to what is here.

The book of Daniel reveals God's program of Gentile dominion. The great image of Ch 2:31-45 is both explicit and implicit that Gentile rule will be under four great powers. Their beginning is also definite, not with Egypt, or Assyria, but with Nebuchadnezzar as the head of gold. It begins not merely with Babylon, but with Babylon under Nebuchadnezzar. Its end would seem to be where it begins, for the image appears to stand in Babylon and falls there. The two powers between revealed as Medo Persia and Greece in Ch 8:20-21, both had Babylon as their seat of authority though Greece had no settled capital city. As we have seen it was here that Alexander met his end. The great prophecy of Ch 8:20-27 gives further details regarding the rise of the final power, the fourth kingdom. After the rapid rise of Alexander to power, he, as the great horn, is broken and in his place four powers divide his kingdom (8:22). These powers are reputed by history to be Lysimachus, Cassander, Seleucus and Ptolemy. Each has a standing in God's prophetic calendar and between them they rule what is often termed the "Prophetic Earth". It is to be noted that the seven names, and seven heads make up the power of Gentile dominion as revealed by Daniel, Nebuchadnezzar, Darius the Mede and Alexander, who is followed by his four generals. Again Dan. 8:9 emphatically state that the final power, the eighth of Rev. 17:11 comes out of one of these "four notable ones" (Dan. 8:8). As we have seen in an earlier chapter, the Man of Sin comes out of Seleucus as revealed in Dan. 11. Is the first king of the north of Dan. 11, who is so prominent until his fall in verse 19, the seventh head out of which the eighth comes? The king of verse 20 seems to be insignificant, for he only continues "a short space". Nevertheless from these rises the vile person, the wilful king, and the eighth of Rev. 17:11.

The problem in all this is the angel's statement in verse 10, "One is". Thus it seems apparent that it is the power that is ruling as John writes. Did Rome rise out of some aspect of Lysimachus's or Cassander's rule? It certainly dominated the realms of three of the four notable ones, though it did not subdue the kingdom of Seleucus, nor did Rome ever control Babylon, which the other powers did. It is their connection with Babylon that marks them out for a place in prophetic history.

Course of the Beast (v. 11)

The revelation of the beast as to his origin and destiny is confirmed in this verse. We are told that the beast is a person, the eighth; he is the head of Gentile dominion in its final stage. He corresponds to the "fourth beast, dreadful and terrible, and strong exceedingly" of Dan. 7:7. This beast is linked with the horns from whom comes the last great world power (see also Dan. 7:19-28). He is also "a king of fierce countenance, and understanding dark sentences" of Dan. 8:23-27. The vision of this beast causes Daniel to be much troubled and his countenance to be much changed within him (Dan. 7:28), also to faint and be sick certain days (Dan. 8:27). John is also caused to marvel at his rise and links with the woman (v. 6), and the beast causes the world to marvel (v. 8).

That he is "of" (*ek*) the seven proves he is from the same root and stock as the kingdoms that portray the times of the Gentiles so vividly recorded in Daniel's five great prophecies. The verse brings before us not only his physical and political rise, but also his catastrophic end "and goeth into perdition".

The Concurrence of the Ten Horns (vv. 12-13)

(a) Their Appearance (v. 12) - It is in the final manifestation of the beast that the horns are seen. In Dan. 2 there is no mention of the toes, (equivalent to the ten horns) in the explanation of the vision (Dan. 2:31-35). It is only in the interpretation of the vision that they are introduced (v. 41) and that with the last kingdom. The prophecy of Dan. 7 again links the horns with the "fourth beast, dreadful and terrible and strong exceedingly" (v. 7). This would correspond with the rise of the horns as revealed here.

They are ten kings that only take a place in the time of the Gentiles in the final phase of its rule under the beast. Unlike the seven heads that have played a major part in world history, these have no prophetic history; they only rise in the end time to fulfil the rule appointed by God. Such is the thought behind the expression "which have received no kingdom as yet; but receive power as kings one hour with the beast" speaking of a future, brief association with the beast.

(b) Their Approval (v. 13) - We are not told who these future kings are, but it can be assumed that they rise from the middle East, and are in close association with each other. Their desire to support and further the cause of the beast is not by force, but mutual consent binds them together. To give their "mind" to the union is to give their purpose, opinion and resolve to put the power of their delegated authority to the support of the beast.

Confrontation with the Lamb (v. 14)

This is introduced here to show the intent of the beast to have supreme authority, with no rival to deny him his desire. The battle itself is recorded in 19:19-21. The beast and his confederate armies are spoken of as being "overcome" here, whereas their utter destruction is seen in Ch 19.

The Sovereign Lord, in association with his saints, must overcome them because of who he is, "Lord of lords and King of kings". The saints, "they that are with him are called, and chosen and faithful", are linked with Christ because his rights to rule are being attacked and in his reign, his saints are fellow heirs. In Ch 19, it is the angel warriors who are linked with him, for there it is the battle that is prominent.

Her Annihilation (vv. 15-18)

And he saith unto me, The waters which thou sawest, where the whore sitteth, are peoples, and multitudes, and nations, and tongues. And the ten horns which thou sawest upon the beast, these shall hate the whore, and shall make her desolate and naked, and shall eat her flesh, and burn her with fire. For God hath put in their hearts to fulfil his will, and to agree, and give their kingdom unto the beast, until the words of God shall be fulfilled. And the woman which thou sawest is that great city, which reigneth over the kings of the earth. (Revelation 17:15-18)

Her Control of the Nations (v. 15)

The woman has absolute sway over the multitudes of humanity in her position as sitting upon many waters as seen in verse 1. This now interpreted for us.

The scene is one of international supremacy. Rome has never known this, and her sphere of authority has only been seen in those nations that have been influenced by their links with the western world. But such is the influence of the doctrines of Babylon that they have polluted all humanity, and it has led to her control of all humanity.

Her Catastrophic End (v. 16)

The AV, following the TR, makes this an act by the ten horns. There is no reason why this should not be, for in their zeal to exalt the beast, who is now in the temple at Jerusalem sitting as God, they want no opposition to his claims. As he is the eighth head, and a resurrected man, this chapter speaks of the final three and a half years of Gentile dominion. Babylon and its religious system must be crushed, as another form of worship is introduced. Not a worship of spirits and the spirit world (1 Cor. 12:2) but of man deified and leading all worship directly to Satan (13:4).

That the beast is in agreement with this destruction cannot be doubted, and may have led to the reading that says, "The ten horns which thou sawest and the beast", rather than the horns "upon" the beast. The point is technical, but makes no difference to the outcome of the hatred that has risen to cause the destruction.

The hatred is intense, it means to loathe in disgust. Such hatred results in her catastrophic overthrow. Every form of religion is opposed; the two witnesses suffer at the hand of the beast in Ch 11, now the harlot suffers at the hands of his cohorts, with whom he is in full collusion. The four expressions about "her" that are used to describe her destruction, would indicate the total devastation that shall befall her. Her wealth is wasted, and she is left desolate, her gorgeous apparel is stripped from her and she is exposed as being naked, her flesh is cannibalised, and she is eaten, and the residue is scorched, and she is burnt with fire". The following chapter gives a graphic picture of the extent of the judgement that befalls her.

Confirming God's Will (v. 17)

God used an unsaved prophet in the Old Testament to reveal His will; Balaam's prophecies are recorded in Num. 23-24. He used an unsaved priest in the New Testament, Caiaphas, to prophesy "that Jesus should die for that nation" (John 11:49-51). Now he takes up those who had links with the whore, to utterly destroy her. Both the destruction of the woman and the alliance of the kings to the beast are in accord with the will of God, "until the words of God shall be fulfilled". Prophecy has foretold all that has happened in this chapter, and the beast and his associates are merely fulfilling the word of God. That the will of God should be carried out by wicked men is not surprising when we consider Prov. 16:4, "The Lord hath made all things for himself: yea, even the wicked for the day of evil".

Consolidating the Prophecy (v. 18)

We are told conclusively, "the woman which thou sawest is that great city which reigneth over the kings of the earth". In Ch 21, we shall see a city that is a bride, but here we have a whore that is a city. Thus the woman is not merely a religious system, but a definite place. It was from this place, Babylon, that all idolatrous teaching arose. It was the seat and centre of teaching regarding evil doctrine. God is going to destroy the source of evil, which has dominated and seduced all nations. Rome, though having great influence in a western world and in nations influenced by the west, has nevertheless never dominated all nations: Babylon has, and does.

The kings of the earth are those spoken of in verse 3, they are the same kings who bemoan her fall (18:9). The beast and the ten kings have been moving in association with her, rather than dominated by her.

Chapter 18
Babylon, her fall recorded

Introduction

Why any should distinguish between these two chapters, and make them separate judgements on two different things I find difficult to discern. Someone states a thing as a fact; and then others think that they see it. This is evidenced in all walks of life, and we see it particularly with the doctrine of evolution, which today seems no longer to be a theory, but is accepted as if it were a proven thesis. That the whore is judged for her great impiety revealed in Ch 17 is obvious. That the whore is a city is expressly and plainly stated (17:18). That, that city is Babylon stands out upon the page for all to read (17:5, 18:2, 18:10 and 18:21). That a city is a commercial centre is the reason for its existence. Zechariah 5:5-11 indicates that a rebuilt Babylon will be the commercial centre of the world in tribulation days. Various reasons have been the means of bringing a city into existence. Manchester England, the city of my birth, rose because of the cotton industry, Stoke-on-Trent where I presently reside was established because of the fine china it produces, with most of the world's great china houses centred there. Babylon's origin was based on religious evil, as taught in Genesis 11, an evil that has influenced every religious system that is opposed to the word of God the world over. The tower of Genesis 11:4 was the dominant feature of Babylon. If God is going to destroy the centre of religious evil, the city must fall with it.

It again seems clear that the judgement is spoken of in this chapter as having already taken place. The angel (v. 2), the monarchs, merchants and mariners (vv. 9-19) are all reflecting on an event that is past. That event took place under the ten kings in Ch 17:16-18. The second angel of Ch 18:21, and the heavenly multitude of Ch 19:1-6 all give their voice to a single judgement that affects both the religious and commercial aspects of one city, Babylon.

One of the main factors that cause expositors to suggest that this is another judgment is that Ch 18 commences with the words "after this" (*meta tauta*). As we have seen, this expression occurs ten times in the book. At each occurrence it would indicate another revelation to John. Charles H. Dyer, however, has set forth a very strong argument that *meta tauta* "can simply be indicating the time sequence in which the visions were revealed to John. The temporal use (as opposed to the eschatological use) of *meta tauta* in the book of Revelation is always indicated by John's inclusion of a verb of perception ('I saw', 'I heard'). In doing this he indicated that the time sequence was in his observation of the visions and not necessarily in the unfolding of future events. When John wanted to indicate a gap of time in future events, he did not include a verb of perception". He then enumerates the verses that have the verb of perception. Ch 4:1; 7:1; 7:9; 11:5; 18:1; 19:1 (Bibliotheca Sacra, 1987). Again he adds, "The four references not associated with verbs of perception seem to indicate chronological distinctions between future events. However, those with verbs of perception only indicate the order in which the parts of the vision were viewed by John. Thus the mere presence of *meta *tauta* in 18:1 does not indicate a chronological distinction between the chapters. It only shows that the events revealed to John by the second angel were shown *after* he had viewed the woman on the beast".

With these things in mind we shall look on the chapter not as another judgement upon a separate place, but as the revealing of the extent, and the effects that are produced by the outpouring of God's wrath upon Babylon itself.

The Cry of the Angel (vv. 1-2)

And after these things I saw another angel come down from heaven, having great power; and the earth was lightened with his glory. And he cried mightily with a strong voice, saying, Babylon the great is fallen, is fallen, and is become the habitation of devils, and the hold of every foul spirit, and a cage of every unclean and hateful bird. (Revelation 18:1-2)

The Character of the Angel (v. 1)

At the fall of Babylon an angelic messenger is sent to proclaim its destruction. It is not surprising that, as with other passages in this book, some would see this angel as the person of Christ because of the glory shining forth at his appearance. Enough has been said on other passages to leave this matter well alone, except to say Christ is never seen as "another angel". As we have said before, he who is exalted far above them will not lower himself again to be equal with them. Again, the book of Revelation gives us great insight into the splendour of angels in their creation, it also unveils the various offices they hold, and the character they bear.

Two things are said of this angel **(a) His Authority** and **(b) His Aura**.

(a) His Authority - He has great power, but this is a delegated power not a power that is inherent, as it would be if this were a divine person that is before us. The word for power here is *exousia* and has this thought associated with it (see Matt. 8:9; 9:8; 10:1; 21:23, 24, 27; 28:18), but it is a great power that is invested in him.

(b) His Aura - The glory that is displayed lightens the earth. The pall of darkness that has held men in its grip from the insidious workings of Babylon has at last been dealt with, and light can now be revealed.

The Collapse of the Adjudged (v. 2)

If the glory of the angel lightens the earth, his voice must carry far and wide the message from heaven. This is the first of six heavenly voices that speak of her fall, each relating to one aspect of the fall as seen by the heavenly host:

18:1-2	-	Her Ruin
18:4	-	The Recovery of the Saints
18:21-24	-	Her Removal

19:1-3   - Her Righteous Judgement
19:4   - The Rejoicing of Heaven's Hierarchy at her Overthrow
19:5-6   - God's Rights to Reign.

Though Walvoord like many others sees two distinct things in Ch 17 and 18, still he distinctly states, "The repetition of the verb 'is fallen', found in the aorist tense indicates a sudden event viewed as completed" (Revelation of Jesus Christ page 258). He goes on to say, "though the context would indicate a future event". Why this must be so is difficult to follow, for this chapter seems to speak of the effect the fall has on various individuals, some who have drunk the wine of her fornication, and others who are thankful to God to see her end. The fall recorded in Ch 17 at the hands of the ten kings has far reaching effects.

The Corruption Attested

There is nothing left now but for Babylon to become what she was always marked by, the habitation and hold of that which would speak of spiritual evil. A home for devils, such is the thought of habitation, and a prison for every unclean spirit and bird. The latter perhaps has in mind Matt. 13:4 and v. 19, where the birds symbolise the activity of the devil, and also vv. 31-32, where we have the parable of the mustard seed that grew so that the birds of the air could lodge in the branches of it, these verses also speaking of spiritual evil. If so, it is little wonder they are said to be "hateful", or as it should be "hated", this is heaven's description of them.

The Cause Announced (vv. 3-8)

For all nations have drunk of the wine of the wrath of her fornication, and the kings of the earth have committed fornication with her, and the merchants of the earth are waxed rich through the abundance of her delicacies. And I heard another voice from heaven, saying, Come out of her, my people, that ye be not partakers of her sins, and that ye receive not of her plagues. For her sins have reached unto heaven, and God hath remembered her iniquities. Reward her even as she rewarded you, and double unto her double according to her works: in the cup which she hath filled fill to her double. How much she hath glorified herself, and lived deliciously, so much torment and sorrow give her: for she saith in her heart, I sit a queen, and am no widow, and shall see no sorrow. Therefore shall her plagues come in one day, death, and mourning, and famine; and she shall be utterly burned with fire: for strong is the Lord God who judgeth her. (Revelation 18:3-8)

The reason for God allowing the ten kings to destroy her is now given; it is because of her sin (vv. 3- 5).

Her Sin (vv. 3-5)

Verse 3 is but a reiteration of what has been stated in Ch 17:2 with the added facts that the merchants of the earth have used the corruptions of Babylon to make themselves rich. The incident recorded in Acts 19:23-27 gives an apt illustration of what is here. For as Demetrius made gain from the silver shrines for Diana, and saw not only his but "the workmen of like occupation" (v. 25) losing their living as a result of the gospel, so here those who profit from idolatrous worship have been made rich with the abundance of her delicacies.

The verse again records what has been seen in Ch 17, where we have the **intoxication of the multitudes**, as they are made drunk with the wine of her evil doctrines that have corrupted their minds and caused them to rebel against all that God has taught in the scriptures of truth.

The **infidelity of monarchs** is another reason for the destruction of Babylon as they have been brought under her corrupting influences, and caused their subjects to receive her evil teaching. What a sad indictment it is of nations that they have rebelled against the truth of God and yielded to the evils of Babylon's doctrines.

We have also the **indulgence of merchants** as they have profited from their merchandise which they have sold. In a visit to the Far East, it was possible to see businesses given over entirely to the sale of idolatrous icons. Many make comfortable livings out of the doctrines of devils.

The Separation of Saints (vv. 4-5)

(a) The Call - The second voice from heaven is now heard, with a call to those who are called "my people". We have before us the prophecy recorded Jeremiah 51:45, "My people go ye out of the midst of her, and deliver every man his soul from the fierce anger of the Lord". Most expositors link the call with Israel alone, but as we have seen from Ch 7, there is a vast multitude from all nations who are redeemed in tribulation days, and this appeal must sound to any of God's people who could be associated with Babylon at that time.

(b) The Consequences - We are told that "evil communications corrupt good manners" (1 Cor. 15:33). That is, our associations affect our lives. The word "partakers" is *koinoneo* - to have in common, but prefixed with the preposition (*sun*) - to be one with. This makes it a very strong word to reveal that any association makes you one with its sins and as a result leaves you open to its plagues. What we condone, we encourage; we must not be linked with anything that is opposed to God. There are lessons here for every believer in any age, but a special call to God's people at that time. The second epistle of John (v. 11) gives a stark warning to any who are associated with those who peddle false doctrine, when even to give them a greeting is to make one a "partaker of his evil deed". The thought behind bidding them God speed in this verse is to give a greeting and by this we become linked to their sin.

(c) The Corruptions - As the tower of Genesis 11:4 sought to reach unto Heaven, so her sins that stem from it have done so. In the tower, men sought to refute all that God had left in the way of truth to men, and the sin of this rejection of his mind is seen and known by those of heaven. God is now bringing to remembrance the iniquity of centuries, and the judgement is to be severe, as verses 6-8 relate. The people of God will do well to separate themselves from such evil.

The Sentence Passed (v. 6)

The truth of Galatians 6:7 readily comes to mind here, "whatsoever a man soweth, that shall he also reap" and, as an old gardener once said to me, "you always get out more than you put in, or there is no point in putting it in". Babylon is to reap a full harvest "double unto her double according to her works". The cup of vengeance, which she hath filled with her wickedness, will be filled to her double.

Her Self Satisfaction (v. 7)

"Whosoever exalteth himself shall be abased" (Luke 14:11) aptly fits the thoughts before us. For the course of history that has marked Babylon brings forth the self-esteem that marks her. Having received the honour of kings and been satiated with the plaudits of nations, it is little wonder we see her as she is here portrayed, as she glorifies herself.

Her Self Exaltation is first exposed as she has sought the glory that belongs to God and Christ. Of the twenty-three occurrences of this word (*doxazo*) in the gospel of John, and the only other occurrence in Rev. 15:14, this is the only place where it is used of anyone other than divine persons. John reserves if for Deity. Of the sixty two references to the word in the New Testament, there are only six other times when it is not used of divine person, and four of those are linked with what is divine; Rom. 11:13 Paul's ministry; 1 Cor. 12:26 the "honour" of saints, that all partake in; 2 Cor. 3:10 the Glory of the Law and 1 Pet. 1:8 of the believer's joy and glory in the Saviour. Elsewhere, Matt. 6:2 and Rom. 1:21 are the only occasions when it is taken from the Lord. The first when sought of man, and the second when men refuse to give God his rightful glory and turn to idolatry.

Her Sumptuous Excesses. Along with the glory she delights in, all the trappings of such a position are fully indulged in, as she "lived deliciously". It is little wonder that her adherents who are duped by her, and become the channels for her doctrines follow the same desires, "These are spots in your feasts of charity, when they feast with you feeding without fear" (Jude v. 12).

Her Secret Exultation. The thoughts of her heart are made manifest as she contemplates the sitting in state that has been afforded her. Surrounded by lovers, she assumes all augurs well for the future. What she cannot foresee is the sorrow she thinks is beyond her, but she is soon to have a spectacular fall. Like other Babylonish monarchs before, Nebuchadnezzar (Dan. 4), and Belshazzar (Dan. 5), she will be swiftly brought down. Of Nebuchadnezzar it is said, "The same hour was the thing fulfilled" (4:33) as the judgement of God swept over him because of his pride. Belshazzar's fall is no less rapid, "In that night was Belshazzar the King of the Chaldeans slain" (5:30). This is revealed in verse 8.

Her Swift Sentence (v. 8)

Her torment and sorrow are seen to come in four ways as God pours out his plagues upon her. **Death, distress**, a **dearth** and utter **devastation** as she is "utterly burned with fire" bringing an end to her existence that will be swift and sudden. The burning of Ch 17:16 is again seen as her end, and, as God is seen to be the author of it in 17:17, using men to fulfil his will, so here it is "the Lord God who judgeth her".

Some have sought to make a distinction between the two chapters, and to strengthen the idea of two separate judgements, they see the destruction of Ch 17 being carried out by the ten kings alone, overlooking the fact that they are acting on the prompting of God, "to fulfil his will" (17:17). They see the judgement of Ch 18 by God exclusively without the involvement of the kings. "In Ch 17 it is the beast and his allies who destroy the harlot Babylon. Here it is God who destroys this aspect of Babylon" (Ryrie - Revelation, page 105).

Calamity for her Admirers (vv. 9-19)

And the kings of the earth, who have committed fornication and lived deliciously with her, shall bewail her, and lament for her, when they shall see the smoke of her burning, Standing afar off for the fear of her torment, saying, Alas, alas, that great city Babylon, that mighty city! for in one hour is thy judgment come. And the merchants of the earth shall weep and mourn over her; for no man buyeth their merchandise any more: The merchandise of gold, and silver, and precious stones, and of pearls, and fine linen, and purple, and silk, and scarlet, and all thyine wood, and all manner vessels of ivory, and all manner vessels of most precious wood, and of brass, and iron, and marble, And cinnamon, and odours, and ointments, and frankincense, and wine, and oil, and fine flour, and wheat, and beasts, and sheep, and horses, and chariots, and slaves, and souls of men. And the fruits that thy soul lusted after are departed from thee, and all things which were dainty and goodly are departed from thee, and thou shalt find them no more at all. The merchants of these things, which were made rich by her, shall stand afar off for the fear of her torment, weeping and wailing, And saying, Alas, alas, that great city, that was clothed in fine linen, and purple, and scarlet, and decked with gold, and precious stones, and pearls! For in one hour so great riches is come to nought. And every shipmaster, and all the company in ships, and sailors, and as many as trade by sea, stood afar off, And cried when they saw the smoke of her burning, saying, What city is like unto this great city! And they cast dust on their heads, and cried, weeping and wailing, saying, Alas, alas, that great city, wherein were made rich all that had ships in the sea by reason of her costliness! for in one hour is she made desolate. (Revelation 18:9-19)

How differently the world sees the judgement of God from those who value divine intervention in human affairs. Those who have had very close links with her, and have used her to their own end, have no sympathy with heaven at Babylon's fall. This section records the effect of Babylon's destruction on monarchs, merchants and mariners.

The Monarchs (vv. 9-10)

That these kings are not the ten who destroyed Babylon is evident. We see here those who have used Babylon to their own satisfaction. These are "the kings of the earth" of Ch 17:2 and 18:3, who "have committed fornication" with her and caused the inhabitants of the earth to have been made drunk with the wine of her fornication.

Their distress is recorded as they bewail and lament her. To bewail is to cry aloud, it is used of Peter as he realises his folly in denying the Lord (Matt. 26:75). The lament is that at being cut down, as the cutting down of a tree (Matt. 21:8, Mark 11:8) and is used of the grief of the women who followed the Lord to his crucifixion (Luke 23:22). These kings feel with intensity the loss of this great city. The loss is irrecoverable; the smoke of her burning displays the hopelessness of the situation.

Their distance is expressed. In the hour of judgement, though unhappy to see her fall, the former nearness in their fornication is now severed "for fear of her torment". They bewail their former paramour but are not prepared to stand with her.

Their declaration points to their distress, "Woe, Woe" and to Babylon's rapid destruction, "For in one hour is thy destruction come". She has dominated the world for centuries, but her fall will be swift and unmistakable.

The Merchants (vv. 11-16)

Their Tears (v. 11) - the overthrow of Babylon brings great grief to the merchants, causing weeping and mourning. The depth of their sorrow is not out of affection for Babylon, they feel the loss not because of the passing of someone loved, but because of the way it affects their business.

Their Trade (v. 11) - it is for personal reasons that they mourn, "for no man buyeth their merchandise any more". It would seem that Babylon has become a great commercial centre, and a centre of distribution for many of the great luxuries of the world. The financial loss will be catastrophic and many will be brought to bankruptcy in an hour. Babylon's fall will affect "the merchants of earth" and their financial collapse will be as rapid as Babylon's judgement.

Their Traffic (vv. 12-14) - the catalogue of goods sold displays the finery of the world. All that would speak of wealth and opulence are traded. The finest of jewels, costly materials, expensive furniture, delightful perfumes, the best of food and lavish entertainments are portrayed. Also that which is needful to ensure that every whim and fancy is satisfied, for it speaks of "slaves and souls of men". Does this reintroduce slavery into the world (if it were ever fully abolished)? Now with all restraint gone under the Man of Sin, the need of those to carry out the desires of men will bring many into forced labour. The margin has "bodies" for "souls" in v. 13, the TR has *soma* (body).

Again the delicious delicacies of the world always desired by the rich and noble. The dainties that please the palate are set forth as the normal diet of Babylon but, as on a former occasion when Babylon feasted and mocked what was of God, the judgement falls. Not now on the king alone, "in that night was Belshazzar the king of the Chaldeans slain" (Dan. 5:30), but the whole city is brought to ruins. Like the city itself in verses 21-24, when six times over it states that things will be found "no more at all" in her, so here, these pleasurable goods shall "no more at all" be found.

The Torment (vv. 15-16)

Like monarchs before them, these who have made great wealth out of Babylon "shall stand afar off". The dreadful sight of Babylon's fall, and the torment she is to endure, causes these merchants to withdraw from her, weeping and wailing. Their cry of woe is because the splendour that marked her has been brought to nothing. The costly array she wears is exactly the same as in Ch 17:4, teaching that one Babylon, not two, is set forth in these chapters. I would judge that the opening sentence of verse 17 belongs to verse 16 and is the reason for the cry of the merchants. All hope of future trade has gone by the rapid destruction, complete and entire, of the city.

The Mariners (vv. 17-10)

Like the kings and merchants before them, the captains, crew and companies in ships lament the sudden catastrophic fall of Babylon. Their distance, distress and future destruction is recorded. No mistake as to the identity of the city can be made, for that which is said of her in Ch 17 is reiterated. In Ch 17:16 she is burned with fire, in verse 18 of this chapter "they saw the smoke of her burning". Again in Ch 17:18 Babylon is called "that great city", so here it is said, "what city is like unto this great city".
Chapter 17 portrays Babylon as a whore and a mother and at least thirty five times the feminine gender is used in Ch 18 to describe Babylon. Expressions such as "her, she, a queen" and "no widow", describe her.

The Vindication of the Saints (vv. 20-24)

Rejoice over her, thou heaven, and ye holy apostles and prophets; for God hath avenged you on her. And a mighty angel took up a stone like a great millstone, and cast it into the sea, saying, Thus with violence shall that great city Babylon be thrown down, and shall be found no more at all. And the voice of harpers, and musicians, and of pipers, and trumpeters, shall be heard no more at all in thee; and no craftsman, of whatsoever craft he be, shall be found any more in thee; and the sound of a millstone shall be heard no more at all in thee; And the light of a candle shall shine no more at all in thee; and the voice of the bridegroom and of the bride shall be heard no more at all in thee: for thy merchants were the great men of the earth; for by thy sorceries were all nations deceived. And in her was found the blood of prophets, and of saints, and of all that were slain upon the earth. (Revelation 18:20-24)

Two classes are asked to rejoice at her fall, those in heaven and those who had responsibility on earth, the holy apostles and prophets. The rejoicing in heaven is described in Ch 19:1-6. The hosts of heaven have always had an interest in earth, and the events that have dishonoured God. The time has now come when the source of opposition is finally destroyed and the dismay at man's rebellion can be turned to delight.

The holy apostles and prophets are those who have had the prime responsibility in God's chief work, the Church. We are built upon their foundation (Eph. 2:20). This is a doctrinal foundation, as they dispensed the truth of God. They have the first place in the Church (1 Cor. 12:28), and would represent all that the truth of God would speak of. Babylon has opposed the truth, and her children are still vehemently against it. Even evangelicals, who profess a love for Christ, will adopt the Babylonish stance of refusing to accept all God's word. They cavil about such truths as headship and subjection. Church order as revealed in 1 Corinthians and 1 Timothy is totally ignored and separation from the world would hardly be recognised. What joy it will give to those now in heaven, who laid the doctrinal foundation, when they see that which has controlled many minds finally destroyed.

The Violent Overthrow of the City (v. 21)

There is no mistaking the severity and finality of Babylon's doom, in the symbolic action by the angel. It is in keeping with Jeremiah's action in Ch 51:63-64 when, after reading the book of prophecy concerning Babylon, he was to "bind a stone to it and cast it into the midst of Euphrates". Here it is "a great millstone" that is cast into the sea. The emphasis is upon the size (*megas*) of the stone, indicating that, when the action is complete, it will plummet to the bottom never to rise again. As any massive rock falling into the sea would cause oceanic disturbance, this is typical of the violence of Babylon's fall, never to rise again.

The Voices Silenced (vv. 22-23)

It cannot be said today that the voice of those whose voice will be heard no more has ceased. Babylon, built by Sadam Hussain, flourishes on the banks of the Euphrates. Raised for his own grandeur, and to immortalise his name, soon it will all perish under the hand of God.

Her music shall be heard no more at all. In keeping with its wealth, Babylon will become a centre for the arts, to gratify the minds of men. The first city, built for Cain's son Enoch, was characterised by music (Gen. 4:21), so will the last city be.

Her manufacturers shall be silenced. Again, the city of Genesis 4 had Tubal-Cain to thank for introducing the craftsman in "brass and iron". Opulence delights in grandeur. Men will seek to satisfy their tastes with the ability of craftsmen to make their homes and premises palatial.

The millstone will cease to roll, and her sound shall be heard no more. The sumptuous feasts requiring the fine flour and wheat of verse 13, along with the wine and oil, will no longer be held.

The mood created by the soft light shall be no more at all. All would speak of the desire of men to live a life of pleasure.

The ministry of preaching will be heard no more at all in her. The Lord "is longsuffering to us-ward not willing that any should perish" (2 Pet. 3:9). The proof of his love for the world is seen in "the voice of the bridegroom and of the bride". The call of God to repent and enter into blessing reaches even to Babylon. It is a sad day for men when the voice of heaven is silenced and the gospel is preached no more.

Sorceries will have deluded the minds of all men. The word sorcery "primarily signified the use of medicine, drugs, spells, then poisoning, then sorcery (AV 'witchcraft')" (Vine's Dictionary of New Testament Words). The rise of the occult with its drug abuse so prominent now will be dominant in Babylon until it pleases God to destroy her.

The Victims of Babylon (v. 24)

Again, the cumulative guilt of her atrocities is pronounced. The saints of all ages are envisaged here. All persecution in all times stems from the Mother of Harlots, their blood is found in her.

Chapter 19
The worship, the wedding, and the war
Introduction

Following the destruction of Babylon, there are eight movements brought to us by the Spirit of God in these chapters (19:1 - 21:8). They bring to a conclusion the third vision, and they express the purpose of God to bring in the new heaven and earth with every opposing element dealt with.

These eight movements are:

19:1- 6	-	The Multitudes Of Heaven
19:7-10	-	The Marriage Of The Lamb
19:11-21	-	The Majesty Of Christ
20:1-3	-	The Manacling Of Satan
20:4-6	-	The Manifestation Of The Kingdom
20:7-10	-	The Madness Of Men
20:11-15	-	The Might Of The Throne
21:1-8	-	The Making Of A New Heaven And Earth

Chapter 19 itself has three divisions, as seen below:

vv. 1-6	-	The Worship
vv. 7-10	-	The Wedding
vv. 11-21	-	The War

The Multitude in Heaven (vv. 1-6)

And after these things I heard a great voice of much people in heaven, saying, Alleluia; Salvation, and glory, and honour, and power, unto the Lord our God: For true and righteous are his judgments: for he hath judged the great whore, which did corrupt the earth with her fornication, and hath avenged the blood of his servants at her hand. And again they said, Alleluia. And her smoke rose up for ever and ever. And the four and twenty elders and the four beasts fell down and worshipped God that sat on the throne, saying, Amen; Alleluia. And a voice came out of the throne, saying, Praise our God, all ye his servants, and ye that fear him, both small and great. And I heard as it were the voice of a great multitude, and as the voice of many waters, and as the voice of mighty thunderings, saying, Alleluia: for the Lord God omnipotent reigneth. (Revelation 19:1-6)

The Anthem (vv. 1-3)

The first six verses belong to Ch 17-18, for though they are introduced with "After this", it is as a result of Babylon's fall that the praise of heaven resounds.

We now hear the first Hallelujahs in the New Testament. Like the first in the Old Testament, (Psalm 104:35), it is connected with the overthrow of the wicked. At last, when that which has led the world in its rebellion against God is judged, the multitudes in heaven rejoice. Their praise is directed "unto the Lord our God". Walvoord points out the fact that the article occurs before each of the words. The praise ascribes to God all that Babylon would have sought. The salvation they proffered is God's alone. The splendour of glory, the status in honour, and the strength of power, none can share.

The Lord our God is never vindictive: if he is to act in judgment it must be "true and righteous". The Whore has been guilty of corruption and violence. The first generally leads to the other (Gen. 6:11).

Is this great multitude comprised of many who were slain at the whore's hands? Are those who cry, "How long, O Lord, holy and true, dost thou not judge and avenge our blood on them that dwell on the earth?" (6:10) among them? For the first two Hallelujahs are uttered by "much people" in heaven.

Such is their joy in seeing the destruction of that which has always opposed God, that a second hallelujah must burst forth from their lips. It is evident from these verses that the saints in heaven will know and see events that are taking place on earth. They will fully acknowledge God's rights in dealing with religious evil, unlike many of God's children today who are associated with it, and some who hold places of prominence in systems that have turned their back on virtually every biblical truth. The excuse that is raised is that if they were to leave there would be no one to stop the progress of evil that they hold; they also profess to hope to win some of these for Christ. They are in the position of Lot, when he sat in the gate of Sodom, seeking to be one of its rulers, and thereby hoping to hold back the evil (Gen. 19:1), and we know that his position there did nothing to halt the progress of evil. The call of Ch 18:4 is still applicable: "Come out of her my people, that ye be not partakers of her sins".

They appreciate the finality of the judgement, for "her smoke rose up for ever and ever". The latter expression, "for ever and ever" has eternal connotations linked with it. In the seven references in the epistles, it is always added to ascriptions of praise to God for his goodness to men (see Gal. 1:5; Phil. 4:20; 1 Tim. 1:17; 2 Tim. 4:8; Heb. 13:21; 1 Pet. 4:11; 5:11). The phrase occurs 13 times in the book of Revelation, of which 9 are to God or Christ, and four to others. Again, of these four, three are linked with the eternal judgement of those who commit evil: Ch 14:11 upon those who worship the Beast, here upon The Whore Babylon, Ch 20:10 the destiny of the wicked unsaved dead. The last reference is markedly different: Ch 22:5 where it is the reign of the saints that is seen. Thus, like all "fours" in scripture, they divide into a three and a one.

The Amen (v. 4)

Those in close association with the throne add their voices to those of the great multitude. This is the last time the four and twenty elders and four living creatures are seen in the book. They first appear when the throne of God is set for judgement (Ch 4), and when that judgement is completed they fade into the background. The future dealings of God with the world are with Christ and his Bride. The Bride is about to come to the fore, linked to Christ. The ministry of these heavenly beings must take a different character. Nevertheless, on the fall of Babylon, with heaven ringing with the rejoicing of the multitude over its judgement, they must give their "Amen"! Though they themselves had not personally suffered at Babylon's hands, they also have witnessed God's rights being rejected, and his people suffering. They must give God thanks for his righteous dealings.

The Anticipation (vv. 5-6)

If the first three hallelujahs are about Babylon's fall, the last would seem to anticipate the marriage of the Lamb. The throne of v. 5 seems to become animated. Is this the voice of God himself calling for his rights? Or is this the four living creatures, who in Ch 4:6 are seen to be in the midst of the throne? Is it they who call for all his servants, and all who fear him, to add to the praise? The answer to these questions is not immediately evident. There is an immediate response to the call from the multitude who acknowledge his claims, powerful and echoing, as the surge of waters, and the sound of thunder. Added to this "Hallelujah" is the cry that, "the Lord God omnipotent reigneth".

The Marriage of The Lamb (vv. 7-10)

Let us be glad and rejoice, and give honour to him: for the marriage of the Lamb is come, and his wife hath made herself ready. And to her was granted that she should be arrayed in fine linen, clean and white: for the fine linen is the righteousness of saints. And he saith unto me, Write, Blessed are they which are called unto the marriage supper of the Lamb. And he saith unto me, These are the true sayings of God. And I fell at his feet to worship him. And he said unto me, See thou do it not: I am thy fellowservant, and of thy brethren that have the testimony of Jesus: worship God: for the testimony of Jesus is the spirit of prophecy. (Revelation 19:7-10)

The Resplendent Groom (v. 7)

This is a chapter of two women, two kings, and two suppers. The praise of v. 6 continues to rise, and the multitude themselves are filled with joy and exultation at the prospect that awaits the Lamb of God. They give glory to him, such is the thought behind the word, "honour" (*doxan*). The day of splendour has arrived for the Lord Jesus. In a western culture, the glory of the wedding day belongs to the bride. Here the glory must belong to Christ; it is his as the Lamb who purchased the bride. The cost of purchasing a bride is recognised; there could be no bride without Calvary. There can be no marriage until all that is spurious is put out of the way. With the whore destroyed, the marriage can take place, and "the marriage of the Lamb is come". Walvoord strangely says, "The marriage of the Lamb is properly the marriage supper of the Lamb" (page 271), but the supper is not until v. 9, and the word for supper (*deipnon*) is certainly not in this verse, nor does a bride make herself ready for the supper, but for the ceremony.

Much has been written as to the identity of the Bride. Some, like Bullinger, would make the Bride to be Israel. But as Thomas has well said, "the difficulty of including Israel along with the church as part of the Bride is a chronological one. Old Testament saints and dead saints from the period of Daniel's seventieth week will rise in time for the Millennium (Dan. 12:1-2), but not in time to join Christ in his triumphal return (19:14)" (Thomas, Revelation, page 368). Israel is seen as a wayward wife, who played the harlot, and is given a bill of divorce (See Jer. 3; Ezekiel 16; Hosea 2). Isaiah 54 records her recovery and restoration as the wife of Jehovah, but Israel could never be the chaste virgin bride that is presented to the Lamb. That honour must belong alone to the saints of this present church age: she, who is so beautifully depicted in Eph. 5:25-33. They are the past object of his love (v. 25), the present object of his cleansing (v. 26), the future object of his glory (v. 27), and the constant object of his care (v. 29).

The first marriage took place on earth, and the bride came from the bone of Adam. The last marriage takes place in heaven and the bride again comes from the wounds of her husband. It is evident that there was no sin in either marriage, and this marriage is indissoluble, the permanent purpose of marriage will be enjoyed. There is no divorce. On earth, the saints of this dispensation are seen as a body, in unity and ministry, now we are seen as a bride in love.

The Radiant Garment (v. 8)

The Bride is seen in a garment that is given, gained, and glorious. "The bride has made herself ready": this would point to the judgement seat of Christ, when, after the rapture the saints must give account to him. Not for sin, for that was settled at the cross, but for service. The beautiful garment of fine linen, clean and white, is said to be, "the righteousness of the saints" (TR), and has justly been put as "the righteous acts of the saints". It is the collective reward displayed by the Bride, given by the hand of Christ. Little deeds of kindness and service, rendered now, will adorn the saints then. What am I sewing into this "gorgeous robe"? For the word "white" is that used of the robe they draped the Lord in when they sent him to Pilate (Luke 23:11). He was a man in rejection, we will be in the nearest place of affection.

The Rejoicing Guests (v. 9)

John is told to write regarding the blessing that will be known by those who are called to the marriage supper. As the one who calls John to write cannot be the multitudes of either v. 1 or v. 6, then we must go back to the angel of 17:1 and 17:15, to identify him, remembering that this angel introduces the third vision, and we are still within its confines. No other angel appears to John after this, until the angel who brings the fourth vision appears (21:9).

The purpose of John's writing is to speak of the blessedness that will be enjoyed by those who enjoy the marriage supper. That there is a distinction between the Bride and the guests is obvious, though some would seek to make them the same, but as seen under different figures. That there is a blessing associated with the call, would indicate these are redeemed people, yet do not form part of the Church, his Bride. From the parables of Matt. 22:1-14, and Matt. 25:1-13, the supper takes place on earth, and ushers in the millennial kingdom. The virgins of Matt. 25 are those of Israel who are awaiting the return of the bridegroom and his bride, though, as here, it is the groom who is prominent, the nation awaits him. One would suggest that the guests are no less than those who will have part in the glorious kingdom of our Lord Jesus, the rule and authority of which will also be shared with the saints of this present church age. The kingdom is seen as a great festive occasion, with the resurrection of Old Testament saints and the raising of tribulation saints, apart from those who will still be alive at the Lord's return, and witness his delivering power from the tyrannies of the Man of Sin. There will be a vast company to rejoice with the Lord at his union with his precious Bride. The certainty of God's word brings it to pass: "These are the true sayings of God".

The Refused Glory (v. 10)

If v. 9 records the faithfulness of John to write, we are now confronted with his folly to worship a created being. The angel, like Peter (Acts 10:25), refuses the homage, and reminds John that he is his equal in office, if not in nature. He also bears "the testimony of Jesus" like John (Ch 1:9). It is a prophetic testimony borne by angels and by men. It unfolds the bringing in of God's King, and God himself must be worshipped.

The Majesty of Christ (vv. 11-21)

And I saw heaven opened, and behold a white horse; and he that sat upon him was called Faithful and True, and in righteousness he doth judge and make war. His eyes were as a flame of fire, and on his head were many crowns; and he had a name written, that no man knew, but he himself. And he was clothed with a vesture dipped in blood: and his name is called The Word of God. And the armies which were in heaven followed him upon white horses, clothed in fine linen, white and clean. And out of his mouth goeth a sharp sword, that with it he should smite the nations: and he shall rule them with a rod of iron: and he treadeth the winepress of the fierceness and wrath of Almighty God. And he hath on his vesture and on his thigh a name written, KING OF KINGS, AND LORD OF LORDS. And I saw an angel standing in the sun; and he cried with a loud voice, saying to all the fowls that fly in the midst of heaven, Come and gather yourselves together unto the supper of the great God; That ye may eat the flesh of kings, and the flesh of captains, and the flesh of mighty men, and the flesh of horses, and of them that sit on them, and the flesh of all men, both free and bond, both small and great. And I saw the beast, and the kings of the earth, and their armies, gathered together to make war against him that sat on the horse, and against his army. And the beast was taken, and with him the false prophet that wrought miracles before him, with which he deceived them that had received the mark of the beast, and them that worshipped his image. These both were cast alive into a lake of fire burning with brimstone. And the remnant were slain with the sword of him that sat upon the horse, which sword proceeded out of his mouth: and all the fowls were filled with their flesh. (Revelation 19:11-21)

We are now brought face to face with the mighty event that all the redeemed wait for, the return in majestic glory of our Lord Jesus. The hosts of heaven also desire to see the Lord glorified, where men have despised and rejected him. There are three divisions to the section:

vv. 11-16   - The Coming Sovereign
vv. 17-18   - The Call To The Supper
vv. 19-21   - The Conquest Of Sinners

His Appearance (v. 11)

We are now introduced to the great event of his coming. The apostle saw "heaven opened". When he was brought into the throne room of heaven (Ch 4:1), it was "a door opened in heaven" that let him in. Now that the King is coming out, Heaven itself rolls aside to reveal his majesty. This thing will not be done in a corner. Every eye is going to see him (1:7). He is coming in flaming fire with the angels of his might (2 Thess. 1:7-8). He is coming in the "clouds of heaven with power and great glory" (Matt. 24:30). He is riding upon a white horse, always the symbol of the conquest of earth. The Man of Sin, unnamed but not unknown (6:2), imitating the Lord, rides upon a white horse, "conquering and to conquer", bringing men to warfare, anarchy, famine and death. Now the true King rides to deliver his people and to establish a glorious kingdom. There are four names associated with Christ in his coming. He is called "faithful and true": the name of **sincerity**, in this his character is manifest; he is faithful to God, and true to all that has been committed to him.

Unlike all other wars, this will be in righteousness. My children recently gave me a book of the century past. A large tome of photographs, the striking thing about it is the brutality of war, scene after scene of carnage and devastation. On a visit to the national war memorial in Canberra, Australia, one could not help but be moved at the violence of humanity, all at the whim of some despot. We must thank our God that all is soon to cease, ungodly men in rebellion must perish, but then the warrior King will usher in a glorious kingdom of peace.

His Adornment (v. 12)

His eyes "as a flame of fire" discern all. Not now the man of sorrows. No tears of compassion as at the tomb of Lazarus, or as those over Jerusalem's missed opportunities (Luke 19:41). The warrior King rides "to execute judgement upon all, and to convince all that are ungodly among them of all their ungodly deeds which they have ungodly committed, and of all their hard speeches which ungodly sinners have spoken against him" (Jude v. 15).

But adorning the once thorn-crowned brow are many diadems. He wears no crown in Ch 1 as the judging priest to the church, but as a warrior king he has "many diadems". The beast has a limited authority of "ten crowns" (13:1). It is unlimited and universal for the Lord.

There are three other names associated with the Lord Jesus at his coming. In this verse we have his **secret** name, "a name written, that no man knows but he himself". It speaks of the fullness of divine nature, which is only known by divine persons (Matt. 11:27). His **sovereign** name is the theme of verse 16.

His Attire (v. 13)

The Lord is seen in "a vesture dipped in blood". Is this a timely reminder of his rejection at Calvary? Are men to realise the reason for their own judgement? Some would link this with Isa. 63:1-6 where the nation sees him coming after the battle "with dyed garments from Bozrah". They speak of it as anticipating the bloodshed to come. But Isa. 63 is after the treading of the winepress, and with victory accomplished; the blood of his enemies will be sprinkled on his garments (Isa. 63:3). This seems to be more in accord with what will happen when "he treadeth the winepress of the fierceness and wrath of Almighty God" (v. 15), rather than at his appearance out of heaven. Seiss would deny any reference to Calvary, or to it being anticipative, but rather, a display of all his past victories as Israel's commander (page 436-437).

The third name is now introduced, not the secret name, but the **searching** name, "his name is called 'The Word of God'." In relation to God he is "The Word" (John 1:1), as regards believers he is "The Word of Life" (1 John 1:1). The present title, "The Word Of God" is to the world. Men will be searched by him and found wanting, the Word of God exposes the true character of the heart of man.

The Army (v. 14)

The Lord will not return alone when he is manifested in glory. He is to be accompanied by the hosts of heaven. Many expositors state that the army is the Bride, the saints of this dispensation, but now revealed as warriors with the great warrior King. Others would link Old Testament saints and tribulation saints with them. The assumption is made from the fact that they wear a garment of "fine linen white and clean". But as we have seen earlier, this is not the attire of believers only. Angelic beings are also so dressed. It is symbolic of the purity that must mark any who are associated with the heavenly courts. One cannot see the church here primarily; for the church is always seen as a compound unit, and never seen as a diverse company of individuals, such as make up an army. That God has a heavenly host is apparent, and these are called "the armies of heaven". Jacob recognised angels as being God's host (Gen. 32:2). Joshua saw "the Captain of the Lord's host" (Josh. 5:13-15). Evidently this was a Christophany, for he would not have had to remove his shoes for an angel. This appearance gave him confidence for the conflict in Canaan. Evidence of God's delivering power by the hand of the host of heaven is seen in 2 Kings 7:6. That the Lord is going to be displayed with "his mighty angels" is clear from 2 Thess. 1:7; Matt. 16:27. If this is so why cannot these be angels here? Angels have been instrumental in bringing great judgements on the earth during tribulation days, why should they not appear for its climax? Those angels that would have come to his aid in the garden of Gethsemane now appear with him in glory. It is to be noticed that this army is not armed. The battle is the Lord's, he alone will deal with men, and the weapons are his alone.

The Arsenal (v. 15)

Three symbols of judgement are borne by the warrior King. "From his mouth goeth a sharp sword". It is the weapon of immediate use, the remnant of the armies of the beast will be slain by it (v. 21). This is evidently the sword of Heb. 4:12, the Word of God. By it he put to silence the ignorance of foolish men, after the Herodians, the Sadducees, and the Pharisees sought to catch him in his words. They "durst not ask him any more questions" (Matt. 22:15-46). Through his word, disease, demons, and death were put to flight. The elements must bow before it and be muzzled (Mark 4:39). Also the army of men who came to take him to trial and crucifixion must fall at his feet in the garden of Gethsemane (John 18:6). It must be seen that it is man who is on the ground in John's gospel, not the Lord Jesus, for he is God in that book.

His governmental authority throughout the millennium is the subject of his second weapon, "a rod of iron", for the Lord is returning to establish his kingdom, which will be inflexible. Sin will be instantly dealt with, obedience will be insisted upon, righteousness will be the sceptre of his kingdom. Peace cannot be enjoyed without it. The saints will also carry the rod (2:27), another pointer that they are not in the army, but will be the administrators of the government of the kingdom.

Finally, "He treadeth the winepress of the fierceness and wrath of Almighty God". This is the fulfilment of Isa. 63:1-6; Rev. 14:17-20. The Lord will crush every enemy beneath his feet, not merely those who gather themselves together to make war against him (v. 19).

His Authority (v. 16)

As the Lord descends in majestic splendour, his title is apparent for all to see. The last of the four names he bears is emblazoned upon his robes. His sovereignty cannot be hid, for he is "KING OF KINGS, AND LORD OF LORDS". It holds the place of the sword, for Psa. 45:3 bids the King to "Gird thy sword upon thy thigh". The sword is the symbol of rule (Rom. 13:4). With the sword proceeding out of his mouth to execute judgement, then in the place of authority is his title of authority. Thomas translates the phrase as "and he has on his garment, even on his thigh, a name written: King of kings and Lord of lords". He further states, quoting Swete, "This gives a better sense than understanding part of the name as written on the garment and part on the thigh. As he sits on his white horse, the part of the cloak covering the thigh is the most conspicuous part and is visible to all" (Thomas, Revelation page 390).

The Call To The Supper (vv. 17-18)

The Figure in The Sun (v. 17)

The apostle constantly draws attention to the position of angels in this book. Where they are is important to him. In Ch 7:1-2 John sees an angel standing on the four corners of the earth, and in v. 2 another comes from the east. In Ch 8:3 he sees one at the altar, in v. 13, one is flying in the middle of heaven to proclaim the woe judgments. Another is in the midst of heaven in 14:6 to proclaim the everlasting gospel. Again in 10:2, he sees the angel with his feet on the sea and the earth. Others are noticed in connection with the temple (14:15, 17; 15:6). This angel is silhouetted in the sun, plain for all the fowls to see and hear.

The Fowl Summoned (v. 17)

The call is, "Come and gather yourselves together". All is in preparation for them to be at God's banquet. The table is yet to be spread, but the guests are called. Unlike those in the parable of Luke 14:16-24, they will not seek to be excused.

Feasting At The Supper

The supper is called, "the supper of the great God". It is a blessing to be called to the marriage supper of the Lamb but dismay and despair for men who will be the meal of fowl. What a sad end for those who refuse the call of the Saviour, to be a meal at the call to this supper.

The Flesh Of Soldiers

Five times over the birds are bidden to eat the flesh of those slain on the battlefield of Armageddon, the hill of slaughter, that we take this scene to be. The pomp, pride, and glory of man are brought to naught, as God has them in derision.

The Conquest of Sinners (vv. 19-21)

The Battle Array (v. 19)

This verse is the fulfilment of Psalm 2:1-3, where the "kings of the earth set themselves, and the rulers take counsel together against the Lord, and against his anointed" (v. 2). We see that "the beast and the kings of the earth" set themselves in direct confrontation with the Lord Jesus Christ. Having removed him from the earth by means of Calvary at the end of his public ministry, there is again a concerted effort to seek his destruction when he appears the second time. "He that sitteth in the heavens shall laugh: The

Lord shall have them in derision. Then shall he speak unto them in his wrath, and vex them in his sore displeasure" (Psa. 2:4-5). How beautifully this describes the scene before us.

The Beast Abased (v. 20)

The verse needs very little exposition; its teaching is self-evident. There is no battle, the two vessels of Satan are summarily taken and dealt with. Such is their sin, that they are immediately cast alive into the lake of fire; the lake of fire is for both the body and soul of men. Of all humanity, they seem to be the only men who do not stand before the judgement throne of God. The enormity of their sin is known, and they become the first occupants of everlasting fire. It is a sad fact that they will soon be joined in that lake by other men and women, who are soon to stand at the judgement of living nations (Matt. 25:31-46). This judgement throne set up at Jerusalem will determine the destiny of humanity, some for the kingdom (the sheep), others for the everlasting fire (the goats). We are informed that the lake of fire is for "the devil and his angels" (Matt. 25:41), yet the first occupants will be men. There is no thought of annihilation with this judgement. The beast and false prophet are seen to be there one thousand years later, "tormented day and night for ever and ever" (20:10). The Gospel of Mark (9:42-48) is most explicit as to the eternal nature of the judgement of ungodly men. "The fire that never shall be quenched" is quoted five times (vv. 43, 44, 45, 46, 48) in the passage. This should give us compassion for men, and cause us to raise a warning voice to them.

If the beast and false prophet are cast alive into the lake of fire, it will be remembered that two in the Old Testament went to heaven without dying: Enoch (Gen. 5:24; Heb. 11:5), and Elijah (2 Kings 2:1-11).

The Battalion Annihilated (v. 21)

The Lord not only deals with the leaders of the final rebellion against him, but with the rest who have been under his control. All these would wear the mark of the beast, or the number of his name. If they set themselves against Christ in all his might, they must feel the full weight of his wrath. It is enough for Christ to speak the word only, and his voice that brought worlds into being, will cause the flesh of men to be the supper of birds. By his actions, two of the great opposing factors are dealt with, the city Babylon, and the Beast and his armies. It only remains for Satan to be dealt with, which is the subject of Ch 20:1-3, and then the millennial kingdom can be ushered in.

Chapter 20

Future destiny settled

Introduction

The chapter break is unfortunate, for there is a continuous theme throughout the whole of this third vision. If the Lord is to rid the world of his enemies, and every evil power that has corrupted the earth, then Satan must be dealt with. The millennial kingdom would not be so glorious as it will be if Satan's influence was not removed. He must, at least for the period of the one thousand year reign, be restrained. We will then see his final end as he is cast into the place prepared for him and his angels. The chapter closes with the last judgement of the wicked unsaved dead, and this opens the way for the eternal state to be ushered in.

The Restraint of Satan (vv. 1-3)

And I saw an angel come down from heaven, having the key of the bottomless pit and a great chain in his hand. And he laid hold on the dragon, that old serpent, which is the Devil, and Satan, and bound him a thousand years, And cast him into the bottomless pit, and shut him up, and set a seal upon him, that he should deceive the nations no more, till the thousand years should be fulfilled: and after that he must be loosed a little season. (Revelation 20:1-3)

The Captor (v. 1)

The simplicity of the opening statement is sublime. It is "an angel" that comes down from heaven. Three times over in this book we see "mighty angels" (5:2; 10:1; 18:21). One would expect that such an angel would be needed to deal with Satan's power. The angel that is sent on the mission is not said to have special powers, it is as if any angel could fulfil the task of subduing Satan. He comes with the necessary means of effecting the captivity. The "key" is the symbol of authority, and the "great chain" that of power.

The Capture (v. 2)

There is no battle here, as in Ch 12:7 when Michael and his angels fought with the dragon and his angels to remove them from the heavenlies. It would seem that, when once cast down to the earth, the devil's power is greatly diminished. He also recognises that his end is near which causes him to have "great wrath" (12:12). Three thoughts are expressed in these verses in connection with Satan's incarceration:

a) The person bound is emphasised. All that Satan is, and every evil he has perpetrated is manifested in the titles given to him. The "dragon" would speak of his ferocious cruelty. The "old serpent" would unveil his subtlety, craft, and cunning. It takes us back to Eden's garden and the advent of sin. What a blessed thought to know that all this will be restrained during the millennium. The "devil" relates to his ministry as the accuser and the tempter, while "Satan" speaks of the enemy of God and man.

It will be a great day for the world when he is bound. The first and last references to binding in the New Testament are to Satan. Matt. 12:29 speaks of the wilderness experience of the Lord, when, as David went to meet Goliath to deliver Israel, so the Lord met Satan and bound him. Only by doing this could he "enter the strong man's house and spoil his goods", the thought being to plunder and take for himself. We see again that Satan is to be bound. If in the Gospels it is to enable the Lord Jesus to effectively fulfil his ministry, at this point of time it is to establish his monarchy.

b) The period of the binding is stressed. It involves the entire millennial Kingdom, of a thousand years. This is the first of six references in the chapter to the duration of the Kingdom of the Lord Jesus. The word of God is specific as to the length of time that the reign of Christ lasts, and no amount of argument by those who hold the a-millennial point of view can remove the simplicity of the statements that it will be for a thousand years. There are many who reject the fact that the Lord Jesus will rapture the saints of this present dispensation away from the tribulation period. They have failed to go beyond what Martha knew in John 11:24, when she said, "I know that he shall rise again in the resurrection at the last day". As we taught elsewhere, all doctrine is progressive, the coming of the Holy Spirit is to lead us into all truth" (Jn. 16:13) and, as the church is not the subject of Old Testament writings, neither could the truths concerning the rapture be the subject of that section of scripture. The New Testament prophets record these truths for us. There are a multitude of scriptures that would plainly refute the thought that there will be only one aspect of the coming of Christ and that all will be one event with no kingdom and just the eternal state brought in. A-millennialism fails to grasp the whole tenor of the word of God.

The Captivity (v. 3)

c) The prospect of Satan is the subject of this verse. Not only bound, but cast into the Abyss, the prison house of demons. A seal is set upon him. Unlike the seal that was put upon the stone of the Lord's grave, this cannot be broken; he will deceive the nations no more till the thousand years should be fulfilled. Yet we are told that release will come briefly at the end of the kingdom to prove that the heart of man does not change in spite of the beneficent reign of Christ. This will be seen in vv. 7-8.

The Reign Of Christ And The Saints (vv. 4-6)

And I saw thrones, and they sat upon them, and judgment was given unto them: and I saw the souls of them that were beheaded for the witness of Jesus, and for the word of God, and which had not worshipped the beast, neither his image, neither had received his mark upon their foreheads, or in their hands; and they lived and reigned with Christ a thousand years. But the rest of the dead lived not again until the thousand years were finished. This is the first resurrection. Blessed and holy is he that hath part in the first resurrection: on such the second death hath no power, but they shall be priests of God and of Christ, and shall reign with him a thousand years. (Revelation 20:4-6)

The Raising Of Thrones (v. 4a)

With all the opposing powers now dealt with, and every hindrance put out of the way, the reign of Christ can begin. The vision that fills John's eyes is not "the throne of his glory" (Matt. 19:28; 25:31), the throne of the Lord Jesus, but rather many thrones occupied by unnamed sitters. Along with them are saints who had suffered martyrdom for Christ and God's word, and "those who did not do homage to the beast, nor his image" (TR) . It would seem then, that there are three distinct companies.

As to the thrones and the sitters, these would seem to point to the saints of this present age, the church. The promise made to the disciples in Matt. 19:28 that they would be associated with the reign of Christ, sitting on twelve thrones, is now fulfilled. Also that promised to the overcomers in Ch 3:21, which puts all his own in close association with Christ when he sits on his throne in the kingdom. The word proclaims that we are "joint heirs with Christ" (Rom. 8:17). Also that when all is gathered up in Christ, "both which are in heaven, and which are on earth, even in him" (Eph. 1:10), of that time it is recorded that "we also have obtained an inheritance" (v. 11). The Holy Spirit is an earnest of it (v. 14). God cannot fail to bring us back with Christ to reign with him and to "judge (govern) the world" (1 Cor. 6:2). Let none deny the clear teaching of scripture as to the future destiny of the church.

The Resurrection of Saints (v. 4b)

John also sees saints who had suffered for their faith linked with the kingdom. The fear and dread of the dark days they had endured are past. Others who had withstood the beast, neither bowing to his claims, nor bearing the brand of his mark, along with them live and reign with Christ a thousand years. The company of Ch 7:9-17, would seem to be made up of those referred to here. In the former passage they "serve him day and night in his temple" (7:15). They are now revealed to be reigning with Christ when the kingdom is established.

The Rest of the Dead (v. 5)

The present verse precludes the doctrine of some who would deny a literal kingdom for the Lord Jesus. Refusing to bow to the plain teaching of the Word of God, they believe the church is an extension of Judaism, and that all God's blessings for the nation are now fulfilled in the church. They see but one final resurrection, which involves all the dead, some of whom will be blessed, and others damned. Such is a-millennialism, but the clear, plain teaching of scripture is to hand. The unbelieving will have no part in the kingdom, and only rise for the Great White Throne judgement of vv. 11-15. The resurrection to blessing is defined as "the first resurrection". This is not a resurrection connected with Time, but with Type. The truth is unfolded in

1 Cor. 15:20-23. The first resurrection covers a large period of time. Christ the firstfruits, belongs to it. Yet his resurrection occurred some two thousand years ago. This is to be followed by "they that are Christ's". The expression covers all known believers from Abel onwards. Yet the scriptures make a distinction between the times of resurrection when it states, "but every man in his own order", that is, in his own rank or file. All do not rise at the same time, but all are at some aspect of the coming of Christ. This again is seen to cover a period of time, all called "the coming". As to the saints of this dispensation, the church, its dead will be raised at the rapture (1 Thess. 4:13-18). We have seen that the two witnesses will be raised three days after their death (Rev. 11:11-12) during tribulation days. Old Testament saints have their resurrection after the tribulation (Dan. 12:2), and the company of tribulation saints of our present passage is also raised at the coming of the Lord Jesus back to earth to establish his kingdom. These verses show that the first resurrection covers a period of time, and is a type of resurrection, as v. 6 pronounces a resurrection to blessing. There is no second resurrection; all that remains is "the last resurrection" when all the lost dead souls will stand at the Great White Throne (vv. 11-15).

Reassurance for the Saints (v. 6)

Those who have part in the first resurrection are said to be "blessed and holy". This relates to their condition and character. The blessing and holiness are both eternal in their character, for "on such the second death hath no power". The second death is that which belongs to those who are to be cast into the lake of fire (v. 14).

Their blessed activity is described as both priestly and regal. Both God and Christ are going to be the subjects of their worship. What a day it will be when "all the earth shall be filled with the glory of the Lord" (Num. 14:21; Psa. 72:19)! Such a time can only be known when, in union with his own, Christ reigns in majesty.

The Release and Removal of Satan (vv. 7-10)

And when the thousand years are expired, Satan shall be loosed out of his prison, And shall go out to deceive the nations which are in the four quarters of the earth, Gog and Magog, to gather them together to battle: the number of whom is as the sand of the sea. And they went up on the breadth of the earth, and compassed the camp of the saints about, and the beloved city: and fire came down from God out of heaven, and devoured them. And the devil that deceived them was cast into the lake of fire and brimstone, where the beast and the false prophet are, and shall be tormented day and night for ever and ever. (Revelation 20:7-10)

The Release of Satan (v. 7)

The thousand-year reign of the Lord Jesus with his saints is needful for the putting down of "all rule and all authority and power - for he must reign, till he hath put all enemies under his feet" (1 Cor. 15:24-25). It is also necessary to establish a rest for God, something God has not enjoyed since the creation week, when sin entered to mar its beauty. From then until the establishment of the kingdom, the words of John 5:17 are appropriate: "My father worketh hitherto, and I work". A work of creation gives way to a work of redemption. When "the redemption of the purchased possession" (Eph. 1:14) brings in the kingdom, then the rest of Heb. 4:9 will be enjoyed.

In the final days of the kingdom, Satan is released from his prison. It is evident that a thousand years has done nothing to change his character, nor that of unredeemed humanity. Seen not as the dragon or the serpent, though moving with ferocity, there is no subtlety. The inveterate enemy of God and man seeks yet again to destroy all that is of God.

The Rebellious Host (vv. 8-9)

That which has been kept in check with the sceptre of righteousness and the rod of iron, will break out again under Satan's leadership. The multitude who gather as the sand of the sea must be children who are born during the millennium, for at its inception only believers go into it (Matt. 25:33-40). This multitude has given passive submission during the kingdom, but not an active willing submission to Christ. These are willing to rebel when they find a leader.

Regarding "Gog and Magog", Baines has written, "Gog and Magog are here used in a wider sphere than in Ezekiel, and their invasion differs in time and details, though agreeing in character and object, with that which he foretells. Ezekiel predicts an incursion by a great northern power called Gog, which from certain geographical indications, is easily identified with Russia. In the Revelation however, Gog and Magog are used to designate the nations, not merely from the north, from all parts, the 'four quarters of the earth' ". Again, the invasion named by Ezekiel is at the beginning of Christ's reign, that in Revelation at the end. The hosts in Ezekiel, too, fall on the mountains, and their bodies are buried; whereas the forces assembled in the Revelation are devoured by fire from heaven" (Serious Christian Vol. 16, page 270-271).

This rebellious host evidently opposes all that is precious to Christ, "and compassed the camp of the saints about, and the beloved city". The beloved city needs no interpretation, evidently Jerusalem is before us, that which is spoken of as "the joy of the whole earth, - the city of the great King" (Psa. 48:2). But what is "the camp of the saints"? This becomes the particular focus of the rebellious horde. The word "camp" is translated "castle" six times in the book of Acts, all are linked with Paul's captivity. It is also used of "the armies of the aliens" who are put to flight by faith (Heb. 11:34). Twice it relates to the camp of Israel, of which our Lord "suffered without the gate" (Heb. 13:11, 13). This evidently relates to Israel as a nation. Grant is thus led to think that the expression "the camp of the saints seems to be that of the heavenly saints, who are the Lord's host around it (that is, Jerusalem)" (Serious Christian Vol. 20, page 24). Could it be that this is the dwelling place of the saints of this dispensation, as they are linked with Christ in his kingdom? It is seen to be the object of the world's enmity along with Jerusalem, but distinct from it. If the saints are to return with their Lord, then there must be a place for them; this could be that place.

It is again noticeable that there is no battle. The millennial kingdom is preceded by a battle in which the opposing forces are summarily executed with the sword, which proceedeth out of the Lord's mouth. It is drawn to a close with another war in which there is no battle. Not with the Son exerting his own rights, but with God sending down fire from heaven and devouring them. By this means, they join the wicked dead who are soon to appear at the Great White Throne.

The Removal of Satan (v. 10)

The trinity of evil are again united, not now in perverse activity, undermining divine authority and seeking to establish their own glory, but in punishment. The lake of fire that is "prepared for the devil and his angels" (Matt. 25:41) at last receives the devil. As we have seen, he follows some men, one thousand years after they have begun their suffering.

There are notable evangelicals among us who deny the fact of eternal punishment. To do so they must flatly reject such scriptures as this, and the following verses. Regarding the portion of the wicked, both satanic and human, the Word of God is abundantly clear. Could God give clearer warning to men, and teaching to his own, than we find in Mark 9:42-48; 2 Thess. 1:9; Jude 9; Luke 16:19-31? Surely even if we had nothing else in scripture which raises a warning voice to men, we have such lovely gospel texts as John 3:16; 3:36; 5:24; though they do not speak of the punishment being eternal, they do remind a sinner he will perish, know God's wrath, and enter into condemnation. There can be no escape for any who refuse to accept the love of God commended to them (Rom. 5:8). Along with the present verses under consideration, they prove that the warnings of God are all eternal in character. We cannot subscribe to the teaching of those who would deny God his rights to execute his word as he has plainly stated. Let us all bow to the plain teaching of the Word of God, and seek to reach the lost before they are beyond salvation.

The devil joins the beast and the false prophet, who have not been annihilated, but seen to be still in the lake of fire and brimstone one thousand years after they had been cast there. Their torment is also recorded in definite terms, "and shall be tormented day and night for ever and ever". Can the Word of God be clearer, and the fate of the ungodly more sure?

The word, "tormented", occurs twelve times in the New Testament, and is variously translated as tormented (Matt. 8:6); tossed (Matt. 14:24); toiling (Mark 6:48); vexed (2 Pet. 2:8); and pained (Rev. 2:2). Together, they describe the eternal suffering that all that are cast into the lake of fire shall know. Should such thoughts not rouse us to live more holily, to be more compassionate, to witness more diligently, as we see our families, friends, and the masses of humanity without Christ? These are to be cast into the lake of fire and brimstone, which Scott states, "are figures of inexpressible torment" (The Revelation, page 409).

The Reward of the Wicked (vv. 11-15)

And I saw a great white throne, and him that sat on it, from whose face the earth and the heaven fled away; and there was found no place for them. And I saw the dead, small and great, stand before God; and the books were opened: and another book was opened, which is the book of life: and the dead were judged out of those things which were written in the books, according to their works. And the sea gave up the dead which were in it; and death and hell delivered up the dead which were in them: and they were judged every man according to their works. And death and hell were cast into the lake of fire. This is the second death. And whosoever was not found written in the book of life was cast into the lake of fire. (Revelation 20:11-15)

The last acts of God in his dealings with the present creation are now described. They are described by two expressions, "I saw". In v. 11 he gets a sight of the throne, from vv. 12-15 he sees those who are to give account before it.

The Solemnity of the Throne (v. 11)

This is not the regal throne of the monarch, but rather a judicial throne. It is not as sovereign but as judge that God sits. The tribulation begins with a rainbow-circled throne in heaven (4:2-3). The present throne is stark; there is no rainbow, and no hope is offered. This is a temporary throne, established for the purpose of the judgement of the wicked unsaved dead. Of all the tribunals of earth, none has ever been marked by the solemnity that surrounds this throne.

The Purity of the Throne

The throne is said to be "white". This is always the emblem of purity. The holiness of God will be paramount. As to his wisdom, Ch 1:14 states, "His head and his hairs were white like wool, as white as snow". In his authority to "reap the harvest of the earth" (14:15), he sits on a white cloud. The warrior King regaining the world for God rides on a white horse (19:11). Finally, when the vile character of man's sin is exposed, he sits on a white throne. His holiness will reveal the true character of the human heart; no feeble excuses will be heard in this court, sin will be apparent.

The Majesty of the Throne

The throne sitter is simply described as "Him". The gospel of John reveals who this will be, "For the Father judgeth no man, but has committed all judgement unto the Son" (5:22). This is further emphasised as Rom. 2:16 records, "In the day when God shall judge the secrets of men by Jesus Christ according to my gospel". This will not be the compassionate Christ of his earthly ministry, who could look upon the multitudes and cry, "Come unto me, all ye that labour and are heavy laden, and I will give you rest" (Matt. 11:28), dispensing blessing and bringing peace and joy.

This will be the Christ whose eyes are as a flame of fire, and feet of burnished brass, out of whose mouth goeth a sharp two-edged sword saying, "I know you not whence ye are, depart from me, all ye workers of iniquity" (Luke 13:27). The suffering Saviour of Calvary becomes the judge of those who refuse his work of grace.

The Authority Of The Throne

Such is the authority that marks this throne that the heavens and earth must flee from before it. In this statement we are informed when the great event of Matt. 24:35; Heb. 1:10-12; 2 Pet. 3:7, 12 takes place. The apparent permanence of the cosmos will quickly dissipate before the Lord Jesus when he sits to judge the wicked dead. At the sight of him the universe must flee. The first reference to this word "flee" is when Joseph took the young child and his mother and fled into Egypt, this is the last. In the former, Joseph fled to preserve the Lord from wicked men, in the last the heavens and earth flee as those wicked men are called into account. What a day of terror when the earth and the sea which have held the bodies of this dead company, disappear from around them! They will be left standing in space with no place to hide, summoned to judgement.

Individuality and Responsibility (v. 12)

Those whom the Bible states are "dead in trespasses and sins" (Eph. 2:1), now rise, but are still spoken of as "dead". They are not seen as living, though evidently in their bodies, and fully aware of that which they must face. All classes of humanity are embraced in the term "small and great". None can escape, no man is too insignificant, and none are supreme enough to avoid their responsibility before God.

Their responsibility is marked by the fact that "the books were opened". That is, the record of human life is now revealed. He that knoweth our thoughts afar off, and before whose eyes all is naked and bare. He that Job feared on such a day as this and said, "Dost thou bring such an one as me into judgment with thee?" (Job 14:3); who recognized, "his days are determined, the number of his months are with thee, thou hast appointed his bounds that he cannot pass" (Job 14:5); that God "numberest my steps: dost thou not watch over my sins? My transgression is sealed up in a bag, and thou sewest up mine iniquity" (Job 14:16-17). At such thoughts of the knowledge of God, it is little wonder he cried out, "O that thou wouldest hide me in the grave that thou wouldest keep me secret, until thy wrath be past" (Job 14:13). There is no hiding place in the grave as these verses prove, but we thank God there is a hiding place in his lovely Son for all who will believe.

There is not only the record of sinful life that is revealed, but also the book of life is opened. This is a witness for the prosecution. There is no possibility of any believer standing at the Great White Throne, and this book is not opened to reveal if any of these were saved while living on earth, but rather as evidence that they refused every call of God to repent. They believed not the gospel, they received not his Son. God ever gives opportunity to every man, and if a man responds to the revelation of God as unveiled to him, he will be saved. There are four fundamental ways in which God has revealed himself during the life span of human history. These are taught in Rom. Ch 1-3. There is the voice of **creation** in Ch 1, the voice of **conscience** in Ch 2, followed by that of the **commandments**, and his final message in **Christ** as seen in Ch 3-4. At all times it is with a view to God revealing himself, that faith may be exercised. From the beginning, men have not wished to retain God in their knowledge, there has been no response to his voice, and the evidence is seen when the book of life is opened.

The works of men will be tried, and God in Christ will judge out of the things which are written, according to their works. It is not how a man is born that is judged, but how he lived. It is not the root, but the fruit of his life that is brought into judgement.

The Inescapability (v. 13)

None can evade meeting with God. The record of God is true, "And thinkest thou this, O man, that judgest them that do such things, and doest the same, that thou shalt escape the judgement of God?" (Rom. 2:3). There is no hiding place on this day. The sea, which has swallowed many victims, yields its prey. Death must give up the body, and hell the soul. It must be remembered that hell is not eternal; it is the abode of the souls of the unredeemed, until the establishment of the great white throne. Nor does hell hold the bodies of men, as these verses prove: the body is either in the sea or the soil. Hell, according to Luke 16:19-31, is a place of torment, and the soul can see, feel, and talk. The memory of earth is fully known, as are relationships, for the rich man in hell remembered his brothers. But at the Great White Throne, the body and soul are reunited - it is to be noticed that there is no mention of the spirit of man being linked with him again. When a man stands before God to give account, and is judged according to his works, the body in which those works were done will also be there.

The Finality (vv. 14-15)

That which has held the body and soul of man will be cast into the lake of fire. Death seen as the last enemy (1 Cor. 15:26) along with hell will no longer be needed. The sin that has marked man will never rise again. Righteousness is going to dwell eternally in the new heaven and earth. The redeemed will never rise against their Lord, and the elect angels will never again fall. Eternal bliss is ushered in, on this ground God can remove forever what was needed for the body and soul during the intermediate state. That is, from the time that sin entered the world and until the bringing in of the new heaven and earth. The casting of death and hell into the lake of fire is another guarantee regarding the eternal security of the believer. Sin will not be known, and failure will not be seen in the eternal state, therefore death and hell can be disposed of.

However one wants to interpret the lake of fire, some say it is symbolic, others insist that it is literal, so far as man is concerned, he must be careful when handling the Word of God, that he does not apply human wisdom to divine revelation. Far better to leave the text as written rather than seek to fathom truth other than as God has revealed it. Hell is spoken of as being "this flame" (Luke 16:24), both the temporary and the eternal are said to be of fire, which is man's greatest dread. The lake of fire is equivalent to "Gehenna" of Matt. 5:22, 29, 30; 10:28. For "Gehenna" is also for the body of man along with the soul. Hades only receives the soul, but eternally the body and soul are united. That there are degrees of punishment is evident from Luke 12:46-48; Matt. 11:20-24, where a difference is made in the punishment received by servants who failed in their responsibility, and in the cities that had received both light and blessing. Greater light brings its commensurate responsibility.

The second death is the inevitable end of those who have never known new birth. They are dead spiritually (Eph. 2:1); they die naturally (Heb. 9:27); the second death is eternal. The solemn statement, "And whosoever was not found written in the book of life was cast into the lake of fire", brings to a conclusion the present dealings of God with this world, and tells of the sad end of ungodly men.

The fact that it is "whosoever" that is cast into the lake of fire, is a stark contrast to the gospel. The call of God goes out to "whosoever will": it is evident that those who could have been saved would not be saved. They must face the consequences of their rejection of Christ and the gospel. Again, the wicked unsaved dead are cast into the lake of fire because of the rejection of the Lord Jesus. On this account their names are not found written in the book of life. They stand before the throne because of their sin, and are judged according to their works, but they find their portion in the eternal fire because they reject the Lord Jesus.

All who are cast out are nameless ones. Only Judas is named with regard to eternal punishment. Though the scriptures would speak of many who perished under the judgement of God, yet their eternal destiny is not spoken of, though assumed. The final destiny of any man must be left entirely with God.

Chapter 21
The descent and description of the city

Introduction

The first eight verses of this chapter bring to a conclusion the third vision of this book, and form an integral part of it. When it has pleased God to "have put down all rule, and all authority and power" (1 Cor. 15:24), then comes the end. With Babylon, the Man of Sin and the false prophet, along with Satan and the wicked unsaved dead having received their just reward, God can now bring in a glorious new world that will function for his pleasure, and according to his will. The final verses from v. 9, describe the blessedness that will be enjoyed by the redeemed, as they enjoy the promises that God has vouchsafed to us in Christ. These verses embrace the final vision of the book, vision number four.

Paradise Restored (vv. 1-8)

And I saw a new heaven and a new earth: for the first heaven and the first earth were passed away; and there was no more sea. And I John saw the holy city, new Jerusalem, coming down from God out of heaven, prepared as a bride adorned for her husband. And I heard a great voice out of heaven saying, Behold, the tabernacle of God is with men, and he will dwell with them, and they shall be his people, and God himself shall be with them, and be their God. And God shall wipe away all tears from their eyes; and there shall be no more death, neither sorrow, nor crying, neither shall there be any more pain: for the former things are passed away. And he that sat upon the throne said, Behold, I make all things new. And he said unto me, Write: for these words are true and faithful. And he said unto me, It is done. I am Alpha and Omega, the beginning and the end. I will give unto him that is athirst of the fountain of the water of life freely. He that overcometh shall inherit all things; and I will be his God, and he shall be my son. But the fearful, and unbelieving, and the abominable, and murderers, and whoremongers, and sorcerers, and idolaters, and all liars, shall have their part in the lake which burneth with fire and brimstone: which is the second death. (Revelation 21:1-8)

The Descent Of The City (vv. 1-3)

Having seen the original creation removed at the establishment of the great white throne, John now sees a new heaven and earth. The promise of God recorded by Peter, "Nevertheless we, according to his promise, look for new heavens and a new earth, wherein dwelleth righteousness" (2 Pet. 3:13), is now fulfilled. In both passages, the word "new" *(kainos)* is used. This word is always linked with the true character of the present dispensation. Unlike the Greek word *neos*, which has the thought of "new in time, youthful, fresh" (Young's Analytical Concordance), *kainos* has the thought of new in nature. It is used in:

Matt. 9:17	-	of the new wine put in new bottles
Matt. 26:28	-	of, "my blood of the new covenant"
Matt. 27:60	-	of Joseph's new tomb
John 13:34	-	"a new commandment I give unto you"
2 Cor. 3:6	-	"able ministers of the new covenant"
2 Cor. 5:17	-	of a man being a new creature in Christ Jesus, and all things becoming new
Gal. 6:15	-	of circumcision, or uncircumcision not availing anything, but "a new creature"
Eph. 2:15	-	making "in himself of twain one new man"
Eph. 4:24	-	"put on the new man"
Rev. 2:7	-	"a new name"
Rev. 5:9	-	"a new song"
Rev. 21:2	-	"new Jerusalem"
Rev. 21:5	-	"Behold I make all things new"

These verses show that the new heaven and earth is not the present universe purged and cleansed. This system has "fled away" (20:11). It will, "wherein the heavens being on fire shall be dissolved, and the elements shall melt with fervent heat" (2 Pet. 3:12), be completely destroyed. After the flood, "the world that then was" (2 Pet. 3:6) changed its character. The new heaven and earth will be changed in nature and composition. Some expositors speak of a rejuvenated world, whereas *kainos* would not allow that idea. As a new dispensation brought in totally new things, so God will make a new heaven and earth for the redeemed.

The new heaven and earth will, like that of Gen. 1:1, bring in a solar system. It will not touch the dwelling of God, "the third heaven" (2 Cor. 12:2). It is evident from v. 2, that that will not be removed, and is the place of security for the saints when the first heaven and earth pass away, for John sees the saints coming down from it. As in the former creation the universe was earth centred, so it will be again. The earth will be the centre of all God's dealings. Christ rejecters would make our present universe heliocentric, stating that all is centred on the sun. Whereas Gen. 1:14-19 brings the heavens into being after the earth, and set them in their place for the earth's benefit, this occurring on the fourth day.

One striking difference marks the new earth, for there will be "no more sea". The Man of Sin rose out of the sea. "The wicked are like the troubled sea, when it cannot rest, whose waters cast up mire and dirt" (Isa. 57:20). The world that perished in Noah's day was overflowed with water. The fact that there is no more sea encourages the heart to know that those things that have opposed God will not have opportunity to rise again. The sea is also a great separator, and in the eternal state there will be no separation.

After the creation of the new heaven and earth, John sees those who will enjoy the chief place in it. Three figures are used to describe the believers of this present dispensation. The first figure is that of a city, "the holy city New Jerusalem". That this city is the believers of the church age is plainly stated by the second figure used, as he states, "prepared as a bride adorned for her husband". He does not state, "prepared for a bride". This is not the dwelling place of the Bride as many suggest, but it is the Bride in another picture form. The third figure is that of a "tabernacle" as seen in v. 3. The Spirit of God has chosen three beautiful things to describe the blessed portion of the saints of God who share Christ's rejection now, but will be glorified then.

Administration of the eternal state

The responsibility of the believers is to administer the eternal state. Along with the creation there is also ordered government. Governmental authority was built into creation, "For by him were all things created, that are in heaven, and that are in earth, visible and invisible, whether they be thrones, or dominions, or principalities, or powers: all things were created by him, and for him" (Col. 1:16). When creating the lights in the firmament, "God made two great lights; the greater light to rule the day, and the lesser light to rule the night" (Gen. 1:16). In the creation of man it was to "let them have dominion" (Gen. 1:26), and that dominion was over created things, and given in the order in which they were created. Satan is known as "the anointed cherub that covereth" (Ezek. 28:14), and Michael is called "the archangel" (Jude 9). Other angels are spoken of as "the prince of Persia" and "the prince of Grecia", even in a seemingly fallen state (Dan. 10:20-21). Dominion and governmental control are not only for a sinful state to control men. They are also seen in the perfect state of heaven and earth, prior to the fall. That the saints of this dispensation are to judge the world, and angels, is taught in 1 Cor. 6:2-3. Along with the inheritance as joint heirs with Christ, is given to us the future administration of the earth, be it in the millennium, or the eternal state.

Jerusalem has always been the centre of God's rule, hence the name, "New Jerusalem". This must not be confused with Jerusalem in modern Israel. It is called "new" here, for in the eternal state, God makes all things new (v. 5). From v. 9, it is called the "holy Jerusalem", for there it is seen in millennial days as we shall see, and in a day when sin is still apparent, holiness will mark the saints, they cannot sin again.

The Destiny of the City (vv. 2-3)

Again, this is recorded in four definite statements, as "coming down", "from God", "out of heaven", "with men". Having been reared with and taught exclusive brethren doctrine, that the church as the heavenly people have their portion in heaven, that Israel as the earthly people will populate the earth, as an enquiring young man I posed the question to many of Britain's leading teachers in assembly fellowship, "Would we, the church, be in the new heaven, and Israel on the new earth?" Having been given the answer, "That is what it seems", or "That is what we think", I was shaken in mind when studying these verses to see the plain, clear, simple statement of scripture that cut across all I had been taught. Perplexed, I took down from my bookshelf "Things To Come" by Dwight Pentecost. Many told me it was the finest book on eschatology at that time. I was somewhat relieved to find him to teach, "Since scripture reveals that the church will be with Christ, it is concluded that the eternal abode of the church will likewise be in the new earth, in the heavenly city, the new Jerusalem, that has been especially prepared by God for the saints. Since the eternal glory of Christ will be manifested in the eternal kingdom, in his eternal rule, it is natural that the church should be there to behold that glorification of Christ forever" (page 562). Though I would presently differ with some of his points, nevertheless, I was thankful to God that others had arrived at the same conclusion. The scriptures are quite plain as to the place we are to occupy.

Affection during the Eternal State

Such is the thought of a bride; affection for Christ will be eternal and undiminished. Seen as a bride one thousand years before the eternal state is ushered in, that first love will never abate, and the freshness of the relationship will not fade. It is noticeable that the Lord Jesus does not appear by name, or by his work. It is not the Lamb's wife as in v. 9, but simply, "a bride adorned for her husband". In keeping with 1 Cor. 15:28, when God is all in all, the person of Christ is not seen. The fact that he is there, and his glory is expressed is revealed in the presence of the Bride. For a bride is of no value without a husband, she complements him.

The Abiding Dwelling Place Of God In The Eternal State (v. 3)

The third figure of the church is brought before us. That which marks us presently, and is suitable to describe our situation: a church in separation, a body in unity, "one new man" in fellowship of Jew and Gentile, a temple as God's dwelling, gives place to the expressions of this chapter. The tabernacle, which appears to be temporary, replaces the temple, which is seemingly permanent. But God goes back to his original intention as seen in Ex. Ch 25-40. God's first intention is his last. The tabernacle, which is "a figure for the time now present" (Heb. 9:9), is that which God uses to take up his dwelling. Scott says the reason God reverts to a tabernacle is because "The tabernacle was a moveable structure; the temple was a fixed one. We gather, therefore, that the tabernacle of God with men intimates that the saints will not settle permanently on the earth, but move to and fro, visiting other parts of God's creation - His inheritance and ours (Eph. 1:10-11)" (Revelation, page 422). This is not the case, the tabernacle was never meant to move, it was to be placed at Shiloh (Joshua 18:1), the place where God would put his name (Deut. 12:5, 11, 13, 14, 18). It was the sin of Israel that caused them to wander thirty-eight years in the wilderness, but it was not God's intention for them. We go beyond the text to make such speculative statements, as Scott.

In this figure of the saints as a tabernacle which becomes God's dwelling place, we learn that "the tabernacle of God is with (*meta*) men". The men are the redeemed of every age from Abel onwards. National distinctions disappear in the eternal state. The millennium sees the fulfilment of all God's promises to Israel. In the eternal state God, who began with man, and made no national distinctions until Gen. 12, will end with man. In Genesis, God came down to walk and talk with man, Adam. In the eternal state he will dwell with men. The saints of this present dispensation will alone remain distinct, as a city, a bride, and a tabernacle. We have in these expressions what the saints of this dispensation will be in administration, affection, and as the abiding dwelling place of God.

God will not only take up residence, but a fixed and eternal relationship will be established, for "God himself shall be with them and be their God". A friend once asked me if I thought in the eternal state heaven would be evacuated. Though we are thankful to know that God will dwell in the saints with men, we must remember that heaven is his throne, the earth is his footstool, and that the heaven of heavens cannot contain him, in whom we live, and move and have our being. But man is not an astronaut for space, or an angel for heaven. Earth is his natural habitat, and God pleases to dwell with him there.

The Deliverance of Creation (vv. 4-8)

And God shall wipe away all tears from their eyes; and there shall be no more death, neither sorrow, nor crying, neither shall there be any more pain: for the former things are passed away. And he that sat upon the throne said, Behold, I make all things new. And he said unto me, Write: for these words are true and faithful. And he said unto me, It is done. I am Alpha and Omega, the beginning and the end. I will give unto him that is athirst of the fountain of the water of life freely. He that overcometh shall inherit all things; and I will be his God, and he shall be my son. But the fearful, and unbelieving, and the abominable, and murderers, and whoremongers, and sorcerers, and idolaters, and all liars, shall have their part in the lake which burneth with fire and brimstone: which is the second death. (Revelation 21:4-8)

The Abolishing Of Pain (v. 4)

Many careless believers and many teachers quote these verses as if they belong to heaven, and though we believe that in the short periods that the saints are in heaven (the seasons when God is judging this world, during tribulation days, and destroying the universe at the end of the thousand year reign of Christ), they will know something of these blessings, nevertheless, they are not linked with heaven, but with the new earth in the eternal state.

All that has left its mark since the advent of sin will be totally removed, never to raise its head again. How blessed to know that tears will be wiped away by the tender hand of God. Tears have been known by:

Mark 9:24	-	Distressed Parents
John 11:33	-	Grieving Families
Luke 7:38	-	A Sinner Worshipping
Acts 20:19-31	-	Ministering Servants
2 Tim. 1:4	-	Sorrowful Saints
Heb. 5:7; John 11:35	-	A Suffering Saviour
Heb. 12:17	-	Despisers Of Blessing

What a blessed hope for the believer, to know that the distress and sorrow of this present world will all be abolished. The thought behind, "crying" is that of hopeless misery, while "pain" relates to distress, both inward and outward. How sad to think of the portion of the lost: "there shall be weeping and gnashing of teeth" (Luke 13:28). It will be because they will see what they have missed, "When ye shall see Abraham, and Isaac, and Jacob, and all the prophets, in the kingdom of God, and you yourselves thrust out".

Abiding State (v. 5)

Not only a new heaven and earth, but also everything connected with it will be made new. It is a decree from the throne; the sovereign rights of God have all been met as far as the old creation is concerned. Those rights will never be challenged in the new, and even "things" are going to be changed and made anew. Such is the assertion as to the permanence of the workings of God, that he commands John to write it, I suppose, for our encouragement. It is a blessing to know these words are, like him, "true and faithful".

Absolute Lord (v. 6a)

As in Ch 1:8, the supremacy of his being is expressed. The original creation is spoken of as a poem: the expression, "the things that are made" (Rom. 1:20) is from the Greek word *poiema*, a poem. The only other occurrence of the word is in Eph. 2:10, where the saints of God in the church "are his workmanship". The two great works of God are his poem written for man (Rom. 1:19-20) and angels (Eph. 3:10) to read. The Alpha and Omega, the first and last letters of the Greek alphabet, the fountain of all wisdom and knowledge, writes a new creation for redeemed men to enjoy. As "the beginning and the ending", he is also the originator, and the one for whom all things were created. In the eternal state, the cry of the four and twenty elders will be realised in all its fullness: "for thy pleasure they are and were created" (4:11).

Abundant Life (v. 6b)

The promise of the enjoyment of abundant life is bound up in the expression, "I will give him that is athirst of the fountain of the water of life freely". The words of the Lord Jesus to the Samaritan woman spring readily to mind, "Whosoever shall drink of this water shall thirst again; but whosoever drinketh of the water that I shall give him shall never thirst; but the water that I shall give him shall be in him a well of water springing up into everlasting life." Does the world sneer at our hope of being with Christ eternally? Let every believer rejoice in the eternal satisfaction that we shall enjoy. The pleasure we find in him will never tarnish or diminish.

Accepted As Sons (v. 7)

The final promise to the overcomer is now introduced: "He shall inherit all things". The margin says, "these things"; the difference is immaterial. All that God has prepared for the redeemed will be enjoyed eternally. As we have seen earlier in this book, the "overcomer" is every born again believer, this is plainly taught in 1 John 5:4. New birth is not merely a New Testament truth

(Ezek. 36:24-27). Nicodemus, the master of Israel, should have known this (John 3:10). What the Lord Jesus proclaimed to Nicodemus was before the church was brought in, and is that enjoyed by all who believe. So that not only the Bride, but also the "men" who enter the eternal state will enjoy these blessings. The blessings will be known in intimacy with God, "I will be their God", and in relationship as sons.

The Abominable Excluded (v. 8)

The final statement from the throne of God in relation to eternal things is the portion that will be known by the lost. God himself categorises them. Of the three verses that bring before us the people who will not share in the blessings of the redeemed (21:8, 27; 22:15), this is the most comprehensive, and all the lists end with liars. It is not concerned with who these people were; it is what they were that assigns them their place for eternity.

The sins enumerated encompass what is mental, sensual, physical, spiritual, and moral. They are headed by the two factors that are the cause of leaving God and Christ out of the life. As a result of godlessness the other sins must follow. The eight sins exposed are:

"Fearful": Dread. This heads the list. The word only occurs three times, and elsewhere it is only used of the disciples in the storm (Matt. 8:26; Mark 4:40), who with the Saviour on hand to preserve them, yet sought by self-effort to save themselves. It is the Lord who said, "Why are ye so fearful?" Such are sinners, the fear of circumstances keeps them from Christ.

"Unbelievers": Dismissive. They refuse to accept the evidence set before them, and fail to respond to every effort of God by his Spirit to bring them to salvation.

"Abominable": Disgusting. Scott simply says, "morally, religiously and physically filthy" (Revelation, page 427). The word simply means "to stink", and only occurs elsewhere in Rom. 2:22.

"Murderers": Destructive. The first such act of man, who found his approach to God by human effort rejected, was by Cain, who "slew his brother" (1 John 3:12). Murder will also characterise the reign of the Man of Sin; the end of human history as we now know it will be marked by the murder of those who believe.

"Whoremongers": Defiled. The word occurs ten times, of which five are translated as here, and five "fornicators". Sensual sins dominate the uncontrolled passions of the unregenerate, as they despise the Word of God, which teaches that sexual relationships should only be known within the marriage bond.

"Sorcerers": Demonology. Man who refuses to seek a relationship with God, nevertheless wants contact with the spirit world. From scriptural teaching regarding its practice over the centuries, it has evidently been sought after in every age. With the drug culture of our modern day, it is not surprising that there is a rise in seeking after those who will bring them into association with the spirit world of witchcraft, spiritism, and devil worship. Those who claim to read man's destiny in the stars, that advertise tarot card reading, are very evident today.

"**Idolaters**": **Deluded**. Those who reject the voice of God must put in his place a worship that is false in its concept. Satanic powers lead men to worship such (1 Cor. 12:2).

"**All Liars**": **Denials**. As we have seen each of the three lists end with liars; it is as if all the foregoing sins are practiced, not because men cannot receive the truth, but being willingly ignorant, their whole life is moulded by one great lie.

Such are said to "have their part in the lake which burneth with fire and brimstone". The fact that it "burneth" indicates that it will never be extinguished or exhausted. Such is "the second death".

A Prospect Revealed (21:9 - 22:6)

The following verses show a marked difference between expositors as to their interpretation. Among pre-tribulationists, there are basically two camps, about equally divided, and with spiritual men linked with either side. Thankfully, essential doctrine is not in question, and whatever side one leans to, the final outcome is of little consequence, and the certainty of interpretation, along with all truth, will one day be known. Nevertheless, one has to be fully persuaded in one's own mind, and must seek to interpret in light of scripture, and not follow men. Though, as all will recognise, what we have read and what we have been taught colours our thinking. I have noticed, in my movements in serving God, that things taught among believers in one country generally hold sway there, while a completely opposite view taught in another country, is generally held among the believers.

Many hold and teach that this section of the Word of God naturally follows what has gone before, and is a further expansion of the eternal state. This I find difficult, if not impossible to conceive. Some also, nay many, following teachings by Larkin and others, make the city descending from God a literal city for the Bride, making it her dwelling place. They would also speak of it as a satellite city hovering in space. This idea not only presents me with difficulty, but seems to border on the absurd, though I must remember that God is able to do anything that he desires, and if God wanted a city in space then God would produce such a thing.

As to what period this is associated with, we first notice that this is another vision to John, the fourth in the book. As we have seen, John receives four distinct visions, all bounded by the expression, "I was in the Spirit" (see Ch 1:10). This condition into which John enters brings another series of revelations to him. It is not uncommon for the book of Revelation to reach a point in tribulation history, to reach a point in time, then go back again over that history. Twice over, as in the sixth seal (6:12-17), and in the seventh trumpet (11:15-18), John sees the Lord return, and Ch 11 particularly, to establish his kingdom. But he reverts to conditions that take place before the Lord Jesus returns. On this basis, it is not inconsistent, having introduced the eternal state, that in this new vision, God should unveil to John the place that the saints of this dispensation shall have, beginning in the millennium, extending to, and continuing in the eternal state. Our sphere of administration does not begin in the eternal state, but from the outset of the millennial kingdom we are in close association with Christ. Nor does it end when the kingdom is delivered to the Father. What begins at the outset of the kingdom will continue eternally.

The terms that are used during the unveiling of this vision are not consistent with what we know of the eternal state, though expositors can deal with them to their own satisfaction, if not to mine. In this vision, as Kelly has pointed out, divine titles are seen. "We have dispensational names, such as the Lord God Almighty and the Lamb; not so in Ch 20:1-8 which discloses eternity, where God is all in all" (The Revelation, page 460). Further, in vv. 1-8 the Lord Jesus himself is only seen in a veiled way as the "husband" of the Bride, whereas the Lamb is prominent in these verses (21:9, 22, 23, 27; 22:1, 3). The millennial kingdom is particularly the day of his glory. Again, nations and kings are present (v. 24; 22:2). There will be no nations in the eternal state for national distinctions will have ended.   There is a problem with the kings, though we are not told who these are, or what is the source of their monarchy, though Ch 20:4 does speak of "thrones". Again, v. 27 would seem to allude to the presence of sin. We know this will be evident in the kingdom, though summarily dealt with. Thankfully it cannot touch the Bride for she, like her Lord, is holy. Thus a new vision, the commencement of our rule, the dispensational names of Deity, and the presence of nations, kings, and sin, leave me with no alternative but to see the millennium in this section.

The interpretation of the literal city is made again by many expositors, men whose understanding of the Word of God causes me to be thankful for them, and for the help they have given me, but here I cannot fathom their reasoning. To seek to make this a literal city seems to be contrary to the plain, simple statement that is before us. The teaching of some may be very imaginative, and in some cases it is certainly speculative, for not a word is recorded in scripture to base their thoughts on. Many would link this city with that which Abraham looked for in Heb. 11:10, when it says, "he looked for a city which hath foundations, whose builder and maker is God". Notice, he did not look for "the city", but "a city". The city of Revelation 21 is said to be "the bride, the Lamb's wife". As we have seen, the Bride is composed of the saints of this dispensation: Abraham had no knowledge of the purpose of God regarding the church age. The epistle to the Ephesians states that this present age is a mystery "which in other ages was not made known unto the sons of men". The great truth of the church was hid from Abraham, and all other Old Testament worthies. "From the beginning of the world" this great truth "hath been hid in God, who created all things by Jesus Christ" (Eph. 3:5, 9). Not only was it "hid in God", but it has "been hid from ages (time) and from generations (men), but now is made manifest to his saints" (Col. 1:26). It is only those who enjoy a portion in the church that can enter into the truth of it.

Abraham, along with "Isaac and Jacob, the heirs with him of the same promise" (Heb. 11:9) was content to dwell in tents as strangers in a strange land, even though he should receive it as an inheritance. These worthies were looking to the day when the nations would be removed, and divine government and glory would fill the land, the time when there would be settled conditions under God, and they would be able to receive their promised inheritance. Until then they were prepared to confess, "that they were strangers and pilgrims on the earth. For they that say such things declare plainly that they seek a country" (Heb. 11:13-14). Simply put, Abraham looked for a kingdom under the rule of God, and not in the hands of the nations who then possessed it. He wanted to see a land built and ruled by God, and not by men. This is what they were persuaded of, and embraced. The truth of the church as a city could not enter their minds.

With these thoughts as the basis for the interpretation of the following verses, we can now turn our attention to them. If vv. 1-8 speak of the descent of the city we are now given,

The Description Of The City (vv. 9-21)

And there came unto me one of the seven angels which had the seven vials full of the seven last plagues, and talked with me, saying, Come hither, I will shew thee the bride, the Lamb's wife. And he carried me away in the spirit to a great and high mountain, and shewed me that great city, the holy Jerusalem, descending out of heaven from God, Having the glory of God: and her light was like unto a stone most precious, even like a jasper stone, clear as crystal; And had a wall great and high, and had twelve gates, and at the gates twelve angels, and names written thereon, which are the names of the twelve tribes of the children of Israel: On the east three gates; on the north three gates; on the south three gates; and on the west three gates. And the wall of the city had twelve foundations, and in them the names of the twelve apostles of the Lamb. And he that talked with me had a golden reed to measure the city, and the gates thereof, and the wall thereof. And the city lieth foursquare, and the length is as large as the breadth: and he measured the city with the reed, twelve thousand furlongs. The length and the breadth and the height of it are equal. And he measured the wall thereof, an hundred and forty four cubits, according to the measure of a man, that is, of the angel. And the building of the wall of it was of jasper: and the city was pure gold, like unto clear glass. And the foundations of the wall of the city were garnished with all manner of precious stones. The first foundation was jasper; the second, sapphire; the third, a chalcedony; the fourth, an emerald; The fifth, sardonyx; the sixth, sardius; the seventh, chrysolite; the eighth, beryl; the ninth, a topaz; the tenth, a chrysoprasus; the eleventh, a jacinth; the twelfth, an amethyst. And the twelve gates were twelve pearls; every several gate was of one pearl: and the street of the city was pure gold, as it were transparent glass. (Revelation 21:9-21)

The Source of the Vision (v. 9a)

The revelation of the whore Babylon was given to John by "one of the seven angels which had the seven vials" (17:1). On that occasion, which of the seven angels it was that ministered the truth to him was not specified. Now when God is going to reveal the vision of the Bride, it is again stated, that, "there came unto me one of the seven angels which had the seven vials full of the seven last plagues, and talked with me saying, Come hither, I will shew thee the bride the Lamb's wife". Why such an angel is chosen we are not told, but it is in keeping with Ch 1:1, where we are informed, "he sent and signified it by his angel unto his servant John". The vision of the whore revealed to John that which bore the glory of man, and which moved in bitter opposition to all that is of God. Now he is to gaze upon that which will glorify God eternally, and bring pleasure to his mind.

The Subject Of The Vision (v. 9b)

In clear, definite, unmistakable words, we are told explicitly that John was to see "The Bride the Lamb's Wife". Such a thought must have filled John with joy. The last time such an angel came, the sight, though inspiring wonder "with great admiration" (17:6), nevertheless must have produced a measure of distaste as he saw, "the mother of harlots" (17:5). But no such thing can occupy his mind again, Babylon's doom has been witnessed, and it is a glorious bride that is to fill his eye. The last time he saw her, she was being presented to her husband in a gorgeous garment (Ch 19). He now views her being presented to the world with administrative duties. So when John sees the Bride, he actually sees a city, holy Jerusalem. The angel does not say he is going to show John "the dwelling place of the Bride" as many expositors take this to mean. Larkin postulated this idea at the beginning of the last century. Himself being an architect, who became a minister in Philadelphia, such an idea would appeal to his mind. It is Larkin who speaks of it as a pyramid, saying that the foundations would not carry a city of such immense proportions. He speaks of the light of the glory of God surmounting the top of it, whereas the whole city displays this according to v. 11. He moves into thoughts of great speculation when he says: "The pyramidal part of the city will doubtless be in the centre of the city, and probably not occupy over one-half of the surface area, leaving the remainder to be divided up into boulevards and broad avenues, with numerous parks and residential sections. We are told that the city itself is of 'pure gold, like unto clear glass' (Rev. 21:18). If this refers to the houses and homes of the inhabitants, then the redeemed are to live in palaces of transparent gold, and the streets are to be of the same material (Rev. 21:18, 21). We cannot imagine a city of such dwellings and streets to be unclean or lack in beauty. The streets are to be lined with trees, as are also the banks of a wonderful river. These trees are not mere shade trees, but beautiful Fruit Trees, called the 'Tree of Life', that bear twelve kinds of fruit, a different kind each month. The fruit of these trees is for overcomers only" (Larkin, Dispensational Truth, page 147).

He also goes on to say: "Somewhere on that 'Pyramidal Mountain' in the centre of the city, probably on its summit, will rest, 'The Throne of God' from under the seat of which will flow down in cascades, from terrace to terrace, the crystal stream that shall feed that wonderful 'River of Life' " (ibid, page 147).

Larkin fills in many things God has not revealed, and paints a very cosy picture, the problem being that not a word of this is said in scripture, it is nothing short of base speculation, founded on gross error. The sad thing is many modern expositors obviously follow his pattern of teaching, and set it forth as if it is divine revelation.

Let us again notice it is "the bride" that John is called to see. He sees the Bride in the figure of a city, for the Bride is the City and the City is the Bride. The present figures used to describe the saints while absent from their Lord, and while bearing testimony in the world, as "the church", "the body", "the temple", will give way to the figures used to describe our future responsibilities as given in this chapter. The terms used here simply describe the saints in their affection to Christ, a bride, and in their future administration of the world, a city. That the saints of this dispensation are not seen in the Old Testament makes it evident why no hint of this is seen there.

The Scene of the Vision (v. 10)

When John was carried by the angel to see the whore of Ch 17-18, he was carried into a waste, barren wilderness. As we saw when looking into those chapters, it was a fitting place to look upon that which opposed all that God desired. So now the contrast is just as startling, and John is carried by the angel, "in the Spirit to a great and high mountain". The location is similarly apt: we recall Moses going up "unto the mountain of Nebo, to the top of Pisgah, that is over against Jericho. And God showed him all the land" (Deut. 34:1). The extent of it is seen in vv. 2-3. Or again, we think of the Lord taking Peter, James, and John into a high mountain, and being transfigured before them. Peter evidently realised that they received a vision of kingdom glory, as they were eyewitnesses of his majesty (2 Pet. 1). John is carried to another mountain, above the world, to see that which God has taken out of the world, the Bride, as a city, a fitting emblem of that which God is going to use in his administrative purpose.

The Significance Of The Metaphors

If this is not a literal city, but the Bride, then the expressions that describe it must be explained. To me, they describe the beautiful conditions that will be seen in the saints as they take the place assigned to them in 1 Cor. 6:2, as those who will rule the future kingdom. Again, in them we have a portrayal of the promises that God has made to the saints, fulfilled in the terms that are used. Paul speaks of the fact "that in the ages to come he might show the exceeding riches of his grace in his kindness toward us through Christ Jesus" (Eph. 2:7). Or again, "When he shall come to be glorified in his saints, and to be admired in all them that believe" (2 Thess. 1:10). That the saints are going to be in close association with Christ, and be a vessel to display his glory was very much in the Spirit's mind when he caused Paul to pen those words. We shall discover that all the figures of speech used describe many facets of God's blessings bestowed upon the saints. Among these are:

The Purity of the Saints (v. 10)

The title used to describe the city is "holy Jerusalem"; this would reveal to us the absolute purity that will be seen in the believers in a coming day. Holiness is not merely the absence of sin, but the impossibility to sin. Nor can sin leave its mark on holiness. The Lord Jesus, "that holy thing which shall be born of thee" (Luke 1:35), could move in a defiling world that affects us presently, but it could not touch holiness. The Lord Jesus was no less pure at the end of his sojourn here than at the beginning, for holiness cannot sin. In the eternal state of vv. 1-8, it is "new Jerusalem". In the millennium, when sin has not been eradicated, it is "holy Jerusalem"; a blessed thought, that we will be so conformed to the Lord Jesus, and having a body like unto his body of glory (Phil. 3:21), sin will never touch us again. Some brethren get a little disturbed to think that the believers will once again be associated with the earth, feeling that the sin that will be present would affect us. But as holiness marked the Lord Jesus, and this world left no stain on him, we can be assured that we will be of the same nature.

Because the verse only sees the saints "descending out of heaven from God", some would uphold Darby's notion that Ch 5:10 teaches we are only to remain "over" the earth, a strange place for saints to be, and as seen when writing on 5:10, this can hardly be the interpretation. We say again, to stir up our pure minds by way of remembrance, that if the twelve apostles are to sit on twelve thrones judging the twelve tribes of Israel (Matt. 19:28), and we are, "to sit with me in my throne" (3:21), the future location of the saints is "on" the earth, reigning "over" it in governmental authority.

The Suitability of the Saints (v. 11)

The saints are said to be, "having the glory of God", that is, what is theirs as a possession. To be able to bear this glory we must be made suitable to carry it. The holiness of the previous verse fits us to manifest that which God has bestowed upon us, even his glory. As this glory radiates before men, the truth of Eph. 3:21 will be known, "Unto him be glory in the church by Christ Jesus throughout all ages, world without end. Amen". That glory shed upon us, will shine forth to the world, to glorify him.

Her suitability is not only seen in her glory, but also in the light she sheds, for it is "like a stone most precious, even like a jasper stone, clear as crystal". The jasper is used to describe the character of God as he sits upon his throne (4:3). The saints are to bear the same features, and would manifest the transparent purity that will be seen in that day, "when we shall be like him" (1 John 1:2). Three times over, jasper is connected with the city; here as she

shines, in v. 18, the wall in its **security** is said to be of jasper, and the first foundation, the **stability** of the saints, is jasper.

The Security of the Saints (v. 12a)

John's eye is drawn to the wall that surrounds the city, as he sees it coming down from God. One of the most blessed truths in the New Testament is the eternal security of the believer. God is expressing it again in the sight that is before us. There are some who would deny this precious truth. When once having fellowship with the Pentecostal movement, Assemblies of God, in my youth, I found that they were very strong in a doctrine of "saved today, and lost tomorrow". As an experiential movement, as are all charismatic movements, they preached that if one did not maintain the things of God they lost their salvation. They would use Matt. 24:13; Heb. 6:4-6; 10:26-31, to promulgate their gospel, which is no gospel. These verses, within the context of tribulation days (Matt. 24), and an apostate Jew who turned his back on the Lord Jesus and the church to revert to finding his hope in Jewish temple worship (Heb. Chs 6, 10), cannot be used to subscribe to such a false gospel. They overlook every gospel section that brings "eternal life" to the believer. How can one lose eternal life? Either we possess it at salvation or it is never ours. Can new birth be lost? To cast aside John 10:27-29, where none can be plucked out of either the Lord's or the Father's hand, by saying we can walk out, is a sad understanding of the Word of God. It also proves how far men will go to bolster a false doctrine. No, the saints cannot be lost, and those who bear the glory of God are now seen in the full assurance of their promised salvation.

The Authority of the Saints (v. 12b)

Such is the thought behind the fact that it has "twelve gates". The number twelve is not without significance, for it is the number of administration. It was to this end that God chose twelve tribes for Israel, and twelve apostles to be with the Lord. Three numbers dominate the city: twelve, four, and three. Twelve is the number of administration, whilst four is the number for the world, and three that of the Godhead. In this city we see a world finally governed according to the mind of God. Every ordered government since creation has failed in its responsibilities to hold things for God. The final form of administration permitted by God prior to this, that of Gentile dominion beginning with Nebuchadnezzar (Dan. 2), ended with the utter rebellion under the Man of Sin. The world will have to wait until it pleases God to establish the kingdom under Christ and his own, until it is governed in a way that will be for its complete blessing.

That the gates speak of administrative authority is plainly taught in the Old Testament. In Gen. 19:1, "Lot sat in the gate of Sodom". He had taken the place of an official to run the political needs of that city. His influence changed nothing; it still fell under the judgement of God, and along with it he lost most of his family. He would have been better had he, like Abraham, "sat in the tent door" (18:1) to control his house, than trying to control the world. It is not for believers to be taken up with the present politics of earth; our responsibilities are in a future day linked to Christ, not presently with ungodly men. Boaz settled the destiny of Ruth before the elders in the gate of the city (Ruth 4).

There are two important additions to the gates: at the gates were twelve angels. Walvoord speaks of them as being there to "serve in this capacity as an honour guard" (page 321), but these angels, who now stand before the throne of God to do his bidding, will in accordance with 1 Cor. 6:3, stand at the gates to do our bidding as they also come under our administrative rule. The words of the Lord Jesus to Nathanael relate to angelic ministry in the millennium, when he said, "Hereafter ye shall see heaven open, and the angels of God ascending and descending upon the Son of man" (John 1:51). The verse proves that the centre of government in the day when heaven and earth are united (Eph. 1:10), will be the earth, with the throne of the Son of Man supreme, but angels ascending teach that they are linked to him. In this verse, they are to act at the discretion of the saints.

The names of the twelve tribes are also written upon the gates. This has led some like Bullinger to link this city and the Bride with Israel, but it would seem to indicate the fact that Israel will have a prominent part to play in the future government of the world. The many Old Testament scriptures that prophesy of Israel's honour in the kingdom are not negated now that the church has been introduced. The promises of God toward them will be fulfilled, but not alone, now in fellowship with the church, who McClain states are the "chief rulers of the kingdom" " ... A body of believers invested with special authority in the future kingdom of heaven" (The Greatness of the Kingdom, page 325). It would seem that in that coming kingdom the government will flow out from Christ and his Bride, to Israel, and then to the nations.

Another thought is introduced with the gates in v. 13, when on the four sides of the city are said to be "three gates". Three, the number of the Godhead, would speak of divine authority being carried to the world. It is a balanced authority carried out in equality. We cannot help but see the inequality with the present system of human government, when it suits the major powers to hold back third world countries, and to use them to their own end. By the huge debts they incur, they then become subject to their controllers. There is no need for famine conditions, there is enough food to sustain the whole of creation if man was faithful to his creator and distributed what was there to meet the need. We can only thank God that the day will dawn when the saints will judge the world. Only then will the government of this world be just and equitable, with the administration from an equal number of gates reaching to the four points of the compass.

The Stability of the Saints (v. 14)

The wall of the city is said to have "twelve foundations and in them the names of the twelve apostles of the Lamb". The basis of all the church is going to be is founded on apostolic ministry. The object of ministry is to prevent immaturity, instability, and gullibility (Eph. 4:14). The gifts of the risen head, the Lord Jesus, to the church were given "till we all come in the unity of the faith, and of the knowledge of the Son of God, unto a perfect man, unto the measure of the stature of Christ" (Eph. 4:13). The object of these apostolic gifts, and of the apostles themselves, is to preserve the saints from satanic attack, and to liken us to Christ. In the coming manifestation with Christ, the truth of God will be seen to have been effectual, and never again will saints be "tossed about with every wind of doctrine".

That the names written are the names of "the twelve apostles of the Lamb" would link in these who were chosen by the Lord in his earthly ministry; that there are other apostles is expressed in 1 Cor. 15:7, when the Lord after his resurrection "was seen of the twelve" (v. 5), "he was seen of James; then of all the apostles". Paul speaks of himself, not as one linked to the earthly ministry of Christ, but as an apostle of Christ Jesus, that is, of an ascended man. That these apostles are seen in the foundation is not that they may lay foundational truth for the saints only (Eph. 2:20), but being closely linked to the earth, it would remind us of their connecting link with Israel, as those who "sit on twelve thrones judging the twelve tribes of Israel" (Matt. 19:28).

The Uniformity of the Saints (vv. 15-18)

God has a delight in measuring what belongs to himself; it is as if he is marking off what is his. We remember the exact measurements that Moses had to follow when building the tabernacle for God. There are the measurements of Ezekiel (Ch 40), and Zechariah (Ch 2), when God's interests in the millennial Jerusalem and its temple are measured. There is also a call to John in Ch 11:1-2 to measure parts of the same city in tribulation days. Three things are to be measured by John: the city, the gates, and the wall. In keeping with the character of the city, a golden reed is used; in tribulation days John uses a reed like unto a rod, a stick or wand. In the dark days of tribulation, a dry stick is in his hand; now the angel carries a golden reed to measure that which is for God's glory.

The Scope Of The City (v. 16)

The city is said to be "four square" with all measurements equal. A perfect cube is before us. God dwelt in such both in the tabernacle and in the temple, and if God is going to be the temple with the Lamb (v. 22), it is fitting that again, consistent with what his glory demands, the saints are seen in perfection, all are equal. One can only see in this beautiful figure the uniformity that will mark us in a coming day. The city must represent the saints in their totality. The present day of the church sees many differences; gift makes a difference, believers make great differences according to wealth, education, social standing, and family relationships. Even the Word of God makes a difference with men and women in the assembly, husband and wife, parent and child in the home, and master and servant in the workplace, but in the City after the rapture all distinctions disappear. The fact that we are all one in Christ Jesus will be manifested to the world.

The result of the measuring with the reed tells us that it is twelve thousand furlongs in length, breadth, and height, each being equal. The number twelve again gives the number of administration, and three and four can divide into it. We are told by expositors that the measurements span a distance of approximately 1500 miles in each direction. Anyone can measure the extent of it on a map, and it will emphasise the vast size that the company of the saints is comprised of. It would portray the vast numbers who have believed the gospel, and also others covered by blood, who died too early to be accountable, or were not in a mental condition to make a positive decision for the Lord.

Many who follow Larkin's teaching would speak of the city as a pyramid, topped by the throne of God with his glory radiating upon the city, rather than the city itself having the glory of God imparted, and belonging to it. The thought of a cube is more in keeping with the presence of God with his own, as seen in the tabernacle and temple. The four square character of the city would also bring the idea of a cube naturally to the mind, unless taught otherwise.

The Size Of The Wall (v. 17)

The angel was to measure the gate after he had measured the city (v. 15), but no record of this is given; he moves directly to the wall, which is seen to be "an hundred and forty and four cubits". A cubit is generally taken to be around 18 inches in length, thus making it 216 feet high. This is sufficient to emphasise both the security of the believers, and also their separation. We are reminded again of the tabernacle in the wilderness with its wall of separation, even the court, which was 5 cubits high, about 7½ ft. tall. God loves to secure and separate his own from everything else.

The measurement is said to be that "of a man, that is, of an angel". This is a difficult expression to grasp the meaning of. Scott says, "the wall is measured separately, but its size is quite disproportionate to that of the city (v. 17); that we can understand; it is 'a man's measure' " (page 435). This can hardly be the reason. Perhaps it is merely expressing that the measurement is the measurement that man would know, even though carried out by an angel, the terms that are used being those that men appreciate.

The Substance of the Wall (v. 18a)

Once again the Spirit of God draws our attention to the wall, when he instructs us that it is of jasper. Enough has been written earlier regarding jasper, the radiance of divine glory now marks the saints; little wonder that we cannot lose our salvation when such splendour is going to be placed upon us.

The Splendour of the City (v. 18b)

If the wall bears that which would speak of the purity of God, the city itself, the saints of God, is said to be "pure gold like unto clear glass". The vessels of the sanctuary in the tabernacle were made of pure gold. The Gold speaks of the essential deity that is expressed in the various vessels as they speak of Christ. The gold always overlays the shittim wood. The shittim wood is a symbol of the Lord's humanity, but the wood is hidden, only gold is seen. By this we are automatically drawn to see and think of him as God. Is it not an amazing thing that the city is also "pure gold"? But "as we have borne the image of the earthy, we shall also bear the image of the heavenly" (1 Cor. 15:49). "It doth not yet appear what we shall be: but we know that when he shall appear, we shall be like him" (1 John 3:2). By new birth, having received the seed of God (1 John 3:9), and being partakers of the divine nature (2 Pet. 1:4), we shall be displayed in all the fullness of what God has made us as sons of God. The transparent purity, "like unto clear glass" will be all about us as we are brought into the place of governmental authority.

The Variety Of The Saints (vv. 19-20)

The foundations of the wall of the city again occupy John's attention. If in v. 14 he is taken up with the number of the foundations, twelve, and also with the names in the foundation, now he records the nature of them, "precious stones". If the foundation would display our stability, here we see the variety that will be seen in the saints. All are very precious, but all are different. The distinct personality that God has given us will not be lost because of the change that will take place at the rapture. The Lord is going to "show the riches of his grace in his kindness toward us through Christ Jesus" (Eph. 2:7). These stones once hidden in the earth, despised and trodden down of men, but sought out by God, are to be polished and set, and given places of honour. The stones would remind us of the breastplate of the high priest bearing the names of Israel upon his heart before God. They speak of the present priestly ministry of the Lord Jesus who in love bears our names before the father. These stones would see the saints in authority in the world, having been kept from the world, and preserved in the world, now reigning over the world. Any encyclopaedia could give the character of each stone, as written by some expositors, but as to the spiritual significance of each stone, I have not discerned that. Sufficient to know that, as in so much in the details recorded, twelve, the number of administration, is seen.

The Beauty of the Saints (v. 21)

Once again the gates are brought before us. If their measurement is not given, though the angel was expected to measure it, we are told what the gates are comprised of: "the twelve gates were twelve pearls; every several gate was of one pearl". Such is the fitting description of the gates, for as we know, the pearl is only formed through suffering. The grain of sand, a piece of dirt, some intrusion that irritates the oyster, causes it to form a coating that eventually becomes a pearl. Is it not so with the saints? The sufferings of our present sojourn are simply preparing us for our future reign. Paul would remind the saints of Galatia, "that we must through much tribulation enter the kingdom of God" (Acts 14:22). While writing to the Romans, he says, "For I reckon that the sufferings of this present time are not worthy to be compared with the glory that shall be revealed in (*eis*) us" (Rom. 8:18). The epistle of 2 Timothy, Ch 2:12 would seem to bring before us the pearl in its forming, "If we suffer, we shall also reign with him". Our present afflictions will be transformed into glorious beauty.

The Unity Of The Saints (v. 21b)

The thought connected with the street is that of unity, for, "Can two walk together, except they be agreed?" (Amos 3:3). We see the severance of Paul and Barnabas over John Mark's ministry that caused them to walk in separate ways in their service for God (Acts 15:36-41). After this division, Barnabas walked right out of scripture, which would seem to indicate he was in the wrong for allowing family ties to hinder unity in service, though Barnabas could have been used in the recovery of Mark, to the point where Paul says "take Mark and bring him with thee: for he is profitable to me for the ministry" (2 Tim 4:11). In a day to come, nothing will mar the fellowship and unity of the saints; we shall walk in perfect harmony one with another. That which began "together" (Acts 2:1), will be caught up "together" (1 Thess. 4:17). The many things that have divided the saints asunder, especially those doctrinal things, as men have given heed to seducing spirits and doctrines of devils (1 Tim. 4:1) which have caused men to depart from the faith, and imbibe that which is not of God, will then be eradicated.

Walvoord says, "The word street (*plateia*) is in the singular, but is used generically to describe all the streets of the city" (page 326). Beloved saints, this will not do, it makes room for his interpretation that this is a literal city, but it is not true to the Word of God. The word is singular: there is only one street, and it cannot be forced to make the many streets that a literal city would need.

The Delights Of The City (21:22 -22:6)

And I saw no temple therein: for the Lord God Almighty and the Lamb are the temple of it. And the city had no need of the sun, neither of the moon, to shine in it: for the glory of God did lighten it, and the Lamb is the light thereof. And the nations of them which are saved shall walk in the light of it: and the kings of the earth do bring their glory and honour into it. And the gates of it shall not be shut at all by day: for there shall be no night there. And they shall bring the glory and honour of the nations into it. And there shall in no wise enter into it any thing that defileth, neither whatsoever worketh abomination, or maketh a lie: but they which are written in the Lamb's book of life. And he shewed me a pure river of water of life, clear as crystal, proceeding out of the throne of God and of the Lamb. In the midst of the street of it, and on either side of the river, was there the tree of life, which bare twelve manner of fruits, and yielded her fruit every month: and the leaves of the tree were for the healing of the nations. And there shall be no more curse: but the throne of God and of the Lamb shall be in it; and his servants shall serve him: And they shall see his face; and his name shall be in their foreheads. And there shall be no night there; and they need no candle, neither light of the sun; for the Lord God giveth them light: and they shall reign for ever and ever. And he said unto me, These sayings are faithful and true: and the Lord God of the holy prophets sent his angel to shew unto his servants the things which must shortly be done. (Revelation 21:22-23:6)

The following verses now bring before us things that will not be in the city, just as the former verses have described what will be there. No temple will be there (v. 22), no light from the sun or the moon (v. 23). Its gates will not be shut, for there is no night there (v. 26). Sin will not be seen in it (v. 27), nor will there be any more curse (22:3).

The Sanctity Of The Saints (v. 22)

The first thing that John realises is that there is no need for a temple. What the saints are now, both in local testimony (1 Cor. 3:16), and in the dispensational aspect of the church (Eph. 2:21), the Lord God Almighty and the Lamb will be. Beginning in the millennium, but going on into eternity, there will ever rise to God the worship of the saints. There will be no need for a place of worship in that day as far as we are concerned, for we will be in direct unbroken communion with the Lord. It seems that there are five gathering centres that God is linked with in the course of human history: the tabernacle, Solomon's temple, Zerubbabel's temple in the restoration of Israel, followed by Herod's temple. This was owned by the Lord Jesus at the beginning of his ministry, "my Father's house" (John 2:16), but disowned at the end of his walk for God here, "Your house is left unto you desolate" (Matt. 23:38), which is explained in the opening verses of Ch 24. Finally, as far as the nations are concerned, the Lord himself will build Ezekiel's temple, but, as the Bride, we will have no need of that to maintain our worship, we shall be in direct communion with the Lord.

"Face to face with Christ my Saviour,
Face to face what will it be..."

The Shining for the Saints (v. 23)

Some have tried to make much out of this verse in their attempts to make this a proof text that this is an eternal scene, and would add that there will be no sun or moon in the new heavens. This is not the point of the verse, neither does it say there is no sun or moon, but, "The city had no need of the sun, neither of the moon to shine in it". In the tabernacle of old, the sun was the light in the court, the lamp lit the holy place, but God himself was the light in the holy of holies. Such will be the communion enjoyed, and the nearness known, that we shall ever abide in the light of his presence. If we presently "walk in the light" (1 John 1:7), we shall then dwell in the light.

Submission to the Saints (v. 24)

Nations and kings are now seen in relation to it: "the nations of them which are saved shall walk in the light of it". Some would omit the words "of them which are saved"; I find no difficulty in accepting the truth of it, even if not qualified to judge the matter textually, for it is only those who are saved who shall enter into the kingdom. The judgement of the living nations is that which determines the destiny of those who remain alive at the manifestation of the Lord Jesus and proves that all that enter the kingdom will be saved (Matt.

25:31-46). The pathway they follow, and the life they live, will be under the direct guidance of saints, who themselves receive the light from divine persons to regulate the lives of those who enter the kingdom.

This will be fully acknowledged by the kings who "bring their glory and honour into it". The saints of God who are presently despised, persecuted, and hated of all men, as they reject the world and its ways in fellowship with Christ, will in that day receive the honour and glory of men. This is the blessed prospect of the believers, and, in the figures used in this city, it proves the wonder of what our salvation has brought us into. There is far more in store for the believer than merely being saved from hell, and going to heaven. May God thrill our souls at the blessed prospect before us.

The Safety of the Saints (v. 25)

The book of Job speaks of the night as the time "when people are cut off in their place" (Job 36:20). When Belshazzar fell it was "in that night was Belshazzar the king of the Chaldeans slain" (Dan. 5:30). Judas also went out to meet the night, for he "went immediately out and it was night" (John 13:30). It was a sad night for Peter when he denied the Lord. But now the saints of God are in the secret place of the most High, and the promise is, "Thou shalt not be afraid for the terror by night" (Psa. 91:5). Eternal preservation will be our portion.

The fact that the gates will never be shut also indicates that the administration of the saints will not cease. We shall never be usurped and overthrown, rather, as verse 26 reveals, the nations, like the kings, shall bring their glory and honour into it.

The Separation of the Saints (v. 27)

No sin in any of its forms, nor any that might practice sin, will ever be seen again affecting the saints of God. All forms of defilement are excluded, and cannot contaminate the believers. Only those who have their record in the Lamb's book of life will be allowed to have fellowship with and enjoy the company of the saints.

Chapter 22
The Final call

The Satisfaction of the Saints (v. 1)

The following verses form an integral part of that which has gone before; there should be no chapter division at this point. Perhaps the fact that the angel "shewed me a pure river of water of life, clear as crystal, proceeding out of the throne of God and of the Lamb", caused the division to be made, assuming that this is another vision.

The water of life is that which the Lord Jesus promised as a possibility to the woman of Samaria for her permanent satisfaction. The Lord also stood and cried on the last day of the feast, saying, "If any man thirst, let him come unto me and drink. He that believeth on me, as the scripture hath said, out of his belly shall flow rivers of living water. But this spake he of the Spirit which they that believe on him should receive:" (John 7:37-39). The water is pure and clear, and its source is the throne of God and the Lamb. It would seem that this stream is for the saints alone, it does not flow beyond the city, and is confined to it. This is not the water that issues from the temple in Ezekiel's vision, Ch 47, for that is for "every thing that liveth, which moveth, whithersoever the rivers shall come, shall live" (v. 9). That water is for all in the millennium.

The verses before us would also take us back to the Garden of Eden, where there was a river moving into four parts of the world. God will ever sustain his creation, how blessed to know that we shall find great satisfaction from the throne.

The Sustenance of the Saints (v. 2)

Again we are drawn to Eden's garden, where in the midst of that garden was the tree of life; now in the midst of the street, the place of fellowship and social communication, and on either side of the river, the source of satisfaction, is the tree of life. There is no sword turning every way at this time, nor cherubim to guard it. On the ground of redemption, when fully recovered to God, the tree of life shall be for our enjoyment. The word for "tree" is the same word that is used for the tree on which they crucified the Lord Jesus. It is translated as, "staves" (Matt. 26:47); "wood" (1 Cor. 3:12; Rev. 18:12); and is simply timber, a stick, club or tree. There is nothing lifeless about this tree, but from the death of him who hung on the tree, we eat of the tree of life. There is no tree of the knowledge of good and evil in association with it. All testing is over; the perfections that mark the saints cannot be spoiled or intruded upon.

The fruit yielded every month is again for the enjoyment of the saints; the fact that months are introduced links this with time, as would its leaves, which are for the healing of the nations. We are not yet into eternity, and nations that have known great affliction will respond to the therapeutic properties that the tree of life produces.

The Sentence Removed for the Church (v. 3)

When sin raised its head in the fair creation of Genesis Ch 1-2, it must bring the curse of God upon Satan for being instrumental in causing Adam and Eve to rebel against him. The ground also was made subject to a curse, though in itself it had no part in the fall, but God brought it into the position that man now occupied, so that a fallen man did not live in an unfallen world. God made the creation consistent with what man had become, but put a hope of recovery in it (Rom. 8:20). The hope being that, when fallen man was recovered, God would recover the creation; it is for this reason that the groaning creation waits for the manifestation of the sons of God (Rom. 8:19). The curse could only be removed by the sufferings of Christ, and in the way that he died, for "Cursed is every one that hangeth on a tree": he was made a curse for us (Gal. 3:13).

There is nothing that will disturb the sovereign rights of God and the Lamb; their throne will continue to have complete sway in the midst of the saints. Never again will anything challenge his authority. There will also be willing service rendered from his bondmen, for such is the word "servants" (*doulos*). As the saints are seen in governmental authority, and radiating with the fullness of the blessing of God, bearing his glory, these bondmen can hardly refer to them. The bondmen must be the redeemed other than those of this church age, who will render true and faithful service to him throughout the millennium. If this term does refer to the Bride, it must relate to the position she takes, and not that given to her.

The Seal of Approval (v. 4)

The priestly blessing of Numbers 6:24-27 has a promise that the Lord will "make his face shine upon thee" (v. 25). The book of Esther (1:4) would show it is the place of privilege and favour when seven princes of Persia and Media "saw the king's face". The blessing of God will be enjoyed by these, and the seal of his favour, "his name shall be in their foreheads". Many of these have refused to take the mark of the beast, and have suffered on account of it, but what a blessed compensation to have the seal of his name, forever marking them out as his!

The Splendour of God's Presence (v. 5)

Again we are told, "there shall be no night there"; the saints of God shall not walk in darkness. When the Lord Jesus came in his public ministry, "the people that sat in darkness saw great light" (Matt. 4:16), for "the light shineth in darkness", only to be unseen, as "the darkness comprehended it not" (John 1:5). The whole realm of Satan's activity is that of darkness, and at the time of the crucifixion, Luke 22:53 records that, "this is your hour, and the power of darkness". The great powers associated with Satan are said to be "the rulers of the darkness of this world" (Eph. 6:12). For the saints to be delivered, the Lord Jesus must know the darkness of Calvary, but as a result of his work on the cross, "there shall be no night there".

Along with the fact that the city has no need of the sun (21:23), the angel reveals that there will be no lamps. As we saw in 21:23, we move in the light of the divine presence, and if "the throne of God and of the Lamb" are seen twice, in v. 1, and again v. 3, we are given the added statement, "and they shall reign for ever and ever": this is the assurance given to the saints, and confirms that the reign of the saints is not merely for the millennial kingdom, but will continue in the eternal state.

The Substantiation of the Vision (v. 6)

The character of the vision is like God and Christ themselves, "faithful and true". They are not spectacular or great, but every believer can depend on the revelation of God being brought to fruition. The God who verified the scriptures of the prophets and caused them to come to pass, gave his authority to this revelation. The strength of the testimony is seen in the use of "his angel to shew unto his servants the things which must shortly be done". Again confirming Ch 1:1, and in keeping with the truths that in the Revelation we have Old Testament titles of God, and the return to earth of the Lord Jesus as revealed in the prophets, so angelic ministry is used to convey truth, as it was in that period of God's dealings with men in Old Testament times, (see Heb. 2:2 and Acts 7:53).

The Promise To Return (vv. 7-21)

The following verses seem to be an epilogue to the book, as Ch 1:1-8 form a prologue. There seems to be no definite division to the verses, but rather certain appeals and warnings as a result of all that has been revealed throughout the unveiling to John. The previous verse could form part of this section, rather than close the great vision of the saints revealed as a city. In the same way, verse seven could also be a closing message with a promise to what has gone before, and be a source of encouragement that the day of Glory that is soon to appear, and in which the saints will share, is at hand and imminent.

Nevertheless, with these things in mind, for ease and help in seeing the truth embodied in this section, we shall make three divisions in the verses, whilst remaining conscious of the fact that they may be somewhat distorted.

7-11	-	The coming and its consequences;
12-16	-	The coming and its consummator;
17-21	-	The coming and its considerations.

The Coming and its Consequences (vv. 7-11)

Behold, I come quickly: blessed is he that keepeth the sayings of the prophecy of this book. And I John saw these things, and heard them. And when I had heard and seen, I fell down to worship before the feet of the angel which shewed me these things. Then saith he unto me, See thou do it not: for I am thy fellowservant, and of thy brethren the prophets, and of them which keep the sayings of this book: worship God. And he saith unto me, Seal not the sayings of the prophecy of this book: for the time is at hand. He that is unjust, let him be unjust still: and he which is filthy, let him be filthy still: and he that is righteous, let him be righteous still: and he that is holy, let him be holy still. (Revelation 22:7-11)

An Unmistakable Prospect (v. 7)

Three times in the final section of this magnificent book that unveils the final dealings of God with the world, the Lord Jesus himself promises that he will come "quickly" (v. 7, 12, 20). The word has the thought of swiftness in it; without delay, soon; or by surprise, suddenly. It occurs thirteen times in the New Testament – six times in the Gospels and seven times in the Revelation. It is not found at all in the Epistles. The occurrences in the Gospels would teach us how the word should be interpreted. Matt. 5:25 - "Agree with thine adversary quickly", 28:7 - "Go quickly and tell his disciples", v. 8 - "They departed quickly from the sepulchre". See also Mark 9:39 "Lightly"; 16:8; John 11:29. Of the seven references in the Book of Revelation, three are written with a warning voice of judgement in them, (2:5, 16 and 11:14). The remaining four carry hope and blessing for the believer, (3:11 and the three occurrences in this chapter).

There are many lovely contrasts between the opening and closing scenes of this book, all of which would give pleasure to the student who is prepared to glean them. Along with the promise that these things will shortly come to pass is the prospect of the blessing that will be received by him "that keepeth the sayings of the prophecy of this book". In Ch 1:3 there is a promised blessing for the public reader, the people that hear it read, and for the doer. The book has now been read but, as always with divine truth, there is a responsibility placed on all who hear, to do. God has no optional extras, all truth is given to promote the character of God and Christ in us, and the blessing of God will only be known by those who seek to conform to his known will. May God give us the grace to do all he would ask of us.

An Untenable Position (vv. 8-9)

How slow we are to learn the truth of God! We may look with surprise at the actions of John in his falling to worship the Angel that had given him such an insight into the great prospect in view for the saints. Had he not done the same thing in Ch 19:10? And there he had suffered a rebuke from the Angel who recognised he was merely a fellow slave doing the will of his master, and that God alone must be worshipped. Yet once again, because of failure to grasp what he had learnt from the Angel of Ch 19:10, he is moved to do the same to another Angel who bears the same character as a fellow bond slave. The Angel himself must keep the sayings of the book, for they stand in the same position as men in relation to the truth of God.

These verses should remind us to take heed to what we hear, that we do not continually make the same mistakes and we should never make too much of those who bring the truth of God. They are only fellow servants, no matter how instructed they are of God, nor how great the truth is that they bring. We have a tendency, like John, to venerate the vessel that God uses, rather than worship God. Men should also beware of seeking to take honours to themselves like Simon of Acts 8:9, "Giving out that himself was some great one". We also remember the fate of Herod when he also took praise from men and "gave not God the glory – and he was eaten of worms, and gave up the ghost" (Acts 12:23).

An Unsealed Prophecy (v. 10)

How blessed are the saints of God in this present Church era, for this prophecy is written to cause the saints to understand the will of God in relation to future events. John was instructed to "write a book and send it to the seven churches which are in Asia" (1:10), whilst verse sixteen of this chapter lays emphasis upon the testimony of "these things in the churches". Unlike the prophetic truth revealed to Daniel regarding Israel's future destiny, when that truth was to be kept hidden from them "to the time of the end", for Daniel was told to "shut up the words, and seal the book" (Dan. 12:4). Israel can in no way understand the great prophetic truth, which has an awesome bearing for that nation in the end times. How privileged are the believers of the present day, for John is told to "seal not the sayings of the prophecy of this book". If we have the blessing of God to know his mind regarding divine truth, how sad when so many are not prepared to give their time to understand the revelation of God to us. Would that we could encourage all to apply themselves to the scriptures "for the time is at hand".

Unalterable People (v. 11)

The present verse does hold a few problems as to when this abiding condition, both of the unjust and unclean, and also the righteous and holy, takes place. Some, like Wiersbe, make it the condition which will prevail after the coming of the Lord, saying, "The angel's words must be understood in the light of the repeated statement 'Behold I come quickly' " (Rev. 22:7, 12), as well as the statement 'For the time is at hand' (Rev. 22:10). Jesus Christ's coming will occur so quickly that men will not have time to change their characters" (Bible Exposition Commentary, Vol. 2, page 625). Walvoord prefers the idea, "In effect, he advocates *status quo* for both the wicked and the righteous. By this he does not mean that men should remain unmoved by the prophecies of this book, but rather that if the prophecies are refuted there is no other message that will work" (page 334). It could simply be that men have made their choice as to the lifestyle they live, so just let them be. If they have chosen to live this way, they will portray what they are.

The two statements regarding both parties relate to, in the first place their practice – "unjust", and then their nature – "filthy". The same things mark the righteous. "Righteous" is his practice, and "he that is holy" relates to his nature or person.

The Coming and its Consummator (vv. 12-16)

And, behold, I come quickly; and my reward is with me, to give every man according as his work shall be. I am Alpha and Omega, the beginning and the end, the first and the last. Blessed are they that do his commandments, that they may have right to the tree of life, and may enter in through the gates into the city. For without are dogs, and sorcerers, and whoremongers, and murderers, and idolaters, and whosoever loveth and maketh a lie. I Jesus have sent mine angel to testify unto you these things in the churches. I am the root and the offspring of David, and the bright and morning star. (Revelation 22:12-16)

Unwavering Decision (v. 12)

Again the voice of the Saviour is heard to say "behold I come quickly". Nothing can hinder the fact of his return. As a blessing was linked with his coming in v. 7 to him that kept the words of this prophecy, so now, he is coming with a reward. I have known able teachers of the Word of God take this to mean that the Judgement seat of Christ will take place in space before we get to Heaven, that when the Church is ushered into Heaven after the rapture our future place in the Kingdom, based on our faithful service will already have taken place and there will be nothing to mar the glory of our entrance. Whether that is so is of little importance, the fact is that "then shall every man have praise of God" (1 Cor. 4:5).

Every believer can anticipate in some small way to receive some reward, for it is "to give every man according as his work shall be" that the Lord returns. The verse is a quotation from Isaiah 40:10, where it is Jehovah Adonahy, the sovereign Lord Jehovah (Newberry Bible).

Unveiled Deity (v. 13)

The fact that the Lord can reward his faithful servants is confirmed by his divine titles brought before us here. For such a one as this will not fail his own. John loves to speak of the Lord Jesus as the "I am" (*ego eimi*). It is not an expression used much by the other Evangelists, occurring only three times of Christ in Matt. (14:27; 22:32; 28:20). Mark also uses the expression on two occasions only of the Lord (6:50; 14:62), whilst Luke makes use of the phrase three times (22:27; 22:70; 24:39). The phrase forms a divine title, being that which God gave to Moses at the burning bush, "I am that I am" (Ex. 3:14). It is used by John in his gospel twenty-three times and, as he closes his writings, he uses it again twice in these verses (see v. 16).

As the book begins so it is drawn to a close. In Ch 1:8, the Lord is the Alpha and Omega, the fountain of all wisdom and intelligence. He is also the beginning and the ending, he in whom everything has its origin, and to which all has its destiny; all came by him and for him. In Ch 1:17 he is the first and the last, not merely in time, but in the place he holds. How blessed to know time does not change our blessed Lord. What he is as John sees him at the beginning, so he will remain when time is no more.

Unhindered Delight (v. 14)

Along with the reward of v. 12 comes the last of the seven blessings of this book. What a precious thought to all his own that, in the midst of the outpouring of the wrath of God, there are constant reminders of the blessings that will be enjoyed by those who are faithful to the Lord. As is often the case, men cannot leave the text alone and here some will insist that the reading should be "they that wash their robes", rather than "they that do his commandments". They state in their writings that the latter phrase would make entrance to the tree of life dependent on works, rather than our redemption as in the former. They seem to forget that "God commandeth all men everywhere to repent" (Acts 17:30), and those who enter into salvation and enjoy everlasting life have obeyed his call. The phrase simply expresses a statement of fact carried out by the redeemed and does not make it a condition of blessing.

The blessing is twofold, to partake of the tree and enjoy a place in the city. John says "that they may have right to the tree of life". The first reference to this word "right" in John's writings is found in John 1:12, "To them gave he power (right) to become the sons of God". As we have rights to a place in the family by receiving his Son, so God has given us rights to eat of the tree of life. Nothing can stop this blessing.

Uncompromising Destiny (v. 15)

There is no place in the sphere of eternal blessing for those who practice the base sins of humanity. Their practice exposes the character of the heart, wherein these have rejected the teachings of scripture and have been motivated by the base nature within them.

To be "without" simply means that they will have no part in the things that God has prepared for those that love him. The word is used of salt that has lost its savour, that is "good for nothing, be to be cast out and trodden under foot of men" (Matt. 5:13). Also in the parable of the dragnet when the good fish are gathered into a vessel, "but cast the bad away" (Matt. 13:48). Always with the things of God there is a within and a without and this principle will extend into eternity.

Six features that mark fallen men are exposed in this final description of the sins that control humanity. They could simply be described as:

Dogs – Personal, what they are in themselves as being unclean and filthy in the sight of God, for this is how dogs are viewed in the word of God.

Sorcerers – Diabolical, man controlled and manipulated by satanic powers, given to witchcraft, the occult and drug abuse. Each of these and more are embraced in the word sorcerers.

Whoremongers – Immoral. This would reveal the moral failure of humanity as they give themselves to all manner of sexual sins to seek to gratify the desires of the flesh. Some men would use the word fornication to cover all aspects of sin and make it a basis for their arguments in the great divorce and remarriage debate, but the word whoremonger seems more appropriate to cover moral failure on the part of man.

Murderers – Unnatural. The Bible would reveal how that men have no regard for life, and what ought to be the natural right for a man to live until it pleases God to remove him; men would play God with the lives of others, whilst not controlling their own.

Idolaters – Spiritual. Having left God out of his reckoning and not wishing to retain God in his knowledge, man must replace the thoughts of God built into his life at creation with the worship of idols. God will have none of it and men will be cast out because of it.

Liars – Ethical. As we have seen earlier, the three lists of the character of men who have no part in the things of God all end with liars. Here they are revealed as "Whosoever loveth and maketh a lie". They lie with a natural affection for it. They follow their father the devil "who abode not in the truth, because there is no truth in him" (John 8:44).

Unfailing Deliverer (v. 16)

Who is it that is going to ensure that all that has been written will come to pass? The answer is both sublime and majestic: "I Jesus". The guarantee that all will be accomplished is in that name. The commission to the Angel "to testify unto you these things in the churches" will come to fruition because of the one who sent him.

The Lord is revealed as both "the root" and the "offspring of David". As the root, David came from him, as the offspring, he came from David. In these expressions is revealed the deity and humanity of the Lord, his eternal being and his earthly experience. Both would tell us that the future destiny of the world will be secure in the hand of him, the seed of David of whom God said "his seed also will I make to endure for ever, and his throne as the days of heaven" (Ps 89:29).

The last "I am" is the one who will bring it all to pass, but if the future government of the world is in his hand, the Church also must enjoy its promised hope. The bright and morning star, the one promised to the overcomer in the Church at Thyatira, will appear to gather us to himself. It has been pointed out by many that the Old Testament closes with "the Sun of Righteousness" arising with healing in his wings (Mal. 4:2), speaking of the Lord in the full blaze of his glory coming in public manifestation, whilst the New Testament closes with the appearance of the bright and morning star, seen before the dawn, to remove the Church from the earth.

The Coming and its Considerations (vv. 17-21)

And the Spirit and the bride say, Come. And let him that heareth say, Come. And let him that is athirst come. And whosoever will, let him take the water of life freely. For I testify unto every man that heareth the words of the prophecy of this book, If any man shall add unto these things, God shall add unto him the plagues that are written in this book: And if any man shall take away from the words of the book of this prophecy, God shall take away his part out of the book of life, and out of the holy city, and from the things which are written in this book. He which testifieth these things saith, Surely I come quickly. Amen. Even so, come, Lord Jesus. The grace of our Lord Jesus Christ be with you all. Amen. (Revelation 22:17-21)

Call to the Thirsty (v. 17)

Some would make the first two of these calls to come, that of the Spirit and the Bride and also those that hear, to be cries to the Lord Jesus to come for them. Ironside, following Kelly, says "it is an invitation to him to return to shine forth and gather his own to himself" (page 365). Though we would not be dogmatic, it does rather seem to be linked to the cry that goes out to the thirsty, the last appeal of God reaching to the lost sinner of the world, to find eternal satisfaction by drinking of the water of life freely (see Isaiah 55:1). With the great event of the coming so prominent, how could those who are to enjoy the fruits of so great a salvation not long for others to enjoy the blessing of God?

Carelessness with the Truth (vv. 18-19)

There is a dual warning from the Son of Man as he continues his testimony to the Churches, he who walks in the midst of the churches in Ch 2-3, and gives warnings for failure in testimony, again warns those who would be careless with truth of the consequences of their actions.

All must beware as to how we handle that which has come from God. No doubt the prophecy of this book is primarily before us, but let all remember that "all scripture is given by inspiration of God and is profitable" (2 Tim. 3:16). No man should tamper with truth, many who are not prepared to submit to the authority of God would speak of certain passages as being "that is only Paul". Could I appeal to every believer that they submit to all that God has revealed and remember Paul said, "If any man think himself to be a prophet or spiritual, let him acknowledge that the things I write unto you are the commandments of the Lord" (1 Cor. 14:37). Many "evangelical" scholars today are casting doubt upon the authority and inerrancy of the Word of God, and by it corrupting many believers. Let us remember the words of warning in these verses, both to the legalist, the man that "adds" to the Word of God, and to the lax, those who would "take away" from it. To one will be added the plagues of this book, to the other "God will take away his part out of the book of life, and out of the holy city, and from the things that are written in this book".

There can be no thought of a believer losing his salvation. That is secured by the death of Christ. Only those who profess rather than possess salvation can carry out these actions of denying the truth of God. A true believer will ever thank God for his word and seek to be submissive to it.

Cry that is Timely (v. 20)

The promise of the Saviour and the desire of the saints combine as this great prophetic book draws to a close. Yet again, like the tolling of the bell, the message rolls down from the throne "surely I come quickly". To it is added "Amen", so be it. This amen gives us the assurance that these events will take place "For all the promises of God in him are yea, and in him Amen, unto the glory of God by us" (2 Cor. 1:20).

The longings of the believers are also expressed, "Even so come Lord Jesus". "It is the utterance of desire in the precise language which the saviour had used, heart responding to heart" (Barnes).

Closing Tidings (v. 21)

As the book begins with the Apostolic Blessing of Grace and Peace (1:4), so as we wait for the Lord to come, we need his grace to sustain us on the journey home. To it must be added the last "AMEN".

Bibliography

Author	Title of Book	Publisher
Adam Ben	The Origin of Heathendom	Marshall Morgan and Scott
Alford Henry	The Greek Testament	Moody Press
Allen J.	The Revelation	Ritchie
Anderson Sir Robert	The Coming Prince	Pickering and Inglis
Ansten B.	Prophetic Events	Christian truth Publishers
Baines T. B.	The Revelation	The Serious Christian
Baxter Sidlow	Explore the Book (Revelation)	Zondervan
Biederwolf William E.	The Prophecy Handbook	World Bible publishers
Bullinger E. W.	The Apocalypse	Samuel Bagster and Sons Ltd
Caldwell R.	Revelation of Jesus Christ	Marshall Morgan and Scott
Chater E. H.	The Revelation of Jesus Christ	Morrish
Clayton R. H.	Future History in the Revelation	Marshall Morgan and Scott
Coates C. A.	Outline of Revelation	Stowhill Bible and Tract Dept
Cohen Dr. Gary C. & Kirban Salem	Revelation Visualized	Moody Press
Darby J. N.	Lectures on addresses to the Seven churches	Morrish
Darby J. N.	Notes on Revelation	W. H. Broom
Dennett E.	Visions of John in Patmos	Morrish
Easton W.	Gleanings in the book of Revelation	Pickering and Inglis
Epp Theodore H.	Practical Studies in Revelation	Back to the Bible
Farrar F. W.	Eternal Hope	
Feinburg Charles I.	Liberty Bible Commentary Revelation	Liberty University
Flanigan Jim	Notes on Revelation	Gospel Tract Publication
Gaeberlain A. C.	The Revelation	Our Hope Publishers
Grant F. W.	Numerical Bible (Revelation)	Loizeaux
Grant P. W.	The Revelation of John	Hodder and Stoughton
Heading John	From Now to Eternity	Everyday Publications Inc.
Hoste William	The Vision of John the Divine	John Ritchie
Hurnard Samuel F.	The Book of Revelation	Marshal Morgan and Scott
Ironside H.	Revelation	Loizeaux
Jukes A.	The Restitution of all things	
Kelly W.	Lectures on Revelation	W. H. Broom
Lang G. H.	The Revelation of Jesus Christ	Oliphants
Langston E. L.	The Last Hour	Henry E. Walter Ltd.
Larkin Clarence	The Book of Revelation	Larkin Estates.
Larkin Clarence	The Greatest Book on Dispensational Truth in the World	Larkin Estates
Lincoln W.	Lectures on Revelation	Hawkins
Lindsey Hal	There's a new world coming	Vision House

Bibliography

Author	Title of Book	Publisher
Lokyer Herbert	Drama of the Ages	Harvest House Publishers
McClain Alva	The Greatness of the Kingdom	B. M. H. Books
Morgan G. Campbell	The letters of our Lord	Pickering and Inglis
Naish R. T.	Talks on Revelation	Chas. J Thynne and Jarvis Ltd.
Neatby Thomas	Our Lord's Coming Again	John F. Shaw and Co.
Newberry Thomas	The Revelation	Gospel tract Publications
Ottman Ford C.	The Unfolding Drama of the Ages	Scripture truth book company
Pentecost Dwight	Things to come	Zondervan
Phillips John	Exploring Revelation	Moody Press
Pink Arthur W.	The Antichrist	Kregal
Ramsey James B.	Revelation	Banner of Truth
Ritchie John	Revelation	Gospel tract Publication
Robertson A. T.	Word Pictures in the New Testament (Revelation)	Eerdman Publishing Co.
Ryrie Charles Caldwell	Revelation	Moody Press
Schofield C. I.	Prophecy made Plain	Pickering and Inglis
Scott Walter	Exposition of Revelation	Pickering and Inglis
Scott Walter	Exposition of Revelation of Jesus Christ	Pickering and Inglis
Scroggie James	The Great Unveiling	Pickering and Inglis
Seiss J. A.	The Apocalypse	Zondervan
Smith Hamilton	The Addresses to the Seven Churches	Central bible Truth Depot
Snell H. H.	Notes on Revelation	W. H. Broom
Stanley Charles	Revelation of Jesus Christ	Morrish
Strauss Lehman	The Book of Revelation	Loizeaux Bros
Tatford F. A.	Prophecy's Last Word	Pickering and Inglis
Tenney C. Merrill	Interpreting Revelation	Pickering and Inglis
Thomas Robert L.	Revelation an Exegetical Comm.	Moody Press
Unger Merrill R.	Zechariah	Zondervan
Various contributors	Pulpit Commentary Revelation	MacDonald
Vincent Marvin R.	Word Studies in the New Testament (Revelation)	Eerdman Publishing cCo.
Walfvoord John F.	Revelation of Jesus Christ	Moody Press
Welch C. H.	This Prophecy	The Berean Publishing Trust
Wiesbe Warren	Be Victorious	Victor Books
Wilmington Dr. H. L.	The King is Coming	
Dyer Charles E.	Identity of Babylon (Paper)	Bibliotheca Sacra 1987